1985

PROGRAMMING PRINCIPLES
AN INTRODUCTION

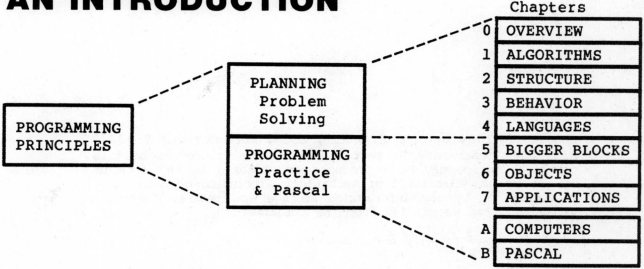

JOHN MOTIL
CALIFORNIA STATE UNIVERSITY
AT NORTHRIDGE

Allyn and Bacon, Inc.
Boston • London • Sydney • Toronto

Library of Congress Cataloging in Publication Data

Motil, John.
    Programming principles.

    Includes index.
    1. Electronic digital computers--Programming.
I. Title.
QA76.6.M69 1983   001.64'2   83-11779
ISBN 0-205-08005-7

Printed in the United States of America

10 9 8 7 6 5 4 3 2   89 88 87 86 85 84

Dedicated
to

Marie
Monique
Jacqueline
Jan
&
Raymonde

```
+--------------------------------------+
|                                      |
|          Table of Contents           |
|                                      |
|                 of                   |
|                                      |
|        PROGRAMMING PRINCIPLES         |
|                                      |
|      ( detailed contents follow )    |
|                                      |
+--------------------------------------+
```

Contents

PROGRAMMING PRINCIPLES

(more detailed contents precede each chapter)

Index

Preface

PROGRAMMING PRINCIPLES

PREFACE:

PROGRAMMING PRINCIPLES

This book introduces the basic ideas of programming, and a structured way of thinking about planning and problem solving. It is intended for a first course in computing for both computer science majors and also non-majors.

The goal is to develop an ability to create algorithms. A sub-goal is to communicate algorithms, as programs, in a language. This sub-goal is considerably easier to attain than the main goal. In fact the sub-goal, of programming in Pascal, is done in an appendix, whereas the rest of the book is devoted to the main goal. Hopefully, it conveys an attitude as well as a methodology.

The approach is very visual, using many diagrams (such as flow block diagrams, flowcharts, data flow diagrams, syntax diagrams, break-out diagrams). Each pair of pages is written as a unit (similar to a program module), with a page of graphics facing a corresponding page of text. The graphics were done with a computer.

Starting with many examples from everday life (involving cooking, business, change-making, calendars, games, etc.), this book creates an "algorithmic" logic of actions, showing how all algorithms can be created from only four building blocks.

Significant concepts (such as structured programming, top-down design, data flow, trees, arrays, records) are introduced simply, in terms of common examples, and then later in terms of computers. In this way, the important programming concepts are not confused with the details of computers or programming languages.

Practice of programming in the Pascal language is considered in a long appendix (of almost 100 pages). This can be studied in parallel with the more general part of the book, but preferably after chapter 3. Computing machines are also included briefly in another appendix.

Many problems, programs, and projects, of varying difficulty, are included after each chapter.

More detailed descriptions of the above ideas follow.

CHAPTER OUTLINE:

PROGRAMMING PRINCIPLES

0.   OVERVIEW: Top-down
   provides a "bird's-eye" overview and introduction to the
   general ideas of programming (algorithms, languages,
   machines, and systems) showing how they are related.

1.   ALGORITHMS: Representations
   provides many common examples of algorithms, along with
   many different ways of representing them, including
   formulas, tables, trees, flowcharts, flow block diagrams,
   data flow diagrams.

2.   STRUCTURE: Form of Algorithms
   considers the basic building blocks and how they can be
   interconnected properly to form algorithms.

3.   BEHAVIOR: Dynamics of Algorithms
   emphasizes the dynamic actions of programs, algorithms
   intended for computers.

4.   LANGUAGES: Communicating Algorithms
   considers concepts common to most high level languages,
   emphasizing the similarities in semantics (meaning or
   actions) despite the differences in syntax (form or look).

5.   BIGGER BLOCKS: More, Different, Deeper Concepts
   describes larger building blocks, more data types, deeper
   nests of loops, and more powerful sub-programs.

6.   OBJECTS: Data Structures
   considers some compound objects (arrays and records) and
   some algorithms (such as sorting and searching) for
   operating on these data structures.

7.   APPLICATIONS: Design, Systems
   considers some computer uses (including simulation and
   graphics) in business, engineering, and other areas. It
   also shows various design methods for larger programs.

Appendices

A.   COMPUTERS: A Low Level Machine View
   introduces a simple but typical computer. Structuring is
   continued in a low level language.

B.   PASCAL: Programming Practice
   introduces a simple high level programming language,
   Pascal, which is very similar to most modern programming
   languages. Many of the programs of the main text are
   shown written in this language. This appendix can be
   read in parallel with the text.

GOALS OF PROGRAMMING PRINCIPLES

WHAT   The goal of this book is to introduce the basic concepts of programming and a structured way of thinking about planning, problem solving, and programming.

WHY   The structured approach aims at plans and programs that are easy to read, understand, write, describe, improve, test, modify, extend, analyse and evaluate.

WHEN   This book is intended for a first course in computing, at an early university level. It should be suitable for students majoring in computing science, as well as those majoring in any other area.

WHERE The concepts studied here are general, not restricted to any particular computer, or language, or system, or application area. There are a great many examples, mainly chosen from everyday life, involving paychecks, calendars, games, statistics, business, cooking, etc.

WHO   This book is intended for the beginner. No previous background in computing is assumed (and in fact may be a disadvantage, for bad habits are hard to break). Extensive mathematical background is not a prerequisite, for most of the required mathematics and logic are developed as necessary.

HOW   The approach taken here could be called the "systems" view, or "top-down" view. It proceeds first from the top "big picture" view, then through intermediate refinements, and ultimately deals with the details.

NON-GOALS

It may be significant to realize what goals were not attempted here (although some of the non-goals may have been achieved).

This book is not intended as a language training manual,
    although a language, Pascal, is introduced in some depth.
This book does not emphasize training in a skill,
    although some skills are acquired in the learning process.
This book is not merely a collection of techniques or tricks,
    although some techniques are encountered within the general unity.
This book is not a picture-book survey of computers,
    although it does have considerable graphics.
This book is not a glorified glossary of computer "buzz words,"
    although some vocabulary is introduced to describe the concepts.
This book is not a study of the hardware aspects of computers,
    although some computer organization is briefly covered.

This book is intended for serious students to develop a view of planning, problem solving and programming using computers at a high human level.

VIEWS or Biases

This book is based on a few simple premises, views or beliefs (my biases, if you wish). They are written so as to seem obvious, but some have been argued considerably.

WE SHOULD LEARN TO READ BEFORE WE WRIGHT (RITE?)!

The creative activity of writing (be it prose, poetry, or programs) should begin by reading good writings of others. We then may analyse them, criticize them, appreciate them, and ultimately venture to write our own. Unfortunately, many people like to start writing programs very quickly, and they end up forming bad habits.

Here we delay the immediate creation and running of programs on computers. We start by reading already created ones, following (or tracing) them. Then we will create algorithms, study them, modify them, and ultimately code them into a language and run them on some machines.

A PICTURE IS WORTH 500 WORDS (OR IS IT 1024?)

Humans tend to understand graphic or diagrammatic structures more easily than written text. For that reason, this book uses many diagrams. In fact almost every second page here consists of diagrams, with a facing page of text (of about 500 words) describing the diagrams. The diagrams and text are equally important.

Diagrams often lead to immediate insight. Flowcharts and flow block diagrams help visualize flow of control. Data flow diagrams describe flow of data and sub-program interaction. Syntax diagrams define language structure. Data space diagrams illustrate parameter passing. Break-out diagrams aid in top-down design. Other diagrams include: state diagrams, trees, and two-dimensional traces.

In the past, many programming books have avoided graphics, often because the diagrams were difficult to draw, but with the aid of computers this difficulty is disappearing. All the diagrams in this book were done with computers.

FLOWCHARTS SHOULD FLOW (OR ELSE GO)

Flowcharts consist of boxes joined by arrows to indicate the flow of action (or control). These diagrams often work well for simple structures, but for more complex structures they could become confusing and prone to errors. It's just too easy to connect an arrow to a wrong box.

Here we insist that flowcharts must flow, and we develop a method and notation to enforce proper flow. Alternatively we develop a flow block diagram and pseudo-code, both of which show the flow structure diagrammatically in quite different but equivalent ways.

MORE VIEWS

LEAVE TO THE MACHINE WHAT BELONGS TO THE MACHINE
      (dirty details, tedious work, repetition)

To use a computer (or car, or clarinet) properly, it is not necessary to know all the details of how it is made. A computer is a very low level device which communicates using the two symbols 0 and 1 only. Humans, however, communicate using the 26 characters of the alphabet, the ten decimal digits, punctuation, and various other symbols. Humans then put together characters into words, words into sentences, sentences into paragraphs, paragraphs into chapters, books, etc.

Here the emphasis will be at the higher, human levels, closer to our applications. Our programming languages will resemble English, mathematics, and symbolic logic. We will, however, consider the computer and its lower level language in sufficient detail to understand the basic concepts, but we will avoid great depth here. The computer, and its low level language, is not introduced too early, for one's first language (be it natural English language, or a programming language) forms the most powerful tool of thought, and if the first language is not at a proper high level, then creativity may be hampered.

Here we will start at a very high diagrammatic level, with flow charts and flow block diagrams. Later we can use intermediate (or higher) levels involving languages such as Pascal, Basic, or Fortran. The computer then translates these languages into its lower level language.

STRUCTURE IS SOUND   (So it works. So what?)

The structure, form or organization of any creative project is important. It is not sufficient that a program works; it should work well. It should be easy to read, write, describe, understand, test, analyse and evaluate. It must also do more, as follows.

Creating programs differs from most other creative activities (such as painting portraits or designing buildings). No one attempts to touch up someone else's completed painting or simply double the number of stories in an already existing building. But in programming there is always the potential for further modification, so programs should be created with such change in mind. Our masterpieces are made to be modified. They should be easy to extend, improve, expand, optimize or transport to other computers. Structured programs created in a top-down manner are usually better for such changes.

SIMPLICITY IS SUPREME

There are usually many ways to create anything, so ultimately a choice must be made. We will invariably choose the simplest, clearest structured way. Experience has shown that beginners often like to use very clever, devious, and difficult ways to program. Ultimately, however, when writing larger programs, the intellectual challenge of programming becomes too great, and only simplicity can keep programs at a manageable level.

OTHER VIEWS

There are many other personal beliefs that have been incorporated into this book. Some of them follow; others I am no longer aware of. Some views (such as "The best length of any unit is one page") correspond to good programming practice as well as good writing and teaching practice.

FIRST THE FAMILIAR

This book begins with common everyday algorithms, and only later gets into computer programs. This way the general fundamental concepts of algorithms are not confused with the particular details of computers or programming languages. The Devil hides in details.

SPIRAL IS SIMPLE

When any concept is introduced here, it is not treated exhaustively in its entirety at that one point. Instead it is first introduced simply; then at a later time is extended and returned to again and again. Each concept is revisited in ever-increasing refinement. This "spiralling" provides for increasing depth, but with breadth for proper "top-down" perspective. So if a concept is not clear to you at first, read on; it will get clearer as you proceed.

DUALITY IS DIVINE

Many concepts, not just programming ones, can be viewed in two ways which are complementary. Some examples are:

      series vs parallel, general vs particular,
      recursion vs iteration, depth vs breadth,
      space vs time, wears tie vs forgets belt,
      top-down vs bottom-up, intuitive vs logical,
      hot vs cool, software vs hardware.

Although some areas of study seem to prefer a specialization, I believe programming requires a balanced view: an intuitive, holistic, spatial, subjective approach for creating programs, and also a rational, logical, defensive, objective approach for analysing, testing and optimizing programs. Programming is both an Art and a Science.

ALL THINGS ARE NOT EQUAL

Not all ideas, concepts, pages and chapters are of equal importance. The significance of each page is indicated in the table of contents preceding each chapter. The more important ideas are usually treated early in a chapter (top-down). Later in each chapter, there are extra challenging concepts (marked optional) which are not necessary for continuing to the next chapters. So if only two-thirds of this book is to be read, then it is best to read the first two-thirds of each chapter. Also, chapters are not equally significant, as shown below where asterisks indicate the relative importance.

STILL MORE VIEWS

TWO DIMENSIONS ARE BETTER THAN ONE
Many concepts of computing appear to have one dimension, to be strung out in a line. For example, an algorithm seems to be a long list of instructions to be done step by step, and a computer program seems to be a long linear sequence of symbols. Actually, it is the structure behind these sequences that is important. It can be brought out by creating two-dimensional schemes such as break-out diagrams, trees and two-dimensional traces. Computers may have a single dimension; humans have many dimensions.

INDENTING IS IMPORTANT
One way of capturing the multi-dimensional form of prose, poetry, or programs is by indenting. In this text a reverse or hanging indent is used, with the most significant matters at the top and farthest to the left; less significant matters are indented farther to the right to show the lesser levels. A similar indentation is used for programs.

SUBS ARE SUPER
The concept of breaking up parts into sub-parts is extremely significant. For this reason, the sub-program concept should be introduced early, before other simpler, but inferior, methods (involving global variables). Through the use of break-out diagrams and data flow diagrams, this early emphasis on sub-programs is possible. Again, the lower details (stacks, parameter-passing methods, etc.) are postponed until later.

THERE IS A TIME
Arrays, while not terribly complex, are treated late in this book. They are not necessary at first, but we may still be tempted to use them because of their power. Also, the dual concept of the array, the record, may be more appropriate. There may be no optimal time to introduce some concepts, but there are non-optimal times.

NAMES ARE NICE
References may be made to things by either number or name. Here, names are preferred; all numbers look alike. Names are given to each chapter, sub-section, page, concept, and even homework problem. Giving good names makes things easier to remember, convenient to refer to, and helpful to manipulate.

BEWARE BEGINNINGS
This book is intended for beginning students, who are not expected to embark on a computing career immediately after reading this book. A surprising number of people believe that everything about programming can be learned in a single course. This book aims at providing a good foundation for continued growth.

Beginners, with their short algorithms and awkward typing, can be forgiven for using short variable names. After all, physics and mathematics have used single-character names for centuries. The advantage of long names becomes obvious to beginners after they start writing long programs. A compromise is used in this book: the smaller general algorithms involve short names, but the Pascal programs involve longer, meaningful names.

USES OF THIS BOOK

This book has been used in many different ways in various courses, and in different schools.

Typically, it has been used in an introductory course on algorithms and programming. It starts with chapters 0 to 3 emphasizing general algorithms, then "detours" to the Pascal appendix, and continues with chapters 4, 5 and 6, done in parallel with the remaining Pascal. Then some of the larger applications of chapter 7 are covered. Finally, the course ends with a brief description of computers and possibly a simulation of a simple computing machine.

Alternatively, this book has been used in a service course (COMP 101) to introduce many non-computer majors to programming. This is done by a shortened version of the above course, covering the general algorithms and some programming in Pascal. This course is followed (in a later semester) by a laboratory experience with emphasis on one particular language (Fortran, Cobol, Apl, PL/I, Basic, etc.). So, when a student wishes to learn more than one language, it is not necessary to repeat the basic principles and algorithms in each language laboratory.

This two semester sequence has much merit. The first course is a lecture (2 units) on fundamentals, with limited Pascal programming. The second course is a laboratory (1 unit) with extensive programming experience. This arrangement separates the principles (algorithms, problem solving) from the practice (language, syntax, system "incantations"), both of which require considerable amounts of time. This avoids the terrible compromises (premature programming, hectic pace, etc.) often encountered in a first programming course. Of course some "hackers" would be unhappy, but most students can abstain from the computer (for about a month), if they are convinced of the importance of this.

Originally, the book served as the basis for three courses: COMP 130SCE (for science and engineering students), COMP 130CSM (for computing majors) and also COMP 130GEN (for general education). The COMP 130SCE course, for example, tended to introduce the computer very early. Although this seemed natural (In the beginning was the computer ...), it led to unfortunate "bottom-up" habits, so now more algorithms are introduced before computers.

Also, the compartmentalizing of students according to the field of their interest tended to result in emphasis on that particular field, rather than on the computing topics.

Significantly, this book has also been used in a pure algorithms course, with no programming language or computer experience. There is sufficient intellectual content for such a course, but only the bravest of computing instructors will want to try that at present.

Additionally, this book has been used by individuals in various ways: as a course in "Pascal as a second language," as a "structured" refresher, as a survey of the "algorithmic method" and as a "top-down" companion to a first course in Pascal.

Undoubtedly other uses of this book are possible.

FORM OF THIS BOOK

The form (layout, format, or syntax) of this book differs from that of most other books. I have tried to reflect the "top-down" view in the design of the book. It has some of the same form that large programs have. I realize that I have not been completely successful in achieving this goal, but, as with most programs, there is room for modification. I am grateful to the publisher, Allyn and Bacon, Inc., for cooperation in making this possible.

BOOKS, in general, consist of chapters which are broken into sub-chapters (sections, parts, etc.) which ultimately are "cut" into equal-sized segments, called pages. This arbitrary cutting into pages often causes pages to start and finish in mid-sentence, a practice that I find annoying (except in novels). It's like breaking up one long program into sub-programs at arbitrary points (every 50 lines).

CHAPTERS in this book are broken into sections, and this break-out is shown in front of each chapter. A chapter is "sandwiched" between a preview at the front and a review following it. A set of problems follows each chapter.

SECTIONS are further split into smaller segments, called page-pairs. There may be two to seven of these segments in a section. Seven (plus or minus two) is a "magic" number often encountered in programming.

PAGE-PAIRS are simply the two pages we face when a book is opened up. The two pages are created to be complementary; one page consists of graphics, and the facing page consists of printed text. Each pair is devoted to a single, isolated concept.

CONCEPTS do not always fit a page easily. When a concept is small, the paragraphs are spaced out to fit the page, so forming blocks of text, adding to the readability. When the concept is large, it is split into sub-concepts, which in turn have their own page.

PAGES consisting of graphics are found at the left of a page-pair, and those consisting of text are at the right. This is consistent with the "split-brain" theory, which states that left and right sides of a brain process information differently.

TEXT PAGES are laid out in a structured way. They consist of "blocks" of text, separated by gaps of white space. Titles are not centered, but instead are allowed to "hang over," out of the blocks of text. Centering hides structure; indentation emphasizes it. Page numbers also hang over the top right of each page for easy reference.

PARAGRAPHS have a reverse indentation, like programs, the better to show the structure. The first sentence is the main or topic sentence, and the first word in it is also made the main or key word. This key word, often capitalized, protrudes into the left margin, so serving as a handle for this concept. This page is an example of such structure. Notice all the blocks, gaps, white space, indentation and capitalization.

PRODUCTION OF THIS BOOK

Computers were very widely used in the production of this book. They ranged from a microcomputer (Apple II) to a "monster" computer (CDC Cyber 170-750).

Graphics were produced interactively on a screen, and then run off on a printer. A student, Luis Castro, created the software for the Apple computer, and then lived with his creation to produce most of the graphics for this book ... almost 200 pages! Marie Alanen took part in the initial stages. My son Jan used this graphic system to create the syntax diagrams. Joe Kwan modified this graphics tool, making it more "friendly" to use.

Text portions of the book were produced originally on the Cyber by Ruth Horgan, and modified over many versions. The Runoff system was then re-created by Luis Castro to conveniently produce proportionately spaced text. Joe Kwan adapted the system to the Apple computer.

Portability between such diverse systems was accomplished mainly because all the tools (for graphics, text, indexing, etc.) were created in the Pascal language. The graphics compatibility among the Spinwriter, Diablo, and Dataproducts printers was a pleasant surprise.

Power of this computer production was rather awesome. I had total control over every aspect. For example, I could specify a diagram roughly, and Luis would enter it into the system, making improvements. Then I could preview the diagram on a screen, and refine it further. I could "tweak" any line, moving it as little as a sixtieth of an inch. Finally, I could get a "hard" copy on paper. To have a human artist re-draw a diagram for any slight change would be prohibitive; to specify a computer to do it was simple. This graphing tool (GRAPH), for creating flow block diagrams, is available from the author.

The text part of the book was developed similarly. I would specify the text initially, and Ruth would edit it before entering it. We had many discussions, leading to refinements which were very easily made to the "soft" copy. The text format was also possible to control in detail. I specified the distance between successive characters, the "leading" or space between the lines, and the space (lots of it) between paragraphs (forming blocks of text). This total control led to a novel indentation scheme, similar to that used for programs. Incidentally, the text in the appendices was not spaced proportionately; you may wish to compare it to the rest of the book.

Complexity of details in such a book could easily become overwhelming. Computers again made the complexity manageable, enabling the dozens of programs, hundreds of pages of text, and thousands of graphics to be readily retrieved, modified, and again stored.

SOURCES (Bibliography)

In this book I have borrowed from many sources. Most of these sources are at a higher level; I have tried to present them at an introductory level. For this reason, most of the following references should be read after this book, not along with it.

Programming, in general, is not covered in many books. One of the few language independent books is "FOUNDATIONS OF COMPUTER SCIENCE", written by M.S. Carberry, H.M. Khallil, J.F. Leathrum, L.S. Levy, and published by Computer Science Press.

Pascal is covered in many books, which often purport to cover problem solving and program design. Most go with very great detail into the Pascal language, and much less detail in developing the ability to create algorithms. A concise coverage of Pascal can be found in the classic "PASCAL USER MANUAL AND REPORT" by K. Jensen and N. Wirth, published by Springer-Verlag.

Data structures are most appropriately covered after this book. Niklaus Wirth has also written a book: "ALGORITHMS + DATA STRUCTURES = PROGRAMS" published by Prentice-Hall. It is concise but at a rather high level.

Machines are well treated in a book by J. Ullman: "FUNDAMENTAL CONCEPTS OF PROGRAMMING SYSTEMS" published by Addison-Wesley. It also links machines to languages.

Languages in general are treated in a unified way using contour diagrams by E.I. Organick, A.I. Forsythe and R.P. Plummer in their book entitled "PROGRAMMING LANGUAGE STRUCTURES" published by Academic Press.

Programming principles of a more theoretical nature are further developed by W. Wulf, M. Shaw, P. Hilfinger and L. Flon in their book "FUNDAMENTAL STRUCTURES OF COMPUTER SCIENCE" published by Addison-Wesley.

Design of programs in a structured way is developed by J.D. Warnier in "LOGICAL CONSTRUCTION OF PROGRAMS". The diagrams developed there have evolved into the break-out diagrams of this text.

Problems, 777 of them, can be found in the text "GRADED PROBLEMS IN COMPUTER SCIENCE" by A.D. McGettrick and P.D. Smith, and published by Addison-Wesley.

Notation for representing algorithms in flow block form evolved from a paper by I. Nassi and B. Shneiderman in the ACM SIGPLAN Notices (Volume 8, Number 8).

Mathematical and engineering systems concepts underlying many discrete structures (Boolean algebra, discrete probability, sequential machines and stochastic systems) are developed in the book "DIGITAL SYSTEMS FUNDAMENTALS" written by John Motil, and published by McGraw-Hill (hardcover) and Ridgeview Press (paperback).

THANKS   (Acknowledgments)

Many persons have contributed to this book, and I wish to thank them
all. None, however, is responsible for any errors. I had total
control over that, and I accept any blame.

First, I must thank Ruth Horgan and Luis Castro, two very hard-working
people, without whom I could not have completed this book. Their
work has been described on a previous page.

Faculty at California State University, Northridge (CSUN) have taught
from many early versions, and offered suggestions, changes, and
encouragement. They include: Jack Alanen, Morteza Anvari, Ronald
Colman, Raymond Gumb, Robert Henderson, Gary Hordemann, Ruth
Horgan, Dorothy Landis, Diane Schwartz, Linda Stanberry, and
Wigberto Yu. Raymond Davidson, Steve Gadomski, Philip Gilbert,
Steven Stepanek, and Rein Turn suffered through very early versions.
Other faculty who did not teach this course also contributed,
including Russell Abbott, Shan Barkataki, Michael Barnes, Fred
Gruenberger, Kenneth Modesitt, Peter Smith, and David Salomon.

Part-time faculty also contributed, especially Richard Kaplan, Robert
Lingard, Georgia Lulovics, Robert McCoard, and Albert Pierce.

Visiting faculty members also taught from this book and provided
differing insights. Thanks to John Van Iwaarden of Hope College,
Michigan, Paul Tavolato from the University of Vienna, and David
Brailsford from the University of Nottingham.

Professors from other departments often audited this course, and
provided unusual feedback. Thanks to Ernest Scheuer of Management
Science, Donald Bianchi of Biology, Edward Hriber and Virgil Metzler
of Engineering, Felix Jumonville and Larry Krock of Physical
Education, Donald Wood of Radio-TV-Film, and Jerrold Gold and Joel
Zeitlin of Mathematics. Richard Truman of Management Science read
some early chapters and eliminated many errors. Jeffrey Sicha of
Philosophy was particularly helpful in many ways.

Administrators at CSUN also helped in their own ways despite severe
resource problems. Thanks to two deans, Charles Sanders and
A. F. Ratcliffe, and to five department chairs (named above) in the
last few years. Sandra Metzger was instrumental in finding
equipment from various local industries. Use of donated equipment
from Dataproducts and Marketron was appreciated.

Participants in a Faculty Development Program were very helpful,
especially about pedagogical matters and the instructor's guide.
They include George Lorbeer of Secondary Education, Nathan Weinberg
of Sociology, Thomas Bader, Thomas Maddux, Alexander Muller, and
Michael Patterson of History. Other participants were Crerar
Douglas of Religious Studies, Richard Smith and James Torcivia of
Psychology and William Vincent of Physical Education. Additional
faculty included Beverly Grigsby of Music, John Miller of Management
Science, and Robert Noreen from the department of English.

MORE THANKS

Secretaries LuAnne Rohrer and Sally Gamon were very helpful, along with many student assistants. Nick Dalton spent many hours copying the graphics. The School technicians, Jack Siano, Bob Allen, Jan Berreitter, Herb Petzold, and Dennis Tibbetts, provided prompt and cheerful aid.

Other colleges have tried preliminary versions, and feedback was appreciated from Margaret Brennan of Glendale Community College, and Ken Stevens of The College of the Canyons. Graduate and senior students Darel Roberts and Ken Clark also contributed ideas and programs.

Reviewers of the manuscript had very helpful advice (some of which I did not take). Thanks to Gary Ford of Arizona State University, Madeleine Bates of Bolt Beranek and Newman, and David Boswell of the University of Waterloo. Very early reviews by Brian Hansche of Arizona State University were useful. Michael Meehan, my original editor, was particularly insightful. Other helpful people from Allyn and Bacon were Gary Folven, Doug Hinchey, Nancy Murphy and Paul Solaqua.

Students from many classes were very good at detecting errors. Encouraged by a small reward for each error or inconsistency, they helped improve the book. I found it interesting that some errors and inconsistencies were not detected by hundreds of students over the years. Some of these imperfections have not been removed in the spirit of "shaboui" - nothing is perfect unless it has some imperfection.

Computer Center staff, directed by Jerry Boles, were often very helpful. Thanks to Mona Clark, Gary Cohen, Jeff Craig, Ann Fuller, Joyce Hayes, J.P. Jones, Nancy Murry, Dave Sansom, Dave Thompson, and Kurt Webb.

Computer store owners Russ and Gene Sprouse from Rainbow Computing provided good information and service when it was badly needed. Lee Castile of California Press was very helpful with the final graphics.

I must also acknowledge Stan Rifkin, who (among other things) initially introduced me to the concept of Structured Programming, by arranging for me to attend a short course given by Edsger Dijkstra. There I was "born again" to programming, which I had previously come to dislike. I also feel privileged to have attended a course taught by Niklaus Wirth.

Finally, I must thank my family and friends for bearing with me during this "obsession."

John Motil

```
Chapter 0

OVERVIEW:
    TOP-DOWN
```

```
PROBLEMS

ALGORITHMS

COMPUTERS

LANGUAGES

SYSTEMS
```

OVERVIEW:
TOP-DOWN

PROBLEMS, SOLUTIONS,
ALGORITHMS, PROGRAMS,
LANGUAGES and MACHINES

* Asterisks indicate the degree of importance *

Chapter 0

OVERVIEW:
  TOP-DOWN

Problems, Solutions,
Algorithms, Programs,
Languages, and Machines

PREVIEW

This chapter provides an overview of programming, showing a brief
  "bird's-eye" view of the general ideas, and how they are related.

PROBLEMS are the main reason for programming, and the algorithmic
  way of solving problems is becoming increasingly important,
  especially for complex problems. Here we introduce ways of
  breaking up a problem into smaller sub-problems. In this
  chapter we will consider only some simple problems, such as the
  computation of part of a weekly payroll.

ALGORITHMS are plans for performing actions on objects. The plans
  may be general (policies, strategies, tactics) having nothing to
  do with computers, but here we will be mainly concerned with
  smaller algorithms and their corresponding computer programs. In
  this chapter we will also consider representations and extensions
  of simple algorithms.

LANGUAGES are methods for representing and communicating algorithms,
  both to humans and also to machines. We will be mainly concerned
  with languages convenient for humans (called high level) rather
  than those closer to machines (low level). Computers can easily
  convert (translate or interpret) a high level programming
  language into a low level computer language. In this chapter we
  will express the payroll program in different languages (Basic,
  Fortran, Pascal, Snobol, APL, and Lisp) to provide an insight
  into the similarities and differences among programming languages.

COMPUTERS are the physical machines than run (or execute) the
  programs. It is not necessary to know much about computers in
  order to use (or program) them. In this chapter we provide only
  a brief introduction into the structure of a computer and also a
  computing system.

Finally, this overview chapter ends with a brief glance at history.
  This view, of both computing history and world history, should
  put the brief lifetime of computing into its proper perspective.

BREAKOUT DIAGRAMS (BODs)

1 TIME

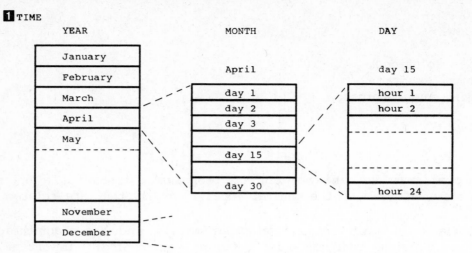

2 SPACE

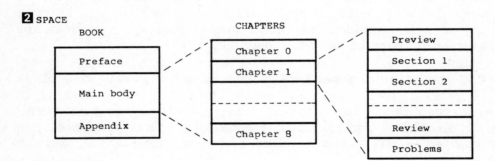

3 ACTIONS

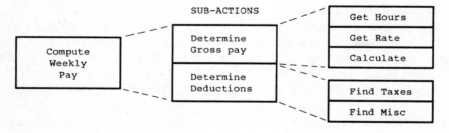

4 OBJECTS

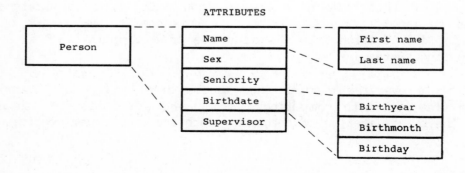

PROBLEMS AND PLANS: Breaking Out

This book is concerned primarily with problem solving and planning; only secondarily is it concerned with computing. The problems may be large and complex (controlling a factory, managing an inventory) or they may be smaller (such as calculating engineering problems, or computing statistics).

Even in simple problems, such as computing a weekly payroll, there could be considerable complexity, involving actions which depend on various changing conditions. Here we will try to develop a way of thinking of such problems, a logic of sequential actions, similar to natural languages, mathematics and logic.

The method of solving a problem is essentially the same as the method of cooking an elephant:

BREAK IT INTO SMALLER PIECES.

But breaking up a problem into smaller sub-problems is not always so easy as it may seem. There are many ways to break up anything; some are better than others. Unfortunately, the pieces required for computing are often so small that the great number of these small pieces creates another problem, that of complexity of quantity. Our challenge is to organize this complexity in our limited heads. This can only be done by looking at a small number of pieces at any one time and seeing how they fit into the "bigger problem."

BREAK-OUT DIAGRAMS (BODs)

One useful method of intellectually managing the complexity of problem solving is to use a tree-like skeleton for viewing problems in levels (or hierarchies). The given figures show four such tree-structures called "break-out diagrams" or call-out diagrams.

TIME can be broken down into years, months, days (and further) as suggested in figure 1. This break-out diagram, if completely expanded, would create one sequence of 365 (or 366) days.

SPACE, as in pages of a book, is shown similarly decomposed first into chapters, then into sections, and ultimately ending with sentences, words and finally letters.

ACTIONS, such as computing a weekly payroll, can be broken down into smaller actions (find the gross pay, find the deductions). Each of these sub-actions can also be split further. In fact, the rest of the chapter will be concerned mainly with this one sub-problem of computing the gross pay.

OBJECTS, such as the data of figure 4, also are easily described by break-out diagrams.

Notice how the same break-out diagrams describe four different entities as varied as space and time, actions and objects. The diagrams essentially show how the long, linear list of small "leaves" at the right is organized or grouped together (into branches) forming a two-dimensional tree.

This method of breaking up a problem is related to many methods such as divide-and-conquer, top-down, stepwise refinement, or the systems approach. It proceeds from the general "bird's eye" view, becoming successively more detailed, and ends at the bottom or "worm's-eye" view.

FIVE REPRESENTATIONS OF ALGORITHMS

1 VERBAL

> GROSS PAY
>   If the hours worked are less than (or equal to) 40, the
>   pay is the product of the number of hours worked and the
>   rate (of ten dollars an hour).   Also, if more than 40
>   hours are worked, the pay is 15 dollars an hour (time-
>   and-a-half) for each of the hours over 40.

2 PSEUDO-CODE

```
INPUT HOURS H
IF H <= 40 THEN
  P IS 10*H
ELSE
  P IS 10*40 + 15*(H-40)
ENDIF
OUTPUT PAY P
```

4 GRAPH (plot)

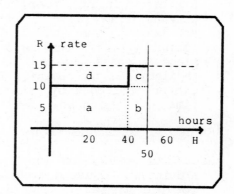

3 FLOWCHART

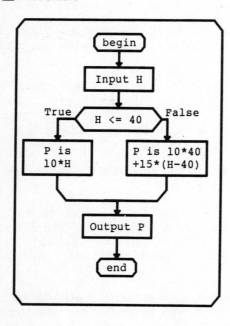

5 DATA FLOW DIAGRAM

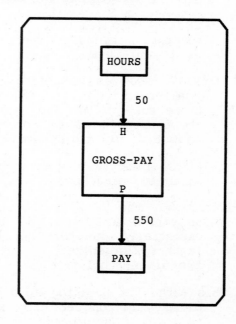

ALGORITHMS: Their Representations

ALGORITHMS are plans (or methods) for performing some actions (or operations) on some objects (items, data, etc.). As an example, we will consider the computation of the weekly (gross) pay of an individual. The objects are numbers; the actions are arithmetic operations of addition and multiplication. This algorithm is not difficult, but it will illustrate many concepts.

VERBAL representations of an algorithm can be given as statements in any natural language. A common pay algorithm is shown in figure 1. The pay rate (of ten dollars an hour) was chosen simply to make multiplication simple for us. Usually, more important reasons determine the pay rate!

PSEUDO-CODE representations of an algorithm are short symbolic descriptions similar to mathematics, logic, and natural language. For example, hours could be symbolized by H, and the pay symbolized by P. Similarly the mathematical operation of multiplication is shown as an asterisk (*), and the symbol for "less than or equal to" is "<=". The pay algorithm, using these symbols, is given in figure 2.

For example, if the hours worked are 25, then the pay is simply determined by multiplying the rate by the hours (10*25=250). But if the hours are 50, then the pay is the sum of two parts. The pay for the first 40 hours is the regular rate multiplied by 40 which is (10*40=400). For the part over 40, the hours over 40 are multiplied by the higher rate of 15 to get (50 - 40)*15 = 150. The total pay is the sum of these regular and overtime amounts (400 + 150 = 550).

FLOWCHART representations of algorithms consist of various boxes joined by arrows as shown in figure 3. Square boxes represent actions, and diamond-shaped boxes represent conditions which determine the arrows to be followed out of the boxes. This form makes it simple for humans to follow the flow of control.

GRAPHS (or plots) are diagrammatic representations that are convenient for humans to understand. The graph of figure 4 shows how the pay rate R depends on the number of hours H worked. The total pay for any number of hours is actually the shaded area under the curve. For example, at H = 50 the total pay corresponds to the rotated L-shaped area, consisting of three smaller rectangles labelled a, b, and c. The pay is:

P = 10*40 + 10*10 + 5*10 = 550.

The pay could also be determined by adding area "a" to the rectangle formed by "b" and "c":

P = 10*40 + 15*(50-40) = 550.

Another way is to take the large rectangle (a+b+c+d) and subtract away the smaller rectangle d.

P = 15*50 - 5*40 = 750 - 200 = 550.

DATA FLOW DIAGRAMS represent algorithms as machines, or black boxes, with data input and output as in figure 5. In this case, data "flows" in at one end (50 hours), and the resulting data (pay of 550 dollars) flows out at the other end. These diagrams hide the details of an algorithm, but they will be useful later to describe interaction among algorithms. Data flow diagrams indicate WHAT is being done, whereas flowcharts indicate HOW it is done.

More representations of algorithms are possible (flow blocks, tables, state diagrams, etc.) and they will be considered in the next chapter.

MODIFYING ALGORITHMS

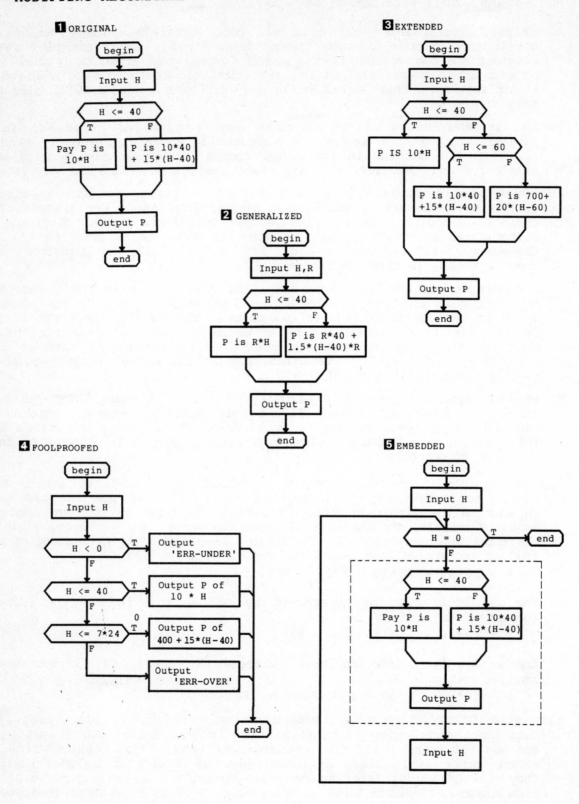

MODIFYING: Generalizing, Extending, Foolproofing, Embedding

Algorithms often go through many changes in their "lifetimes." Sometimes they are made more powerful, or more useful, more convenient, more efficient, or more foolproof. Sometimes they are used as parts of larger algorithms.

GENERALIZING algorithms is the process of making them apply to more and more examples. For instance, the previous pay algorithm, repeated in figure 1, applies only to people making a constant rate of 10 dollars an hour. This could be modified by allowing the input of any rate, say R, in addition to the hours H. This modification, shown in figure 2, now applies to more people (working at any rate), and is said to be more general.

EXTENDING algorithms to include more cases is also very common. For example, the original algorithm pays an overtime rate (time and a half) for any hours greater than 40. Often after more hours are worked (usually 60) there is a greater overtime rate, twice the regular rate. This extension of the original algorithm is shown in figure 3.

FOOLPROOFING is a process of making an algorithm more reliable or failsafe, by anticipating erroneous input or other difficulties. For example, if the hours were input as negative numbers, then an error message should be output. Also, if the hours input are more than the number of hours in a week (7*24=168) then another error message should be output. The resulting foolproofed, or robust, algorithm is given in figure 4.

EMBEDDING an algorithm is the process of using that algorithm within another algorithm. For example, the original pay algorithm is shown embedded within a loop in figure 5. While the input values for hours H are not zero, this algorithm computes the pay and keeps repeating. When a value of zero is input, the repetition or looping ends. This concept of looping is extremely useful and will be treated in great depth in the next chapters.

Notice that each of these figures shows a single modification of the original algorithm. If all four modifications were shown on one figure, the resulting algorithm would be considerably more complex than the original algorithm.

The realization that algorithms can be modified throughout their lifetimes is important, for it means that algorithms should be created so as to allow for modification. When algorithms are structured properly, their modification can lead to better algorithms; otherwise the modification can be disastrous.

COMPUTING MACHINES

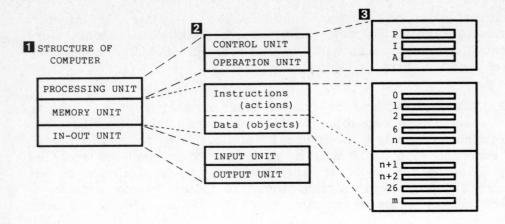

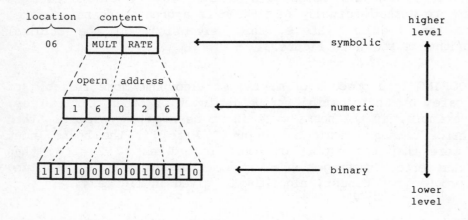

1 STRUCTURE OF COMPUTER

PROCESSING UNIT
MEMORY UNIT
IN-OUT UNIT

2 CONTROL UNIT
OPERATION UNIT

Instructions (actions)
Data (objects)

INPUT UNIT
OUTPUT UNIT

3 P
I
A

0
1
2
6
n

n+1
n+2
26
m

4 STRUCTURE OF INSTRUCTION

location   content

06 | MULT | RATE | ← symbolic   higher level

opern | address

| 1 | 6 | 0 | 2 | 6 | ← numeric

| 1 | 1 | 1 | 0 | 0 | 0 | 0 | 0 | 1 | 0 | 1 | 1 | 0 | ← binary   lower level

5 STRUCTURE OF DATA

location   content   name

26 | + | 10 | RATE   ← decimal value

sign | number

| 0 | 0 | 0 | 1 | 2 | ← intermediate value (octal, base 8)

| 0 | 0 | 0 | 0 | 0 | 0 | 0 | 0 | 0 | 0 | 1 | 0 | 1 | 0 | ← binary value

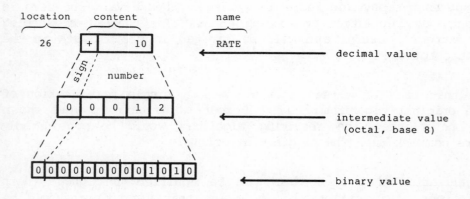

COMPUTERS: A Low Level View

Although computers differ in details, they have a common structure. They can be viewed as being composed of three units: a processing unit, a memory unit, and an input-output unit. These units are not always physically separate, but it is useful to view them functionally this way. Each unit can be further split into sub-units as shown in the break-out diagram of figure 1.

PROCESSING UNITS consist of a control part for "supervising" the behavior, and an operation part for carrying out the required operations. The operation unit is often called an ALU, arithmetic and logic unit.

MEMORY UNITS can also be viewed as two parts: one part containing the instructions, and the other containing the values that the instructions operate on. This concept of a "stored program" is extremely significant, for it makes possible a general purpose machine: changing the program in memory literally changes the behavior of the machine.

INPUT-OUTPUT UNITS serve either to input information (from keyboards or card readers) or to output information (to line printers or graphic displays).

REGISTERS, the basic building blocks of units, are shown in figure 3. The processing unit has few registers: a program register P, which points to the instruction being performed, and an instruction register I, which holds that present instruction. The operation unit contains working registers (such as the accumulator, A). The memory unit contains many registers, each given by a numerical address (or location).

INSTRUCTIONS in this computer (a typical single-address machine) have two parts, an operation part (such as MULTiply), and an address part (such as RATE) as shown in figure 4. These two parts are represented symbolically at the top level, and then each is broken into a corresponding numeric code where MULT has a numerical value of 16, and RATE has a value of 26 (referring to register 26). At the last level the numeric values are represented by their binary values: everything, to the computer, is ultimately zero or one.

DATA has a somewhat different structure, as shown in figure 5. This data (of location 26) could represent the rate of pay (which has a decimal value 10). It is first broken up into a sign part and a numeric part. At the next lower level the sign is converted to a binary value (zero for positive, 1 for negative), and the value of 10 is converted into an intermediate number (in base 8). Finally, at the lowest level everything is again in base 2, or binary.

More details on computers can be found in Appendix A.

PAY PROGRAM: IN SIX PROGRAMMING LANGUAGES

1 BASIC

```
100 REM   SIMPLE PAY IN BASIC
110 REM   H IS HOURS
120 REM   R IS RATE
130 REM   P IS PAY
140 INPUT H,R
150 IF H > 40 THEN 180
160    LET P=H*R
170 GOTO 190
180    LET P=40*R + (H-40)*1.5*R
190 PRINT 'GROSS PAY IS ',P
200 END
```

4 SNOBOL

```
*       SIMPLE PAY IN SNOBOL
        RATE = INPUT
        HOURS = INPUT
        GT(HOURS,40)        :S(OVER)
REG     PAY = HOURS * RATE :(OUT)
OVER
        PAY = 40 * RATE +
+       (HOURS - 40) * 1.5 * RATE
OUT     OUTPUT = 'GROSS PAY IS ' PAY
END
```

2 FORTRAN IV

```
C    SIMPLE PAY IN FORTRAN
     REAL   HRS,R,PAY
     READ(60,10) HRS,R
  10 FORMAT(2F10.2)
     IF(HRS.LE.40.0) PAY=HRS*R
     IF(HRS.GT.40.0) PAY=40.*R
  $     +(HRS-40.)*1.5*R
     WRITE(61,20) PAY
  20 FORMAT(14H GROSS PAY IS ,
  $            F10.2)
     STOP
     END
```

5 APL

```
          ∇ PAYROLL
[1]  ⍝ SIMPLE PAY IN APL
[2]  H ← □
[3]  R ← □
[4]  → (H>40)/7
[5]  P ← H×R
[6]  → OUT
[7]  P ← (40×R)+1.5×(H-40)×R
[8]  OUT : 'GROSS PAY IS ' P
          ∇
```

3 PASCAL

```
Program Pay( Input, Output);
 (* Simple pay in Pascal *)
Var  hours, rate, pay: real;
Begin
  Read( hours, rate );
  If hours <= 40 then
    pay := hours*rate
  else
    pay := 40*rate +
           (hours - 40)*1.5*rate;
  Write( 'gross pay is ',pay:6:2)
end.
```

6 LISP

```
(PAY  (LAMBDA (HOURS,RATE)
   (COND
     ((GREATERP 40 HOURS)
          (* HOURS RATE))
     (T (+ (* 40 RATE)
        (* (- HOURS 40)
           (* 1.5 RATE))
        )
   )))
 )
```

LANGUAGES: Communicating Algorithms

Programming languages are notations for communication of algorithms between humans and machines. There are now hundreds of such languages; six of the more lasting ones are shown in the figure, all expressing the same payroll algorithm. These examples are not intended to be thoroughly understood now, but are only to suggest similarities and differences.

All of these programs have a similar meaning (semantics) but differ greatly in the details of their form (syntax). For example, they all input the hours and rate, but each specifies this input differently: Basic and Snobol use the verb INPUT, Fortran and Pascal use READ, APL uses a rectangular "quad" box, and Lisp has no input operation. Lisp is always very different!

BASIC (Beginner's All-Purpose Symbolic Instruction Code) was developed by John Kemeny at Dartmouth College (around 1967). It is a simple programming language, designed to be easy to learn and to use. It is intended for convenient "conversational" (interactive) computing, whereby the user gets immediate response to what is typed.

FORTRAN (FORmula TRANslation), developed by John Backus (around 1957), was intended for engineering and scientific computations. It is still extensively used for numerical work.

PASCAL, created by Niklaus Wirth (around 1970), was based on an international language called Algol 60. It is similar to both Basic and Fortran, but incorporates many refinements in structure. Its clarity, simplicity, and unity make it suitable as a first programming language.

SNOBOL (StriNg Oriented symBOlic Language), developed by Ralph Griswold (around 1963), is a language that is particularly suited to handling strings of characters. It is useful in text processing and linguistics.

APL (A Programming Language), developed by Kenneth Iverson (1962), was initially only a concise mathematical notation (with many exotic symbols), which was later converted into a programming language.

LISP (LISt Processor), developed by John McCarthy (about 1960), is a very unusual language for processing trees (or lists). It is mainly used in artificial intelligence.

COBOL (COmmon Business Oriented Language), developed by a committee (CODASYL) in the late 1950s, is a language particularly suited to business applications.

Other programming languages have been created. Some of the surviving ones are: PL/I, Simula, Algol 60, and Algol 68, in addition to those listed above. Another language is Ada, based on Pascal.

More details on languages can be found in Chapter 4, and more on the Pascal language is in Appendix B.

A COMPLETE COMPUTING SYSTEM

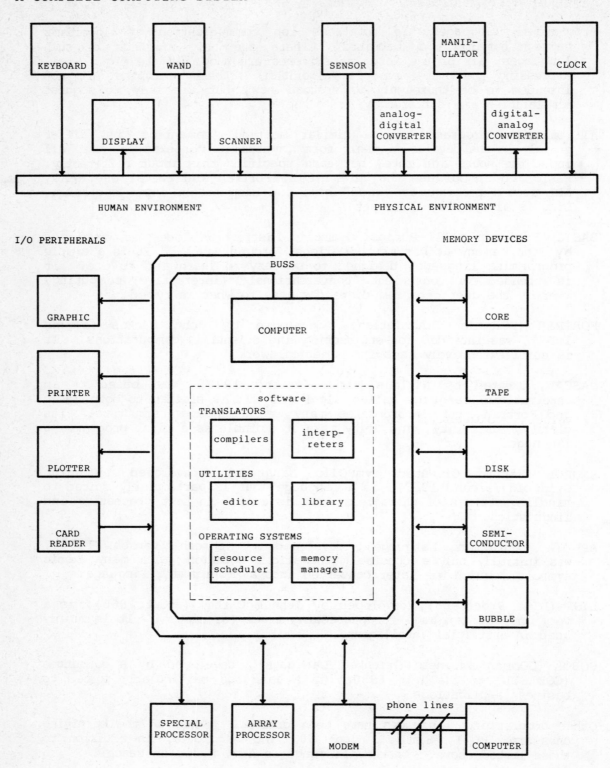

SYSTEMS: And Their Environments

COMPUTER SYSTEMS are described here to put computers into a
    proper perspective. A diagram of a computing system is shown;
    notice that the computer is one small component (in the
    center). The systems view takes a broader look at computing in
    terms of interacting with environments, both human and
    physical.

HUMAN ENVIRONMENTS, such as a business system, are shown to the
    left of the figure. Humans communicate through input devices
    such as keyboards, card readers, and "wands" (which can sense
    data, or can be touched onto appropriate places on a display).
    Humans receive outputs on video displays, printers, or
    plotters. These and other input-output devices connect to the
    system through an input-output buss, or channel.

PHYSICAL ENVIRONMENTS, such as a manufacturing plant, are shown
    at the top right of the figure. It communicates through
    transducers, such as a sensor to input a temperature, and an
    output manipulator to regulate the source of heat. Other
    devices, such as analog-to-digital converters, can transform
    some physical quantities (distance, pressure, time) from their
    analog or continuous values to equivalent discrete or digital
    values. Similarly, digital-to-analog converters transform
    digital values into continuous values.

MEMORY of a computer can be extended by auxiliary memory devices
    as shown to the right of the figure. Such devices include core
    memory, magnetic tape, disk, semiconductor, bubble memory, and
    any other types which can be "plugged onto" the memory buss.
    Other auxiliary devices may be "hung onto" this system (as
    shown on the bottom of the figure), including special array
    processors, and even other computers.

HARDWARE is the term which refers to these many physical devices
    of the system. Since humans and mechanical devices operate
    thousands of times slower than electronic devices, the computer
    can service all the devices ("polling" them hundreds of times a
    second), so appearing to simultaneously operate all the devices
    at the same time.

SOFTWARE is the term which refers to all the programs required to
    operate the system. This includes the translators (to convert
    high level languages into machine languages), utility programs
    (for convenience of editing, program storage and retrieval,
    etc.), and operating programs (for loading application
    programs, scheduling resources, and managing memory).

STAGES OF PROGRAMMING AND PROGRAMS

1 SMALL PROGRAM

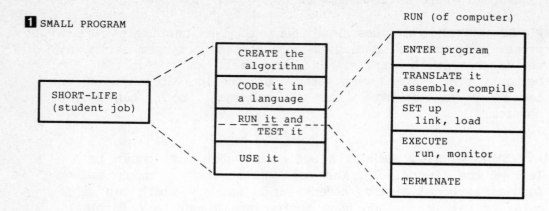

RUN (of computer)

SHORT-LIFE (student job)

| CREATE the algorithm |
| CODE it in a language |
| RUN it and TEST it |
| USE it |

| ENTER program |
| TRANSLATE it assemble, compile |
| SET up link, load |
| EXECUTE run, monitor |
| TERMINATE |

2 MEDIUM PROJECT
style profile

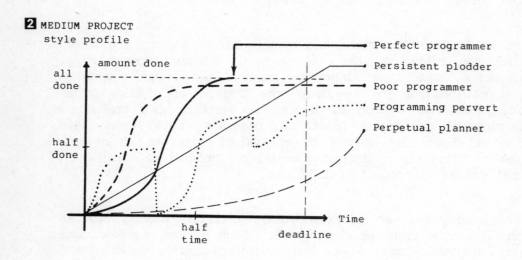

Perfect programmer
Persistent plodder
Poor programmer
Programming pervert
Perpetual planner

3 LARGE PRODUCT

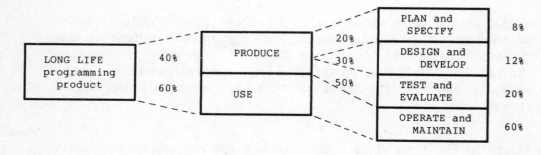

LONG LIFE programming product		PRODUCE		PLAN and SPECIFY	8%
	40%		20%	DESIGN and DEVELOP	12%
	60%	USE	30%	TEST and EVALUATE	20%
			50%	OPERATE and MAINTAIN	60%

LIFE CYCLES: Stages of Programming

Programs, like all dynamic things, are created, live, and then ultimately die. Small programs often have a different life cycle from larger ones, not necessarily shorter or longer.

SMALL programs, created simply for learning purposes, have a very simple life, as shown in figure 1. First the algorithm is created, and only then is coded or translated into a programming language. It is run and tested (sometimes repeatedly) on a computer. Finally small programs are used and ultimately thrown away. Sometimes they are modified and included within larger programs.

The run (or execution) done by the computer is shown in the last break-out diagram of figure 1. First the program (called a task or job) is entered or input, either by typing it in directly, or indirectly by punching onto cards. It is then translated (compiled or assembled) into the lower level language of the computer. This version is loaded into memory and linked to other programs (from a library of programs). The job is then run and monitored for time duration, space access, and errors. It finally terminates with some results (output data or error messages, with information on resources used, cost, etc).

MEDIUM programs, those that can be created by one person, have various styles of creation as shown in figure 2. It shows the work done (only the visible progress) as a function of time.

Perverted Programmer spends no time on creating an algorithm, but starts coding immediately. This leads to frequent throwing away of code and re-starting. The program is seldom finished in time.

Poor Programmer spends little time on planning the algorithm, rushes to coding, and spends most of the time testing. This programmer is "90 percent finished for over 90 percent of the time."

Persistent Plodder spends more time planning the algorithm, starts slower on the coding, requires less time for testing, and finishes just in time.

Perpetual Planner starts very slowly, spends much time in design, and never gets far into coding before the deadline.

Perfect Programmer spends a reasonable amount of time in creating the algorithm, which results in fast coding, and testing, and may be finished before the deadline.

LARGE PROGRAMS are those involving more than a single person. They are usually complex, and made more complex by the communication problems among people. Also, after they are completed, they are invariably modified throughout their lives. This modification, or maintenance, is shown as taking 60 percent of all the time, money and effort spent on a program, but it often takes over 70 percent!

The Life Cycle of a large programming project is shown in figure 3. Planning and specification involves studying the problem, analysing the requirements, specifying functions (actions) and data (objects).

Design and Development involves decomposing the whole project into parts, refining the parts, coding them, and documenting (describing) the design.

Test and Evaluation involves verifying the function, testing the performance, optimizing (improving time or space), and validating usefulness.

Operation and Maintenance involves the training of users, the operation, and the fixing of errors. It also includes extending the uses, optimizing, and modifying to transport the program to another computer or system.

HISTORY: EARTH, A TOP-DOWN PERSPECTIVE

1 Geological levels

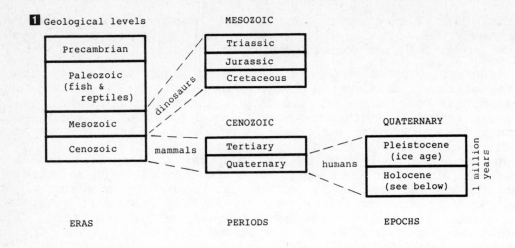

ERAS   PERIODS   EPOCHS

2 CREATIONISM

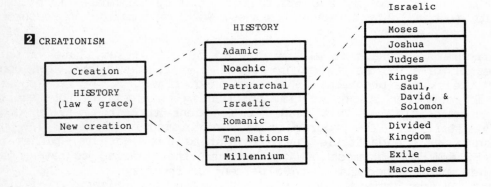

3 Archeological Levels **4** Classical Levels A.D. **5** Computing Levels

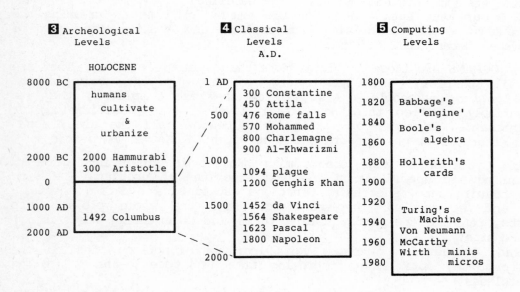

HISTORY: Of Programming and the Earth

Computers have been commercially available for only about thirty years, so their history is recent. To put this history into perspective, we will first view the complete history of the earth, and end with the history of computing. This view will again illustrate the break-out diagrams.

History of the earth could start with the geological levels called eras, which break up into periods, which in turn break up into epochs as shown in figure 1.
Alternately, a Creationist view of history (His-story) is given as a break-out diagram shown in figure 2.

More recent history is briefly shown in figures 3 and 4. You may wish to add your favorite historical events. Notice that the classical levels (the last 2000 years) are a very small part of the history of the earth. An even smaller part is the history of computing shown in figure 5.

AL-KHWARIZMI, a ninth century mathematician, studied sets of rules which are now called algorithms (named after him).
CHARLES BABBAGE, in the 1820s, created the first general-purpose "calculating-engine" with a sequential control using rotating wheels.
GEORGE BOOLE, in the 1840s, discovered that the symbolism of mathematics could be applied to logic. His algebra forms a basis for both the hardware (interconnections of components) and also the software (programs with compound conditions).
HERMAN HOLLERITH, around 1900, developed the punched card and its uses in data processing. The size of punched cards used even now is based on his choice, the size of a dollar bill of that time.
ALAN TURING, in 1937, introduced a conceptual model of computability and a theoretical device called a Turing Machine, which indicated limits on what is computable.
JOHN VON NEUMANN, around 1945, introduced the concept of a stored program, where instructions and data are both stored in memory.

Later developments are too recent to be objectively put into historical perspective. They include

    JOHN McCARTHY with a model of computing,
        and a language Lisp,
    EDSGER DIJKSTRA with a methodology of structured programming,
        and a structured operating system,
    NIKLAUS WIRTH with a methodology of stepwise refinement,
        and the language Pascal.

Other pioneers in the field of computing are: John Atanasoff, John Backus, Noam Chomsky, J. Presper Eckert, Robert Floyd, Fred Gruenberger, Tony Hoare, Grace Hopper, Donald Knuth, Ada (Byron) Lovelace, John Mauchly, Blaise Pascal, Herb Simon.

REVIEW: of Chapter 0

OVERVIEW: TOP-DOWN

Problems, Solutions, Algorithms,
Programs, Languages, and Machines

This chapter provides an overview of problems, planning, and programming.

Problems are solved by breaking them into sub-problems, and further subdividing the sub-problems. Break-out diagrams are particularly useful devices for breaking up the problems. These two-dimensional tree-like diagrams reduce complexity by showing how sub-parts relate to the whole. Break-out diagrams were used here to describe many things: space, time, objects, actions, as well as computers, stages in the life of programs, and the "flow" of history.

Algorithms are plans for performing actions on objects. They are shown represented in a number of ways (verbal, pseudo-code, graphic, flowchart, and data flow diagram). More representations are given in the following chapter. Algorithms are often modified (by generalizing, extending, foolproofing, and embedding) and so must be created to allow future modification.

Computers are the devices that perform the operations that are specified by algorithms. They, too, were briefly described by break-out diagrams. Computers are only one part of a system, which includes hardware (printers, plotters, sensors, etc) and also software (editors, compilers, schedulers, etc).

Languages for programming are many, and are illustrated here briefly by six languages (Basic, Fortran, Pascal, Snobol, APL, and Lisp). Most programming languages are quite similar in what they do (behavior, or semantics) but are very different in looks (form, or syntax).

Many concepts of this chapter are very general and not very detailed. This follows the top-down view: first we see the whole picture; then we get deeper into details. This allows us to see how the detailed parts fit into the big picture. The "bottom-up" view starts with the details, often getting lost in them. It does have its place, but that place is not at the beginning.

PROBLEMS: on Chapter 0

1. SCISSORS SEARCH
    Indicate which of the following verbal algorithms is better for finding some object (such as the "good" scissors), and explain why:
    a. Look on the rightmost end of the lower shelf of the middle cabinet in the garage.
    b. Look in the garage, in the middle cabinet, on the lower shelf, at the rightmost end.

2. BREAK-OUT PROBLEMS
    Create break-out diagrams describing four of the following:
    a. a telephone number
    b. arrangement of items on a shelf
    c. performing some process (laundry, cooking)
    d. your entire past life
    e. plan of your present day
    f. plan of the next five years
    g. layout of newspaper sections
    h. electromagnetic frequency spectrum
    i. anything else of interest to you.

3. MORE PAY   (page 0-6)
    a. If the condition for overtime in the original payroll problem was changed, from (H <= 40) to (H < 40), does this change the amount of pay?
    b. If hour H is input as a negative amount (say -50 by mistake), is the output correct except for its sign?
    c. Extend the extended pay algorithm for triple-pay when the hours are greater than 80. Draw the corresponding graph and flow chart.
    d. Modify the embedded pay algorithm by including the foolproofing of figure 4, the extensions of figure 3, and the generalizations of figure 2.

4. LANGUAGE LOOK
    Even without knowing any programming languages, you can now meaningfully make comparisons among the six presented in this chapter.
    a. Is multiplication indicated by an asterisk (*) in all of these languages?
    b. What different symbols represent the relation "is greater than"?
    c. What different verbs describe the output instruction?
    d. When some statements (formulas, etc.) are too long to fit on a line and continue onto another line, how is this indicated (in Snobol, Fortran, Pascal)?
    e. Statements called comments are intended for communication to humans, rather than machines. How are such comments indicated in each language?

5. PRICE BREAK
    Suppose the price P of something (say peanuts or power) depends on the quantity Q that is purchased. For example, if the quantity is less than or equal to three, then the price is four dollars per unit (each); otherwise, it is three dollars per unit.
    a. Create a flow chart where quantity Q is input and the total price T of this amount is output.
    b. Extend the above flow chart when there is another price break, where the unit price is 2 dollars if the quantity is over five.
    c. Represent the above algorithm as a graph of P versus Q. Does the area under this curve represent the total cost?
    d. Draw a graph of T versus Q, when Q varies from 0 to 8.
    e. How do the above graphs change if the quantities are non-divisible (such as pens, pumpkins or puppies)?

CHAPTER 0: PROBLEMS

6. THINK BIG

Suppose that entire computers became as small as bugs (roaches or integrated circuits), and had the ability to move around and manipulate things (carry, measure, cut, etc). Write a brief essay indicating possible uses and potential benefits of such programmable bugs (PRUGS).

For example, many functions could be performed differently. Lawns could be maintained, not by mowing, but with an "army" of PRUGS roaming around randomly, measuring each individual blade of grass and cutting it off at a precise length.

7. THINK WELL

Write another brief essay anticipating the negative consequences of the PRUGS in the previous problem.

8. BAD BODS (BEWARE)

The following BODs are not proper. Why not? Redraw each of them in a better form.

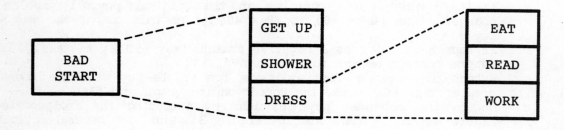

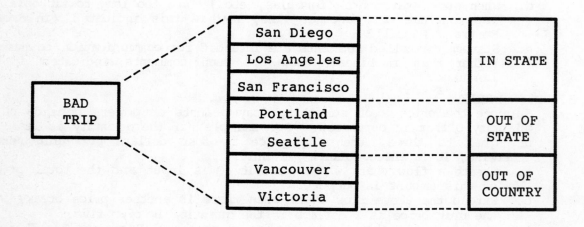

Chapter 1

ALGORITHMS:
REPRESENTATIONS

VERBAL FORM

ALGEBRAIC FORM

TABULAR FORM

TREE FORM

FLOW CHART FORM

FLOW BLOCK FORM

DATA FLOW DIAGRAM

STATE DIAGRAM FORM

ALGORITHMS:

REPRESENTATIONS

* Asterisks indicate degree of importance *

Chapter 1:

ALGORITHMS

Representations

PREVIEW

In this chapter, we define algorithms, indicate their properties, provide simple examples of them, and present various representations. Representations of algorithms are many, including verbal, algebraic, and tabular forms, as well as various diagrams (flowcharts, flow block diagrams, data flow diagrams, state diagrams). Not all of these forms are equally important; they are given as a brief survey. Ultimately, you will come to prefer some of the representations over others.

ALGORITHMS: Definition and Properties

An algorithm is a plan (method or procedure) for performing some actions (operations or processes) on some objects (items or data). Examples of algorithms are:

            Prepare a meal (breakfast or dinner)
            Change a tire (on a car)
            Change money (from a dollar)
            Charge people (for admission)
            Sort names (alphabetically)
            Plan a schedule (for a day or week)
            Play a game (of cards or a sport)
            Pay a loan (mortgage)
            Average some numbers (grades, mileage)
            Operate a device (camera, campstove)
            Specify a last will (trust)
            Follow a process (develop film)

Notice that each algorithm specifies an action and an object to be acted on. Many of these algorithms will be considered later in detail, but now it is sufficient to see that algorithms are quite common and do not necessarily involve computers.

GENERAL PROPERTIES OF ALGORITHMS

Algorithms, to be useful, must satisfy four main properties: generality, completeness, consistency, and finiteness.

GENERALITY means that an algorithm solves a class of problems, not simply one problem. An algorithm to average numbers should average not just 4 numbers, nor 44, but any number N of them.

COMPLETENESS means that an algorithm must be defined for all cases; no cases should be left unspecified. For example, the algorithm:

        "Charge $2 for people under 12, and $3 for people over 12"

is not complete since it does not specify a charge for twelve-year-olds.

CONSISTENCY means that an algorithm must be uniquely defined; there must not be two or more conflicting behaviors. For example, the algorithm:

        "Charge $2 for people 12 or under, and $3 for people 12 or over"

is not consistent since it specifies two rates for twelve-year-olds.

FINITENESS means that an algorithm must be restricted to occupying a limited space, and taking a limited time to perform. For example, consider an algorithm to determine if there are 7 consecutive 7s in the decimal expansion of PI (3.14159...). If the algorithm proceeds simply by searching through the entire (infinite) expansion, then it may never halt, and so may not be finite.

ALGORITHMS REPRESENTED VERBALLY

---

1   CHARGE Admission

Children (under 12)
pay 2 dollars; all
others pay 3 dollars

---

3   DAYS - in a month

Thirty days hath September,
April, June and November.
All the rest have thirty-one
Except February alone
Which has four plus twenty-four
And every leap year one day more

---

2   LEAP year

A leap year is divisible
by 4, but if it is also
divisible by 100 it is
not a leap year unless
also divisible by 400.

---

5   DICE game (simple craps)

First, two dice are thrown.
If their sum is 7 or 11 you win, and
if the sum is 2 or 3 or 12 you lose,
otherwise remember the sum (point)
and keep throwing until either
the point comes up (and you win)
or a 7 comes up (and you lose).

---

4   PLAY BALL (baseball)

The game goes on when
the inning is less than
or equal to 9 or the
score is tied, and
it is not raining.

---

6   ISBN checksum code

Find the sum of:
 the first digit and
 two times the second digit,
 three times the third
 and so on to...
 nine times the ninth digit.
Then divide this sum by 11,
 and find the remainder.
If it is less than 10 it
becomes the checksum,
 otherwise the checksum
 is the character X.

---

7   LOAN - repayment of amount A

While a balance B remains, make
a payment P each month, and
adjust the balance accordingly
(including an amount of
interest at some rate R of the
remaining balance).

VERBAL REPRESENTATION OF ALGORITHMS: Common Examples

We will consider many algorithms and their representations in this chapter. For each representation there are many examples so that you may find at least one of interest to you. They are meant to communicate to humans; later some may be modified to run on machines. It is not required that you understand all the algorithms. You should be able to follow every algorithm, for that is precisely what computers do.

Some very common examples of algorithms are specified in the given figures. They appear here in a simple verbal form (representation), and will be put into other forms later. For any particular algorithm one representation may be much better than another, so it is worth getting familiar with a number of alternative forms.

CHARGE, of figure 1, specifies an admission charge, which depends on the age of the person being admitted. It was previously considered and has the properties of consistency and completeness.

LEAP, of figure 2, indicates a method of determining if a given year is a leap year. Usually it is sufficient to see if 4 divides evenly into the year, but in the case of a century year the algorithm is more complex. For example, the year 1900 was not a leap year, but the year 2000 will be a leap year.

DAYS, of figure 3, is a simple poem which aids us in determining the number of days in any month.

PLAY BALL, of figure 4, shows an algorithm to determine if a baseball game is to continue or not.

DICE, of figure 5, indicates how a simple game is played, using two cubes (dice) having one to six dots on each side.

ISBN, of figure 6, describes the International Standard Book Number. Most recent books are given a special ten-digit ISBN code such as
    0-205-08005-7   (hyphens are not important)
The first nine digits are assigned by the publisher, and the last digit is a checking digit which is computed from the nine preceding digits as shown in the figure. For example, the "weighted sum" of the above number is:

$$0 + 2*2 + 3*0 + 4*5 + 5*0 + 6*8 + 7*0 + 8*0 + 9*5 = 117$$

Dividing this sum by 11 yields a remainder of 7, which is the checksum. This code is used for error checking, for example in ordering a book. If the checksum computed does not equal the last digit, then an error has been made in copying this book number.

LOAN, of figure 7, indicates how an initial loaned amount A (say $100) is to be repaid, with payments P (say $20), and an interest rate R (of say 10%). This algorithm could be used to determine the total time required to pay off the loan.

ALGORITHMS REPRESENTED AS FORMULAS

---

1 CHARGE admission

C = 3*A + 2*B
where
   A is the number of adults
   B is the number of babies

---

5 TIME: Days, Hours, Mins to seconds

T = S + 60*M + 60*60*H + 24*60*60*D
       or alternately
T = S + 60*(M + 60*(H + 24*D))

---

2 MAXimum of two values X,Y

$$MAX = \begin{cases} X \text{ if } X > Y \\ Y \text{ otherwise} \end{cases}$$

---

6 MEAN and VARIANCE of X1,X2,... XN

M = (X1 + X2 + X3 +...+ XN)/N
V = [(X1-M)^2+(X2-M)^2+...+(XN-M)^2]/N

---

3 TEMPerature conversion

C = (5/9)*(F-32)
F = 9/5*C + 32

---

7 SINE with FACTORIAL sub-formula

SIN(X)=X - X^3/3! + X^5/5! - X^7/7! +...
WHERE:
   N!=N*(N-1)*(N-2)*...*3*2*1

---

4 SQUARE S of integer N

A) S = N*N

- -

B) S = N + N + N +...N

- -

C) S = 1 + 3 + 5 + 7 +...

---

8 BASE conversion

a) binary
  $(a_n,...,a_3,a_2,a_1,a_0)_2 = \sum a_i*2^i$
  $=a_0+a_1*2^1+a_2*2^2+a_3*2^3+...+a_n*2^n$

- -

b) general
  $(a_n...a_2a_1a_0)_b = \sum a_i*b^i$
  $=a_0+a_1*b^1+a_2*b^2+...+a_n*b^n$

ALGEBRAIC REPRESENTATION: Expressions and Formulas

Many algorithms, especially in mathematics and engineering, are given in algebraic form as expressions or formulas. This is often a very brief form, convenient for computers. Some examples of this algebraic form follow.

CHARGE, represented again in figure 1, probably is most simple as this formula.

MAX is a very useful algorithm; here it describes how to find the maximum value of two numbers. The example shows how the maximum value MAX of X and Y is determined, by selecting one of the two formulas depending on the comparison between X and Y. Later we will use MAX to find the maximum value of three or more numbers.

TEMP shows the typical temperature conversion formulas.

SQUARES, of figure 4, indicates three different algorithms to compute the square of any positive integer number N.

First, N could be simply multiplied by N.
Secondly, if multiplication is not possible or convenient, the number N could be added to itself N times.
Finally, the square of an integer N can be determined by summing the first N odd integers. For example

$$7^2 = 7*7 = 1 + 3 + 5 + 7 + 9 + 11 + 13 = 49.$$

This SQUARES example illustrates the fact that there may be many ways to do something. In fact, there are other ways of finding this square, which we shall see later.

TIME is an algorithm for converting days, hours, minutes, and seconds into seconds. This is done in two ways. The first way seems natural; the second way comes from factoring out common terms, and results in half as many multiplication operations.

OTHER ALGEBRAIC FORMS (Optional)

MEAN and VARIANCE are statistical measures. The mean, M, is a central value (of N given values), and the variance, V, indicates the amount of variation of the values about this mean value. Expressions involving such sums are often written in a short but complex notation such as:

$$M = \sum_{i=1}^{N} X_i / N \quad \text{and} \quad V = \sum_{i=1}^{N} (X_i - M)^2 / N$$

SINE of an angle X may be computed by a few terms from the formula indicated in figure 7. Notice that it refers to a sub-formula for computing the factorial (denoted N!).

BASE is a formula to convert binary numbers into decimal (or base 10) numbers. For example, the binary number 1101 becomes:

$$(1101)_2 = 1*2^3 + 1*2^2 + 0*2^1 + 1*2^0 = 13 \text{ (in decimal)}$$

A more general formula for any base, b, appears in figure 8b.

ALGORITHMS REPRESENTED AS TABLES

 1 DAYS

Month	Days
1	31
2	→
3	31
4	30
5	31
6	30
7	31
8	31
9	30
10	31
11	30
12	31

2 LEAP

LEAP YEAR	FEB DAYS
NO	28
YES	29

3 RESISTOR

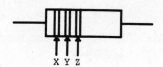

X Y Z

$$R = (10*X + Y)*10^Z$$

COLOR	CODE
Black	0
Brown	1
Red	2
Orange	3
Yellow	4
Green	5
Blue	6
Violet	7
Gray	8
White	9

4 CHARGE

A	B	C
1	0	3
1	1	5
1	2	7
1	3	9
2	0	6
2	1	8
2	2	10
2	3	12
3	0	9
3	1	11
3	2	13
3	3	15

5 CHARGE IN 2 DIMENSIONS

A＼B	CHARGE 0	1	2	3
1	3	5	7	9
2	6	8	10	12
3	9	11	13	15

6 MAJORITY

A	B	C	MAJ
0	0	0	0
0	0	1	0
0	1	0	0
0	1	1	1
1	0	0	0
1	0	1	1
1	1	0	1
1	1	1	1

7 DECISION TABLE

MAJ Decision Table					
A	Y	Y	-	N	N	-
B	Y	-	Y	N	-	N
C	-	Y	Y	-	N	N
MAJ	Y	Y	Y	N	N	N

8 BINARY

A3	A2	A1	A0	B
0	0	0	0	0
0	0	0	1	1
0	0	1	0	2
0	0	1	1	3
0	1	0	0	4
0	1	0	1	5
0	1	1	0	6
0	1	1	1	7
1	0	0	0	8
1	0	0	1	9
1	0	1	0	10
1	0	1	1	11
1	1	0	0	12
1	1	0	1	13
1	1	1	0	14
1	1	1	1	15

TABULAR REPRESENTATION: Tables, Arrays, Matrices

Tables (also called arrays or matrices) are rectangular grids having entries (values) within the grids. Tables are often convenient for representing algorithms.

DAYS, previously indicated verbally, is shown as a table in figure 1. Here the months are represented as integers from 1 to 12. Corresponding to each such integer is a number indicating the number of days in that month. However in February, there is another tabular form given in figure 2, showing that one algorithm may be a sub-algorithm of another algorithm.

RESISTOR, of figure 3, indicates how the three colored bands on an electrical resistor can be read to determine the value of the resistance. For example, if the bands are Red, Yellow, and Orange, the corresponding codes from table 3 are 2, 4, and 3, yielding a value of $24*10^3$, or 24,000 ohms.

CHARGE, also encountered earlier (for admission of $3 per Adult and $2 per Baby), could be computed once for the most common numbers of A (Adult) and B (Baby), and then referred to thereafter to save further computation. For example, in the alternate version, figure 5, the charge corresponding to A adults (say A=2) and B babies (say B=1) can be determined by moving along the row (for A=2), and down the column (for B=1). The point at which the row and column intersect (C=8) indicates the amount to charge for this combination. Notice that this algorithm is not complete, but it is still convenient and useful for it specifies the charge for the most common combinations of adults and babies.

MAJORITY compares three variables A, B, and C (which have only two values, 0 or 1), and indicates which value appears two or three times. For example, if A = 1, B = 0 and C = 1, then the MAJority value is 1, as indicated in the third from last row of figure 6.

DECISION TABLES, as shown in figure 7 (for the MAJority decision), are an alternative form of table 6. They are used in many business applications, for they are easy to check for completeness and consistency, since all combinations are listed. The main difference is in the notation; A, B, and C are called conditions, and MAJ is called an action. Each of the six combinations of A,B,C are called rules. For example, consider the first column (rule); if A and B conditions are both Yes, then regardless of condition C (the dash indicating don't care) the MAJority action is Yes.

BINARY, of figure 8, is a listing of some binary (base 2) and decimal (base 10) equivalent numbers.

Indices refer to a position in a table. For example, the tables corresponding to DAYS, LEAP, and RESISTOR have only one index each. CHARGE has two indices labelled A and B. MAJ has three indices labelled A,B,C. BINARY has four indices labelled A0, A1, A2, and A3. Indices are often called subscripts.

ALGORITHMS REPRESENTED AS TREES

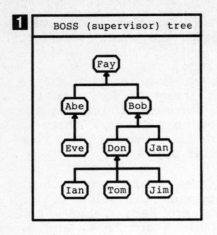

1 BOSS (supervisor) tree

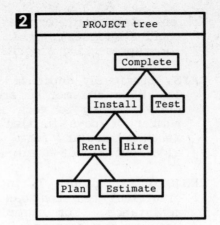

2 PROJECT tree

EXPRESSION trees

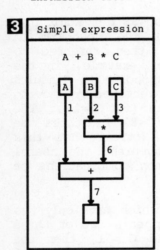

3 Simple expression

A + B * C

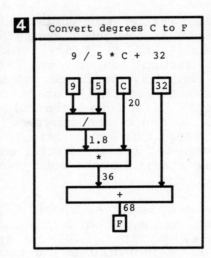

4 Convert degrees C to F

9 / 5 * C + 32

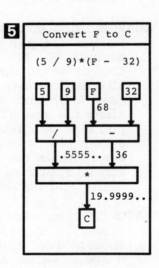

5 Convert F to C

(5 / 9)*(F - 32)

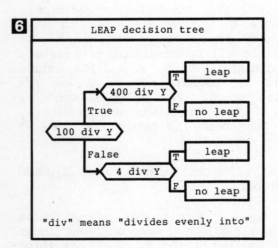

6 LEAP decision tree

"div" means "divides evenly into"

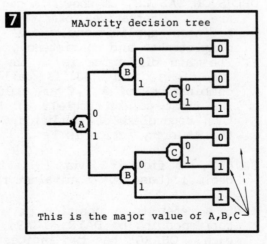

7 MAJority decision tree

This is the major value of A,B,C

TREE REPRESENTATION: Levels and Hierarchies

Trees are extremely important in computing. They have a great many applications, only a few of which we can appreciate now. Trees are also very convenient for humans, for everyone has some idea of a tree, and the notation (of trunk, branches, nodes, and leaves) is self-explained. Trees are a useful way of showing a break-up into levels.

Unfortunately, in computing, trees are not always drawn in the "natural" way with the trunk rooted at the bottom, and the leaves reaching upward. For example, the trees in figures 1 and 2 have their trunks above the leaves, and the trees in figures 6 and 7 are laid on their sides. Only the trees in figures 3, 4, and 5 are shown in their natural positions.

BOSS, of figure 1, is an organization chart which may be viewed as a tree with arrows on each branch indicating who is the boss or immediate supervisor of each person. Note that the top person supervises itself.

PROJECT is another "hierarchical" diagram showing how a problem COMPLETE (of a building project) is broken down into sub-problems (first INSTALL, secondly TEST), with each sub-problem broken down further again.

EXPRESSIONS, of figure 3,4,5, show trees of arithmetic expressions or formulas, indicating how numbers are grouped. The most common convention (called precedence) is that multiplication is done before addition and subtraction. For example 1 + 2 * 3 is 7, as shown in figure 3. When multiplication and division appear together in a term, it is evaluated from the left to the right as in figure 4.

Parentheses can be used to override these conventions. Figure 5 shows how formulas within parentheses are to be evaluated first.

Notice that figure 4 converts 20 degrees C to 68 degrees F, and figure 5 converts this resulting 68 degrees F to 19.9999... degrees C. This illustrates a problem of possible inaccuracy when dealing with repeated unending decimals, such as 5/9 (or similarly 1/3).

LEAP, of figure 6, shows how to determine if a given year Y is a leap year, by following certain branches depending on the conditions at the nodes. For example, consider the year 1984. First, 100 does not divide evenly into 1984, so the lower branch is followed to the node asking if 4 divides 1984 evenly. Since it does, the next upper branch is followed to the resulting conclusion, that 1984 is a leap year.

MAJority is a decision tree, similar to LEAP. The path taken out of each node depends on the value (0 or 1) associated with that node.

ALGORITHMS REPRESENTED AS FLOWCHARTS

1 ACTIONS

| Charge $3 | Sum N values | Output result |

2 CONDITIONS

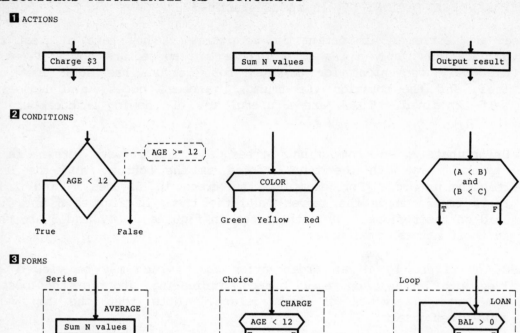

3 FORMS

Series

AVERAGE

Sum N values

Divide by N

Sub forms

AVERAGE

Choice

CHARGE

AGE < 12

T   F

CHARGE $2   CHARGE $3

CHARGE

Loop

LOAN

BAL > 0

T   F

make PAY
change BAL

LOAN

4 COMBINED FORMS

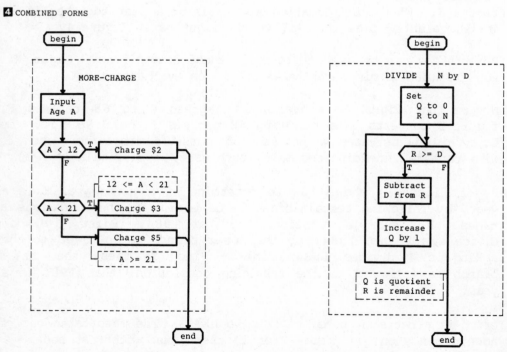

FLOWCHART REPRESENTATION: Flow of Control

Flowcharts are a common representation of algorithms. They consist of boxes joined by lines (arrows). The boxes are of various shapes depending on whether they represent actions, conditions or assertions.

ACTIONS denote processes (such as input, output, calculate) and are represented as rectangular boxes, as shown in figure 1.

CONDITIONS indicate possible events (decisions or tests such as AGE < 12, color) which have a number of outcomes (usually true or false). Conditions are represented by diamonds (or flattened diamonds) with one outgoing arrow labelled for each outcome, as in figure 2.

ASSERTIONS are comments or facts (such as "Age >= 12") indicating the situation (truth) at any point of a flowchart. They are shown by dotted boxes pointing to the places where the assertions hold true.

FORMS indicate the ways actions and objects may be connected. There are only four fundamental forms, as illustrated in the following examples.

AVERAGE (really MEAN in disguise) simply has two actions in series (or cascade), one following the other.
CHARGE involves a choice of actions depending on whether the condition "AGE < 12" is true or false.
LOAN involves a loop depending on the condition "Balance greater than 0," abbreviated as "BAL > 0". While this condition is true, a payment is made and the Balance changed accordingly (each month). Only when the Balance is finally reduced to zero is this loop left.

The above examples can each be put into a box (with double vertical sides) and considered a single action (sub-action) within other flowcharts, as shown below each form of figure 4.
These same examples illustrate the basic building blocks (or four fundamental forms: Series, Choice, Loop, and Sub) from which all algorithms can be made. Notice that each of these four forms has a single entry and a single exit.

MORE CHARGE, of figure 4, shows a slightly more complex algorithm. It is an extension of the previous CHARGE algorithm, which has been modified to include a third category (that of adult, those 21 or over). This form of an algorithm, going through many decisions (cases) in a sequence until one succeeds, is called a CASE form. Notice the assertions in the dotted boxes.

DIVIDE, of figure 5, is an algorithm to divide one whole number (N, the numerator) by another nonzero whole number (D, the denominator) to produce a quotient Q and remainder R. This is done by successive subtractions, going around a loop adding 1 to Q for each time that D is subtracted from remainder R, until this remainder is less than D. Notice that this is very different from the way humans divide.

COMBINED FORMS

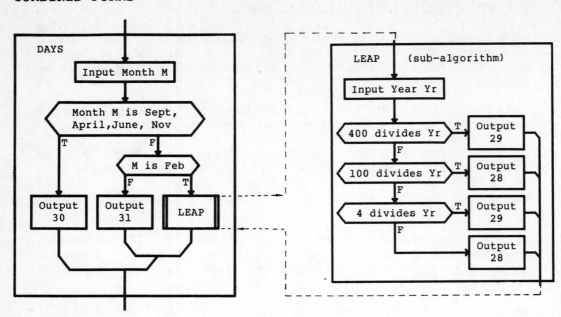

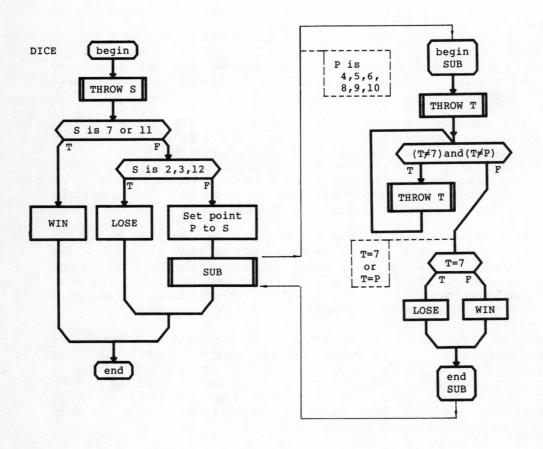

LARGER FLOWCHARTS: Use of Sub-algorithms

As algorithms become larger it is often convenient to split them into smaller connected algorithms. Each sub-algorithm may then be considered separately, making the entire algorithm more intellectually manageable. Two such "decomposed" algorithms follow.

DAYS is an algorithm which determines the number of days in any month M. It does this first for all the months except February. Since that month is rather complex, it is separated from the original algorithm as a sub-algorithm called LEAP.

LEAP simply decides if a year is a leap year by determining if the year can be divided evenly by various numbers (400, 100 and 4), as shown in the figure. Notice that the sub-algorithm LEAP may seem more complex than the "main" algorithm DAYS.

DICE is a simple game called craps, which is played with two dice (cubes having each side marked with 1 to 6 dots). The two are thrown ("rolled") with the resulting sum of dots from 2 to 12. The rules for this game are:

> First, two dice are thrown.
> If their sum is 7 or 11 you win.
> If the sum is 2, 3 or 12 you lose.
> Otherwise, remember the sum (called the point).
> Keep throwing the dice, until either
> this point comes up (and you win) or
> until a 7 comes up (and you lose).

The given flowchart describes the game. The main algorithm describes the first throw, and the sub-algorithm SUB describes all subsequent throws (if any). A third sub-algorithm THROW is shown below.

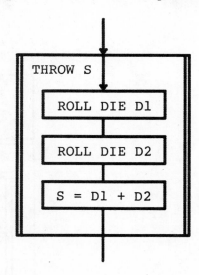

THE RELATION BETWEEN FLOWCHARTS AND FLOW BLOCKS

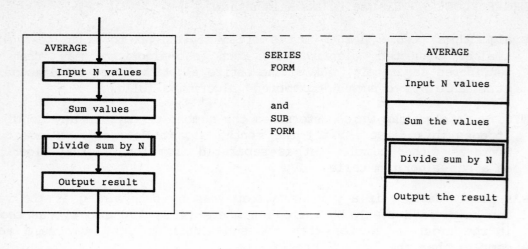

SERIES
FORM

and
SUB
FORM

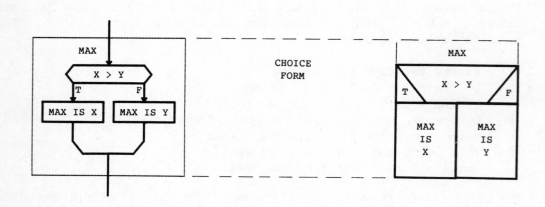

CHOICE
FORM

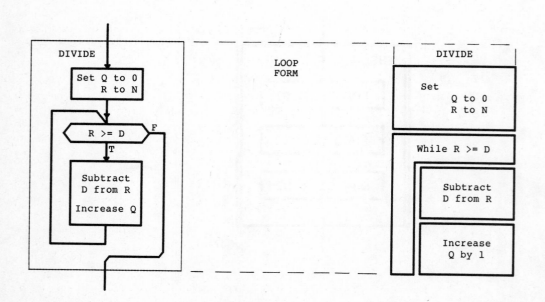

LOOP
FORM

FLOW BLOCK DIAGRAM REPRESENTATION: Alternatives to Flowcharts

Flow block diagrams are alternative diagrams to flowcharts. Flowcharts can be useful for humans to create and communicate
algorithms. However, flowcharts often do not flow! The lines
joining the boxes often meander in complex paths, making an
algorithm difficult to understand, and so destroying the simple
beauty of the graphic form. Also, when creating flowcharts, many
dangling lines (arrows) can easily get connected to the wrong
boxes, resulting in error-prone algorithms.

Flow blocks (or structure charts or Nassi-Shneiderman Diagrams) are
graphic alternatives to flowcharts. They consist of a series of
rectangular boxes, which are easier to draw than flow charts. The
boxes can be placed (connected) only in certain patterns, usually
one above the other (so the single exit of one is the single entry
of another), thus preventing bad structures. So the blocks flow!

Algorithms illustrating flow block diagrams are given in the figure.
They are shown next to their equivalent flowcharts for comparison.

SERIES forms (illustrated by AVERAGE) simply have all the lines
removed, so the boxes sit on top of one another. Note that the
boxes can be enlarged, for room need not be left for the arrows.

CHOICE forms (illustrated by MAX) evolve from the flowchart by
distorting the decision "diamond shape" into a triangular shape
with the entry at the top. Then, depending on the condition in
this triangle, the exit is by one of the two sides of the triangle
into one of two boxes below. Finally, the two paths join again at
the bases of the two boxes.

LOOP forms (illustrated by DIVIDE) consist of a "reversed L-shaped"
box which encompasses the body or that part which is to be
repeated while the condition is true.

SUB forms (such as DIVIDE shown in the AVERAGE program) are now
denoted by a box within a box, which are easier to see than the two
vertical lines of the flowchart sub-algorithm.

DAYPLAN, on the following page, shows another, larger flow block
diagram describing the plan of one student's day. It needs no
further explanation.

DICE, also on the following page, contrasts flowcharts with flow block
diagrams.

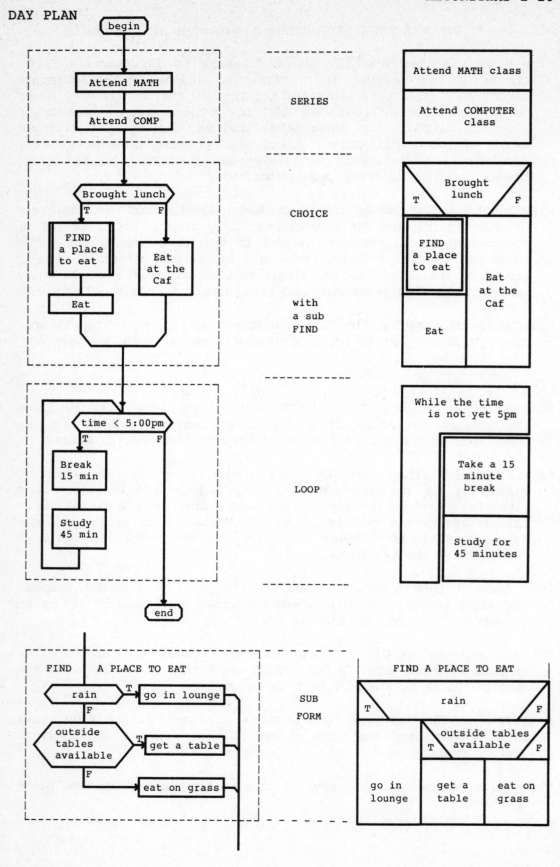

DAY PLAN

FLOWCHARTS VS FLOW BLOCKS: A Comparison

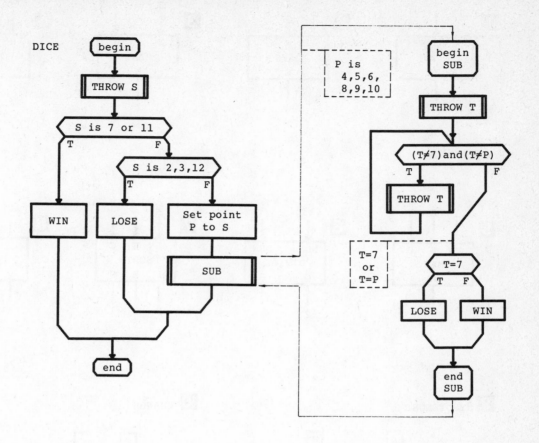

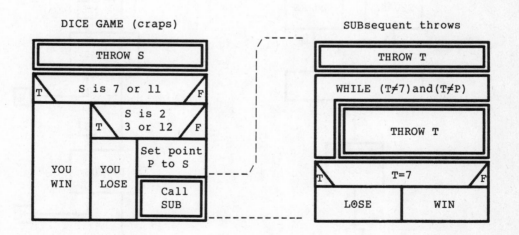

DICE GAME (craps)   SUBsequent throws

ALGORITHMS REPRESENTED AS DATA FLOW DIAGRAMS

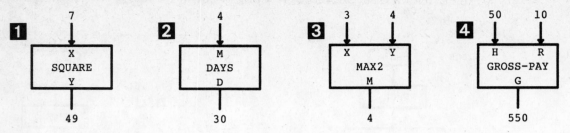

1
```
        7
        ↓
   ┌─────────┐
   │   X     │
   │ SQUARE  │
   │   Y     │
   └─────────┘
        ↓
        49
```

2
```
        4
        ↓
   ┌─────────┐
   │   M     │
   │  DAYS   │
   │   D     │
   └─────────┘
        ↓
        30
```

3
```
     3    4
     ↓    ↓
   ┌─────────┐
   │  X    Y │
   │  MAX2   │
   │   M     │
   └─────────┘
        ↓
        4
```

4
```
    50    10
     ↓     ↓
   ┌──────────┐
   │  H    R  │
   │GROSS-PAY │
   │   G      │
   └──────────┘
        ↓
       550
```

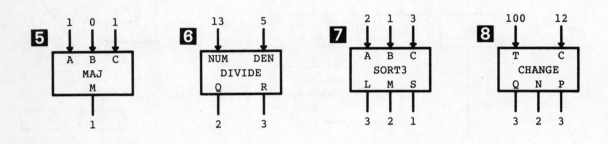

5
```
   1   0   1
   ↓   ↓   ↓
 ┌───────────┐
 │ A   B   C │
 │    MAJ    │
 │    M      │
 └───────────┘
      ↓
      1
```

6
```
  13       5
   ↓       ↓
 ┌───────────┐
 │ NUM   DEN │
 │  DIVIDE   │
 │ Q      R  │
 └───────────┘
   ↓       ↓
   2       3
```

7
```
   2   1   3
   ↓   ↓   ↓
 ┌───────────┐
 │ A   B   C │
 │   SORT3   │
 │ L   M   S │
 └───────────┘
   ↓   ↓   ↓
   3   2   1
```

8
```
  100      12
   ↓        ↓
 ┌───────────┐
 │ T       C │
 │  CHANGE   │
 │ Q   N   P │
 └───────────┘
   ↓   ↓   ↓
   3   2   3
```

9 HYPOTENUSE

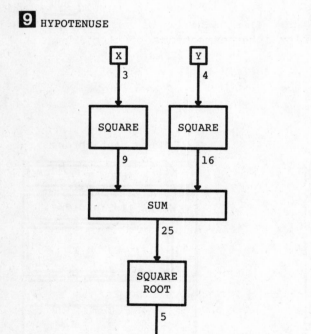

10 CHANGE

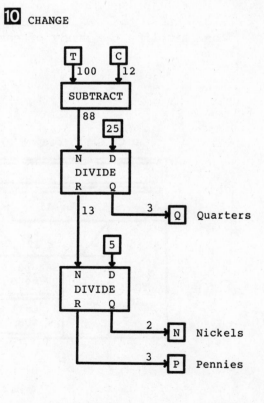

DATA FLOW DIAGRAM REPRESENTATION: Flow of Data

DATA FLOW DIAGRAMS represent algorithms as machines or black boxes, with emphasis on the input-output data flow. This view is in direct contrast to flowcharts, which emphasize the flow of control. Data flow diagrams are concerned mainly with the function of the algorithm: what it does, not how it does it.

SQUARE, of figure 1, is a simple example showing an input value of 7 "flowing" into the box, and the resulting data value of 49 being output. It does not indicate how the square of N was computed within the box; it could have been done by N successive additions of N, or by summing the first N odd integers.

Examples of other previous algorithms are given as data flow diagrams in the figures. Notice the differing numbers of data inputs and outputs. DAYS has a single input and output. MAX and GROSS PAY both have two inputs and an output. MAJority has three inputs and an output. DIVIDE has two inputs (numerator and denominator) and two outputs (quotient and remainder). SORT3 shows three input values, which have been sorted (ranked) as three output values (Large, Middle, Small). CHANGE has two inputs and three outputs. We input the cost C of an item, and some money tendered T. The output is the amount of change, a certain number of Quarters Q, Nickels N, and Pennies P.

Data flow diagrams are mainly used to show the interaction among a number of algorithms. Since they hide the inner details of individual algorithms, they simplify the study of complex interconnections of algorithms.

HYPOTENUSE, of figure 9, shows the computation of the hypotenuse H of a right triangle (with sides X,Y). If the details of the SQUARE and SQUARE ROOT algorithms were shown, this HYPOTENUSE algorithm would look very complex.

CHANGE, of figure 10, shows an algorithm to make change using division and subtraction. Let us follow the data flow for an amount tendered of a dollar (T = 100), and for the cost of items, C, = 12 cents. The first data flow diagram subtracts C from T leaving 88 cents as change. This is divided in the first DIVIDE box by 25, yielding a quotient Q of 3 (output as quarters), and a remainder of 13 cents which enters the second DIVIDE box. This value of 13 divided by 5 now yields a quotient of 2 (output as 2 nickels) and a remainder of 3 (output as pennies).

Stepwise refinement also applies to data flow diagrams. For example, the CHANGE algorithm of figure 10 is the refined version of figure 8. Notice that humans would never use such an algorithm for making change; division is too difficult. Humans make change by avoiding even subtraction. Humans often do things differently than computers do.

Data flow diagrams will be very useful later when we consider sub-programs. Also, many of the more common data flow diagrams (such as SQUARE, SQUARE ROOT, MAX, DIVIDE, etc.) are available (as functions) in higher level languages. Additionally, data flow machines are now being built, and may be very significant in the future.

MORE DATA FLOW DIAGRAMS

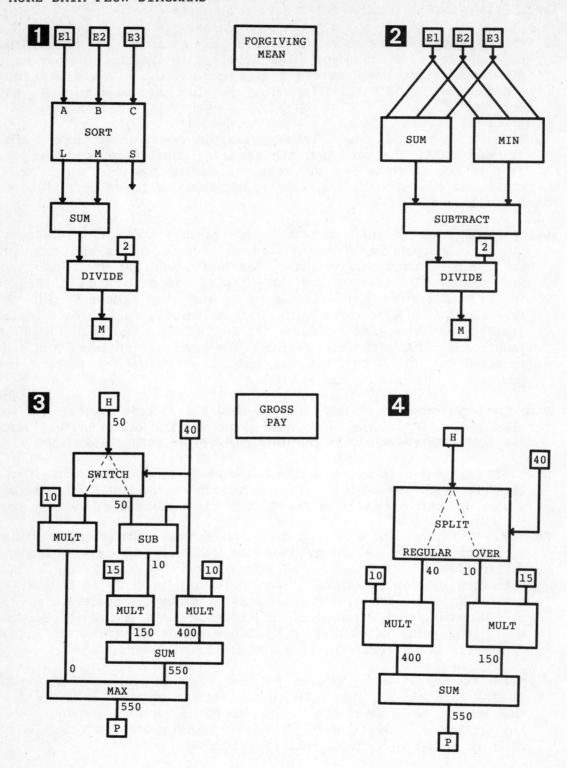

FORGIVING
MEAN

GROSS
PAY

MORE DATA FLOW DIAGRAMS: Data Flow Components

A big problem with creating algorithms is that we often get into details
    very quickly, and get bogged down in them. Data flow diagrams
    prevent this tendency, or at least tend to postpone it. They allow
    us to think in bigger blocks.

FORGIVING MEAN is an algorithm to average the exam grades of a student,
    when the lowest grade is excluded (forgiven). This could be done in
    two different ways, as will be shown for the case of three grades.

Figure 1 first sorts the three exam grades E1, E2, E3 into order with
    the largest labelled L, the middle value labelled M and the smallest
    S. Then the highest two values L and M are added, and this sum
    divided by two to get the resulting mean M.

Figure 2 finds the sum of the three, and the minimum value of the
    three. It then subtracts the minimum from the sum and divides this
    result by two to get the resulting mean M.

It is not important to know which of these two methods is preferable; it
    is important to realize that there are often a number of ways to do
    anything. The first method may seem simpler, but it may be slower
    or more costly. The choice between methods depends on more
    knowledge of cost, speed, availability, etc.

Notice that the operations of SUM and MIN may be done at the same time
    (in parallel, or concurrently), although our present machines and
    languages do not take advantage of this. In the future, our systems
    may find this parallelism to be useful and efficient; they need not
    wait for the SUM to be done before they start on the MIN.

STILL MORE DATA FLOW DIAGRAMS (Optional)

GROSS PAY shows two more data flow diagrams for a previous algorithm.
    In this example, a choice of paths is to be made depending on how
    the number of hours compares to 40. There are again a number of
    ways to do this.

Figure 3 shows a SWITCH component, which "steers" the hours to flow on
    one of two paths depending on whether the hours are greater than 40.

Figure 4 shows an alternative and simpler algorithm which uses a
    component called SPLIT to divert the regular pay along one path, and
    the overtime pay (if any) along another path.

Again, whether the choice is done with a switch or with a splitter (or
    some other flow component) is not as important as the fact that
    there are many ways to do most things.

ALGORITHMS REPRESENTED AS STATE DIAGRAMS

1 GENERAL STATE DIAGRAM

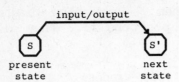

input/output

S — present state

S' — next state

2 DISPENSE-15

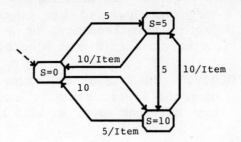

3 TRACE

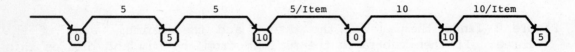

4 DISPENSER (of 15¢ items) with CHANGE output.

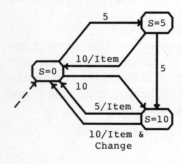

5 DISPENSER-15 (as Table of transitions)

State	s	0	0	5	5	10	10
Coin	c	5	10	5	10	5	10
Item	I			T	T	T	
Change	C						T
Next State	s'	5	10	10	0	0	0

start ⟶

6 WORD COUNT

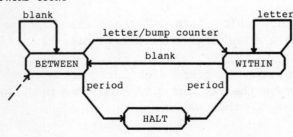

7

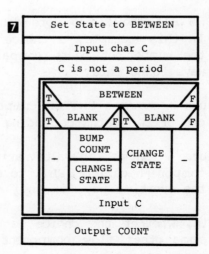

| Set State to BETWEEN |
| Input char C |
| C is not a period |

BETWEEN

BLANK / BLANK

BUMP COUNT / CHANGE STATE / CHANGE STATE

| Input C |
| Output COUNT |

STATE DIAGRAM REPRESENTATION: A View of Streams (Optional)

State diagrams (sometimes called finite state machines, sequential circuits, or regular automata) are very useful to describe communicating, controlling and computing. Here we will use state diagrams to describe algorithms. They are most convenient when inputs come in a sequence, such as a string of characters, or a stream of coins.

State diagrams consist of circles representing states, and arrows indicating the changes between states as shown in figure 1. Each arrow has an input value, and could have a corresponding output, which is separated from the input by a slash.

DISPENSE-15, of figure 2, shows the behavior of an algorithm which accepts sequences of nickels (5 cents) and dimes (10 cents), and outputs an item when the accumulated sum reaches 15 cents. The states in this case represent the amounts of money (0, 5, 10) accumulated at any time. The initial state (shown by a dotted arrow) is state 0. Then when a nickel is input, the state changes to 5, but when a dime is input, it changes to 10. Similarly, if the state is 10 (indicating an accumulation of 10 cents) and a nickel is input, then an item is output and the next state is 0.

State changes (transitions) caused by input sequences of coins can be shown by a trace as in figure 3. Notice that there is no change output by this machine, so that when the state is 10 and a dime is input, then an item is output and the next state is 5 (crediting the 5 extra cents to the next transaction). An alternative dispenser, which outputs change also, is shown in figure 4. It is represented as a table in figure 5.

WORDCOUNT is an algorithm which counts the number of words in a sentence. As the characters are entered, one at a time, the state (situation) changes from being BETWEEN words to being WITHIN words. For example, when the state is WITHIN and the input is a blank, then a word counter is bumped, and the next state becomes BETWEEN. Ultimately, when a period is input (regardless of the state), the algorithm halts. A corresponding flow block diagram is shown in figure 7.

State diagrams as described here are useful and yet more general than seen in other applications. The inputs correspond to conditions, and it is easy to check that all possibilities are considered. Also, the outputs correspond to actions, including the "empty action" where nothing is output for some inputs. Other, more limited versions of state diagrams require an output for every input.

REVIEW: of Chapter 1

ALGORITHMS: REPRESENTATIONS

ALGORITHMS are plans for performing some actions on some objects. The actions or objects need not have anything to do with computers.

PROPERTIES, which must hold for all algorithms, generally are:
GENERALITY, ability to apply to a class of problems
COMPLETENESS, defined for all cases, exhaustive
CONSISTENCY, defined uniquely, non-contradictory
FINITENESS, restricted to limited time and space.

REPRESENTATIONS of algorithms are ways or forms of describing, denoting, or presenting them. There are many such ways, some better than others, so it is important to try various representations.

VERBAL forms involve words, in sentences and paragraphs. This representation is usually very verbose, long, and often not accurate.

ALGEBRAIC forms involve mathematical symbols in expressions or formulas. This is usually a very concise representation.

TABULAR forms involve rectangular grids (tables, arrays or matrices) with entries in the grids. This method is useful for summarizing large selections.

TREE forms involve diagrams resembling natural trees. Many structures have this hierarchical, level-oriented form.

FLOWCHART forms involve boxes joined by lines, describing the flow of control of actions. They are very clear for smaller algorithms, but could become confusing if not structured well.

FLOW BLOCK forms involve only rectangular boxes, with very limited (but significant) ways of connecting them. They also describe only the flow of control of actions.

DATA FLOW forms also involve boxes, but describe the flow of data. This form is most useful at higher levels when dealing with sub-algorithms.

STATE DIAGRAM forms describe state changes, depending on "streams" or sequences of inputs.

OTHER representational forms are also possible (including a very important PSEUDO LANGUAGE, in a chapter by itself), but are not considered here. Not all forms are equally important. In the past, most forms emphasized control flow (flowcharts, flow blocks), but now data flows are beginning to get equal emphasis.

PROBLEMS: on Chapter 1

1. BAD MIN
What is wrong with the following definition of MIN, the minimum of two values X and Y?

$$\text{MIN} = \begin{cases} X, \text{ if } X < Y \\ \qquad \text{or} \\ Y, \text{ if } Y < X \end{cases}$$

2. BINARY
Convert the following binary numbers to decimal:
a) 101010
b) 101010101
c) 1100100

3. SIMPLE BINARY
Find the decimal equivalents of the binary numbers:
a) 11111111
b) 100000000
Use the above to find a simple way to obtain the decimal equivalent of a binary number consisting of any number N of ones in succession.

4. OCTAL
Convert the following octal (base 8) numbers into decimal:
a) 177   b) 200   c) 333

5. ISBN CHECK
Check whether the following ISBN numbers are proper numbers:
a) 0-387-90144-2   b) 0-13-215871-X
c) 0-574-21265-4   d) 0-88236-115-5
e) 3-540-90144-2

6. BAD PLAY
If the comma is misplaced in the PLAY BALL algorithm (following the "or"), how is the game affected? Draw the flow chart corresponding to each of these algorithms.

7. PATRIOTIC RESISTOR
If a resistor has colors Red, White and Blue, then what is its resistance?
What if the colors were in the reverse order?

8. PROJECT SEQUENCE
For the PROJECT tree, on page 1-8, list the actions in the order they should be done.

9. BOSS TABLE
Convert the BOSS tree of page 1-8 into a simple table listing all persons alphabetically, along with their corresponding immediate supervisor.

10. METRIC and NON-METRIC
a) Give a formula to convert yards, feet, and inches into inches.
b) Give a formula to convert meters, decimeters, centimeters, and millimeters into millimeters.

11. EXPRESSION TREES
    Create a tree corresponding to each of the following expressions:

    a) 3*A + 2*B   b) X*X + Y*Y

    c) S + 60*M + 60*60*H   d) S + 60*(M + 60*H)

    e) A*8 + B*4 + C*2 + D   f) 2*(2*(2*A + B) + C) + D

12. PLAY BALL TABLE
    Fill out the following decision table, and create its equivalent
    baseball table with fewer than eight columns (rules). Draw a
    flowchart describing this algorithm.

        I<=9   F T F T F T F T
        TIED   F F T T F F T T
        RAIN   F F F F T T T T
        PLAY

13. LEAPING AGAIN
    Represent the LEAP algorithm of page 1-12 as a table, with three
    conditions (4 divides Y, 100 divides Y, and 400 divides Y) and
    eight rules (combinations). Then create another table with fewer
    rules. (A solution follows on page 3-22)

14. CHANGE CHANGE
    Modify the data flow diagram describing CHANGE, on page 1-18, to
    allow for dimes and half-dollars.

15. DRINK
    a) Write a formula to convert a given number of cups, pints,
    quarts, and gallons into cups.
        (2 cups = 1 pt, 2 pts = 1 qt, 4 qts = 1 gal)
    b) Create a data flow diagram to convert a given number of cups
    into gallons, quarts, pints, and cups. Show the flow for 57
    cups.

16. HOT ONE
    Since humans hate division, they often create algorithms to avoid
    it. For example, instead of converting temperatures by:
        F = 9/5*C + 32
    sometimes the following algorithm is used.
        First, multiply C by 2 and subtract from this amount
        its first (most significant) digit. Then add 32 to
        this, and the result should be the Fahrenheit value.
    For example, 20 degrees C becomes:
        40 - 4 + 32 = 68
    Check this algorithm for some numbers, and indicate any
    limitations, problems, or inaccuracies.

17. DISPENSE20
    Draw the state diagram describing the dispenser of 20-cent items
    (with change), if inputs are sequences of nickels (5 cents) and
    dimes (10 cents) with only one coin entered at a time. Also,
    represent this dispensing algorithm in one other way.

```
Chapter 2

STRUCTURE:
  FORM OF ALGORITHMS
```

```
STRUCTURED PROGRAMMING

FOUR FUNDAMENTAL FORMS

OBJECTS  AND  ACTIONS

TOP-DOWN DESIGN
```

STRUCTURE:

FORM OF ALGORITHMS

 * Asterisks indicate the degree of importance *

Chapter 2:

STRUCTURE

Form of Algorithms

PREVIEW

STRUCTURE, or form, of algorithms is the main concern
   in this chapter. Structure is particularly
   important for large algorithms, but even smaller
   structured algorithms are usually simpler to
   understand, explain, modify, test, analyse, and
   ultimately prove.

STRUCTURED PROGRAMMING is a method of organizing
   algorithms in a simple way, using a small number of
   building blocks, with a simple interconnection
   between them.

FOUR FUNDAMENTAL FORMS (called Series, Choice, Loop,
   and Sub) are the building blocks used to create all
   algorithms. Initially we will use flowcharts to
   describe these structures. Eventually the emphasis
   will shift to flow block diagram representation.
   These diagrams make it difficult to create poorly
   structured algorithms.

TOP-DOWN DESIGN is another significant concept that is
   introduced here. It is the process of creating
   algorithms in stages, by successively refining them
   into smaller sub-algorithms.

OBJECTS AND ACTIONS described by our algorithms are
   common everyday objects, again showing that
   algorithms need not involve any computers or
   mathematics. In the following chapter, computing
   algorithms (or programs) will be considered and
   their objects (numbers) will actually be simpler
   than the "common" ones treated here. For this
   reason we make our objects very detailed and
   explicit here.

THE FOUR FUNDAMENTAL FORMS
   all having a single entry and a single exit

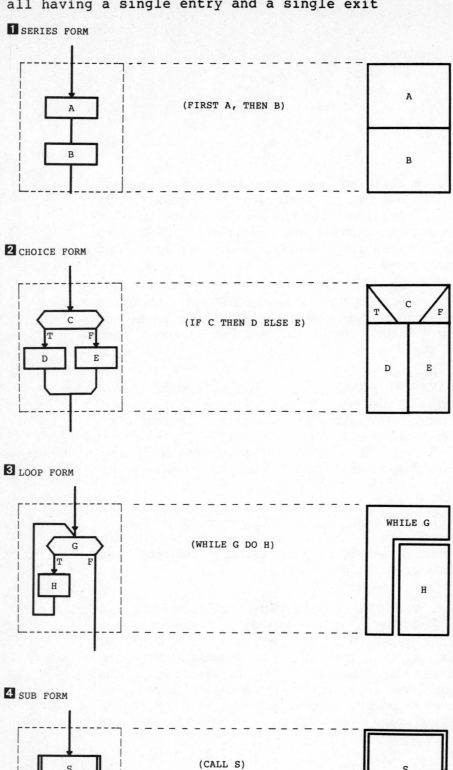

1 SERIES FORM

(FIRST A, THEN B)

2 CHOICE FORM

(IF C THEN D ELSE E)

3 LOOP FORM

(WHILE G DO H)

4 SUB FORM

(CALL S)

STRUCTURED PROGRAMMING: The Four Fundamental Forms

Structured programming is a method of organizing algorithms using only a small number of building blocks. All algorithms can be constructed from just four forms (SERIES, CHOICE, LOOP and SUB). Other forms are unnecessary but sometimes convenient; they are considered later. All these forms have a single entry and a single exit, making the path of flow very evident. These four fundamental forms are shown in both flowchart form and flow block diagram form in the figures.

SERIES is a form (also called Sequence or Concatenation) which simply indicates the linear sequence in which actions are to be done. The order of doing things is usually significant, but even if the order is not important, doing things one at a time means something must be done first.

CHOICE is a form (also called Conditional, Alternation, or Selection) which simply poses a condition C. If this condition is true, then one action D is done; otherwise another action E is done. The actions D and E may be complex. After whichever of the two "detours" is taken, the paths join again, yielding a single exit. This form is called the IF-THEN-ELSE, for it may be stated verbally as "IF C THEN D ELSE E" in most modern programming languages.

LOOP is a form (also called Iteration or Repetition) which begins by posing a condition G. While this condition is true the action H is repeated and the condition G re-tested. When this loop condition finally becomes false, the repetition stops and the single exit is taken. This form is also called the WHILE, for it may be stated verbally as "WHILE G DO H" in most languages.

SUB is another form (called Sub-algorithm or Abstraction) which corresponds to grouping some parts together, giving the grouping a name, and referring to this grouping by the name, as if it were a single simple action. This enables a useful algorithm to be defined once, and then whenever it is needed it is called by its name. For example, we could compute various statistics (say, AVERAGE) by calls such as:

CALL AVERAGE   or   PERFORM AVERAGE   or   simply   AVERAGE

Other forms than these four are possible (including UNTIL, FOR, CASE) and may be useful or convenient, but they are not necessary or fundamental. They will be introduced later when appropriate or convenient.

EXAMPLES OF THE FOUR FORMS

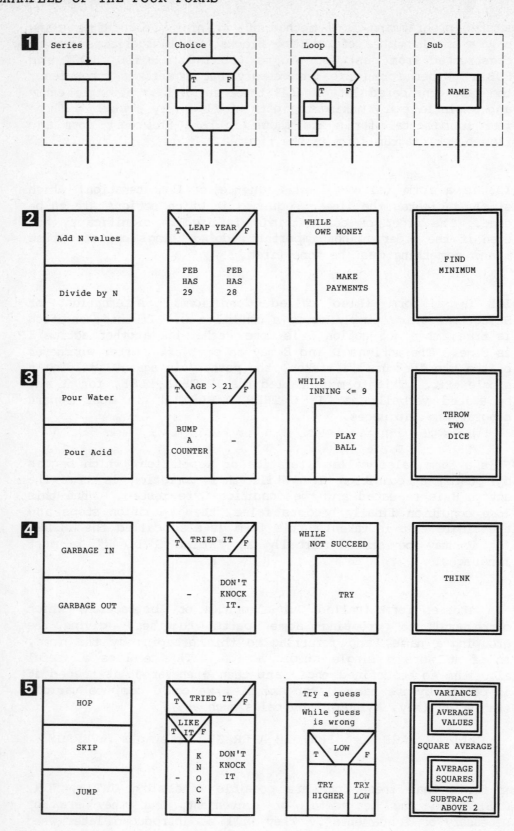

Problem Solving and Proving

It is interesting to note that the four fundamental forms are related to the four methods of problem solving and the four methods of proving.

The four methods of problem solving are:
      SERIES   break a problem into steps, and do the steps in order,
      CHOICE   consider each case or alternative separately,
      LOOP   repeat steps, successively becoming more successful,
      SUB   use a previously solved problem as a sub-part of another.

The four methods of proof in Logic are also similar:
      SERIES   proof by steps, linear deduction,
      CHOICE   proof by enumeration of cases, or truth tables,
      LOOP   proof by induction,
      SUB   proof by appeal to previous results, sub-theorems.

Examples of the four fundamental forms are shown in the given figures.

Row 1 repeats concisely the flowcharts corresponding to the four forms.

Row 2 repeats some previously considered algorithms, and some slightly
   modified ones.

Row 3 indicates some old algorithms in a new form:
         Always pour acid into water, not vice versa.
         If the age is greater than 21, bump the counter.
         While the inning is less than or equal to 9, play ball.
         Throw the dice.

Incidentally, actions may be trivial (for example, do nothing when Age
   <= 21), and conditions can be quite complex. For example, a more
   reasonable condition for playing ball is the compounded condition:

         (Inning <= 9 OR score tied) AND NOT raining.

Row 4 puts into algorithmic form some common sayings:
         Garbage-in, Garbage-out.
         If you haven't tried it, don't knock it.
         If at first you don't succeed, try, try again.
         Think. (The ultimate sub-block!)

Row 5 takes slightly more complex combinations of the forms:
         A series combination of three steps.
         A choice involving another choice within it.
         A loop including a choice.
         A sub-form containing sub-forms.

More complicated examples follow. Actually, it is more difficult to
   create algorithms about such common examples, than about more
   computer-related examples.

CASCADING AND NESTING THE FOUR FORMS

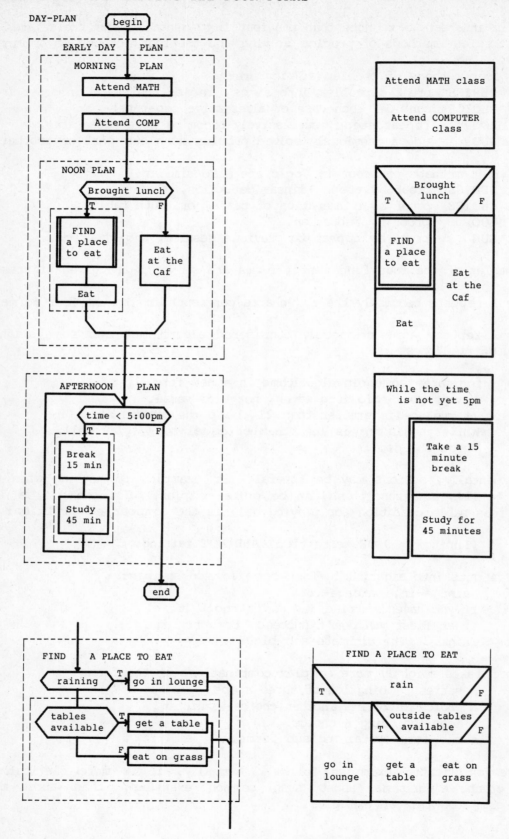

Building with the Four Forms

The Four Fundamental Forms are rather small and simple blocks, but they are sufficient to create all algorithms. Virtually all the algorithms in this book are written using only these four forms.

Interconnection of the four forms is possible in only two ways: cascaded (one following the other) or nested (one within another). There is no "sharing" of parts between blocks. This method of interconnecting yields a composition where all blocks, especially larger ones, have a single entry and a single exit.

CASCADING of forms is illustrated by the MORNING PLAN, where ATTEND MATH is followed by ATTEND COMPuter Class. This cascading also applies to larger boxes, so the MORNING PLAN could be cascaded with the NOON PLAN to create an even larger box (possibly called EARLY DAY PLAN). Then again this EARLY DAY PLAN could be cascaded with the AFTERNOON PLAN.

NESTING of forms is illustrated by the NOON PLAN part of the figure. It shows a series form nested within a choice form. Another nested example is the FIND sub-algorithm at the bottom of the page, which shows a choice form nested within another choice. Again note that every box (dotted and undotted) has a single entry and a single exit.

This sort of interconnection could continue for many levels; what is important is that each box have a single entry and a single exit, and that the boxes be either cascaded or nested. After some experience the dotted boxes need not be drawn, for you can tell the form of interconnection simply by inspection. However, inspection is sometimes deceiving, so in complex cases you may need to revert to drawing such dotted boxes.

It is also important to realize that if a flowchart is well structured it can be converted into a corresponding flow block diagram. If it is not well structured, it cannot be put into the flow block form. So a good test for structuring is to draw the flow block diagram.

The block diagram for DAY PLAN is shown to the right of its flowchart. It is often a clearer way of showing that an algorithm is structured.

NESTED COMBINATIONS OF FORMS

1 CHOICE NESTED IN A CHOICE

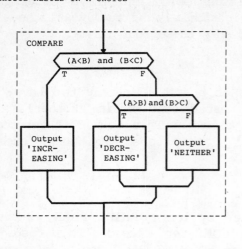

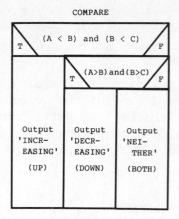

2 LOOP NESTED IN A CHOICE

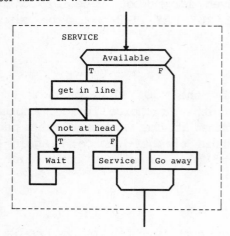

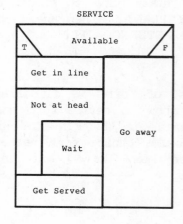

3 CHOICE NESTED IN A LOOP

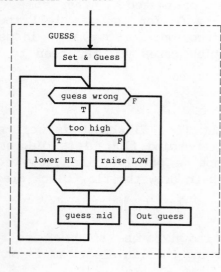

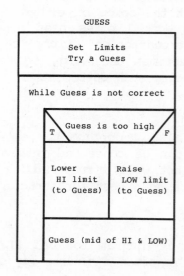

Nested Forms

Of the two methods for combining forms, cascading and nesting, the method of nesting is more complex. The given diagrams show some nests, as both flowcharts and block diagrams.

COMPARE, of figure 1, is an algorithm which compares values of A, B, and C to determine if the values are:
    increasing (such as 1,2,5 or -1,0,3),
    decreasing (such as 5,2,1 or 3,0,-4), or
    neither (such as 1,0,2 or 1,1,1).

This algorithm should not be viewed as five boxes (two conditions and three actions), but should instead be viewed as two forms, a choice nested within a choice. This view, looking at forms rather than parts of forms, keeps algorithms simple. In this case, the COMPARE algorithm was not very complex, but in slightly larger examples, 13 boxes could be confusing, whereas the equivalent seven or eight forms could be understood.

SERVICE, of figure 2, is an algorithm to describe a queue or waiting line. It illustrates a loop form which is nested within a choice.

GUESS, of figure 3, is an algorithm to determine some value by a series of guesses; each guess gets closer to the final correct result. This method will be used later in algorithms called Bisection and Binary Search. Here it simply illustrates a choice form nested within a loop.

PAY, shown below, illustrates a deeper level of nesting, where a choice has within it a choice within a choice. It is shown to be well structured in figures 5 and 6.

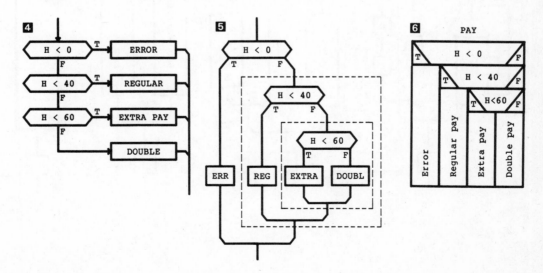

COMPLEX NESTS: In Structured Form

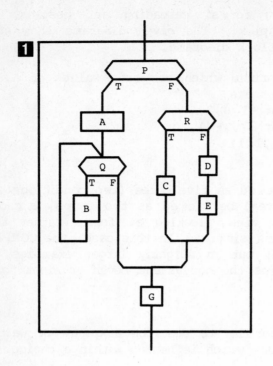

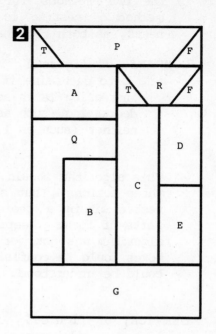

DECOMPOSITION OF STRUCTURE

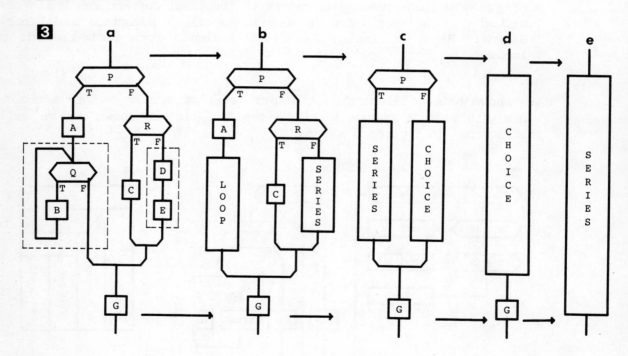

Complex Nests

Complex nests are illustrated by the example of figure 1. The actions (A,B,C,...,G) and conditions (P,Q,R) are symbolized to keep the diagram simple. This example will be used to show some methods of proving proper structure.

Conversion of this example into a flow block representation is shown in figure 2.

Decomposition of this algorithm, in great step-by-step detail, is shown in figure 3. The original figure is copied in figure 3a. Figure 3b shows how the loop (with Q and B) and the series (with D and E) are each considered as one block at the next level. Then that loop with A is a new series block at the next level (figure 3c). This process continues until finally, at the last level of figure 3e, the form is that of a single series block.

This process of "hiding" the detailed structures level by level is useful to understand now; it is not always necessary to do it. It does, however, provide a view of "hierarchical" design, which may be useful later.

SET VIEW: Contours (Optional)

Nested structures can also be viewed as sets, and drawn as closed dotted curves (or contours). The sets can be labelled by the actions or conditions within them, as in the figure below. The resulting sets are either completely nested within one another, or are totally separated from one another; the sets do not intersect.

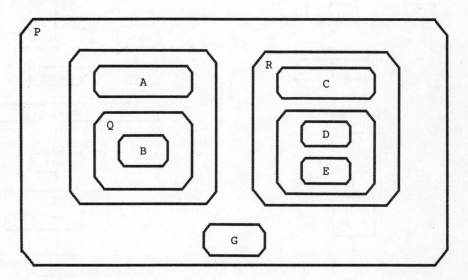

OBJECTS AND ACTIONS: Chili Recipe

1 OBJECTS

3 SECRET SAUCE - sub-recipe

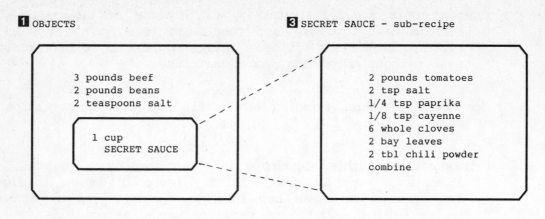

```
3 pounds beef
2 pounds beans
2 teaspoons salt

    1 cup
    SECRET SAUCE
```

```
2 pounds tomatoes
2 tsp salt
1/4 tsp paprika
1/8 tsp cayenne
6 whole cloves
2 bay leaves
2 tbl chili powder
combine
```

2 FLOW OF ACTIONS

4 FLOW OF OBJECTS

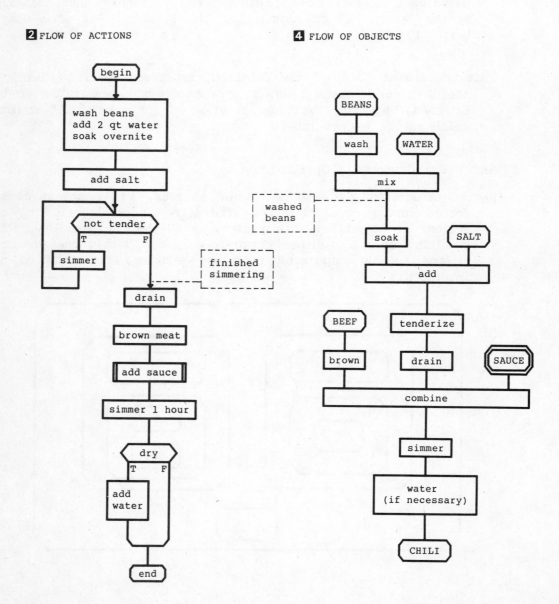

OBJECTS AND ACTIONS: Recipe for Chili

Algorithms were defined as plans (methods) for performing actions
  (operations) on objects. The emphasis in algorithms is often
  on the actions, and not the objects. This is because the
  objects initially seem simpler than actions; later we will find
  much more difficult objects. Just to emphasize objects in the
  next few examples we will provide more than "equal time" to
  objects.

RECIPE is a typical cooking algorithm for making Chili. First, in
  figure 1, the ingredients (objects) are specified (declared).
  Then, in figure 2, the instructions (actions) indicate the
  sequence of operations to be performed on the ingredients.

SECRET SAUCE is a sub-recipe, listed as a part of the objects
  (in figure 1), and then defined as a separate sub-algorithm
  (in figure 3). It can be viewed as either an object or an
  action! Such a recipe is an ideal model of programs in many
  modern programming languages. This same order, of objects
  (followed by sub-actions) followed by the main actions, is
  identical to the structure of programs written in the Pascal
  programming language.

Flow of objects, shown in figure 4, is in contrast to the previous
  flow of actions. Notice how this diagram resembles a tree,
  where the leaves are objects, with each node indicating how
  objects "flow together" to make new objects, finally arriving
  at a final node (trunk of a tree) indicating the final object,
  Chili!

Difference between the two diagrams (flowchart and data flow
  diagram) is great. One describes flow of control (actions);
  the other describes flow of data (objects). One has loops; one
  hasn't. At any line (arrow between boxes) we can make an
  assertion (shown dotted) which describes an action on the
  lefthand flowchart, and describes an object on the rightmost
  data flow diagram.

Again, the overemphasis on objects in this example is simply to
  remind us about objects. We now return to a more balanced
  emphasis on actions.

MAGIC AND CONVERSION

1 CARD TRICK

OBJECT: Array of cards
3 columns of 7 rows

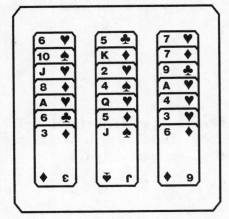

3 CONVERT: decimal-to-binary

OBJECT: variable N
(integer number)

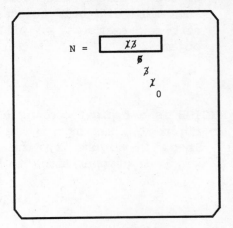

2 ACTION

```
Arrange 21 cards
   face up as shown

Have a person think of a card
   and indicate its column
```

```
While column is indicated
   3 or less times
```

```
Pick up columns with
the indicated one
sandwiched in middle

Arrange cards again
   (row by row)
into 3 columns & 7 rows

Have the column
indicated again
```

```
Pick up the cards
   in 'sandwich' order

Count off 10 cards

Show the eleventh card

It is the required card!
```

4 ACTION

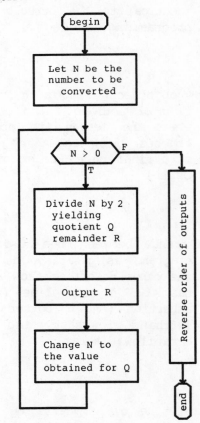

Card Trick and Binary Conversion

CARD TRICK is an example having a reasonably complex structure of objects. In this example, cards are placed in a two-dimensional order with 7 rows and 3 columns, as is best shown in the diagram of figure 1. Such a structure is often called an array. The cards in any column are overlapped to maintain the order of cards, and to ease picking up a column quickly.

You allow a person to think of one of the 21 cards, without telling you which. The person does, however, indicate the column that the card is in. Then you arrange the cards (as shown in the algorithm) and the column is indicated again. The cards are rearranged and the column determined again, for the third and last time. Finally you count off 10 cards, and the 11th one is the selected one. You pick it out, from the back, without even looking at its face!

The trick is entirely described in the figure. Try it. Notice that it doesn't take any knowledge or skill on your part, just the ability to follow directions!

CONVERSION (Decimal to Binary) is one method for converting a positive integer number in base 10 to its equivalent in base 2. It has a particularly simple object, one number N, called a variable, which keeps changing during the computation. This number is repeatedly divided by 2 (and the remainder output) until it reaches zero. The output values (always 0 or 1) when taken in reverse order make up the required equivalent binary numbers.

For example, let us convert the decimal number N=13.

```
13/2 = 6 with remainder (output) of   1
 6/2 = 3   "        "           "    " 0
 3/2 = 1   "        "           "    " 1
 1/2 = 0   "        "           "    " 1
```

The binary equivalent of 13 is 1101.

There are other methods to convert decimal numbers to binary. They will be considered later.

PEASANT PEBBLE PRODUCT

1 OBJECTS

HALVES
PILE

DOUBLES
PILE

PRODUCT
PILE

(7 pebbles)   (4 pebbles)   (0 pebbles)

2 ACTIONS

PRODUCT P OF X,Y

Make 3 piles of pebbles
HALVES having X pebbles
DOUBLES having Y pebbles
PRODUCT having no pebbles

While the HALVES pile
is not empty

T \ the number in HALVES pile is ODD / F

Duplicate the doubles pile, and put it onto the <u>PRODUCT</u> pile	Duplicate the doubles pile, and put it back on the <u>DOUBLES</u> pile
Remove <u>one</u> pebble from the HALVES pile	Remove <u>half</u> the pebbles from the HALVES pile.

The product is
the number of pebbles on the PRODUCT pile

3 'SNAPSHOTS' OF OBJECTS
AFTER EACH LOOP

HALVES   DOUBLES   PRODUCT

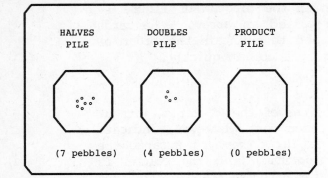

Peasant Pebble Product

An ingenious method of multiplication was developed long ago by
Ethiopian peasants. It involves manipulation of three piles of
pebbles. The algorithm is shown in the figure.

First, the two numbers to be multiplied are represented by two
piles of pebbles named HALVES and DOUBLES. A third pile
(called PRODUCT) is initially empty. Then the following
process is repeated while the HALVES pile is not empty.

If the HALVES pile has an odd number of pebbles, then each pebble
on the DOUBLES pile is duplicated and added to the PRODUCT
pile. Also, one pebble is removed from the HALVES pile.

Alternatively, if the HALVES pile has an even number of pebbles,
the DOUBLES pile is duplicated again, but now it is added to
the DOUBLES pile, so doubling it. Also, the number of pebbles
on the HALVES pile is halved.

This sequence of actions ends when the HALVES pile is empty; the
product is represented by the number of pebbles on the PRODUCT
pile. A series of "snapshots" of a typical Product computation
is shown to the right of the algorithm. Such a sequential
description of the series of actions is called a TRACE. This
entire process may seem unusual, but it works (the reasons for
it are given later in Chapter 3, along with other such
products).

Notice that we need not understand such an algorithm in order to
follow it; computers always follow instructions well, yet they
don't "understand" them. Of course we must understand
algorithms in order to design them. But now we are still at
the stage of experiencing and appreciating algorithms; design
will come later in this chapter.

Notice that this PRODUCT has certain limitations. First, it
applies only to whole numbers, called integers (peasants dealt
with whole animals). It also does not apply to negative
numbers. Also the piles of pebbles could grow very large.

GUESSING GAME

1 GUESSEE OBJECTS

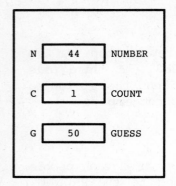

3 GUESSOR OBJECTS

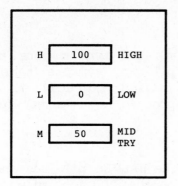

2 GUESSEE ACTIONS

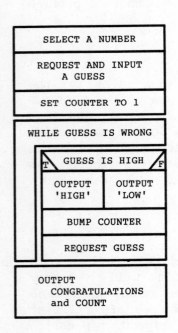

4 GUESSOR ACTIONS

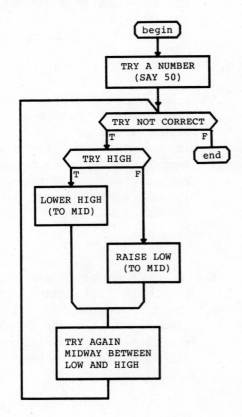

Guessing Game: Intelligent Trial and Error

A common guessing game involves two parties (either human or computer). One party (called GUESSEE) selects a number, say between 0 and 99, and the other party (called GUESSER) tries to guess it, in the fewest number of tries. The only information conveyed is whether the guessed number is higher or lower than the selected number.

GUESSEE is an algorithm which could be followed by one party. It selects the number, indicates the comparison, and keeps count of the number of tries.

GUESSER is an algorithm describing one possible way of making guesses. It simply keeps track of the high and low values and guesses the mid value, the average of these two values. Depending on the outcome of the guess, one of the limits is changed (to this mid value). This method of halving the correct range of values at each try is called Bisection. It will also be useful in solving equations, and efficiently searching through data. In n tries, this algorithm can select between 2^n numbers. So in ten tries, we can guess any number between 0 and 1023.

Notice that both algorithms have a similar form, but are drawn in two ways, consisting of a choice within a loop. Both also involve only three numbers as objects. The GUESSEE must know the number N selected, the count C, and the value G guessed. GUESSER must know the HIGH and LOW values, and from these computes the MID or "try" value.

Random Numbers   (Optional)

Random number generators (RNGs) are methods for producing sequences of numbers which appear to be unpredictable (occurring by chance). Such an RNG could be used by the GUESSEE to select numbers for the guessing game. One method of creating a series of such numbers follows:

First start with a random number R, say 711 (called a seed).
   Multiply R by 343.
   Divide the above result by 1009; keep the remainder, called R.
   This R is the next random number, to be used in the above.
Each selected value RN (between 0 and 99) is the remainder
   when each R is divided by 100.
This algorithm generates the following sequence of R values:
   711,   704,   321,   122,   etc.
from which we use values RN:
   11,   4,   21,   22

This method generates random numbers between 0 and 99. Such a sequence is called "pseudo random," for it ultimately repeats (or cycles). In this case the constant 1009 was chosen for the convenience of division (for humans). As a result, this sequence starts repeating after a few dozen values. More on random number generators can be found in chapter 7.

EQUIVALENT ALGORITHMS: Many Ways to Leap

1

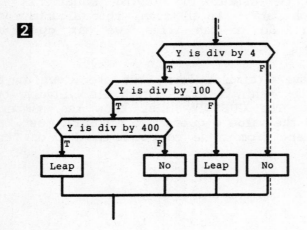

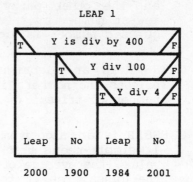

LEAP 1

T Y is div by 400 F			
	T Y div 100 F		
		T Y div 4 F	
Leap	No	Leap	No
2000	1900	1984	2001

2

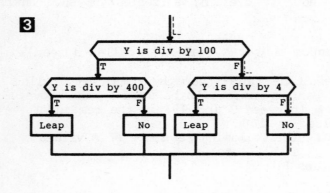

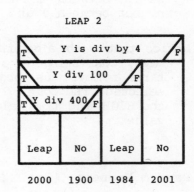

LEAP 2

T Y is div by 4 F			
T Y div 100 F			
T Y div 400 F			
Leap	No	Leap	No
2000	1900	1984	2001

3

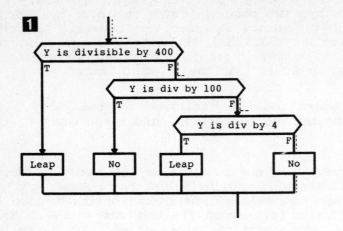

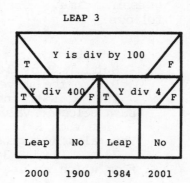

LEAP 3

T Y is div by 100 F			
T Y div 400 F		T Y div 4 F	
Leap	No	Leap	No
2000	1900	1984	2001

Equivalent Algorithms (or, many ways to leap)

It is important to realize that two algorithms may behave the same, but may be structured differently. For example consider the following algorithms for determining whether a year Y is a leap year.

LEAP1 (considered previously) begins by first asking if Y is divisible by 400. It has two other choices nested within it. This algorithm is tested for the four typical years: 2000, 1900, 1984, and 2001. For example, the year 2001 follows the rightmost path (shown dotted in the flowchart) and requires three decisions to be made. The paths taken by the four test cases are indicated by the dates at the exits of the flow block diagrams.

LEAP2 begins exactly the opposite of the above algorithm by first asking if Y is divisible by 4. Note here that the year 2001 again corresponds to the rightmost path (shown dotted on the flowchart) but it requires only one decision or choice. The flow block diagram at the right shows the outcome for the four typical years.

These two algorithms are identical in behavior for they now produce the same outcomes in all possible cases. They are, however, different in structure for they encounter different numbers of decisions for the same test cases. Which algorithm do you prefer?

The important thing now is not what you prefer, but that you have a choice to prefer one or the other. If two things are equivalent in one sense, this is an opportunity for selecting the optimal one in another sense. The selection depends on your goals.

For efficiency reasons (minimizing time with fewer decisions) you might prefer LEAP2, because in the most common cases (when the year is not divisible by 4, occurring about 75 percent of the time) the number of decisions are smaller (one decision for LEAP2 compared to three decisions for LEAP1).

Efficiency, or speed, is not always the best goal. Other goals include human convenience, beauty, ease of communication, robustness, and others which will be considered later.

LEAP3 shows yet another algorithm which is equivalent to the above two algorithms. It begins by asking if the year is divisible by 100. The structure is quite different from the others, for every input case goes through exactly two tests: there are no short paths here.

There are even more algorithms to determine if a year is a leap year; they will be considered later. The important idea here is not that you should try to optimize anything now; you should simply realize that there may be many ways of doing the same thing!

TRIANGLE CLASSIFICATION

1 OBJECTS

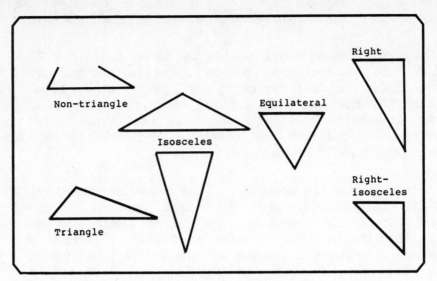

ACTIONS

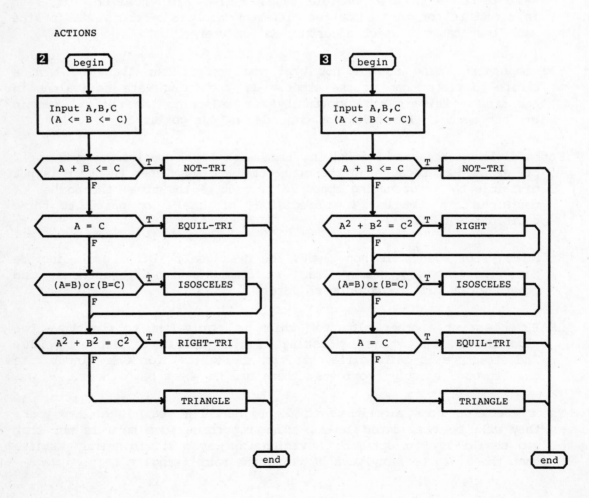

Alternative Algorithms (Triangle Classification)

There are often alternative ways of creating algorithms, some ways more convenient or better than others. The following example illustrates alternative algorithms, which are not equivalent. The problem is to determine whether three given numbers A,B,C (representing lengths of sides) could create a triangle, and if so whether it is isosceles (two sides equal), or equilateral (all three sides equal), or a right triangle (one 90 degree angle).

First, let us determine if the three sides make a triangle. From figure 1 (the non-triangle) we can see that a triangle is possible only if the sum of the shortest two sides exceeds the longest side. If the sides are given in increasing order (say A <= B <= C) the condition is:

(A + B > C)

Similarly, for an equilateral triangle the general condition is:

(A = B) AND (B = C)

But if A,B, and C are in order this condition becomes simply:

(A = C)

For an isosceles triangle the general condition is:

(A = B) OR (B = C) OR (A = C)

which becomes, when sides are ordered:

(A = B) OR (B = C)

This example illustrates the fact that if the data has some structure, this structure could be used to simplify the algorithm. Notice particularly that the conditions are not equivalent! The simpler conditions can be used as alternatives to the more complex conditions only if the values are in order. The values could be input initially in that order, or they could go through an algorithm to put them into order. (This algorithm, called SORT3, will be done later.)

Alternative algorithms for classifying the triangles are shown in figures 2 and 3. Figure 2 first tests for the equilateral property, and if it holds it exits (without indicating that it is also isosceles, since all equilateral triangles are isosceles). Figure 3, alternatively, first tests for isosceles triangles, and if found tests for equilateral. So in this case an equilateral triangle indicates both properties, equilateral and isosceles. This may be more redundant, but sometimes it is clearer than having to recall that one property implies (or covers) another property. Either algorithm can be used.

A TYPICAL INTERACTIVE SYSTEM

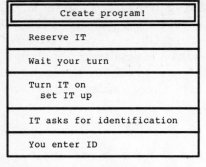

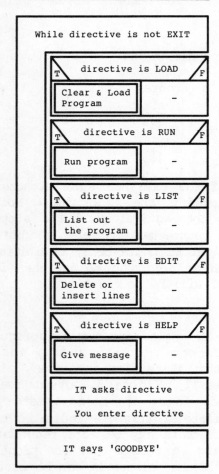

A TYPICAL CONVERSATION

(with US-Unsuspecting Student
and IT-Interactive Terminal)

IT: PLEASE IDENTIFY YOURSELF

US: JOHN MOTIL

IT: SORRY, TRY AGAIN

US: 19,84, SESAME

IT: WELCOME

IT: ENTER A DIRECTIVE
(IF UNSURE TYPE HELP)

US: HELP

IT: PROPER DIRECTIVES ARE:
LOAD, EDIT, LIST
RUN, EXIT, HELP.
ENTER DIRECTIVE

US: LOAD

IT: ENTER PROGRAM

US: 10 - - -   ⎫ program
      20 - - -   ⎬ (say to
      25 - - -   ⎪ compute
                 ⎪ SQUARE)
      99 END   ⎭

IT: ENTER DIRECTIVE

US: RUN

IT: ENTER VALUE

US: 7

IT: OUTPUT IS 49

IT: ENTER DIRECTIVE

         etc.

IT: ENTER DIRECTIVE

US: EXIT

IT: GOODBYE

Interactive Computing

The interactive method of using a computer can be described by an algorithm. This method involves a direct dialogue or conversation between a user and a computer system by means of a typewriter-like terminal. Actually, many terminals are often "shared" at the same time with a single computer (called time-sharing), each taking only a small portion of the computer's time.

A typical interactive session is shown in the figure. First the algorithm should be created, planned, refined, and coded into some language. This creative process should not be done at the terminal: it short-circuits the thinking process! Only after this planning stage do you go to the terminal, set it up, and "log on" to the system.

IT, the interactive terminal, typically asks for identification (user number and password). If given an improper identification, it usually repeats this log-on process for at least a few times. After recognizing and accepting the identification, it usually gives a welcoming message, indicating the current time and perhaps some news about the system. Then it requests a command (or directive) from you. If you are uncertain, you type "HELP" and it provides a message listing the possible directives.

ENTER is a directive which allows a program to be entered from the keyboard. It also allows some minor corrections (changing spelling, etc.). One simple way of entering a program is to precede each statement by a line number. The line number refers to a statement, so that when another statement is typed with the same line number, the new statement replaces the old one.

RUN is a directive which executes the program, immediately printing any results at the terminal. If the results are in error, the EDIT directive allows changes to be made to the program. These changes include inserting, deleting, and appending lines or blocks of lines.

LIST is a directive which prints out the entire program. It is also possible to print out only selected parts of a program.

All the directives (ENTER, RUN, LIST, EDIT, and HELP) can be used, and re-used, repeatedly in any order as aids or tools in programming. There are also other directives available on various systems, including:

    SAVE, to store a program for future use,
    OLD, to retrieve any saved program,
    NEW, to create another new program,
    KILL, to destroy a previously saved program.

Finally, the EXIT directive halts the entire operation, usually providing some indication of the resources used.

THE TOP-DOWN VIEW

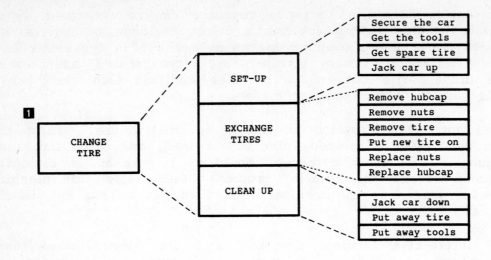

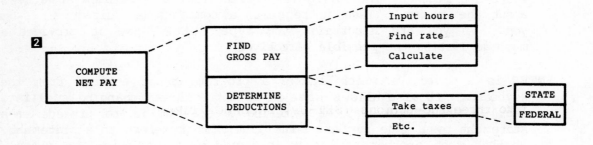

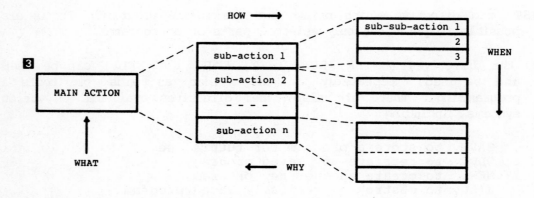

GENERAL

TOP-DOWN DESIGN: Stepwise Refinement

At this point we have seen many algorithms, and many representations of them. We should now be ready to create algorithms properly. There are two general approaches to this design: top-down and bottom-up.

The TOP-DOWN view is a significant way of approaching algorithms. Simply stated, it starts at the top, general, and bird's-eye view and then proceeds to lower levels by successively splitting (or refining) the larger blocks into smaller, more manageable blocks. Finally, at the lowest levels it treats the fine details.

The BOTTOM-UP view starts conversely with the details (often getting bogged down in them) and then proceeds to higher levels by combining smaller blocks. Unfortunately, by concentrating on the details first, the building process may quickly become unmanageable.

STEPWISE REFINEMENT is another name for top-down design (as are iterative multi-level modelling, and hierarchical programming). It is often pictured with break-out diagrams as shown in the given figures.

First, the algorithm is created as a single big action. Then the action is broken down (refined) into a small number of sub-actions. The sub-actions are independent of one another, and not too detailed. This process continues by further refining each sub-action into sub-sub-actions (gradually getting more detailed).

CHANGE TIRE, of figure 1, shows the one action CHANGE TIRE, broken into three sub-actions (SET-UP, EXCHANGE TIRES, CLEANUP). At the third level, each of these previous sub-actions is refined further. Ultimately a stage is reached where every action is understood.

NET PAY, of figure 2, shows a more computer-oriented example. The last stage of stepwise refinement will be in terms of some programming language.

GENERAL, of figure 3, shows how answers to four important questions (what, how, when, and why) are found on the break-out diagrams.

WHAT main action is being done is shown furthest to the left.
HOW an action is done is shown broken out at the right of an action.
WHEN the actions are done (the sequential order) is specified along the far right of the diagram.
WHY a sub-action is done is found to the left of the action.

Although sometimes only the step-by-step sequence of actions is wanted (the WHEN at the right) it is important to see the rest of this structure.

It is very important to realize that each level is complete, as far as it goes. It may need refinement, but it does not need addition or appending. In other words, it expands to the right; it does not expand downward!

JOB: A TYPICAL 'ORDER TAKER' AT A FAST FOOD PLACE

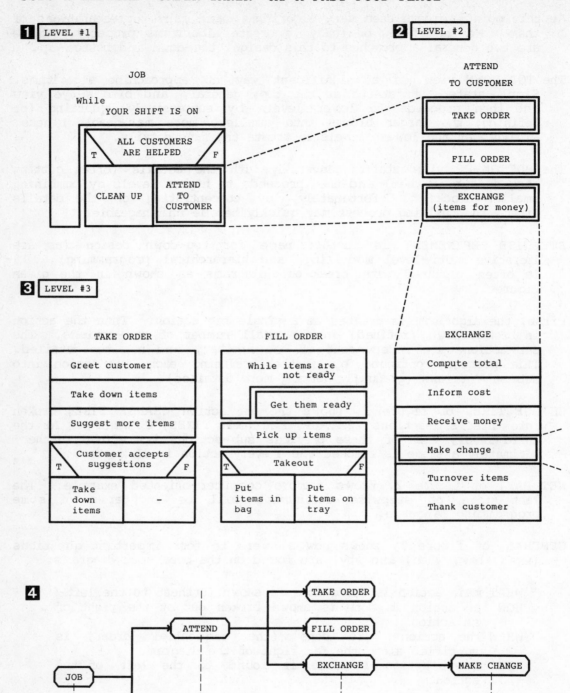

1 | LEVEL #1

JOB

```
While
    YOUR SHIFT IS ON

        ALL CUSTOMERS
        ARE HELPED
    T                      F

    CLEAN UP    ATTEND
                TO
                CUSTOMER
```

2 | LEVEL #2

ATTEND
TO CUSTOMER

TAKE ORDER

FILL ORDER

EXCHANGE
(items for money)

3 | LEVEL #3

TAKE ORDER

Greet customer

Take down items

Suggest more items

```
        Customer accepts
        suggestions
    T                      F

    Take
    down        -
    items
```

FILL ORDER

```
    While items are
    not ready

        Get them ready
```

Pick up items

```
    T        Takeout        F

    Put         Put
    items in    items on
    bag         tray
```

EXCHANGE

Compute total

Inform cost

Receive money

Make change

Turnover items

Thank customer

4

```
                          TAKE ORDER

           ATTEND         FILL ORDER

JOB                       EXCHANGE ───── MAKE CHANGE

           CLEAN UP
```

Level 1   Level 2   Level 3   Level 4

Top-down Example: Job Description

JOB, working at a fast food place, is described in a top-down manner in the given figures. It is developed in levels, to show the convenience of the "sub" blocks in the top-down view.

The first level, of figure 1, is a high level, having no details, but refers to sub-block ATTEND at a second lower level. Then ATTEND, in figure 2, is further broken down into three sub-blocks TAKE ORDER, FILL ORDER, and EXCHANGE. Finally these three sub-blocks are spelled out in detail, in figure 3.

If the detail is still not sufficient, then more levels must be created. For example, the last algorithm EXCHANGE could refer to a sub-algorithm CHANGE, which spells out in detail how the change is to be made. This CHANGE algorithm will be done shortly.

The top-down method forces us to devise a general overview of a system before getting into its details. It also shows the segmenting of a larger system into smaller modules. This segmenting often makes the complexity more understandable and manageable. The segmenting into modules could take the form of a tree, as shown in figure 4 for the case of an order-taker at a fast food place. It could also take the form of nested sets as shown below.

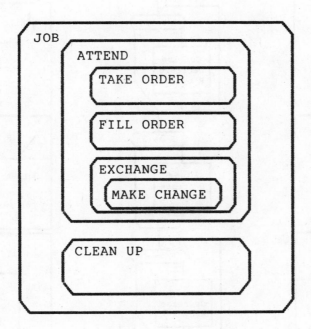

CHANGE MAKER: From the Top

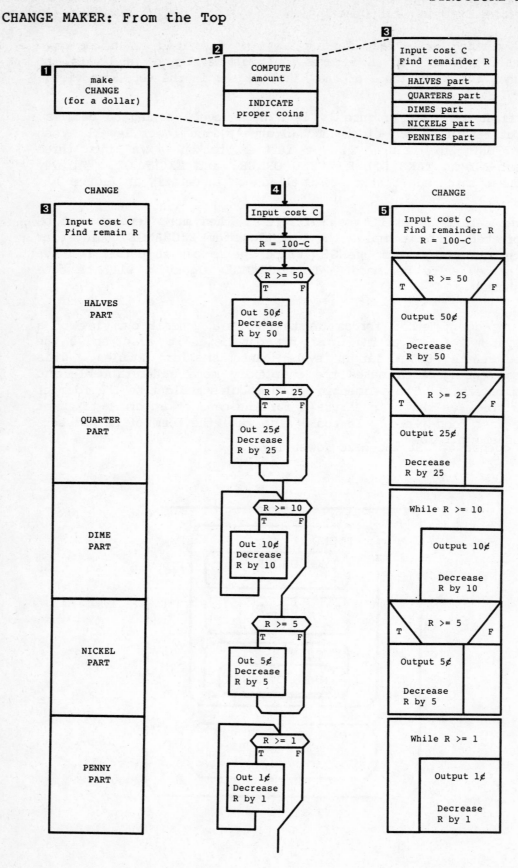

Top-down Algorithm: CHANGE

The top-down design of an algorithm will be illustrated with the design of a change-maker CHANGE. It is required to make change from a dollar for an item costing C cents. The coins to be output are pennies (1 cent), nickels (5 cents), dimes (10 cents), quarters (25 cents), and half-dollars (50 cents).

There are many ways to solve this problem. One way is to subtract the cost C from 100 and output the remaining amount all as pennies. This is a solution, but not a good one; we would prefer to have fewer coins output.

Actually humans usually avoid computing the remaining amount because they prefer not to subtract! They often use another method in which coins are added from the amount C up to a dollar. This method will be treated in the next chapter.

A simple CHANGE algorithm is developed top-down in the given figures. At the first level there is a simple action labelled CHANGE. At the next level this action is split into two sub-actions: COMPUTE the amount of change, and INDICATE the proper coins. At the third level we expand the part indicating the coins. Since we wish fewer coins to be output, we first consider large coins, half-dollars, then quarters, followed by dimes, nickels and pennies. What we do for each coin is a detail not considered at this level. Drawing the boxes for each coin tends to hide the detail; the boxes will be "opened up" at the next lower level.

The final level of refinement is shown completely in figures 4 and 5 as both a flowchart and a flow block diagram. The first block simply computes the amount of change, R, remaining. The next block, for half-dollars, tests this remainder R. If R is less than 50 cents, it leaves this block (with no output); otherwise it outputs the 50 cents, and decreases the remainder by 50 cents. The next block checks for quarters similarly.

The block for considering dimes differs from the above because more than one dime could be output. So it loops (outputting 10 cents, and decreasing R by 10 during each loop) while the remainder is larger than or equal to 10 cents.

The nickel block is again a simple choice form because only one nickel can be output. The penny block is a loop, for more than one penny may be output.

This CHANGE algorithm can be modified in many ways. It can be generalized by allowing the input of any amount T tendered (rather than just a dollar). It can also be extended to more denominations (five and ten dollars), and it can be foolproofed to test that the input values are in the proper range (C is positive, and amount tendered is greater than the cost). Notice that the block form suggests that modifications can be done by inserting or substituting blocks, so encouraging "modular" design.

FIFTY: A Dice Game

1 OBJECTS: Dice

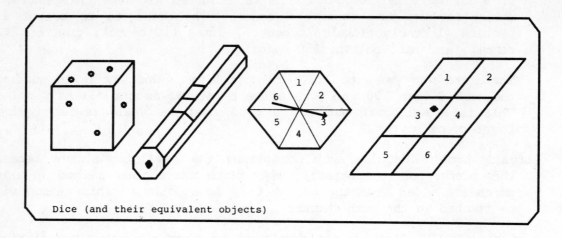

Dice (and their equivalent objects)

2 ACTIONS:

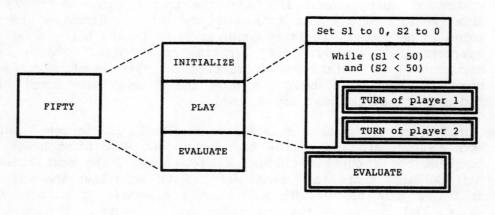

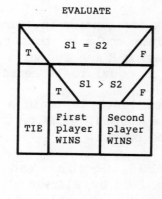

Top-down Dice Game: FIFTY

Games often provide simple examples of algorithms which may be used to show top-down design. Dice games especially have been used for thousands of years.

DICE, the objects of many games, usually consist of cubes (of bone, ivory, sugar, etc.) made with 1 to 6 dots on a side (so that opposite sides add up to 7). Dice games have also been played by rolling a six-sided "cylinder" (pencil), spinning an arrow, or throwing a pebble onto an area marked off in six sections. Another way of getting 1 to 6 randomly is to throw a handful of pebbles on a table, and keep separating off seven at a time until fewer than seven pebbles remain. The given figures show dice and their equivalent objects. The eight-sided rod has two sides without marks; if these come up, then it is rolled again.

FIFTY is a game played with two dice and two people. The players each take a turn in one round, and the rounds continue while neither person's score has reached 50.

During a turn, a player throws the two dice once. There is no change in score unless two identical numbers come up. If both dice are sixes, then 25 points are added to that player's score. If both dice are threes, then that player's score is reset to zero. If any other doubles are thrown, five points are scored. The winner is the one whose score after a round is the highest and 50 or over. A tie is possible.

TOP-DOWN design of FIFTY is shown in the given figures. At the top level it is drawn as a simple, single action. Then it is broken into three sub-actions: INITIALIZE the scores, PLAY a game, and EVALUATE the outcome.

INITIALIZE simply sets the two scores S1, S2 to zero. Notice that the order of playing is not important; the player who goes first does not have an advantage, since both players get a turn during every round.

PLAY loops through a round, where each person gets a turn, while neither one scores 50 or more.

EVALUATE is a choice form which determines which player is winner. It includes the possibility of a tie (equal score).

TURN, at the next lower level, is a sub-algorithm which describes actions during each throw of the two dice, where scores of the players may be modified.

THROW A,B is a final sub-algorithm called to determine the values of the two dice A, B.

STRUCTURED DATA

1 CARD DECK

SUIT

| ♣ clubs |
| ♦ diamonds |
| ♥ hearts |
| ♠ spades |

RANK

| Ace |
| 2 |
| 3 |
| 4 |
| |
| 10 |
| Jack |
| Queen |
| King |

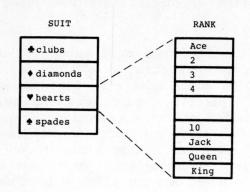

SUIT   RANK

3 TEXT

PAGE

| line 1 |
| line 2 |
| |
| line i |
| |
| line 30 |

LINE

| ch 1 |
| ch 2 |
| |
| ch j |
| |
| 70 |

CHAR

0	bit 0
1	bit 1
0	bit 2
0	
0	
1	
0	
1	bit 7

30*70*8 = 16,800

4 TIME

YEAR

| Jan |
| Feb |
| Mar |
| |
| |
| Dec |

MONTH

| day 1 |
| day 2 |
| 3 |
| 4 |
| . |
| . |
| n |

28-31

DAY

| hour 1 |
| 2 |
| |
| |
| hour 24 |

24

5 PEOPLE

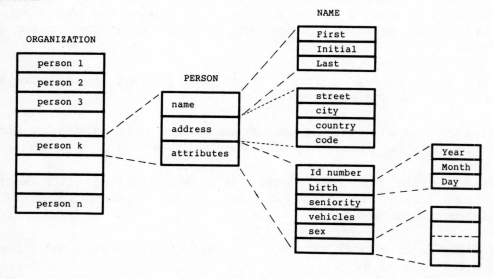

ORGANIZATION

| person 1 |
| person 2 |
| person 3 |
| |
| person k |
| |
| |
| person n |

PERSON

| name |
| address |
| attributes |

NAME

| First |
| Initial |
| Last |

| street |
| city |
| country |
| code |

| Id number |
| birth |
| seniority |
| vehicles |
| sex |
| |

| Year |
| Month |
| Day |

MORE STRUCTURE: Structured Data

Emphasis so far has been on the structure of control, or actions, but objects or data can be structured also. Structured data can also be described by break-out (or call-out) diagrams.

DECKs of playing cards consist of 52 cards, broken into four suits, each having thirteen ranks. Figure 1 shows a deck as a break-out diagram: a simple, self-explained structure. The tree of figure 2 attempts to show the deck completely, doing so in a complex way, so hiding the basic simplicity.

TEXT, of figure 3, similarly shows how a page of text consists of lines, which further break up into characters, which in turn break up into binary digits (bits). This simple structure shows a page of 30 lines, each having 70 characters, with each character represented by 8 bits. So each page uses a total of 30*70*8 or 16,800 bits.

TIME, of figure 4, shows how a year can be split up into months, which in turn split into days, and then hours. Notice that there is not a constant number of days in a month; it varies from 28 to 31 as shown in the break-out area.

PEOPLE, of figure 5, shows an organization of persons, each specified by name, address, and attributes. Then each of these three is broken out further. Notice that at the first level all the break-outs were of the same form, but at the second level each break-out has a different form.

Structured data again will be largely ignored in the next chapters, but will be important in later chapters, especially Chapter 6.

PROBLEM SOLVING: With Trees - Top Down

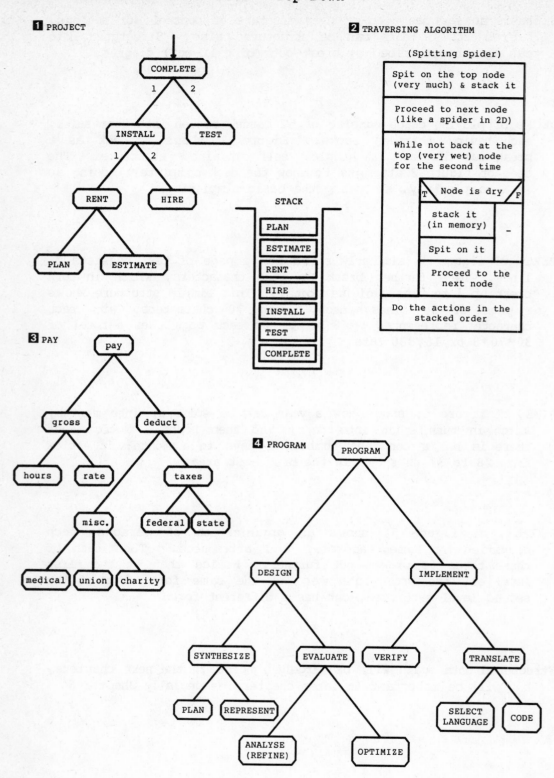

1 PROJECT

```
            COMPLETE
           1        2
      INSTALL        TEST
     1       2
  RENT        HIRE
 PLAN  ESTIMATE
```

2 TRAVERSING ALGORITHM

(Spitting Spider)

Spit on the top node (very much) & stack it
Proceed to next node (like a spider in 2D)
While not back at the top (very wet) node for the second time

T Node is dry F	
stack it (in memory)	-
Spit on it	
Proceed to the next node	

| Do the actions in the stacked order |

STACK

```
PLAN
ESTIMATE
RENT
HIRE
INSTALL
TEST
COMPLETE
```

3 PAY

```
            pay
       gross    deduct
    hours  rate    taxes
              misc.   federal  state
        medical union charity
```

4 PROGRAM

```
                PROGRAM
         DESIGN          IMPLEMENT
    SYNTHESIZE  EVALUATE  VERIFY  TRANSLATE
   PLAN REPRESENT                SELECT   CODE
                                LANGUAGE
      ANALYSE      OPTIMIZE
      (REFINE)
```

Problem-solving with Trees   (Optional)

Problem-solving can be viewed as an algorithmic process. Big problems can be split into smaller sub-problems, and each sub-problem again split into further sub-problems. This subdivision of a problem into smaller problems can be drawn as a tree as shown for PROJECT. This tree illustrates, for example, that the main problem COMPLETE is split into two sub-problems, first to INSTALL, and then to TEST (in that order, given from left to right). Similarly, the INSTALL problem could be split into RENT the tools, and then HIRE the people to use them. Also the TEST problem could be split into three sub-problems, of CALIBRATE, APPLY, and EVALUATE. It was not split up, to keep things simple.

To put these sub-problems into the proper ordered sequence (as in a program) is rather simple, as shown by the algorithm in figure 2. It can be viewed as the path of a spitting spider crawling along a (two-dimensional) tree. The spider simply puts each activity (sub-problem) on a stack the very first time he encounters it (the spitting keeps track of this). Then finally, the reverse order of his encounters (or the order in the stack) specifies the order of doing the activities.

So, merely putting boxes (activities, problems, or instructions) into a sequence is not a significant skill (even a spider can do that, in reverse order yet). The initial plan or design of the structure, splitting the bigger problems into smaller ones, is significant! The proper sequence simply "falls out" from a good design. Notice that the design (tree, in this case) is created from the top down!

PAY, the algorithm of figure 3, is similarly done as a tree. For example, at the top, to determine the pay we need to know the gross earning and the deductions. Then to determine the gross pay we need to know the hours worked and the rate of pay. This process of decomposing the problems continues until the sub-problems are simple, and can be done easily. When these boxes are ordered by the given traversing algorithm, they take the form:

    HOURS, RATE, GROSS, etc.

This sequence represents the more detailed operations:
    GET THE HOURS
    MULTIPLY HOURS BY RATE
    STORE THIS AS THE GROSS PAY
    etc.

PROGRAM, the final algorithm of this chapter, describes the process of programming, from a top view. You traverse it to determine the algorithm for programming!

TREE TRAVERSING is also useful to convert algebraic formulas into various forms (prefix, reverse polish, postfix) which will be considered later, in chapter 4.

RESTRUCTURING UNSTRUCTURED FORMS: Last and Least

1 The NODE-PULLING Technique

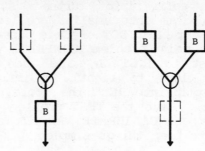

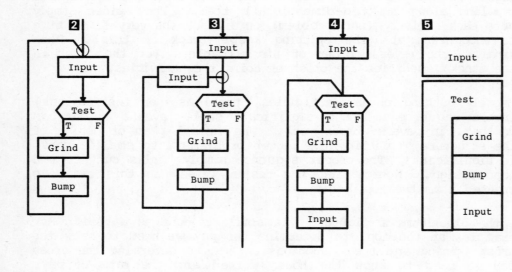

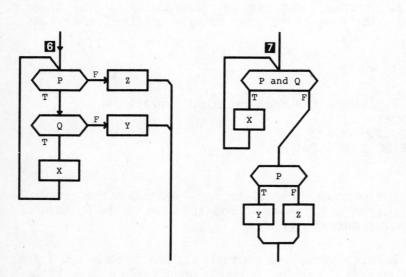

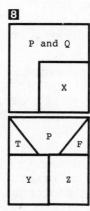

Restructuring Unstructured Algorithms   (Optional)

It is sometimes necessary to convert unstructured algorithms into well structured ones. There are some techniques for doing this restructuring, but the best advice is not to create the unstructured form in the first place.

NODE-PULLING, as shown in figure 1, is one technique for modifying algorithms. Any time two branches intersect at a node, the following box may be "pulled" through the node and repeated on each branch. This may seem trivial and even wasteful, but it is often useful for restructuring algorithms.

For example, consider the very common algorithm of figure 2. It is represented as a flowchart, but it cannot be converted into a block structured diagram because it is not well structured. Applying the node-pulling technique to the circled node (at the top) allows the input box to be pulled through, as shown in figure 3. This is redrawn slightly in figure 4, and the new converted algorithm is shown as a flow block diagram in figure 5. The "cost" of this structure is the addition of one extra input box, not a bad price to pay for structure.

This method of node-pulling will not convert all forms into structured forms. There are other methods, but usually a little creativity is sufficient.

Consider, for example, the algorithm of figure 6. It involves two exits out of a loop; but all well structured forms have only one exit! This is easily remedied by creating a single exit, governed by a single condition which is simply the logical AND combination of the two other conditions. Finally, the rest of the algorithm must be fixed up to account for the above changes. A choice form following the loop determines the actions depending on the condition P. Ultimately, we arrive at the well structured forms of figure 7 and figure 8.

More Restructuring

TWO-LOOPS, of figure 9, seems to have one loop within another. But it it is actually a single loop, as shown in figue 9b. The one condition for looping is that either P OR Q must be true. Then within that loop either action A or B is chosen depending on the condition P. Figure 9c shows the flow block diagram of the resulting very simple algorithm.

FIGURE-EIGHT, of figure 10, shows a rather complex algorithm with a loop criss-crossing in the shape of a figure eight, but having two exits. In such complex examples, an intermediate "flag" variable F is introduced to control the main loop of the new structured algorithm. When an exit is taken in the old algorithm, it is replaced by setting a flag, and returning to the loop test box in the new algorithm. This is shown in figure 10b.

MORE RESTRUCTURING

9 TWO-LOOPS?

10 FIGURE-EIGHT

PROBLEM 2 (page 2-42)

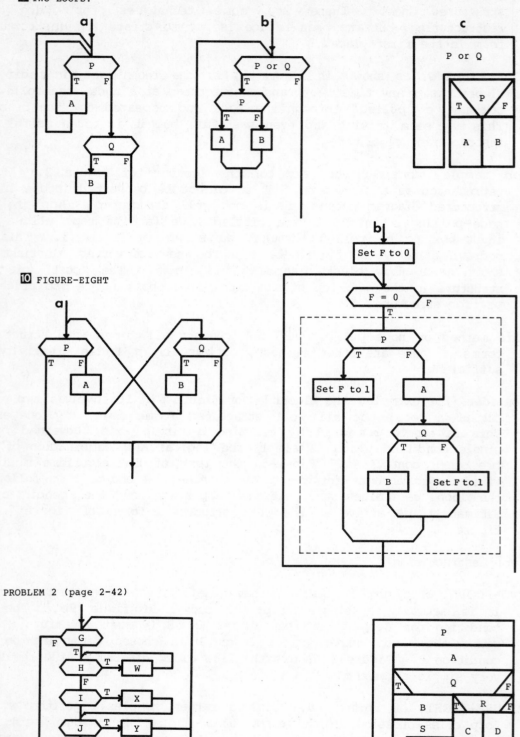

REVIEW: of Chapter 2

STRUCTURE: Form of Algorithms

This chapter develops the two main ideas of Structured Programming and Top-down design. This development is done using many common examples, to illustrate the generality of this approach. It also keeps in perspective the concepts of objects as well as actions.

THE FOUR fundamental forms (Series, Choice, Loop, and Sub) are considered, along with their two methods of connection (cascaded and nested). From these, all possible algorithms may be created. Other building blocks (Until, For, and Case) will be introduced in later chapters.

Structured Programming is a method of organizing algorithms in a simple form, involving a small number of building blocks, with a simple limited interconnection between them. It usually results in algorithms which are clear, orderly, understandable, efficient, modifiable, and provable.

Top-down development is the process of approaching the design of algorithms by starting at the top, splitting it into a few parts (modules), and proceeding stepwise, refining all parts, ultimately ending up at the details. It is important to realize that each stage or level is complete; it may be general but still specifies all. This top-down planning provides a tree-like (hierarchical) structure to algorithms where high level goals and lower level details are both kept in perspective.

Actions and objects are both considered in this chapter, but the emphasis is on the structure of actions (control flow). There is, however, constant brief mention of the structure of data, to keep the two in perspective. Data (or objects) are also capable of stepwise refinement (with break-out diagrams).

PROBLEMS: on Chapter 2

1. CHILI BLOCK
    Convert the Chili recipe flowchart, of page 2-21, into a flow block diagram.

2. CONVERT
    Convert the two flowcharts describing triangle classification (of page 2-23) into flow block diagrams.

3. RE-CONVERT
    Convert the flow block diagram at the bottom of page 2-40 into a flowchart, and convert the given flowchart into a flow block diagram.

4. DISPENSE
    Create an algorithm (in flowchart or flow block form) to dispense items selling for 15 cents. It accepts a sequence of input coins (nickels, dimes) and outputs the item and appropriate change.
    a) Do this using the choice form only.
    b) Do this using a loop form.

5. ANOTHER DAY
    The number of days D in any month M can be determined by knowing if the month is even or odd, and if it is greater than seven or not. Of course, the second month is a special case, given by LEAP sub-block. Create an algorithm to determine the number of days D in any given month M. Create a second different algorithm to do the same thing by simply changing the order of testing the conditions. Create a third equivalent algorithm.

6. BETTER PAY
    If a person works over eight hours in one day, these extra hours should be paid at the overtime rate (even if the total weekly hours are fewer than 40). Create an algorithm to input the hours worked for each of the seven days in a week, and to output the total pay.

7. TRI-AGAIN
    Triangles may be classified by their angles as: equilateral, isosceles, right, obtuse (one angle greater than 90 degrees), and acute (all angles less than 90 degrees). Create an algorithm to do this classification.

8. QUADRILATERALS
    Four-sided figures may be classified according to their angles as: quadrilaterals, trapezoids, isosceles trapezoids, parallelograms, or rectangles. If the four angles (in degrees) are input, starting with the smallest, and continuing clockwise to adjacent angles in order, create an algorithm to identify the figures.

9. CLOCK
    Create an algorithm to "tell time" from a "non-digital" clock which has a long hand L and a short hand S. The inputs to the algorithm are these two variables: L and S (both having integer values ranging from 1 to 12), indicating which value each hand is on, or has passed. The output is to be one of the following four forms, whichever is most appropriate:
    H 'O'CLOCK'
    M 'MINUTES AFTER' H
    'HALF PAST' H
    M 'MINUTES BEFORE' H
    where M and H are the required minutes and hours.

GENERAL PROBLEMS ON TOP-DOWN

Design an algorithm, top-down, for four of the following. Show the break-out diagrams for three to four levels only.

1. Start a car.
2. Make a phone call.
3. Shave (face or leg).
4. Shampoo your hair.
5. Operate a combination lock.
6. Set an alarm clock.
7. Check out a library book.
8. Parallel park a car.
9. Balance checkbook.

10. Launder clothes.
11. Register for your courses.
12. Repair a flat bicycle tire.
13. Shop for groceries.
14. Replace flashlight batteries.
15. Apply artificial respiration.
16. Mix a drink (screwdriver).
17. Set a trap (for mice).
18. Clean a fish.
19. Paint a wall.

20. Saddle a horse.
21. Unclog a toilet.
22. Mow a lawn.
23. Change a light bulb.
24. Take medication.
25. Make a picture frame.
26. Change diapers.
27. Make a bed.
28. Sharpen a pencil.
29. Travel from home to school.

30. Tie a knot (bow).
31. Find a name in a telephone directory.
32. Take an exam.
33. Shift gears in a car manually.
34. Make a left turn with a car.
35. Use a dispensing machine.
36. Assist a choking person.
37. Wallpaper a room.
38. Fold newspapers to create a hat.
39. Decide which four of the above to do.

ROLL-YOUR-OWN

Create an algorithm describing something of your own choice.
Develop it in a structured top-down manner.
Some examples are:
    operating a machine, camera, camp stove, projector, computer
    going through a process, repairing something, developing film
    playing or scoring a game, bowling, tic-tac-toe, hide and seek

MORE PROBLEMS

1. BINARY-TO-OCTAL
    There is a very simple algorithm to convert binary numbers into
    their equivalent octal (base 8) numbers. Try to discover it from
    observing a few equivalents, such as:
        100011 = 43,   010110101 = 265,   1111 = 17
    Write this algorithm in any convenient form.
    Hint: Try grouping the binary numbers.

2. CHANGE-CHANGE
    Modify the CHANGE algorithm of page 2-30:
        a) if half-dollars are not given.
        b) if, in addition, the algorithm is to test for improper
            inputs (negative values, or over a dollar) and output
            appropriate messages.
        c) if loop forms cannot be used.
        d) if choice forms cannot be used.
        e) if any amount T can be tendered (input), and loop forms
            can be used.

3. MORE-TIME
    Create an algorithm to convert a given number of seconds S (say
    one million) into the equivalent number of days D, hours H,
    minutes M, and seconds S. Do this in two different ways, one way
    similar to CHANGE, and one as a data flow diagram.

4. INCHES
    Create an algorithm to convert a given number of inches into its
    equivalent number of yards, feet, and inches. Do this in two
    different ways, both represented as data flow diagrams.

5. ROMANO
    Create an algorithm to convert Arabic numbers (ordinary positive
    integers) into their corresponding Roman numbers.
        a) if at most four consecutive occurrences of a single symbol
            are allowed (where 9 is VIIII and 44 is XXXXIIII).
        b) if at most three consecutive occurrences of a single
            symbol are allowed (9 is IX, and 44 is XLIV).
    Assume inputs less than 300. Hint: See the CHANGE algorithm.
    Note: I=1, V=5, X=10, L=50, C=100.

6. ONAMOR (ROMANO in reverse)
    Create an algorithm to convert Roman numbers into Arabic numbers,
    according to the two above systems.

7. LAST WILL
    Create a "last will" algorithm for someone (such as yourself, a
    friend, an enemy, a fictitious character, a well-known person).

8. BLACKJACK
    Create an algorithm describing the rules of the card game called
    Blackjack (or 21). Create another algorithm describing some
    simple strategy for playing this game.

9. PING
    Create an algorithm describing the game of table tennis.

DICE PROBLEMS

Create algorithms (top-down and structured, of course) describing the following dice games.

1. ROTATION DICE

The game of ROTATION is played with two dice and two people. The players each take a turn for a round. There are 11 rounds in a game, one for each of the combinations: 2,3,4, up to 12. During the first round, the goal is to throw a 2, during the second round it is to throw a 3 -- and so on up to 12. Each time a player is successful, that number of points is added to that player's score; otherwise nothing is added. The winner is the player with the highest score after the 11 rounds.

2. PIG DICE

The game of PIG is played with one die and two people. The players each take a turn for a round, and the rounds continue while all scores are less than 100. During a round each player throws the die, and accumulates the sum, as long as he wishes, or until a 1 comes up. If the 1 comes up the sum is lost; otherwise it is added to the player's score. The winner is the one whose score is the highest.

3. DICE CLIMB

Create an algorithm describing the following game involving two players and one die. The players try to roll a 1, then a 2, a 3, and so on up to 6, in that order but not necessarily one number immediately following the other. First they roll a die to determine who goes first (the highest). Then they alternate turns, stopping as soon as one player (the winner) reaches the value 6. During each turn a player rolls the die once, and keeps rolling only when he gets the numbers he requires.

4. DICE 21

The game of DICE21, or dice blackjack, is played with one die and any number of players. Each player in turn rolls the die until the accumulated sum is 16 or over. If the sum is over 21 the player "goes bust" and is eliminated from the game. The winner is the player (or players) whose score is closest to 21.

5. DICE BASKETBALL

The game of basketball can be simulated with two dice and two players. The game consists of four quarters; during each quarter each player throws the two dice four times, increasing the score by the sums on the dice. The winner is the player with the highest score after four quarters. If tied, extra quarters are played.

6. DICE BASEBALL

The game of baseball can be simulated with one die and two players (teams). It consists of nine innings (rounds) with each team taking a turn during each inning. A throw of the die determines the play as follows:

  a throw of 1,2, or 3 advances a player that many bases (and others already on base advance ahead of this player),
  a throw of 4 is a home run,
  a throw of 5 is a strikeout,
  a throw of 6 is a fly out.

After three outs in a turn (half inning) the other team gets a turn. The game continues for at least nine innings, and additional innings if the score is tied.

MORE GAMES

1. ARCHERY SCRAM

Create an algorithm describing the following game of skill involving two players shooting arrows at a target. The target consists of nested circles labelled with values from 1 to 6; value 1 is farthest out, and value 6 is in the center, or Bull's eye.

The players shoot one arrow each. The one who comes closest to the center becomes the "stopper", and the other becomes the "scorer." They then take turns, each shooting three arrows per turn. The stopper aims to close a sector by hitting it. The scorer aims to get as many points as possible before all sectors are closed. When all sectors are closed, the players swap roles. The winner is the player who scores the highest.

2. DARTS

Create an algorithm describing the following simple dart game. It involves two people throwing darts at a circular target that is divided into different scoring areas. The first turn goes to the player who throws a dart closest to the center of the target. Each player throws three darts in a turn, starting with a given score (say 101), and attempts to reduce the score exactly to zero. If a player's turn takes the score past zero, the score does not change. The first player to reach zero wins.

3. UNSNARLING PROBLEMS

Transform the given unstructured algorithms into equivalent structured algorithms, using only the four fundamental forms. Try creating some other equivalent structured algorithms for these.

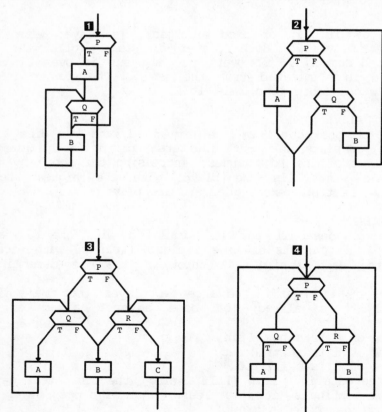

Chapter 3

BEHAVIOR:
  DYNAMICS OF ALGORITHMS

PROGRAMS
   Objects and Actions
SERIES FORM
   and Traces
CHOICE FORM
   and Proofs
LOOP FORM
   and Invariants
SUB FORM
   and Data Flows
MIXED FORMS
   and Applications

BEHAVIOR:

DYNAMICS OF ALGORITHMS

 * Asterisks indicate the degree of importance *

Chapter 3:

BEHAVIOR

Dynamics of Algorithms

PREVIEW

In this chapter we finally begin to consider programs, which are algorithms that are intended for computers. All the previous concepts of algorithms apply to programs, including the properties, representations, and the Four Fundamental Forms.

Objects now will be viewed uniformly as boxes of various types. Actions, including arithmetic operations, input and output, and assignment, will be limited to such objects.

The Four Fundamental Forms will be considered in more detail, from a behavioral view, concentrating on the dynamic (moving) actions, rather than the static (fixed) structure. We will not be concerned with a single run or path through an algorithm, but rather all possible paths. We will see that there may be many different structures, each having the same behavior in all cases.

Choice forms, and their equivalence, are studied and verified by methods from symbolic logic (such as truth tables).

Loop forms have considerably more complex behaviors. They are described by a two-dimensional trace, which yields insight into the dynamic behavior. Loop Invariants are considered briefly. Later in this chapter the invariants are used to improve programs. They can also be used to prove programs correct, but that is not done here.

Sub-forms are considered as data flow diagrams. This view, as a black box or machine, provides an easy and early introduction to an otherwise complex mechanism.

Nesting of forms is not emphasized in this chapter; only simple nests are considered. In the next chapters we consider larger programs and their design.

PROGRAMMING OBJECTS

1 INTEGER (type)

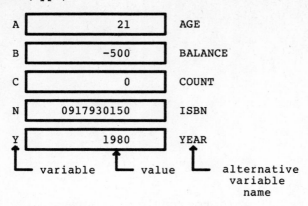

A	21	AGE
B	-500	BALANCE
C	0	COUNT
N	0917930150	ISBN
Y	1980	YEAR

└── variable   └── value   └── alternative variable name

2 CHARACTER

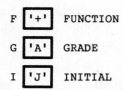

F	'+'	FUNCTION
G	'A'	GRADE
I	'J'	INITIAL

3 REAL

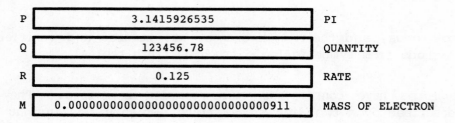

P	3.1415926535	PI
Q	123456.78	QUANTITY
R	0.125	RATE
M	0.00000000000000000000000000000911	MASS OF ELECTRON

4 ETC.

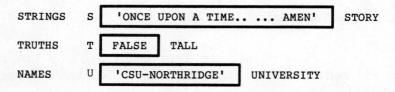

STRINGS	S	'ONCE UPON A TIME.. ... AMEN'	STORY
TRUTHS	T	FALSE	TALL
NAMES	U	'CSU-NORTHRIDGE'	UNIVERSITY

COMPUTER ALGORITHMS (Programs): Objects

The algorithms considered until now have been quite general, involving objects that are as diverse as people, dice, cards, resistors, pebbles, triangles, recipes, and money.

Programs are algorithms which are intended for computers; they have limited objects to manipulate. The programming objects are viewed as labelled boxes (variables) of various sizes (types) with contents (values) that may be examined, copied, or replaced. The physical nature of the boxes may be electronic, or magnetic or chemical or other, but this is unimportant for programming.

Identifiers are symbolic names (or labels) associated with the programming objects. Here in our short programs we use short names (such as A, B, C, or AGE) for convenience; in actual programs we use longer, descriptive names (such as MINIMUMAGE or COUNT_OF_SHEEP) for communication.

TYPE is a description of an object, indicating a range or set of values that an object may have. We could view the type as the size or shape of the box representing a data object. In this chapter we will consider three main types: integers (medium-sized boxes), reals (large-sized boxes) and characters (small-sized boxes). Some examples are shown in the figures.

INTEGERS result from the process of counting, where the values are whole or integral numbers (such as 0, 1, 2001, -7, etc.). Integers could describe populations, dice throws, days in a month, and the age of people. Actually, computers have a limit to the largest size of integer, which may be as small as 32,000 (2^{15}), but is usually much larger. Integers will be the most common type in this chapter.

REAL numbers result from the process of measurement, where values may be portions of a unit. For example, the radius of a circle could be a real value, and the constant PI (3.14159...) is also a real value. Some real numbers can only be approximated by computers.

CHARACTERS result from the process of communication. A character is any single letter, digit, punctuation, or other symbol from a keyboard. The character type would correspond to a very small box, holding only one single symbol selected from dozens on the keyboard. Character values are indicated within quotes, to eliminate confusion between values (such as 'A') and variables (such as A).

LOGICAL, or Boolean, types come from decision-making, where there are only two values, TRUE and FALSE. Logical expressions are usually found as conditions in either the Choice or Loop forms.

Other types often used include the string type, consisting of a sequence of characters. Complex number types are also found in some languages. Programmer-defined types, enabling programmers to create their own types, are available in new languages. Compound objects (such as arrays and records), consisting of combinations of smaller objects, are considered in later chapters.

ACTIONS: Operations on Objects

1 ASSIGNMENT (PUT)

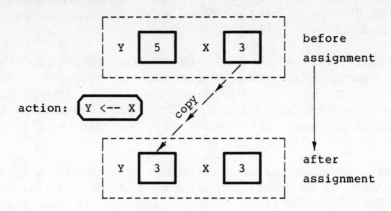

1a INCREMENT (BUMP)

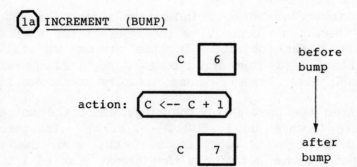

1b ACCUMULATE (SUM)

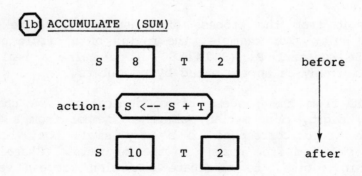

2 INPUT (READ)

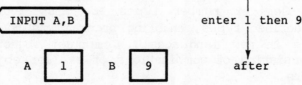

Actions on Programs (Computer Algorithms)

Operations, or actions that can be performed on programming objects, depend on the type of objects. For example, objects of the type real may be added, subtracted, multiplied and divided, yielding results of type real. Logical operators are AND, OR, and NOT; they do not apply to numbers. Similarly, arithmetic operations should not act on variables of type logical or character; dividing two characters should be meaningless.

COMPARISON is a common operation between objects of the same type. Operations such as "is equal to" or "is less than" apply to numbers, but they also have meaning for characters. Characters are assumed in alphabetical (or lexicographical) order, so character 'A' is less than 'B' (or any other alphabetic character).

ASSIGNMENT is a significant action which operates on all data types. It is the process of giving a value to a variable, the act of putting some content into a box. The assignment operation is represented by a leftward arrow as in

$$X \longleftarrow 3$$

which puts the number 3 into the box labelled X. If the box contained anything else before, it will be destroyed, and replaced by the new value 3.

More generally, the assignment notation involving two variables

$$Y \longleftarrow X$$

could be read as "Y gets X" or "Y becomes X" or simply "Y is assigned X." It specifies that the value be copied from box X (without destroying it), and put into box Y (destroying the previous value of Y). A snapshot of the values of variables X and Y is shown in figure 1, both before and after the assignment. If X had not previously been given a value, then this assignment would be meaningless. If the right side is an expression (say a mathematical formula), then it is evaluated, and the resulting value is assigned to the variable at the left.

INCREMENT, of figure 1a, shows how the value of a variable C is increased by a constant. This could be used to "bump" a counter. It should be viewed as one action, rather than as many smaller actions (such as get C, add one to it, and put the result into C).

ACCUMULATE, of figure 1b, is another convenient operation where a value of T is added to the value in S, replacing that value in S.

INPUT, of figure 2, is a useful action which does not directly use the assignment operator. It allows an external value to be read into a variable. Similarly, the OUTPUT action prints a value.

Other actions on programming objects (variables) include special functions (such as finding the square root, or the trigonometric sine), which may be considered later, as necessary.

AN AVERAGE PROGRAM

1

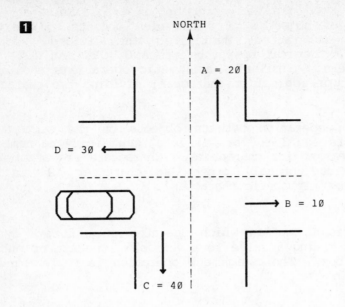

2 AVERAGE Algorithm

```
S <-- 0
S <-- S + A
S <-- S + B
S <-- S + C
S <-- S + D
M <-- S / 4
```

3 TRACE of Algorithm

STEP	S	M	A	B	C	D
1	0	?	20	10	40	30
2	20	?			40	30
3	30	?				30
4	70	?				
5	100	?				
6	100	25	20	10	40	30

unchanged

4

OBJECTS	ACTIONS
Data structure	Algorithm structure

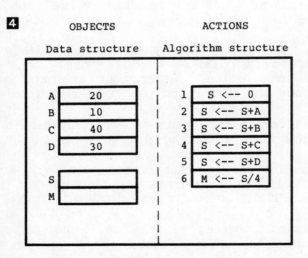

A	20	1 S <-- 0
B	10	2 S <-- S+A
C	40	3 S <-- S+B
D	30	4 S <-- S+C
		5 S <-- S+D
S		6 M <-- S/4
M		

SERIES FORMS: AVERAGE

The simplest computer algorithms (programs) involve a series of actions. The simplest series program would perhaps involve similar actions (such as accumulation). Such an example follows.

Let us consider an algorithm to compute the average or mean value M of four values labelled A, B, C, and D. For example, each of the four values may represent the traffic density (number of cars per minute) passing through some intersection in the four directions: North, South, East, and West, as shown in figure 1. A single number measuring the activity of the intersection could be determined by summing all four values and dividing by 4, yielding the mean value. This number could be computed each minute and printed out.

AVERAGE, an algorithm to compute this mean value, M, is given in figure 2. First a variable S is set to zero. Then the value in A is added to it, and replaces this sum S. At the third step, the value of B is added into S (or accumulated). Similarly, the values of C and D are accumulated in steps 4 and 5, ultimately yielding the sum of 100 in S. Finally, at step 6, this value of 100 is divided by 4 to yield the mean value of 25.

TRACE of an algorithm is a series of "snapshots" of the data values as they vary. A trace of AVERAGE is shown in figure 3, with the data values shown to the right of each step of the algorithm. Since the values of A, B, C, and D do not change at each step, they are not repeated. Traces will be very useful for studying the behavior of algorithms, especially more complex ones.

Structures of two kinds are shown in figure 4. The data structure consists of six boxes, and the algorithm structure consists of six instructions. To average 50 numbers this way could require 52 boxes (one for S, one for M, and one for each data item), and also 52 instructions (one for initializing S, one for dividing, and one for each accumulation). For large amounts of data, this method is horrible; later we will find a better method to do this repetitive action using the loop form. For few numbers, this series form of averaging is sufficient.

The average could also have been represented (at a high level) by the single action:

$$M \longleftarrow (A + B + C + D)/4.$$

SERIES EXAMPLES

SALES

1 PROGRAM   **2** Comments

1. INPUT P   Enter price P
2. INPUT Q   Enter quantity Q
3. S <-- P*Q   Compute selling price S
4. R <-- 0.06   Get the tax rate R
5. T <-- R*S   Compute tax T
6. C <-- S + T   Find the cost C
7. WRITE C   Write out the cost

SWAP

3 Data (registers)   **4** Algorithm   **5** Trace

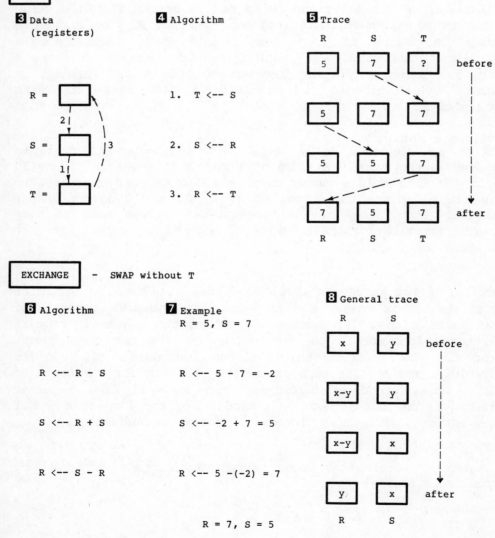

4 Algorithm

1. T <-- S
2. S <-- R
3. R <-- T

EXCHANGE   -   SWAP without T

6 Algorithm   **7** Example   **8** General trace
R = 5, S = 7

R <-- R - S   R <-- 5 - 7 = -2

S <-- R + S   S <-- -2 + 7 = 5

R <-- S - R   R <-- 5 -(-2) = 7

R = 7, S = 5

More Series Programs

SALE, of figures 1 and 2, is a simple program (algorithm) consisting of a series of assignments. It describes the selling of a single item, and includes a computation for sales tax.

SWAP, of figures 3 and 4, is an algorithm to interchange the values of two variables, R and S. It uses a temporary variable labelled T. The algorithm behaves as follows:

> First   the value of S (a 7) is put into T.
> Then   the value of R (a 5) is put into S
>   (destroying the 7).
> Finally the value of T (a 7) is put into R
>   (destroying the 5).

A trace of this SWAP algorithm is shown in figure 5. Such traces are useful for keeping track of the changing contents of variables.

The purpose of the temporary variable T is to save the value of S, which gets destroyed in the second step. Actually, it is possible to swap the contents without using a temporary variable such as T. Try it; then read on.

EXCHANGE, of figure 6, shows another algorithm to interchange the contents of R and S without using any temporary variable such as T. It also consists of three steps, involving variables R and S having values x and y.

> First   R is replaced by (R - S),
>   which has the value (x - y).
> Then   S is replaced by (R + S),
>   which is (x - y) + y, or x.
> Finally R is replaced by (S - R),
>   which is x - (x - y), or y.

An example of the EXCHANGE algorithm is shown in figure 7. The corresponding trace of figure 8 is general, showing the algorithm to work for any numeric values x and y.

Notice that EXCHANGE uses the arithmetic operations of addition and subtraction, so it should not be used with characters, logical values, or other data types that cannot be added. So the SWAP algorithm is more general, applying to all data types.

These two algorithms both require three steps; the steps of EXCHANGE are more complicated than those of SWAP, but SWAP requires the extra variable T. In general, there is a trade-off between efficiency (number of steps), space (number of variables or boxes), and complexity (the kinds of steps).

SOME SIMPLE CHOICES

ABSOLUTE VALUE: (often denoted: Y = |X| or Y = ABS(X)).

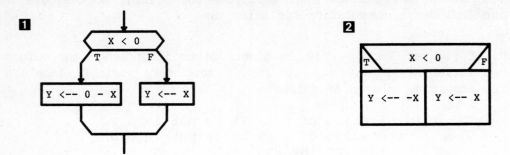

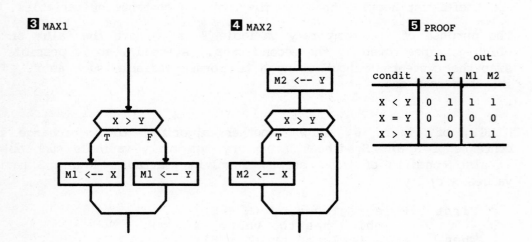

BIG and SMALL (MAX-MIN)

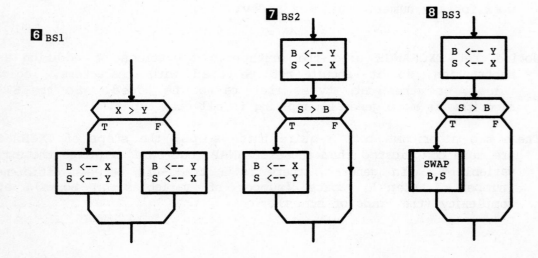

CHOICE FORMS

The ABSOLUTE value of a number (positive or negative) is the number without its sign. An algorithm to remove this sign of variable X producing Y is shown in figure 1. Its corresponding flow block diagram is given in figure 2.

MAX algorithms of figures 3 and 4 show two ways of finding the maximum value of X and Y. MAX1 is the previously considered algorithm, but MAX2 is new.

MAX2 initially assigns Y to be the maximum value; then it tests to see if that was actually so. If X is greater than Y, the algorithm re-assigns the maximum value to be X. This example illustrates a commonly used method or paradigm of computing: first make an estimate (guess), then refine (correct) it, if necessary.

Proof of the equivalence of these two algorithms is given in figure 5. It consists of a table summarizing all possible conditions (three combinations of values of X and Y). For each of the three combinations (conditions), typical values of X and Y are chosen, and the outcomes, M1 and M2, of each algorithm are evaluated. If these outcomes (actions, outputs) are the same in all these three possible cases, then the algorithms MAX1 and MAX2 are equivalent.

These MAX examples again illustrate the fact that there can be algorithms that have the same behavior but different structure. In this example, one structure is not particularly preferable over the other. Later we will see that in some programming languages (Algol, Pascal) the first algorithm MAX1 is preferable, but in other languages (Fortran, Basic) the second algorithm MAX2 is slightly more preferable.

BIG-SMALL algorithms of figures 6, 7, and 8 are slight extensions of MAX. They not only find the maximum or biggest value B, but also the smallest value S.

Algorithm BS1 of figure 6 is very similar to algorithm MAX1. Algorithm BS2 of figure 7 is structured like algorithm MAX2.

Algorithm BS3 begins much like BS2 by making an initial, and arbitrary, assignment to B and S. Then it tests to see if the assignment was proper and, if not, the values of B and S are swapped. So this final algorithm uses a sub-algorithm SWAP, which has been defined previously. It could also use the previous EXCHANGE algorithm, which is equivalent to SWAP.

SOME CHOICE PROOFS

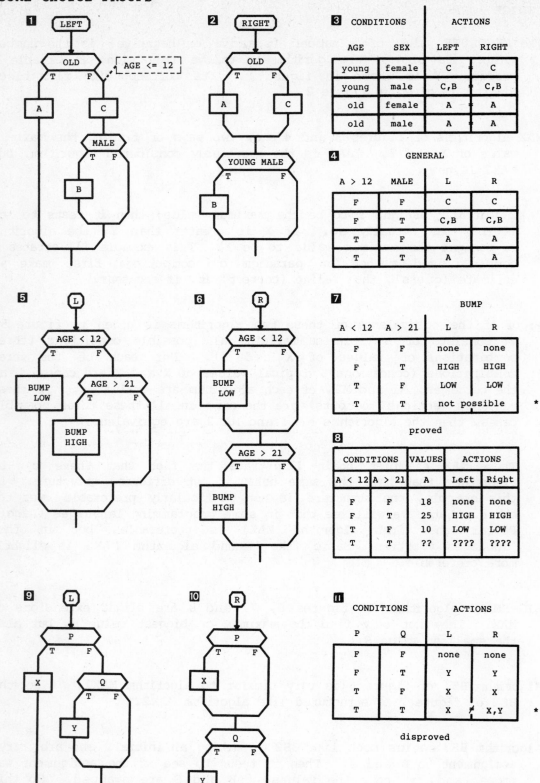

1 LEFT

2 RIGHT

3

CONDITIONS		ACTIONS	
AGE	SEX	LEFT	RIGHT
young	female	C	=	C
young	male	C,B	=	C,B
old	female	A	=	A
old	male	A	=	A

4 GENERAL

A > 12	MALE	L	R
F	F	C	C
F	T	C,B	C,B
T	F	A	A
T	T	A	A

AGE <= 12

5 L — AGE < 12 — BUMP LOW — AGE > 21 — BUMP HIGH

6 R — AGE < 12 — BUMP LOW — AGE > 21 — BUMP HIGH

7 BUMP

A < 12	A > 21	L	R
F	F	none	none
F	T	HIGH	HIGH
T	F	LOW	LOW
T	T	not possible	*

proved

8

CONDITIONS		VALUES	ACTIONS	
A < 12	A > 21	A	Left	Right
F	F	18	none	none
F	T	25	HIGH	HIGH
T	F	10	LOW	LOW
T	T	??	????	????

9 L — P — X — Q — Y

10 R — P — X — Q — Y

11

CONDITIONS		ACTIONS	
P	Q	L	R
F	F	none	none
F	T	Y	Y
T	F	X	X
T	T	X ≠	X,Y	*

disproved

Proofs Involving Choices

Algorithms involving Choice forms can be proved equivalent by testing them for all possible combinations of values. This is similar to the "truth table" proofs of symbolic logic.

Consider the algorithm of figure 1, involving two conditions (of age and sex). There are three actions A, B, C corresponding to three categories: A for aged, B for boys, and C for children. This algorithm could be used within a larger algorithm where A, B, and C are variables that act as counters. For example, every girl causes the C variable to be bumped, and every boy causes both the B and C variables to be bumped.

The algorithm of figure 2 also involves the two conditions of age and sex, and the three actions A, B, C, but they are arranged differently. These two algorithms can be proved equivalent in behavior by creating a table of all possible combinations of conditions, and testing if the resulting actions are the same in both.

The table of combinations is shown in figure 3; in all four cases the two algorithms behave identically. Figure 4 shows this table of combinations converted into a truth table which is more symbolic. Either table may be used as the proof of equivalence. Either one of these algorithms can be substituted for the other; usually cascaded choices are preferred over nested choices.

A second example shows nested choices in figure 5 with cascaded choices in figure 6. The table of figure 7 shows all four combinations. The first combination, for example, includes all ages from 12 to 21, inclusive. However, the last combination (A < 12 and A > 21) has no ages satisfying it. This logical combination is not physically possible, so it need not be considered. All the other conceivable combinations are possible, and have identical actions, so the algorithms are equivalent. An alternative truth table showing some typical test values is shown in figure 8.

A third set of examples of figures 9 and 10 have a similar form to the above figures 5 and 6, consisting of a nesting of Choices and a series of Choices. The two pairs differ, however, in their conditions. The table of combinations, figure 11, shows one combination (the last) where the behaviors differ. This one case is sufficient to disprove the equivalence.

All the examples on this page involved only two conditions (tests, or decisions), so at most four combinations needed to be tested. If there were three such conditions, then there would be eight combinations to test. Such an example will be considered next.

MAJORITY OF THREE: A,B,C

0 Definition of MAJORITY

A	B	C	M
0	0	0	0
0	0	1	0
0	1	0	0
0	1	1	1
1	0	0	0
1	0	1	1
1	1	0	1
1	1	1	1

1

A = 1 (T/F); B = 1; C = 1

M <-- 1, M <-- 1, M <-- 1, M <-- 0, M <-- 1, M <-- 0, M <-- 0, M <-- 0

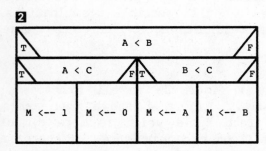

2

A < B (T/F); A < C; B < C

M <-- 1, M <-- 0, M <-- A, M <-- B

3

A = B (T/F); B < C

M <-- A; M <-- A, M <-- C

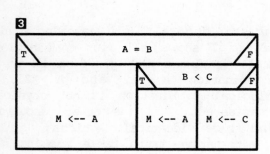

4

S <-- 0

A = 1 (T/F)

S <-- (S + 1)

B = 1 (T/F)

S <-- (S + 1)

C = 1 (T/F)

S <-- (S + 1)

S >= 2 (T/F)

M <-- 1, M <-- 0

5

(A + B + C) >= 2 (T/F)

M <-- 1, M <-- 0

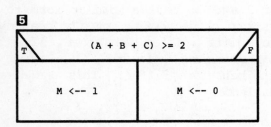
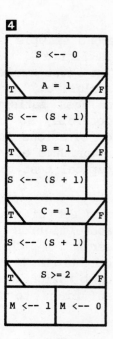

Bigger Choices: MAJORITY

Consider the problem of creating an algorithm to act on three binary variables A, B, and C (having values 0 or 1 only), and to output the MAJORITY value of the three. This process is often called Triplication or Majority Vote-taking. A table describing the MAJORITY is shown in figure 0.

Again, there are many possible algorithms to do this, as shown in the figures.

Method 1 is a systematic, exhaustive, and exhausting enumeration of all possible values. It involves a total of seven tests (count them).

Method 2 is shorter and simpler, involving three tests. Note that the conditions test whether one variable is greater than another (whereas Method 1 tests the value of each variable).

Method 3, simpler yet, involves only two tests, both testing the equality of variables. Essentially, if any two of the three values are equal, then that value is the MAJORITY value.

Method 4, a "thin and long" version, simply accumulates in S the number of times the value of 1 appears in the three cases. Then if this accumulated sum S is greater than or equal to 2, the MAJORITY value is 1; otherwise it is 0.

Method 5, the simplest version, views the values as numbers 0 and 1. It has a single but complex condition, which asks if the sum (A + B + C) is greater than or equal to 2. If so, the MAJORITY is 1; otherwise it is 0.

It is interesting to notice the different conditions in each method.
> Method 1 compares a variable to a constant.
> Method 2 compares two variables for size.
> Method 3 compares two variables for equality.
> Method 4 compares a variable to a constant.
> Method 5 uses a more complex condition.

In this case, a more complex condition resulted in a simpler algorithm. This is often true in general.

Extending the MAJORITY to five variables would be interesting. Some of these methods extend more easily than others. Try it.

Proofs of such MAJORITY algorithms are considered next.

PROOFS OF EQUIVALENCE

1 <u>MAJORITY</u> again - M is the most often occurring value of A,B,C.

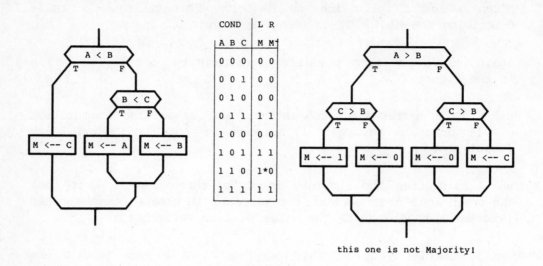

COND	L R
A B C	M M
0 0 0	0 0
0 0 1	0 0
0 1 0	0 0
0 1 1	1 1
1 0 0	0 0
1 0 1	1 1
1 1 0	1*0
1 1 1	1 1

this one is not Majority!

2 <u>MAXIMUM</u> - B is the largest (big) value of X,Y,Z.

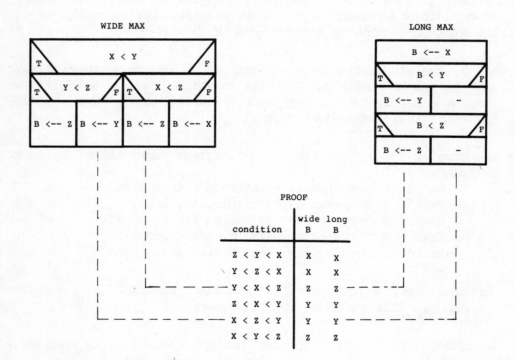

WIDE MAX

LONG MAX

PROOF

condition	wide B	long B
Z < Y < X	X	X
Y < Z < X	X	X
Y < X < Z	Z	Z
Z < X < Y	Y	Y
X < Z < Y	Y	Y
X < Y < Z	Z	Z

Larger Proofs

As algorithms have more variables, they involve more combinations. For example, consider the two given algorithms in figure 1, which are claimed to find the MAJORITY. The three variables A, B, and C each have one of two values, so yielding a total of 2^3 or eight possible combinations, as enumerated in the table. Notice that the binary values are listed systematically, corresponding to the binary numbers zero through seven.

The table (between the algorithms) contains a column labelled "Left M", which shows the values of M evaluated for the algorithm on the left. Similarly "Right M" shows the values assigned to the algorithm at the right. If these two "output" columns had the same value for all combinations, then the two algorithms would be equivalent. However, in this example they behave differently in one case (shown starred), and that is sufficient to disprove the equivalence of these two algorithms. Actually, only the algorithm on the left is a MAJORITY algorithm. Notice that it is a modification of figure 2 of page 3-15.

This algorithm involving three binary variables required 2^3 rows. An algorithm involving n binary variables requires 2^n rows. So for 10 variables, there are 1024 rows, and for 20 variables there are over a million rows. This exhaustive method is very exhausting when the number of variables becomes large.

Figure 2 shows two algorithms for computing the MAXimum of three values X, Y, and Z. The "short and wide" MAX at the left is to be proved equivalent to the "long and thin" MAX at the right. If the values are limited to binary values (say 0 and 1, or any other two values), then eight combinations would be required for the proof of equivalence. However, we would like to prove the equivalence for all (infinitely many) possible combinations of values! This proof is still possible by taking all possible ranges of values. In this case, there are only six possible ranges or conditions, as shown generally in the lower figure at the left. Evaluating both algorithms for all these combinations yields the identical behavior.

Another proof of equivalence can also be done, less abstractly, using six sets of test values (say 1,2,3) as shown below. Any other set of test values could be used; for example, the combination 10, 20, 300 gives the same results as 1, 2, 3 or any other increasing sequence of three values. In the most general situations, when some values may be equal, more combinations must be tested (such as 113, 131, 133, 311, 313, 331, 333).

COMBINATION	X Y Z	W L
Z < Y < X	3 2 1	3 = 3
Y < Z < X	3 1 2	3 = 3
Y < X < Z	2 1 3	3 = 3
Z < X < Y	2 3 1	3 = 3
X < Z < Y	1 3 2	3 = 3
X < Y < Z	1 2 3	3 = 3

GRADES: NESTING OF CHOICES

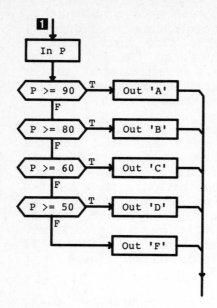

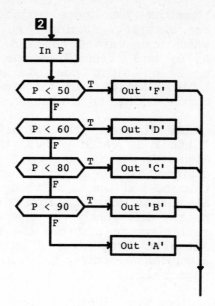

Identical condition

Equivalent series of choices.

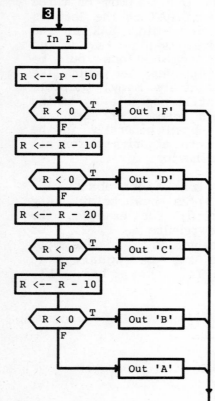

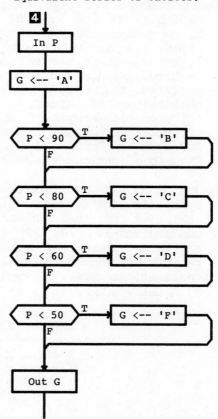

Nested Choices

Nesting of choices is illustrated by the following GRADES algorithm which assigns students grades based on percentage scores. It could be argued that this is not a good way to assign grades, but it is a good example to illustrate many nesting concepts. The specification for the GRADES algorithm is as follows:

    A score of 90 to 100 gets a grade of 'A'
    A score of 80 to 89 gets a grade of 'B'
    A score of 60 to 79 gets a grade of 'C'
    A score of 50 to 59 gets a grade of 'D'
    A score of less than 50 gets a grade 'F'

Many methods are possible for implementing this algorithm; four methods are given in the figures.

Method 1 first tests the largest percentage range, and keeps testing the ranges in decreasing order until the proper range is found, and the corresponding grade is output.

Method 2 is similar but starts from the smallest percentage range.

Method 3 makes the very same test (R < 0) at each stage. This is useful for machine level programming since machines can compare values to zero very easily.

Method 4 involves a series of choices, unlike all the above methods which involve nested choices. This method is often simpler to program in languages having a limited IF structure (such as Fortran). Notice that this method requires the assignment of characters; none of the other methods uses assignment.

Other methods can be used; at least two other different structures are possible.

Modification of all the above algorithms is possible. The constant values (50, 60, 80, 90) could be replaced by other symbolic values (PA, PB, PC, PD) which are assigned the constants initially. Then if the grading "constants" are to change, they may be modified in this one place, at the beginning of the program, rather than in various places in the middle of the program.

EFFICIENCY of algorithms describes the speed of their operation. The speed, or time to do an algorithm, could be determined by counting the number of operations (such as decision boxes). For example, the last algorithm (figure 4) always requires four decisions; every path through this algorithm encounters every decision. All the other three algorithms require four decisions only in the worst case; often the algorithms are left after fewer decisions. So the fourth algorithm is less efficient than all the others.

Analysis of efficiency depends on the values provided. For example, given an input value of 95, method 1 requires only one decision, whereas method 2 requires four. In general, the analysis should not be done for just one such value, but for many values, a distribution of values. For example, if the grade distribution is high, then method 1 would be faster on the average. If, however, most grades were C, then another algorithm could be created with the first decision box testing for the C grade. Try it.

COMPOUND CONDITIONS: Simple Logic

1 CONJUNCTION (logical AND)

a <u>Algorithm</u>   **b** <u>Verbal description</u>   **c** <u>Truth table</u>

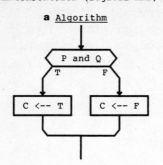

The conjunction C
  is true
  when
  both

P is true
  and
Q is true

P	Q	C
F	F	F
F	T	F
T	F	F
T	T	T

2 Alternative "atomic" algorithms

2a

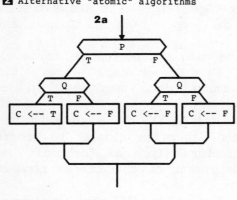

2b

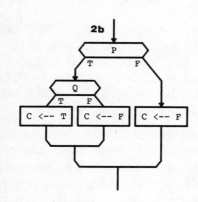

2c

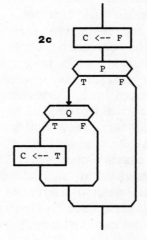

2d

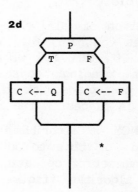

*

3 Other logical compound conditions (connectives)

a DISJUNCTION
        (OR)

P	Q	D
F	F	F
F	T	T
T	F	T
T	T	T

b EXCLUSIVE-OR
        (XOR)

P	Q	E
F	F	F
F	T	T
T	F	T
T	T	F

c IMPLICATION
        (CONDITIONAL)

P	Q	I
F	F	T
F	T	T
T	F	F
T	T	T

d NEGATION
        (NOT)

P	N
F	T
T	F

Logical Choices (Optional)

All the values used so far have been numbers (integer or real), but in
most languages other types of values are possible. A useful type is
the logical (or Boolean) type, having only two values (true, false).
Expressions involving combinations of logical variables are very
common as conditions in Choice and Loop forms. These conditions
often involve the logical operations of AND, OR, and NOT.

CONJUNCTION is a logical operation (connective) denoted as (P AND Q).
It is used as the ordinary AND as in the condition

    (I < J) AND (J < K)

which holds true when I, J, and K are in increasing order. This
logical AND is shown in figure 1 as an algorithm, a verbal
description, and a truth table (table of combinations).

Alternative algorithms for expressing this AND, using only simple
conditions (as is necessary in low level languages), are given in
figure 2. These can be proved equivalent by drawing the
corresponding truth tables. Notice especially the simplicity of the
very last algorithm, 2d. It says, essentially, if P is true then the
conjunction C has the value of Q; otherwise C is false.

Other logical connectives are listed in figure 3. The logical
disjunction, OR, is true when either P or Q, or both, are true. The
"EXCLUSIVE OR" is true when only one or the other of the variables
is true. The logical IMPLICATION, which is not very common in
computing, is false only when the first variable P is true and the
second variable Q is false. The negation, or NOT, reverses the
logical truth value of any variable.

MORE LOGICAL PROOF

It is sometimes useful to prove that two logical statements are
exactly opposite to each other. For example, the condition for
remaining in a loop is the opposite of that for leaving a loop. In a
previous CRAPS dice game, the condition for looping (and throwing)
is:

    (T = 7) AND (T = P)

and the assertion after leaving the loop is just the opposite:

    (T ≠ 7) OR (T ≠ P).

This corresponds to a general result called DeMorgan's Theorem:

    (NOT X) AND (NOT Y) = NOT (X OR Y)

where X, Y are any logical variables. In this case

    X is (T = 7)   and   Y is (T = P).

Proof of DeMorgan's Theorem is shown in the following truth table having
four rows. The proof proceeds column by column (in the numbered
order). Finally columns 3 and 5, corresponding to the left and
right sides of DeMorgan's Theorem, are seen to be identical.

X Y	NOT X	NOT Y	NOT X AND NOT Y	X OR Y	NOT(X OR Y)
F F	T	T	T	F	T
F T	T	F	F	T	F
T F	F	T	F	T	F
T T	F	F	F	T	F
	1	**2**	**3**	**4**	**5**

MORE CHOICES: LEAP AGAIN

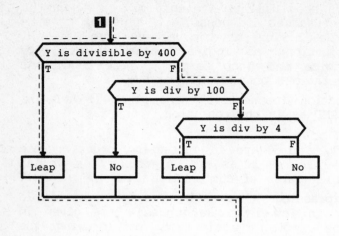

1

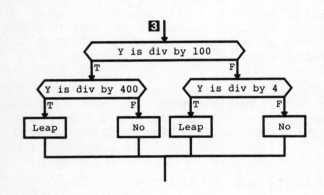

C1 = (Y D 400) OR (Y Ø 100 AND Y D 4)

2 LEAP 2

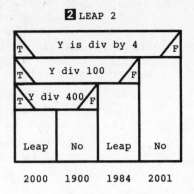

2000   1900   1984   2001

C2 = (Y D 4) AND (Y Ø 100 OR Y D 400)

3

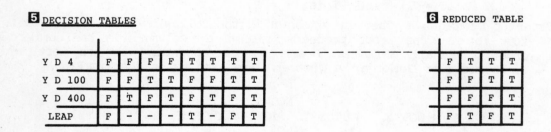

C3 = (Y D 100 AND Y D 400) OR (Y Ø 100 AND Y D 4)

4

	Ci	
T		F
LEAP		NO

5 <u>DECISION TABLES</u>

Y D 4	F	F	F	F	T	T	T	T
Y D 100	F	F	T	T	F	F	T	T
Y D 400	F	T	F	T	F	T	F	T
LEAP	F	–	–	–	T	–	F	T

6 REDUCED TABLE

F	T	T	T
F	F	T	T
F	F	F	T
F	T	F	T

Larger Logical Equivalences   (Optional)

Logical conditions involving N logical variables can be proved equivalent by truth tables of 2^N rows. For example, let us consider the logical "Distributive law":

$$(A \text{ OR } B) \text{ AND } (A \text{ OR } C) \ = \ A \text{ OR } (B \text{ AND } C)$$

The three logical variables yield 8 combinations. The left side L and right side R are evaluated, and found identical in all cases as follows:

A	B	C	L	R
F	F	F	F	F
F	F	T	F	F
F	T	F	F	F
F	T	T	T	T
T	F	F	T	T
T	F	T	T	T
T	T	F	T	T
T	T	T	T	T

TRADING OFF COMPLEXITY

It is possible to make algorithms simpler by making conditions more complex. This trade-off can be illustrated by the LEAP algorithms.

LEAP algorithms (to determine whether a given year Y is a leap year) were given in a previous chapter and are repeated in figures 1, 2, and 3. The equivalence of these three can be proved by using the truth table (decision table) of figure 5. Notice that many conditions are not possible, for example in column 3 (Y not divisible by 4, but divisible by 100).

All three of these algorithms involve three separate conditions. If the conditions were allowed to be more complex, the resulting algorithm could be as simple as the algorithm of figure 4. In fact, there are three such different but simple algorithms, one corresponding to each of the three complex flowcharts.

Consider the first flowchart, of figure 1. There are two paths through it leading to a leap year: when Y is divisible by 400, or when Y is not divisible by 100 and is divisible by 4. Putting this symbolically leads to one larger condition:

$$C1 = (Y \text{ D } 400) \text{ OR } (Y \text{ } \emptyset \text{ } 100 \text{ AND } Y \text{ D } 4)$$

where $\emptyset$ means "D is not divisible by".

The other complex conditions developed from the other algorithms are shown under the corresponding flowcharts. Attempt to convince yourself of these two. As a last resort, you could use truth tables.

THE WHILE FORM: Repetition

1 Structure

2 Behavior (trace)

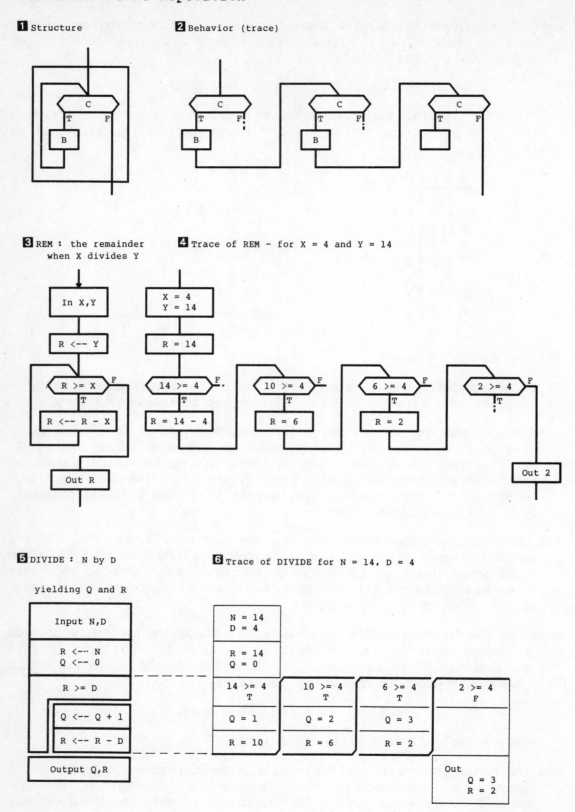

3 REM : the remainder when X divides Y

4 Trace of REM - for X = 4 and Y = 14

5 DIVIDE : N by D yielding Q and R

6 Trace of DIVIDE for N = 14, D = 4

LOOP FORMS

Algorithms with loops are significant in computing, especially when there is much repetition. In fact, many algorithms are purposely made repetitious to make use of a loop form.

Structure and behavior of the loop form is shown in figures 1 and 2. The structure is static (still) but the behavior is dynamic (moving). The structure indicates that while the condition C is true, the body B is repeated. The behavior shows this series of actions by means of a "trace" to the right of the structure. The body B is repeated, until the condition C is changed (to False), so ending the repetition.

TRACE is a series of "snapshots" showing the behavior of an algorithm. In the trace of figure 2, the result of each step is written directly to the right of that step in the algorithm. This creates a series of "stages", one stage (or column) for each time through the loop. More convenient traces, in the form of flow block diagrams, will be introduced next. Such systematic two-dimensional traces will prove to have great uses.

REM, of figure 3, is an algorithm for computing the remainder when Y is divided by X. It illustrates this for the value 14 divided by the value 4. It proceeds by repeatedly subtracting away 4 from 14 until the result is less than 4 (leaving a remainder of 2 in this example). The remainder is often called the modulus, and this operation is represented as the MODULO function:

R = Y MOD X   or sometimes   R = MOD(Y,X)

DIVIDE, of figure 5, shows an algorithm which divides the numerator N by the denominator D, yielding a quotient Q and remainder R. The trace shows how 14 divided by 4 yields a quotient of 3 and a remainder of 2.

This is done by subtracting away the denominator from the numerator (re-named R, the remainder), counting the number of times, Q, that this is done while the remainder is greater than or equal to the denominator.

DIVIDE differs from the division operation available in most programming languages. Usually, division of two real numbers (written Y/X) yields another real number, and the result is expressed in decimal form. The division of two integer values usually yields only the quotient; the remainder is lost (or can be obtained from the above MODULO operation).

SQUARE AND SQUARE ROOT

1 ODD-SQUARE

Input N	
S <-- 0	
I <-- 1	
B <-- 1	
While I <= N	
S <-- S + B	
B <-- B + 2	
I <-- I + 1	
Output S	

N =	6						
S =	0						
I =	1						
B =	1						
	1 <= 6 T	2 <= 6 T	3 <= 6 T	4 <= 6 T	5 <= 6 T	6 <= 6 T	7 <= 6 F
S =	1	4	9	16	25	36	
B =	3	5	7	9	11	13	
I =	2	3	4	5	6	7	Output 36

Trace of ODD-SQUARE.

(which computes the square S of any integer N by summing the first N odd integers).

note

$1 + 3 = 2^2$

$4 + 5 = 3^2$

$9 + 7 = 4^2$ ←

generally

$$S + B = I^2$$

$36 + 13 = 7^2$

also: $S = (I - 1)^2$ and $B = I + I - 1$

2 SQUARE-ROOT
(Newton-Raphson)

Input X,L	
G <-- X / 2	
G*G - X > L	
Q <-- X / G	
G <-- (G + Q)/2	
E <-- G*G - X	
Output G	

X = 20					
G = 10					
	100 ≠ 20 T	36 ≠ 20 T	21.8 ≠ 20 T	20.1 ≠ 20 T	20 ≠ 20 F
Q =	2.0	3.33	4.29	4.47	
G =	6.0	4.67	4.48	4.47	
E =	16.0	1.77	0.04	0.00+	Output 4.47

note: G*G - X = E and E > L

Tracing and Invariants

The trace of an algorithm can yield many insights. Often it indicates errors in algorithms; sometimes it suggests improvements in algorithms, or even suggests alternative algorithms. The trace also shows useful relationships among variables. These concepts are illustrated in the next two pages.

ODD SQUARE, of figure 1, shows one algorithm to find the square of any integer N by summing the first N odd integers. It is not a very significant problem, but it avoids multiplication and it also illustrates some important concepts.

Observing a trace often reveals relationships among variables. For example, at each stage adding S and B yields the square of I.

$$
\begin{aligned}
\text{At stage 1,} \quad & 1 + 3 = 2*2 \\
\text{At stage 2,} \quad & 4 + 5 = 3*3 \\
\text{At stage 3,} \quad & 9 + 7 = 4*4 \\
\\
\text{In general,} \quad & S + B = I*I
\end{aligned}
$$

LOOP INVARIANTS are relations (such as the above $S + B = I*I$) which hold during every stage of looping. All the variables may be changing but the relationship among the variables is constant, or invariant.

Further observation of this trace yields another formula that holds at every stage:

$$S = (I - 1)^2$$

There is still another formula that holds, a third invariant:

$$B = 2*I - 1 \quad \text{or} \quad B = I + I - 1$$

This relation between B and I suggests that both these variables are not necessary. In fact, such a simple algorithm having only one of these variables, I, is possible: try it.

In this example there were many invariants, and they were rather easy to observe. In general, loop invariants are not always easy to find; there is no foolproof technique for finding them. At present, they mainly provide insight into the behavior of algorithms. Also, they are a challenge, making traces interesting. Later in this chapter, they are used to improve algorithms. They can also be used to prove algorithms.

SQUARE ROOT, of figure 2, is a more practical algorithm used to compute the square root of any input value. It does this by successively refining a guess G until the square of this guess is sufficiently close to X.

The condition for remaining in the loop is that the error E (which is $G*G - X$) be greater than some limit L (say 0.01). Alternatively, the assertion after leaving the loop is that the magnitude of the error E must be less than the limit L.

TWO FACTORIALS

1 FACT1

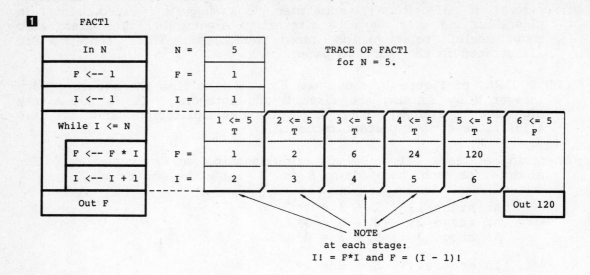

TRACE OF FACT1
for N = 5.

NOTE
at each stage:
I! = F*I and F = (I - 1)!

2 FACT2

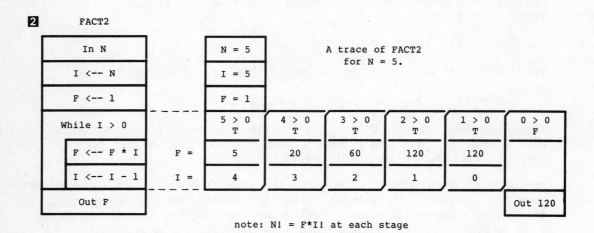

A trace of FACT2
for N = 5.

note: N! = F*I! at each stage

More Tracing, and Insight

FACTORIAL is a common concept found in probability, statistics, and counting types of problems. The FACTORIAL of any nonnegative integer N is written as N! and defined as:

N! = N*(N − 1)*(N − 2)*(N − 3)* ... *3*2*1

The products could be done in either increasing or decreasing order such as:

5! = 1*2*3*4*5   or   5*4*3*2*1

leading to two different algorithms, FACT1 and FACT2.

FACT1, of figure 1, initially sets a variable F to 1, sets another variable I to 1, and then loops. While I is less than or equal to the input value N it multiplies F by the value of I, increases I and continues looping. Ultimately, when variable I finally is "bumped" past N, it leaves the loop and outputs the final value of F.

The trace shows this computation for an input value of N = 5. At a glance it shows that as 1 increases gradually, the value of F increases dramatically. Just doubling the value of N to 10 would produce an output value of 3,628,800. Such a computation can quickly exceed the bounds of any computer, so we must beware of taking large factorials.

Observing this trace leads to two loop invariants:

I! = F*I   and   F = (I − 1)!

These two relations can be combined into a third relation:

I! = (I − 1)!*I

This is a recursive definition of factorial, which will be treated later.

FACT2, of figure 2, proceeds in just the opposite way from FACT1. It starts the counter I at a high value of N, and loops, decreasing this value until it reaches zero. During each loop it multiplies F by this decreasing value of I.

Observing this trace, we can see that at each stage the following invariant holds:

N! = F*I!

Notice that this loop invariant for FACT2 is very different from the previous invariant for FACT1. Different ways of computing the same algorithm may have different loop invariants.

Notice also that if the condition (I > 0) was incorrectly written as (I >= 0) the resulting value of factorial would be zero, for F would ultimately get multiplied by this lowest value of I (of zero). It is often easy to make such a slight error in a condition, which can result in a very large error in the final result. Tracing helps to find such errors.

Tracing in this two-dimensional way is useful in many ways.
1. Tracing provides output by simulating computers.
2. Tracing yields insight into dynamic behavior of algorithms.
3. Tracing detects errors (such as the notorious "off by one").
4. Tracing yields interesting relations among variables.
5. Tracing suggests other algorithms.

PRODUCT ALGORITHM

1 BAD PRODUCT

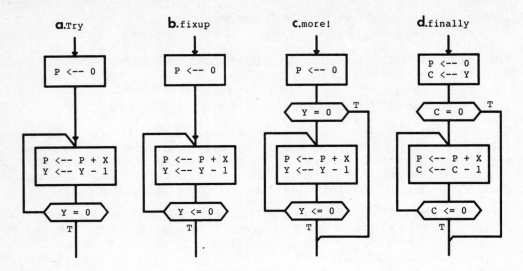

2 BETTER PRODUCT

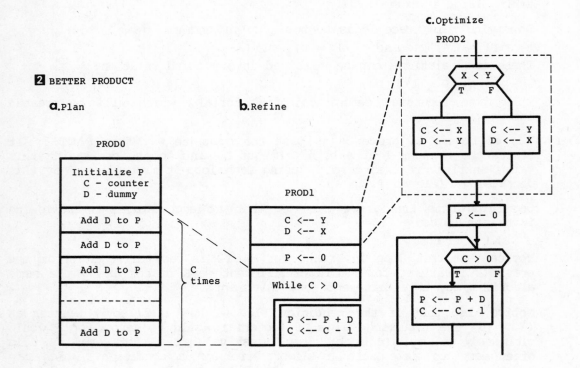

Creating Products, Good and Bad

Let us consider creating an algorithm to find the product P of two nonnegative integers X and Y. It is to be done by successively adding the value X for a total of Y times. This product is not necessarily a very useful algorithm, but it illustrates many concepts, both good and bad.

BAD product, shown in figure 1, does not use the fundamental "while" loop form; it performs the test after doing the body (called post-test) instead of performing the test first (called pre-test). Now let us see how the unfortunate consequences of this post-test do multiply!

Algorithm 1a works well for most values, but not if Y is 0. In that case Y is first decreased to -1, then Y is tested to see if it reached 0. But Y has already passed 0, so it keeps looping, and Y keeps decreasing forever!

Algorithm 1b "fixes up" this infinite loop by leaving the loop when Y is less than or equal to zero. So it doesn't loop forever, but it still doesn't compute the correct result in one case. When Y is zero the algorithm first sets P to zero, and then immediately increases it by X and halts. So multiplying any value by zero does not yield a zero!

Algorithm 1c "patches up" this unusual case by first testing for it, and immediately circumventing the loop. But this algorithm still has a problem! By using one of the variables Y as a counter, it destroys the original value of Y. This "side effect" of the algorithm may not always be harmful; but if Y is to be used again later in the program, its value will have been changed to 0. So if Y is to be a constant rate of pay (say 10 dollars an hour) and it is to be multiplied by various hours X which are input, then the first product of X and Y will yield a correct answer; all other products of any X with Y will yield zero.

Algorithm 1d finally fixes this side effect by first making a copy of Y, calling it C, and using C as a counter.

This process of trial and error followed by many fix-ups and more errors is entirely unnecessary. Some prior plan and refinement using the four fundamental forms yields a better product as shown in figure 2.

BETTER PRODUCT, of figure 2a, starts out at a very primitive level, setting up not only a counter C, but also a "dummy" variable D. Then the successive additions are shown as a series of accumulations.

Algorithm 2b is a simple refinement of the previous algorithm, which replaces the series of accumulations by a while loop. This could be the final algorithm; there is nothing more to it! By using the proper structures in the proper way we have created a better Product. In fact since we are saved time from fixing and patching, we might take some time to optimize the finished product.

Algorithm 2c shows an optimized product, where the counter C is first chosen to be the smaller of the two values X and Y. It thus loops the fewest number of times. Time is saved for the machine, but not necessarily for the human programmer.

LOAN: A Problem of Interest

1 Top view

Set up AMOUNT, BALANCE RATE, DURATION PAYMENT

Loop for a
duration of
5 years:
 	
. Computing
  INTEREST
 	
. Modifying
  BALANCE

Output BAL

2 Refined

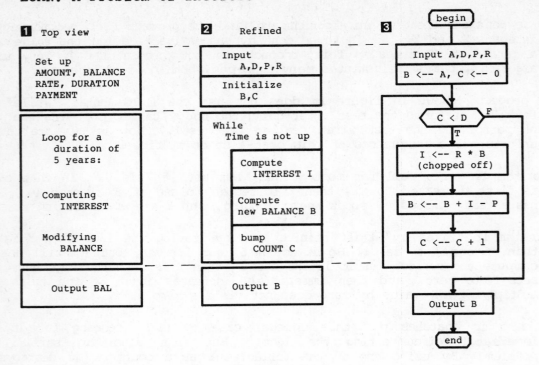

3

4 TRACE (run)

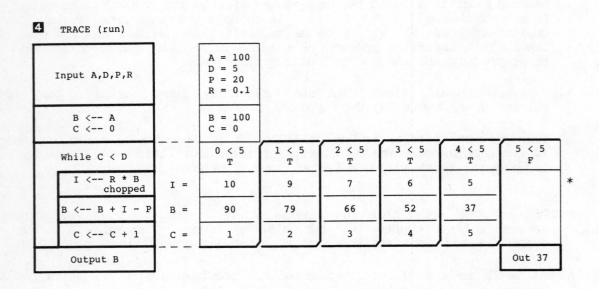

5 STATE TRACE

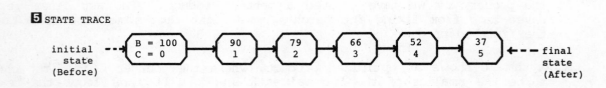

A Business Application

LOAN -- A Problem of Interest

Borrowing money usually involves interesting algorithms. As an example, let us consider making a loan of amount A (say 100 dollars) for a duration D (say five years). The amount of each regular payment is P (say 20 dollars), and the interest rate is R (say 10 percent of the remaining balance B). This amount of interest is chopped off to the next lower dollar. All these numbers and conditions have been chosen for our convenience in making the trace. Later, when using a computer, we can be more realistic.

After making the payments for the duration, there is still an amount to repay at the end; this amount is called the balloon payment, for it "balloons" into a much larger amount than we expect. Our problem is to compute the balloon payment. You may wish to guess the value before reading on.

The development of the algorithm is shown in the given figures.

Figure 1 shows the very top view, first setting up the variables, then looping, and then outputting the final balance (the balloon).

Figure 2 refines each of these three blocks, but still not in detail. It shows the loop explicitly and introduces two new variables (I for the interest at each stage, and C for counting the stages).

Figure 3 finally spells out each step in all its detail.

Figure 4 represents the previous flowchart as a flow block diagram, with a trace to its right. It shows a solution of 37 dollars as the balloon payment.

Incidentally, if the payment is ten dollars (equal to the interest) then the balloon payment equals the original loan amount (of 100 dollars), regardless of the duration. This is called an "interest-only" loan.

Another way of computing this balloon payment is possible from observing the trace. It results from realizing that after the five payments of 20 dollars the entire loan amount has been paid off, and the balloon payment is due only to the interest. The total interest can be determined by summing the individual interest I computed each year. It is:

$$10 + 9 + 7 + 6 + 5 = 37$$

This corresponds to summing the second row of the trace (shown starred). Notice that this alternative method works only if the sum of the payments alone equals the amount borrowed.

A STATE TRACE following the detailed trace is a shorter form of the trace, showing only the really relevant (dynamic) variables. It includes only the balance B and the count C, the only variables necessary to continue the process should it be interrupted at any step.

SUB-ALGORITHMS

1 Definition and representation (for MAX example)

a. Interior view **b.** Data flow view **c.** Control flow view

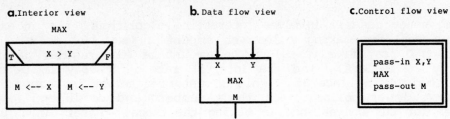

2 Structure and interconnection of sub-forms
(L is the largest of A,B and C)

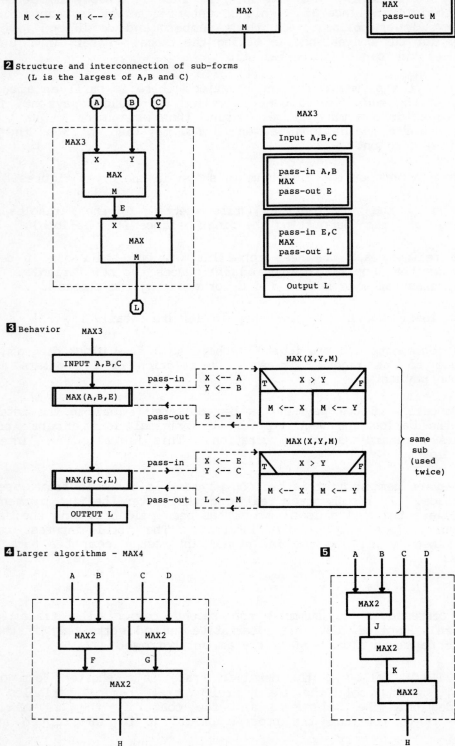

SUB-FORMS

Sub-algorithms (or sub-forms) are simply algorithms which are parts of other algorithms. A sub-algorithm is "called" or invoked by giving its name and indicating the objects that it involves. The most significant use of sub-forms is to simplify a large algorithm by breaking it down into smaller pieces. A sub-algorithm could also be used to avoid repetition of a commonly occurring block, by referring to this sub-block repeatedly.

A sample sub-algorithm MAX is given in figure 1. It is first defined internally in all its detail. It is also viewed externally in figure 1c as a "black box" called MAX, having three variables X, Y, and M. Another representation is the data flow diagram of figure 1b, where it is viewed as a machine or box with two inputs X and Y and an output M. Here M can be thought of as being "connected" to either X or Y, whichever is the largest.

MAX3, of figure 2, shows how the maximum of three variables A,B, and C can be created by interconnecting two of the smaller MAX sub-algorithms. Notice that each MAX sub-algorithm always internally involves variables X,Y, and M (called formal parameters), which are "connected" to other variables A,B,C,E,L of the calling algorithm. These variables of the calling algorithm (or main algorithm) are called actual parameters. The process of connecting, or making a correspondence between, formal and actual parameters is called "passing" parameters. We say that the actual parameters A and B are passed-into MAX, and E is passed-out of MAX.

Correspondence between formal and actual parameters in most languages is indicated by the order of the parameters within parentheses. For example the MAX sub-algorithm is defined by the form:

        MAX(X,Y, M)   where X,Y, and M are formal parameters

and when it is called, or referred to as MAX(P,Q,R), then it makes P correspond to X, Q correspond to Y, and R correspond to M so that R becomes the maximum value of P and Q. Input parameters are often (not always) listed first, and separated from the output parameters by a space.

The algorithm for MAX3 can be written in this notation as:

        INPUT A,B,C
        MAX(A,B, E)
        MAX(E,C, L)
        OUTPUT L

Behavior of such a sub-algorithm is illustrated by the flow of control (shown dotted) in figure 3. Each time a sub-algorithm is called, the flow of control is diverted to the sub-algorithm, the input parameters are passed to the sub-algorithm, some actions are done there, the resulting values are passed back to the calling algorithm, and then control returns back also. The sub-algorithm MAX is shown twice, but it could be one occurrence of it, used twice.

MAX4 can be created similarly from MAX2 sub-forms, in two different ways as shown in figures 4 and 5. Notice that the algorithm at the left could allow the two MAXes to be done at the same time (if such "parallel" operation is available). The algorithm at the right could not make use of such parallelism. With parallelism (concurrency) the algorithm at the left could take two time units, whereas the one at the right must take three time units.

SECONDS WITH SUB-ALGORITHMS

1 DIVIDE-SUB

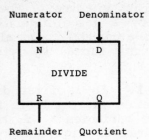

2 DIVIDE IMPLEMENTATION

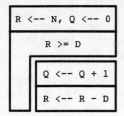

3 FIRST-SECONDS

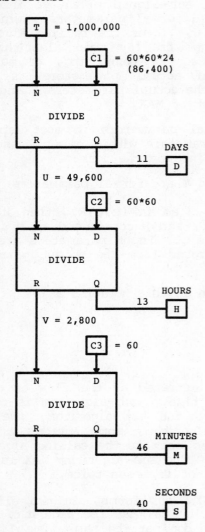

4 SECOND-SECONDS

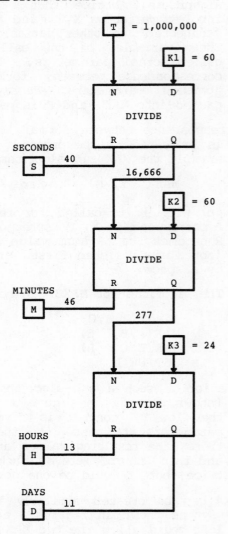

Sub-form Examples: SECONDS

Suppose you were asked to convert a given number of seconds (say T = 1,000,000 seconds) into days, hours, minutes, and seconds. You could proceed as follows.

First you divide T by the number of seconds in a day (86,400), yielding a quotient which is the number of days, say D, and some remaining number of seconds.

Then this remainder from above is divided by the number of seconds in an hour (60*60), yielding the number of hours, say H.

Finally, the above remainder is divided by the number of seconds in a minute (60), yielding a quotient which is the number of minutes, M, and a remainder which is the number of seconds S.

An algorithm to do this conversion can easily be created from the above verbal statements. The main building block of this algorithm is the DIVIDE sub-algorithm.

DIVIDE-SUB is shown in figure 1 first as a data flow diagram, with two inputs (numerator N and denominator D) and two outputs (quotient Q and remainder R). It could be implemented in a number of different ways, one shown in figure 2.

FIRST-SECONDS, of figure 3, shows the above described algorithm for converting seconds T into days D, hours H, minutes M, and seconds S. This algorithm could be written in program form as:

```
INPUT T
DIVIDE(T, 60*60*24, D, U )
DIVIDE(U,  60*60,   H, V )
DIVIDE(V,   60,     M, S )
OUTPUT D, H, M, S
```

Notice that the products such as 60*60*24 need not be evaluated by us; the computer can do that.

SECOND-SECONDS, of figure 4, shows another algorithm to do this same conversion in another way by producing the results in the opposite order, first SECONDS and last DAYS. It first divides the total of one million seconds by 60 to yield a quotient of 16,666 minutes and a remainder of 40 seconds. The minutes are then divided by 60 to yield a result of 277 hours and a remainder of 46 minutes. Finally, the 277 hours are divided by 24 to yield a quotient of 11 days and a remainder of 13 hours.

At this time we are not concerned with which of the above methods is better; we should realize only that there may be many possible algorithms. We need not stop at the first one we create.

INTERCONNECTIONS OF SUB-ALGORITHMS

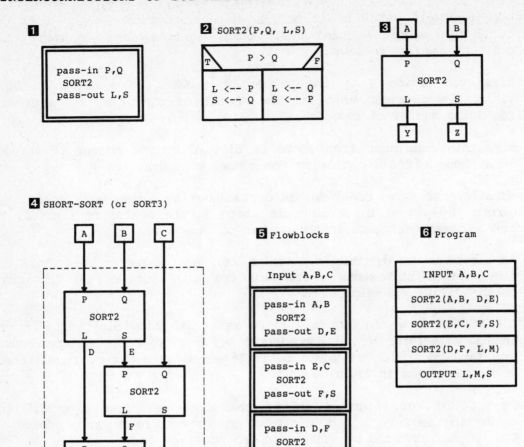

1
```
pass-in P,Q
SORT2
pass-out L,S
```

2 SORT2(P,Q, L,S)

T	P > Q	F
L <-- P		L <-- Q
S <-- Q		S <-- P

3
```
    A        B
    |        |
    P        Q
      SORT2
    L        S
    |        |
    Y        Z
```

4 SHORT-SORT (or SORT3)

```
   A      B      C
   |      |      |
   P      Q
     SORT2
   L      S
   D      E
          P      Q
            SORT2
          L      S
                 F
   P      Q
     SORT2
   L      S
   |      |      |
   L      M      S
```

5 Flowblocks

Input A,B,C
pass-in A,B SORT2 pass-out D,E
pass-in E,C SORT2 pass-out F,S
pass-in D,F SORT2 pass-out L,M

Output
  L (largest)
  M (medium)
  S (smallest)

6 Program

INPUT A,B,C
SORT2(A,B, D,E)
SORT2(E,C, F,S)
SORT2(D,F, L,M)
OUTPUT L,M,S

DATA FLOW DIAGRAMS (with same pass-in and pass-out)

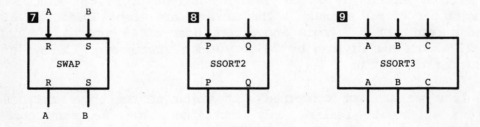

7
```
   A      B
   R      S
     SWAP
   R      S
   A      B
```

8
```
   P      Q
     SSORT2
   P      Q
```

9
```
   A    B    C
     SSORT3
   A    B    C
```

More Sub-forms: Short Sorts

SORTING is a process of putting objects into order, either increasing or decreasing. It is a frequently used algorithm in computing. Here we will consider only small sorts (of two, three, four, or five values); later we will extend this. Now our main interest in sorting is to illustrate more concepts of building with sub-algorithms.

SORT2 is an algorithm to sort the contents of two variables, P and Q, with L becoming the larger and S becoming the smaller. Figure 2 shows the internal details of the algorithm, and figure 3 shows the data flow diagram. The data could be viewed as flowing directly from P to L and Q to S, or it could be flowing from P to S and from Q to L.

SORT3 is an algorithm which sorts three values. Figure 4 shows how SORT3 can be created using SORT2 sub-algorithms. First A and B are sorted, with the largest called D and smallest E. Then E and C are sorted, so the smallest value of all three variables is S. Finally D and F are sorted, so the largest of the three values is L, and the remaining value is the mid value M. If you are not convinced, the table of combinations can be created for all six orderings of A, B, and C; in each case L, M, and S will be in sorted order. Figure 5 shows the flow block representation of SORT3; figure 6 shows how the program is written.

In most cases variables are passed either by input or by output. In some cases, however, values may be passed by both input and output. For example the SWAP algorithm of figure 7 has two values called A and B which are input, swapped, and output as A and B. Similarly, the SORT2 sub-algorithm can be modified into another SSORT2 sub-algorithm, where both inputs and outputs are P and Q, as shown in figure 8. This decreases the number of variables, but it also destroys the initial values of P and Q -- a side effect. Finally, the sort of three values, SSORT3, as shown in figure 9, could be done using three variables.

SORT5, a sub-program to sort five objects using SORT3, is shown on the following page. Notice that there are many ways to do this sort.

DIFFERENCE between two times, given in military form on 24-hour clocks (such as 2030 or 0250), is given by an algorithm on page 3-41. It calls a sub-algorithm CONVERT twice (to convert each time into minutes past midnight). CONVERT also calls BREAKUP to split up the given time into hours and minutes.

The minimum difference between any three such times is given in figure 2. You may wish to create a third algorithm to determine which two times are closest together.

These examples show that we should not create all examples from "scratch"; we could build on already created sub-algorithms.

BIG SORTS FROM SMALL ·SORTS

1 SORT5 FROM SORT3

2 MORE SORT5

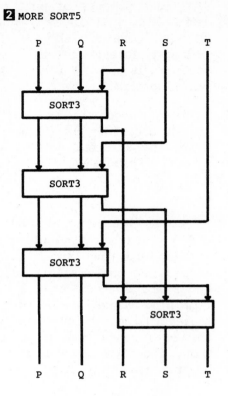

Other ways of getting big sorts from small sorts

3

SORT3 P,Q,R
SORT3 Q,R,S
SORT3 R,S,T
SORT3 Q,R,S
SORT3 P,Q,R

4

SORT3 P,Q,R
SORT3 P,S,T
SORT3 R,S,T
SORT3 Q,R,S

5

SORT3 P,Q,R
SORT3 R,S,T
SORT3 Q,R,S
SORT3 P,Q,R

SUBS INVOLVING TIME

1 TIME-DIFFERENCE Algorithm - with SUBS

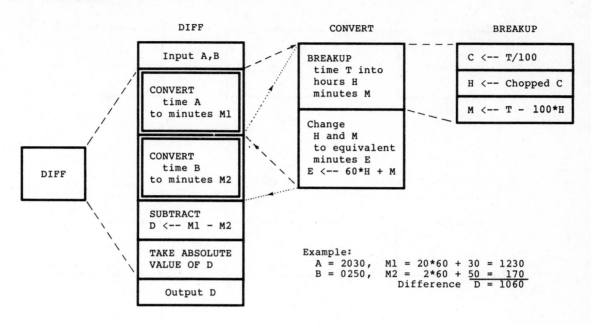

	DIFF		CONVERT		BREAKUP

DIFF

Input A,B

CONVERT
time A
to minutes M1

CONVERT
time B
to minutes M2

SUBTRACT
D <-- M1 - M2

TAKE ABSOLUTE
VALUE OF D

Output D

CONVERT

BREAKUP
time T into
hours H
minutes M

Change
H and M
to equivalent
minutes E
E <-- 60*H + M

BREAKUP

C <-- T/100

H <-- Chopped C

M <-- T - 100*H

Example:
A = 2030, M1 = 20*60 + 30 = 1230
B = 0250, M2 = 2*60 + 50 = 170
              Difference D = 1060

2 MINIMUM TIME DIFFERENCE between 3 times X,Y,Z.
using the above DIFF(A,B,D)

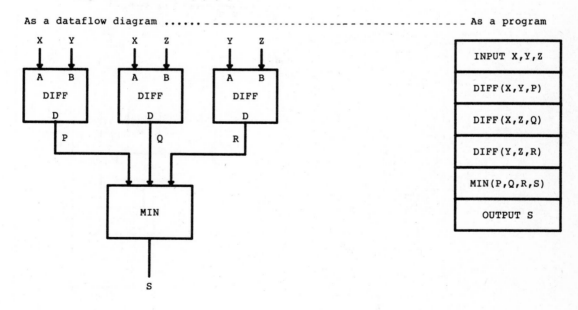

As a dataflow diagram ......_____ As a program

X   Y   X   Z   Y   Z

A   B   A   B   A   B
  DIFF   DIFF   DIFF
D   D   D

P   Q   R

MIN

S

INPUT X,Y,Z

DIFF(X,Y,P)

DIFF(X,Z,Q)

DIFF(Y,Z,R)

MIN(P,Q,R,S)

OUTPUT S

FUNCTIONS vs PROCEDURES

1 Simple Subs - with single outputs

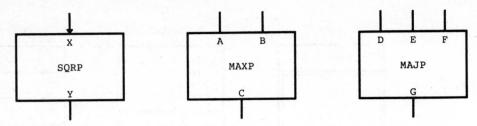

2 Functions - corresponding to above subs

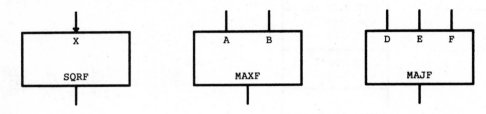

3 Hypotenuse

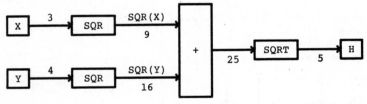

4 MAX4

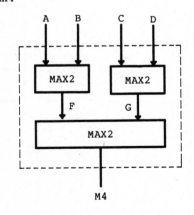

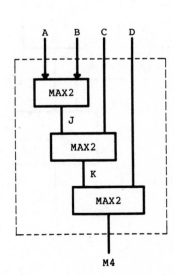

Simpler Sub-forms: Functions

Sub-algorithms in general may have any number of output variables. The general sub-algorithms are called procedures (or subroutines). Many sub-algorithms have only a single output, and they may be viewed as simpler forms called functions.

Figure 1 shows three sub-algorithms (Square, Maximum, and Majority) each involving only one output variable. These three can be represented generally as procedures:

SQRP(X, Y)   MAXP(A,B, C)   MAJP(D,E,F, G)

Functions are another simpler way of representing these sub-algorithms, as shown in figure 2. As functions, the name of the action is chosen to be the name of the output variable (and the output variable is not listed within the parentheses), in the form:

Y <--- SQRF(X)   C <--- MAXF(A,B)   G <--- MAJF(D,E,F)

Functions can be used wherever variables or expressions are used in statements such as the following formula for the hypotenuse of a right triangle:

H <--- SQRTF(SQRF(X) + SQRF(Y))

The maximum MAX4 of four variables A,B,C, and D can be written in two ways as:

M4 <--- MAX2(MAX2(A,B), MAX2(C,D))

M4 <--- MAX2(MAX2(MAX2(A,B), C), D)

which are shown in figure 4. If the first of these is written using procedures, it would be less convenient, requiring three statements:

MAX2(A,B, F)
MAX2(C,D, G)
MAX2(F,G, M4)

Many other such functions are possible, and are available as convenient built-in functions in most programming languages. Some typical functions are:

ABS(N)   which computes the absolute value of number N
SIN(A)   which computes the trigonometric sine of angle A
ODD(I)   which determines if integer I is odd
LOG(X)   which computes the logarithm of X

CHOP(R) is a another useful function which operates on any real number R and returns only the integer part of that value. For example, CHOP(4.56) is 4 and CHOP(-4.56) is -4. The CHOP operation is often called truncate and is sometimes denoted $\lfloor R \rfloor$. A similar function ROUND(X) returns the next nearest integer to X.

In summary, functions are used very differently from procedures. Functions are viewed as objects, whereas procedures are viewed as actions. From the view of languages, procedures are viewed as statements (sentences), whereas functions are viewed as expressions (phrases or parts of statements). We do not need functions, but they are often convenient; procedures are more general, but they are often inconvenient.

BEHAVIOR OF INTERCONNECTED SUBS

1 FLOW OF CONTROL of SIGNED PRODUCT

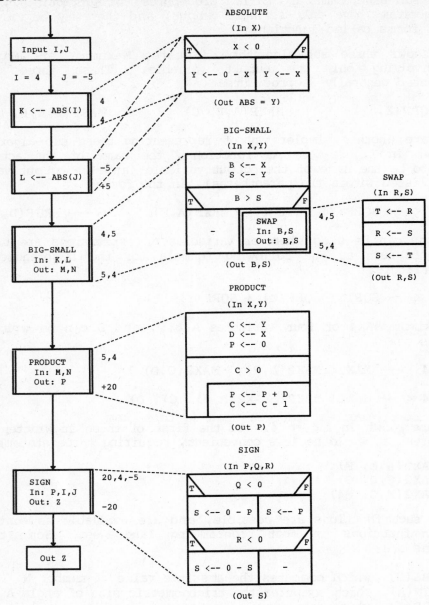

2 FLOW OF DATA

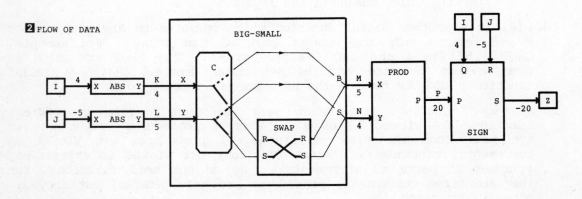

Interconnected Sub-algorithms

Algorithms which consist of many sub-algorithms can be traced in two ways. One way is to emphasize the flow of control, and use flowcharts. The other way is to emphasize the flow of data, and use data flow diagrams. Both ways are shown in the following example.

SIGNED PRODUCT is an algorithm to compute the product of two integers, which may be positive or negative. It proceeds by first taking the absolute value of the integers, selecting the smallest of these in order to loop the fewest times, and finally affixing a sign to the resulting product. This method is one of many ways to do this (you try others); it is shown here to emphasize sub-algorithms.

FLOW OF CONTROL, of figure 1, is described by a flowchart showing the path as one sub-program calls other sub-programs. The values passed between the subs are also shown on the dotted control paths.

FLOW OF DATA, of figure 2, is described by a data flow diagram, showing the paths of data flow between subs. Notice that within BIG-SMALL there is a choice box, C, which compares the values of X and Y, and "steers" this data throught (into) SWAP or around (bypassing) SWAP.

Functions and procedures are both used in this example. Some of these sub-programs having only one output (ABSOLUTE, PRODUCT, or SIGN) are implemented as functions; others, having more than one output (BIG-SMALL and SWAP), must be implemented only as procedures.

NAMES, or labels, are in great abundance. The data flow diagram particularly shows how the same data (such as B,S and M,N and X,Y) may have three different names in the three sub-algorithms. It also shows how the same name (such as S) corresponds to three different variables (indicating the small value in BIG-SMALL, one of the swapped variables in SWAP, and the sign variable in SIGN). This multiplicity of names has been exaggerated in this example to show what could be done, but what should not be done for the sake of clarity.

In most programming languages, names can be longer than one character, so S would be labelled SIGN in one sub-algorithm, and SMALL in another, thus preventing confusion. But even if we inadvertently use the same name in two different sub-algorithms for different variables, they will be treated as different variables.

SOME COMPOUNDED FORMS

1 GREATEST COMMON DIVISOR

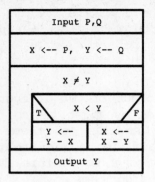

```
┌─────────────────────────┐
│        Input P,Q        │
├─────────────────────────┤
│   X <-- P,  Y <-- Q     │
├─────────────────────────┤
│          X ≠ Y          │
├─────────────────────────┤
│  T        X < Y      F  │
├────────────┬────────────┤
│   Y <--    │   X <--    │
│   Y - X    │   X - Y    │
├────────────┴────────────┤
│        Output Y         │
└─────────────────────────┘
```

Trace of GCD of 111 and 259.

X = 111				
Y = 259				
111 ≠ 259	111 ≠ 148 T	111 ≠ 37 T	74 ≠ 37 T	37 ≠ 37 F
111 < 259 T	111 < 148 T	111 < 37 F	74 < 37 F	
Y <-- 148	Y <-- 37	X <-- 74	X <-- 37	Output 37

Loop Invariant: GCD(X,Y) = GCD(P,Q)

2 CONVERT
decimal to binary

```
┌─────────────────────────┐
│         Input X         │
├─────────────────────────┤
│        P <-- 16         │
├─────────────────────────┤
│        Y <-- X          │
├─────────────────────────┤
│         P > 0           │
├─────────────────────────┤
│       D <-- Y - P       │
├─────────────────────────┤
│  T        D < 0      F  │
├────────────┬────────────┤
│            │  Output    │
│            │   "1"      │
│  Output    ├────────────┤
│   "0"      │  Y <-- D   │
├────────────┴────────────┤
│      P <-- ⌊P/2⌋        │
└─────────────────────────┘
```

Trace of conversion of decimal integer 13 to binary number 01101

	X = 13					
	P = 16					
	Y = 13					
	16 > 0 T	8 > 0 T	4 > 0 T	2 > 0 T	1 > 0 T	0 > 0 F
D =	-3	5	1	-1	0	
	-3 < 0 T	5 < 0 F	1 < 0 F	-1 < 0 T	0 < 0 F	
Out	[0]	[1]	[1]	[0]	[1]	
		Y <-- 5	Y <-- 1		Y <-- 0	
P =	8	4	2	1	0	

3 SIGNED PRODUCT (again)

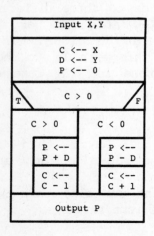

```
┌─────────────────────────┐
│        Input X,Y        │
├─────────────────────────┤
│        C <-- X          │
│        D <-- Y          │
│        P <-- 0          │
├─────────────────────────┤
│  T        C > 0      F  │
├────────────┬────────────┤
│   C > 0    │   C < 0    │
├────────────┼────────────┤
│   P <--    │   P <--    │
│   P + D    │   P - D    │
├────────────┼────────────┤
│   C <--    │   C <--    │
│   C - 1    │   C + 1    │
├────────────┴────────────┤
│        Output P         │
└─────────────────────────┘
```

	C = -4				
	D = +5				
	P = 0				
	-4 > 0 F				
	-4 < 0 T	-3 < 0 T	-2 < 0 T	-1 < 0 T	0 < 0 F
P =	-5	-10	-15	-20	
C =	-3	-2	-1	0	
					Output -20

MIXED FORMS: Nested Loops and Choices

Until now, the algorithms of this chapter have involved only simple forms; now we will consider some combinations of the four fundamental forms. More complex combinations, and their design, will be considered in the next chapters.

GCD, of figure 1, is an algorithm which illustrates a loop form with a choice form nested within it. It computes the greatest common divisor, denoted GCD. This algorithm is similar to one created by Euclid, over 2000 years ago.

The GCD of two integers P and Q is the largest number that divides both of them. For example, the GCD of 111 and 259 is 37, as shown computed in figure 1. One use of the GCD is for sharing or partitioning of two kinds of "whole" items, such as pebbles or cans of goods, which cannot be split further. For example, if we have 111 cans of one kind of item and 259 cans of another kind, then the largest number of identical piles of cans equals the GCD, which is 37. Each of the 37 piles would have 3 cans of one type (111/37=3), and 7 cans of the other type (259/37=7). Many other uses of the GCD are also possible, but are usually more complex.

CONVERT, of figure 2, is an algorithm for converting decimal integers into their equivalent binary form. For example, it converts the number 13 into 1101. Notice first the following binary "break-up" of the number:

13 = 1*8 + 1*4 + 0*2 + 1*1

The algorithm does the conversion by extracting various powers of 2, starting from the highest power. Here it starts from the power of 2 just higher than the number to be converted. For example, to convert 13, it starts with power P = 16.

First, there is no 16 in 13, so the output is 0.
Second, there is an 8 in 13, so the output is 1.
Third, there is a 4 in the remaining 5, so the output is 1.
Fourth, there is no 2 in the remaining 1, so the output is 0.
Finally, there is a 1 in the remaining 1, so the output is 1.

The resulting output sequence 01101 is the binary equivalent of 13.

For larger values, this algorithm cannot start with P = 16, but with a power of 2 that is just larger than the number to be converted. This could be done with a separate sub-algorithm, called INITIALIZE. It would start with P equal to 2, and would loop, each time doubling P until P exceeded X.

SIGNED PRODUCT, of figure 3, is an algorithm for multiplying two integers, which may be positive or negative. It is an alternative to the algorithm of page 3-45. This example illustrates the form of loops nested within a choice.

CHANGE: MANY WAYS

CHANGE - from a dollar - for an item costing C cents.

- outputs the number of quarters Q, nickels N and
  pennies P (no dimes, and no half dollars).

1 CHANGE BY
       SUBTRACTION

```
┌─────────────────────────┐
│ INPUT C                 │
│ R <-- 100 - C           │
├─────────────────────────┤
│        Q <-- 0          │
├─────────────────────────┤
│        R >= 25          │
│  ┌──────────────────────┤
│  │ Q <-- Q + 1          │
│  │ R <-- R - 25         │
├─────────────────────────┤
│        N <-- 0          │
├─────────────────────────┤
│        R >= 5           │
│  ┌──────────────────────┤
│  │ N <-- N + 1          │
│  │ R <-- R - 5          │
├─────────────────────────┤
│        P <-- R          │
├─────────────────────────┤
│      Out Q,N,P          │
└─────────────────────────┘
```

3 CHANGE BY
       ADDITION

```
┌─────────────────────────────┐
│ INPUT C                     │
│ S <-- C                     │
├─────────────────────────────┤
│         Q <-- 0             │
│         N <-- 0             │
│         P <-- 0             │
├─────────────────────────────┤
│   S not divisible by 5      │
│    ┌────────────────────────┤
│    │ P <-- P + 1            │
│    │ S <-- S + 1            │
├─────────────────────────────┤
│   S not divisible by 25     │
│    ┌────────────────────────┤
│    │ N <-- N + 1            │
│    │ S <-- S + 5            │
├─────────────────────────────┤
│          S ≠ 100            │
│    ┌────────────────────────┤
│    │ Q <-- Q + 1            │
│    │ S <-- S + 25           │
├─────────────────────────────┤
│       Out Q,N,P             │
└─────────────────────────────┘
```

2 CHANGE BY
       DIVISION

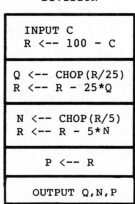

4 CHANGE BY DECISIONS

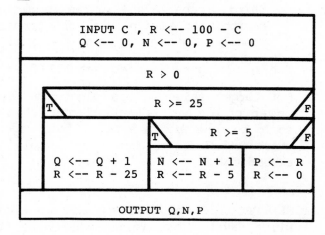

More Change

Change may be made in many ways, illustrating many combinations of forms. As an example, let us consider a slightly modified CHANGE maker which provides a count of the quarters, nickels, and pennies in exchange for a dollar when buying an item costing C cents. There are no dimes or half-dollars involved.

Figure 1 shows an algorithm using the method of subtraction. It is very similar to the previously described method of Chapter 1. It consists of a series of loops, starting at the higher denominations (quarters), and subtracting away these denominations, counting as it proceeds.

Figure 2 shows Change done by a method of division. It is essentially the same as the above method; it simply recognizes that the above method is really doing division in disguise.

Figure 3 shows Change done by a method of additions. It is the way humans usually prefer naturally, for it involves only addition. Here the algorithm starts with the cost C and the lower denominations. Pennies first are added until the sum is a multiple of five. Then nickels are similarly added until the sum is a multiple of 25. Finally, quarters are added until the sum reaches a dollar.

Figure 4 shows Change done with a single loop, having nested choices within it. Otherwise, this method is quite similar to the first method of subtraction; it simply trades off a series of loops for a nest of choices.

All of these four methods can be extended to include more denominations such as dimes, half-dollars, two dollars, etc. They should also be extended to accept any amount T tendered. Some of these methods extend much more easily than others.

More methods of making change are possible; they are considered later.

Invariance Again   (Optional)

It may be interesting to note that at any point in the change-making process all the variables T, C, R, Q, N, P are related by a single invariant, which is:

$$T = C + R + 25*Q + 5*N + P$$

Initially, for example, when no change is given, the invariant holds.

$$Q=0 \quad N=0 \quad P=0 \quad \text{and} \quad T = C + R$$

Finally, when all change is given, the remainder is zero and the invariant again holds true:

$$T = C + 25*Q + 5*N + P$$

During each stage, the invariant also holds, serving as a check and balance; R decreases as one of Q,N,P increases until R ultimately reaches zero.

MAXIMUM ELECTRICAL POWER

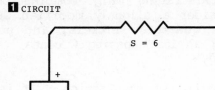

1 CIRCUIT

S = 6

+

E = 120

L

2 RELATIONS

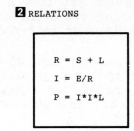

R = S + L

I = E/R

P = I*I*L

3 PLOT

POWER (Watts)
P

800

600 .... M = 600

400

200

halfpower

L

LOAD
(ohms)

10   20   30   40

L = 1

B = 6

H = 34

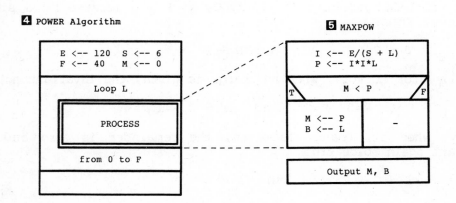

4 POWER Algorithm

E <-- 120   S <-- 6
F <-- 40   M <-- 0

Loop L

PROCESS

from 0 to F

5 MAXPOW

I <-- E/(S + L)
P <-- I*I*L

T   M < P   F

M <-- P
B <-- L   -

Output M, B

Engineering Applications: POWER   (Optional)

A common problem in engineering is to analyse the effect of some variables on other variables. This could lead to the best or optimal values of the variables.

CIRCUIT, of figure 1, is an electrical network, consisting of a voltage source of E volts, providing power to a load resistor L through a series resistor S. We wish to determine the value of the load which would provide the maximum power to the load.

Relations among the variables are given by the formulas of figure 2 (determined from knowledge of Ohm's law and Kirchoff's laws). The behavior of such a system, given in figure 3, shows how the power P (in watts) varies depending on the resistance L of the load (in ohms). From this graph we see that the best value B of the load resistor L is 6 ohms, resulting in a maximum power M of 600 watts.

POWER, of figure 4, is an algorithm for analysing this system. It is a simple loop which varies the load resistance L from zero to some final value F, computing the corresponding value of power P. The box marked PROCESS could simply output the L,P combinations. This box could also compute the maximum power M and the corresponding best resistor B, as shown in figure 5.

PROCESS could possibly find the half power points: those two values of R (say, low L and high H) at which half power is sent to the load. Any load value between these two would result in more than half power delivered. Notice that the half power points are not equally distant about the maximum power point B. It is also possible to create an algorithm that plots the power P versus load resistor L. Such plots are considered in a later chapter.

Other engineering systems can be analysed similarly. For example, we may wish to find the optimal angle to shoot some object so that it goes the farthest distance. Or we may wish to compute the best combinations of decisions to make optimal profits.

Alternative methods sometimes exist for analysing systems. For example, it can also be proved (using calculus) that the maximum power occurs when the load resistor L equals the series resistor S. But if the system was more complex (say non-linear), then computer methods may be better than the analytic methods.

BISECTION: To Compute Roots

1   SQRT1

Input X
Set limits
Guess (mid M)
M*M ≠ X
Guess M is too high   T / F
lower upper limit / raise lower limit
Guess mid M
Output M

2   SQRT2

Input X
L <-- 0   H <-- X
M <-- (H + L)/2
M*M ≠ X
M*M > X   T / F
H <-- M   L <-- M
M <-- (H + L)/2
Out M

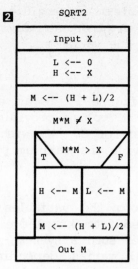

3

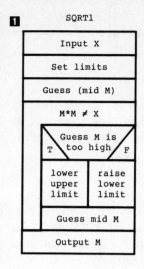

TRACE (trajectory) of ranges

(HI, LOW, and MEDIUM values) for the square root of 24

H = 24

M = 12   H = 12

L = 0

H = 12   L = 0

H = 6   L = 0

H = 6   L = 3

H = 6   L = 4.5

H = 5.25   L = 4.50

4   SQRT3

In X
H <-- X, L <-- 0   E <-- .01
M <-- (H + L)/2
|M*M - X| > E
M*M > X   T / F
H <-- M   L <-- M
M <-- (H + L)/2
Out M

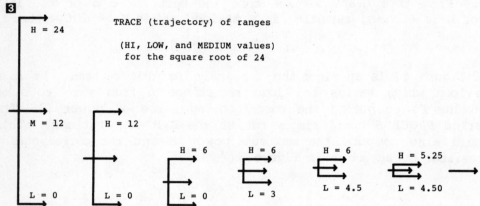

X =	24			
H =	24		Trace of square root of 24.	
L =	0			
M =	12			
	120 > .1 T	12 > .1 T	15 > .1 T	3.75 > .1 T	etc...
	144 > 24 T	36 > 24 T	9 > 24 F	20.25 > 24 F	
	H <-- 12	H <-- 6	L <-- 3	L <-- 4.5	
M =	M <-- 6	M <-- 3	M <-- 4.5	M <-- 5.25	

Bisection (Bracketing)

Bisection is an algorithm (also known as Bracketing, or Half-Interval
Method) which is very useful for solving many types of problems. It
proceeds by taking two limiting values and adjusting them successively
to bracket the required result. This method was used in the
GUESSER-GUESSEE algorithm of page 2-19.

Bisection is illustrated in the given figures which compute the square
root of some number X, say 24. Figures 1 and 2 show the top-down
development of the algorithm, but its behavior is best shown by
looking first at figure 3.

First, a high limit H = 24 and a low limit H = 0 are assumed. The
mid-point M = 12 is chosen as a first guess at the solution. Since
this guess is too high (12*12 > 24) the higher limit is lowered to
the mid value. If the guess were too low, the lower limit would
have been raised (to the mid value). This same process is now
repeated for the new limits. The repetition continues until the two
limits narrow down (or bracket) the solution to any degree of
precision required.

More formally stated, the looping continues while the square of the
guessed root of X differs (in absolute value) from X by more than
some allowable error amount. This constant of precision (or error)
E is initially chosen to be some small value, such as 0.01 or
0.00001, but the smaller its value, the more looping is required to
attain that precision.

Symbolically, the loop condition is written as

$$|M*M - X| > E$$

Figure 4 shows another trace of the algorithm for computing the square
root of 24. Notice that this method of bisection is not limited to
just square roots! It can equally compute the cube root by simply
changing the conditions to compare M*M*M with the value X. This
Bisection Method can also be used to find the roots of equations.

Limitations of this Bisection method sometimes exist. For example, the
given square root algorithm does not work properly if the input value
of X is between 0 and 1. Try a trace to see why.

Bisection is a very general method which will be useful later in many
problems. For example, we will use it again in chapter 6, to search
quickly through a sorted list.

IMPROVING PRODUCT

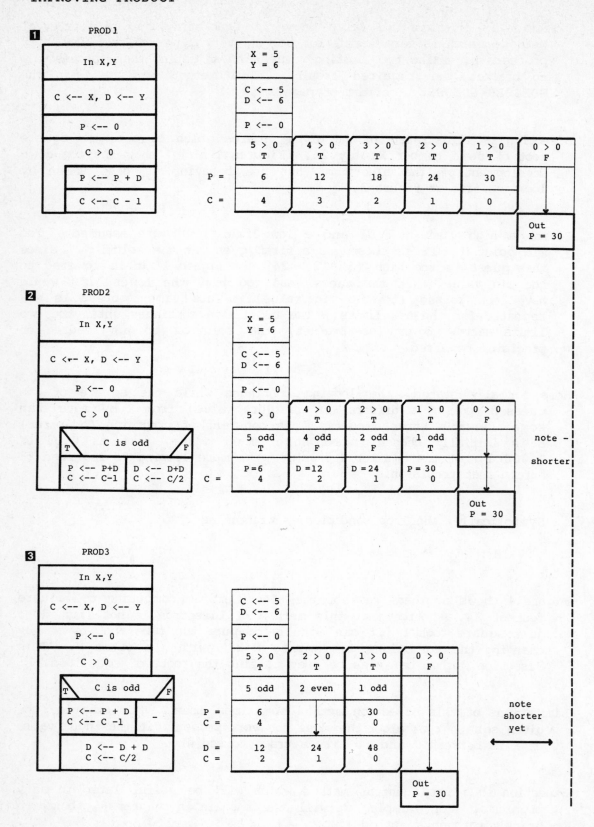

PROD 1

| In X,Y |
| C <-- X, D <-- Y |
| P <-- 0 |
| C > 0 |
| P <-- P + D |
| C <-- C - 1 |

| X = 5 Y = 6 |
| C <-- 5 D <-- 6 |
| P <-- 0 |

	5 > 0 T	4 > 0 T	3 > 0 T	2 > 0 T	1 > 0 T	0 > 0 F
P =	6	12	18	24	30	
C =	4	3	2	1	0	

Out P = 30

PROD2

| In X,Y |
| C <-- X, D <-- Y |
| P <-- 0 |
| C > 0 |
| C is odd |
| P <-- P+D / C <-- C-1 | D <-- D+D / C <-- C/2 |

| X = 5 Y = 6 |
| C <-- 5 D <-- 6 |
| P <-- 0 |

	5 > 0	4 > 0 T	2 > 0 T	1 > 0 T	0 > 0 F
	5 odd T	4 odd F	2 odd F	1 odd T	
C =	P=6 4	D =12 2	D = 24 1	P = 30 0	

Out P = 30

note – shorter

PROD3

| In X,Y |
| C <-- X, D <-- Y |
| P <-- 0 |
| C > 0 |
| C is odd |
| P <-- P + D / C <-- C -1 | - |
| D <-- D + D / C <-- C/2 |

| C <-- 5 D <-- 6 |
| P <-- 0 |

	5 > 0 T	2 > 0 T	1 > 0 T	0 > 0 F
	5 odd	2 even	1 odd	
P = C =	6 4		30 0	
D = C =	12 2	24 1	48 0	

Out P = 30

note shorter yet

IMPROVING PROGRAMS: Using Invariants (Optional)

Loop invariants are any assertions (relations, conditions, equations, etc.) which remain constant (true) during every loop. They will be used here to improve the speed of algorithms. As an example, consider the previous PRODUCT algorithm shown in figure 1. The loop invariant is:

$$X * Y = P + C * D$$

This invariant has an intuitive meaning here; the product of X and Y at any point is determined by summing the partial product P and the remaining C * D that is yet to be added into P. This breakdown into two parts (an already computed part, and a part yet to be computed) is often useful for determining invariants.

A significant aspect of loop invariants is that the actions within the body of a loop do not change the invariant. For example, the actions within the PRODUCT algorithm are:

$$P \longleftarrow P + D \quad \text{and also} \quad C \longleftarrow C - 1$$

Substituting these two into the original relation:

$$X * Y = P + C * D$$

yields

$$= (P + D) + (C - 1) * D$$
$$= P + D + C * D - D$$
$$= P + C * D$$

This yields again the original invariant! The invariant holds at the beginning of the body of the loop, and also at the end of it. In other words, this relation remained invariant through the computations in the body of the loop. This is rather significant, as we shall see next.

It is interesting to see whether we can find other assignments in the body of the loop to keep the given relation invariant. One such pair of assignments is:

$$C \longleftarrow C/2 \quad \text{and} \quad D \longleftarrow 2 * D \quad (\text{or } D \longleftarrow D + D).$$

In other words, if C is halved and D is doubled, their product will remain the same. And incidentally, this halving and doubling is a faster way of finding the product than is the previous method, of adding a single D and subtracting one from the counter C.

Of course, this halving can only be used if C is an even number, so for odd numbers we could still use the original pair of assignments. If we then modify the body of the loop to choose between these two assignments (both of which keep the relation invariant), we obtain a very efficient product algorithm as shown in figure 2. Incidentally, this is the same algorithm previously described as the Peasant Pebble Product. A slightly more efficient algorithm is given in figure 3, by doing the doubling and halving during every loop.

Efficiency of these algorithms can be illustrated by considering the product of two numbers about the size of a million. PROD1 would take about 1,000,000 loops, PROD2 would take about 40 loops, and PROD3 would take about 20 loops! Notice particularly that this efficiency came from rather simple algebraic manipulation of the loop invariant, showing it to be a very useful concept.

REVIEW: of Chapter 3

BEHAVIOR OF ALGORITHMS

In this chapter we considered the dynamic behavior of algorithms, as opposed to the previous static structure. These algorithms, which are intended for computers, are called programs.

OBJECTS involve concepts of variable, value and type. A variable is viewed as a labelled box containing a value of some type. In this chapter, types were mainly limited to numbers: integer and real.

ACTIONS involving these objects include assignment, input, output, comparison and various arithmetic operations. These combine to yield complex actions and algorithms.

SERIES forms are quite simple, but still can show that different structures (such as SWAP and EXCHANGE) can have the same behavior.

CHOICE forms are capable of more complex behavior, but the class of all behaviors (or paths through) is finite. It is possible to compare two choice forms and determine equivalent behavior by comparing all paths.

LOOP forms have considerably more complex behaviors. This behavior is described by a form of tracing: a two-dimensional typical path. Tracing yields insights into dynamic behavior by showing a typical trajectory, by detecting errors, by yielding interesting relations among variables, and by suggesting other equivalent algorithms.

LOOP INVARIANTS are relations which hold true during every stage of the looping process. They are useful for providing some insights; they can also be used to both prove and improve programs.

SUB-forms were introduced by data flow diagrams describing their behavior. They emphasize higher level views: what is being done, rather than how it is done.

Creation of algorithms was shown for some simple examples, which do not involve much nesting. In Chapter 5, algorithms will be created having considerable complex nesting of loops and choices.

The most fundamental concepts of computing have been introduced in this chapter; most later chapters are simply extensions of these principles.

PROBLEMS: on Chapter 3

1. SIMPLE SERIES

   Describe briefly what the following algorithms do (but not how they do it).

   a. A <--- 2   b. E <--- A   c. Z <--- A
       B <--- A + A   A <--- B   Z <--- B + Z + Z
       C <--- B + B   B <--- C   Z <--- C + Z + Z
       D <--- C + C   C <--- D   Z <--- D + Z + Z
       E <--- D + D   D <--- E   Z <--- E + Z + Z

2. INTERCHANGE

   Create another algorithm to exchange the contents of two variables, say R and S, without using any temporary variable. Use the arithmetic operations of multiplication and division.

3. CHARGE AGAIN

   Create an algorithm to compute a charge C, given by the formula:

   C = 4*B + 6*A

   for A adults and B babies, without using multiplication, and without any looping. Do this in two ways, using a different number of additions each time.

4. SERIES PROOF

   Prove (or disprove) that the following two series algorithms are equivalent in producing the same output E.

       C <--- A * A   C <--- A + B
       D <--- B * B   D <--- A - B
       E <--- C - D   E <--- C * D

5. SMALLER MAJORITY

   Modify the majority algorithm of figure 3, page 3-14, by eliminating one choice form.

6. LOTSASWAPS

   What does the following sequence of swaps do?
       SWAP(A,B)
       SWAP(B,C)
       SWAP(A,B)
   Do the same thing more simply.

7. DISJUNCTION

   Create an algorithm expressing the logical OR (of page 3-21) by using only single, simple conditions. Do this also for the exclusive OR.

8. LOGICAL PROOF

   Prove (or disprove) the following logical expressions.
   a. NOT(P AND Q) = (NOT P) OR (NOT Q)
   b. (P AND Q) OR (P AND R) = P AND (Q OR R)
   c. P OR (NOT P AND Q) = P OR Q
   d. (P AND NOT Q) OR (NOT P AND Q) =
                              (P AND Q) OR (NOT P AND NOT Q)
   e. (NOT P) XOR (NOT Q) = NOT(P XOR Q)

PROBLEMS ON CHOICE FORMS AND PROOFS

1. **EQUALITY OF CHOICE**
    Compare the following two algorithms, and try (intuitively) to determine if they are equivalent. Then prove, or disprove, this equivalence formally.

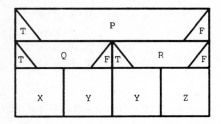 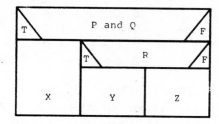

2. **BIGGER EQUIVALENCE**
    Prove whether or not the given algorithms are equivalent.

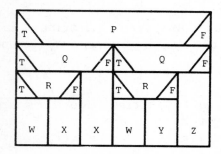 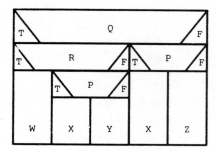

3. **TRADE-OFF STRUCTURE FOR CONDITION**
    Create an algorithm equivalent to each of the following by combining the conditions with logical operations.

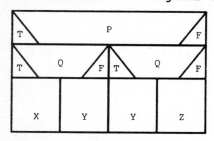 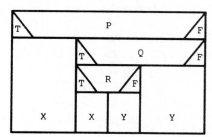

4. Prove (or disprove) equivalence of the following algorithms, assuming integer values A, B, C, with none equal.

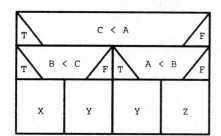

MORE CHOICE PROBLEMS

1. **MANY WAYS TO GRADE**
   Create a GRADE algorithm equivalent to the ones on page 3-18, but starting with the first condition being (P >= 80). Create another algorithm with the first condition being (P >= 60). Indicate the smallest set of values necessary to test this Grading algorithm.

2. **COMPLEMENTS**
   Prove (or disprove) that the given two conditions are opposite (complementary) in behavior.

   ```
   (X<=30) AND ( (X>20) OR (X<=10) )
   (X>10)  AND ( (X>30) OR (X<=20) )
   ```

3. **TEST EQUIVALENCE**
   Prove whether or not the following algorithms are equivalent in behavior.

   FIRST   SECOND   THIRD

   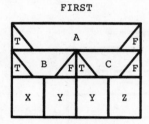 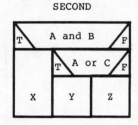 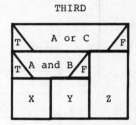

4. **TEST SORT**
   Prove whether or not the following algorithm sorts variables having unequal values.

   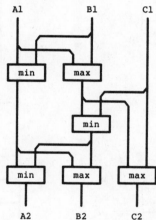

5. **DICE POKER**
   The game of dice poker (or Indian Dice) involves the throwing of five dice, and the evaluation of the throws (or "hands") in the following order. Create an algorithm to evaluate each hand, assuming SORT5 is available.

   a. Five of a kind, means all dice have the same value,
   b. Four of a kind, means 4 dice have the same value,
   c. Full house, means 3 are of one value, 2 of another,
   d. A straight, means the 5 values are in consecutive order,
   e. Three of a kind, means three dice are of one value,
   f. Two pairs, means 2 dice of 1 value, and 2 of another,
   g. One pair, means only two dice have the same value,
   h. No pairs, means none of the above.

TRACING PROBLEMS

1. **CON**
   Trace algorithm 1 for X = 13, and describe its general behavior briefly. Assume integer values.

2. **WOW**
   Trace algorithm 2 for X = 13 and Y = 2. Find its loop invariant.

3. **PIE SQUARE**
   Trace the following algorithm, which computes the square of PI, and indicate what formula it computes (but do not work out the arithmetic). Also describe briefly how it works.

4. **REFINE PRIME**
   A prime number is defined to be any positive integer which is divisible only by 1 and itself. Algorithm 4 indicates whether any value X is prime or not. Modify this algorithm in at least two ways, so that it does less looping.

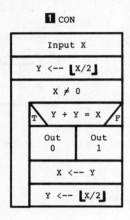

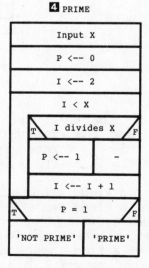

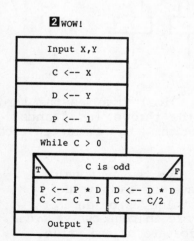

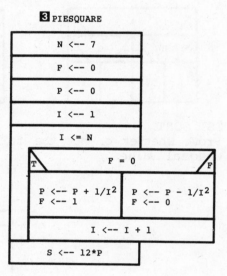

PROBLEMS ON CREATING LOOPS

1. **SQUARE AGAIN**

    The square of an integer N can be computed by summing all the integers from 1 to N and then back down to 1. For example
    $$4^2 = 1 + 2 + 3 + 4 + 3 + 2 + 1 = 16$$
    Create an algorithm to compute the square of any integer N by such a method.

2. **POWER**

    Create an algorithm to find the Nth power, P, of any number X, where N is a nonnegative integer. Then modify this algorithm to work for any integer N.

3. **FIBONACCI**

    One simple model of population growth (of rabbits) is given by the series:
    $$1 \quad 1 \quad 2 \quad 3 \quad 5 \quad 8 \quad 13 \quad 21 \quad ...$$
    where the new population P at one month is determined by summing the previous two months' populations (called latest L and second latest S). Create an algorithm to determine the population at month M, where M > 2.

4. **DIVIDE AND CONQUER**

    Create an algorithm to divide any integer A by another integer B, yielding a quotient Q and a remainder R. Do this in the following ways:
    a. use multiplication
    b. use bisection (as well as multiplication)
    c. use some other way.

5. **ANOTHER SIGNED PRODUCT**

    Create yet another algorithm for the SIGNED PRODUCT described on page 3-44. For example, if the loop variable C is negative, change the signs of it and the dummy variable D.

6. **EXTEND CHANGE**

    Extend the CHANGE algorithm of figure 3 on page 3-48, to output the count of dimes also.

7. **EXPO and SINE**

    Create an algorithm to compute the SINE and exponentiation functions from the first N terms of the following series:

    $$EXPO(X) = 1 + X + X^2/2! + X^3/3! + X^4/4! + ...$$

    $$SINE(X) = X - X^3/3! + X^5/5! - X^7/7! \, ...$$

8. **BISECT WALLACE**

    Use the BISECTION algorithm of page 3-52 to solve equations such as Wallace's Equation:

    $$X^3 - 2*X - 5 = 0$$

PROBLEMS ON SUB-FORMS

1. MAX7 FROM MAX3
   Given data flow blocks for MAX3, the maximum of three variables, use them to create the maximum of seven variables, in two ways.

2. MINS FROM MAXES
   If you are given a data flow diagram MAX3, use it along with sign inverters (sign changers) to create MIN3, which finds the minimum value of any three variables.

3. MID3
   Create a data flow diagram showing how the middle value MID of three values A, B, C can be created using the data flow diagrams of the MAX, MIN, SUM, and DIFFerence. Do this again using only MAXs and MINs.

4. SCORE
   In some sporting events, a number of judges each gives a score. The overall score is determined by dropping the highest and lowest scores, and averaging the remaining scores. Create a data flow diagram to determine the score S for an event having five judges giving grades A, B, C, D and E (each having values ranging from 0 to 10).

5. MORE MAJORITY
   Draw a data flow diagram for the following formulas.
   a. M = MAX (MIN(A,B), MIN(B,C), MIN(A,C))
   b. M = A*B + A*C + B*C - (2*A) * (B*C)
   first using only binary functions (having two inputs), then using functions of any number of inputs (i.e., using a four-input product). Prove that both of these formulas behave as a MAJORITY.

6. BIG MAJ FROM LITTLE MAJs GROWS?
   The given data flow diagram shows four MAJORITY units MAJ3 connected in an attempt to create the majority U of five variables P,Q,R,S, and T. Indicate whether the given algorithm does find the majority of five variables. If it does not do it, then disprove it; otherwise show how you would prove it.

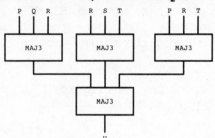

7. DEMILITARIZE TIME
   Represent the TIME-DIFFERENCE algorithm of page 3-41 as a data flow diagram using sub-operations such as ADD, SUBT, MULT, and the two-output DIVIDE.

8. WHAT IS IT?
   Draw a data flow diagram for the following formula, and indicate briefly its behavior for all integers.
       M = (ABS(A + B) - ABS(A - B))/2

9. ONE MORE DAY
   The following formula is supposed to compute the number of days D in any month M. Draw the data flow diagram of it, and show what it does in a tabular form.
       D = 30 + ((ABS(2*M - 15) MOD 4) MOD 3)

LOOPS AND INVARIANCE

1. INVARIANCE OF DIVISION
    Find the loop invariant of the DIVIDE algorithm, figure 5 of page 3-24.

2. INVARIANCE OF SQUARE
    Create an algorithm to compute the square of any nonnegative integer N by successively adding N for a total of N times. Find the loop invariant.

3. INVARIANCE OF POWER
    Create an algorithm to compute the power, P, of any number X raised to some integer value N, by looping N times and multiplying. Find the loop invariant, and use it to improve this algorithm.

4. INVARIANCE OF A CUBE
    The given algorithm computes the cube of any positive integer N. Trace it for N = 5. Then indicate which of the following is the loop invariant.

    a. $C^3 = A + B + C + 6$

    b. $C = B + D^3$

    c. $C = B + (A/6)^3$

    d. $D^3 = A^3 + B^2 + C + 6$

    e. $A + B + C + D^3 = 6$

5. INVARIANCE OF LOAN
    Find the loop invariance of the LOAN algorithm, figure 4 of page 3-32. You need to introduce more variables, representing some sums.

6. MORE INVARIANCE
    Trace the following algorithms FIRST and SECOND, and find their loop invariants. Find two invariants for SECOND.

CUBE

```
+-------------------+
|     Input N       |
+-------------------+
| A <-- 0           |
| B <-- 1           |
| C <-- 1           |
| D <-- 1           |
+-------------------+
|      D < N        |
|  +--------------+ |
|  | A <-- A + 6  | |
|  | B <-- A + B  | |
|  | C <-- B + C  | |
|  | D <-- D + 1  | |
|  +--------------+ |
+-------------------+
|     Output C      |
+-------------------+
```

FIRST

```
+-------------------+
| B <-- 50          |
| J <-- 1           |
+-------------------+
|      B < 300      |
|  +--------------+ |
|  | B <-- B + B/J| |
|  | J <-- J + 1  | |
|  +--------------+ |
+-------------------+
```

SECOND

```
+---------------------+
| N <-- 7             |
| C <-- 0             |
| S <-- 1             |
+---------------------+
|        C < N        |
|  +----------------+ |
|  | C <-- C + 1    | |
|  | S <-- S + C + N| |
|  | N <-- N - 1    | |
|  +----------------+ |
+---------------------+
|      OUTPUT S       |
+---------------------+
```

APPLICATIONS (to business, engineering, etc.)

1. BALLOONLESS LOAN
    Modify the LOAN algorithm of page 3-33 to determine the time to
    pay off the entire loan.   Compute also the total interest paid.
    Modify it further if the interest rate changes after a certain
    balance has been reached.   Modify this again if the payment is
    increased by a certain percentage after each year.

2. GROWTH (of population, money, etc.)
    The growth of various quantities (money, population, disease) is
    often a fixed portion of the present quantity.   For example, the
    yearly interest gained on an amount of invested money is given by
    a fixed rate R of interest, which is multiplied by the present
    amount A (or balance) each year.
    Create an algorithm to determine the number of years required for
    the money to double.
    Modify the algorithm to determine the number of years to reach a
    certain final amount F.

3. RELIABILITY (of systems)
    The reliability R of a system of N independent series components,
    each having Probability P is determined by:

        R = P*P*P*P...*P   (where there are N Ps)

    For example, consider a chain made of links each having a
    probability P of .99 of successfully withstanding a certain load.
    If N=70 of these are connected together, the probability of all
    the links successfully withstanding the load is:

        R = .99*.99*.99*...*.99 = .50

    Create an algorithm to determine the number of components N (each
    having given probability P) to reach a given reliability R.

4. ECOLOGY
    The population movement between three parts of a city labelled A,
    B, C (representing a swank neighborhood, a suburb, and a slum) is
    described by the following equations:

        A(t+1) = 0.4*A(t) + 0.3*B(t) + 0.1*C(t)
        B(t+1) = 0.6*A(t) + 0.5*B(t) + 0.3*C(t)
        C(t+1) =   0.2*B(t) + 0.6*C(t)

    Create an algorithm to find the population A(T), B(T), C(T) for
    any time T (say T = 5), given any initial population percentages
    such as:

        A(0) = 20%, B(0) = 50%, C(0) = 30%

Chapter 4

LANGUAGES:
    COMMUNICATING ALGORITHMS

SYNTAX AND SEMANTICS

PSEUDO-LANGUAGES

PROGRAMMING LANGUAGES

CODING AND CONVERSION

LOGIC AS A LANGUAGE

BNF NOTATION

LANGUAGES:

COMMUNICATING ALGORITHMS

* Asterisks indicate the degree of importance *

Chapter 4:

LANGUAGES

Communicating Algorithms

PREVIEW

Languages are briefly introduced in this chapter. We start
generally with an overview of natural languages. Then we
consider pseudo-languages and programming languages. After
this chapter, you may wish to study a particular language in
more detail, while proceeding in parallel with the rest of this
book.

Natural languages, such as English, are considered first. They
are used for humans to communicate with other humans. Such
languages introduce concepts such as syntax (form of a
language) and semantics (meaning of a language). They also
illustrate the differences between interpretation and translation.

Pseudo language, or pseudo-code, is then introduced to communicate
algorithms from humans to computers, and also among humans.
It is similar to many actual programming languages, but more
convenient and "forgiving" of errors. Pseudo-code is a model
of programming languages; it can be easily converted into many
existing programming languages.

Programming languages are surveyed by comparing six "real"
languages: Basic, Fortran, Pascal, Snobol, Apl, and Lisp.
This overview provides an insight into the significant
similarities among languages despite their differences.

Coding, the process of converting an algorithm into a program in
some programming language, is also illustrated. Fortran is
used to illustrate coding in a structured manner.

Particular languages are not developed in the main text. Pascal,
however, is considered in greater detail in an appendix.

SYNTAX OF LANGUAGES

SYNTAX TREES

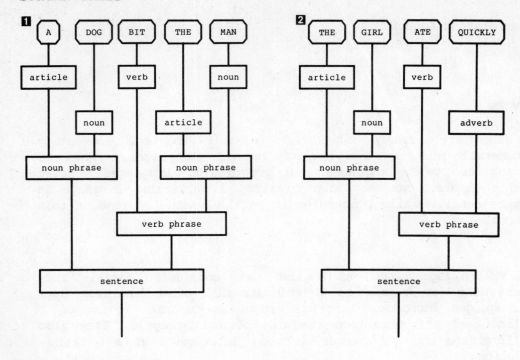

SYNTAX DIAGRAMS

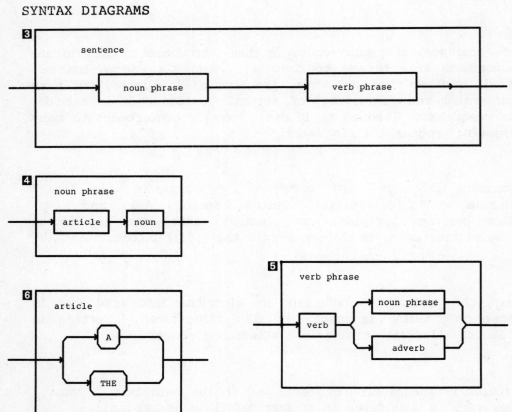

SYNTAX AND SEMANTICS

Languages in general involve sequences of symbols arranged in a linear
    stream. Natural languages, such as English, French, and Latin,
    involve symbols called words joined together as sequences called
    sentences. These sequences are intended to communicate, and so have
    meaning (called semantics) and have form (called syntax).

SEMANTICS is the study of meaning, actions, function, and behavior of a
    language. Syntax is the study of the form, representation, grammar,
    and structure of a language. Briefly, semantics describes what a
    language does, and syntax describes how it looks. For example,
    consider the following two sentences:
       'A DOG BIT THE MAN'
       'A MAN BIT THE DOG'
These two statements have very different meanings (semantics), for
the first would seldom appear in a newspaper, whereas the second is
sufficiently unusual to become a headline. These two statements,
however, do have the same sentence structure (syntax) with only the
two nouns (DOG and MAN) interchanged.

SYNTAX trees are convenient diagrams to describe the form of a language
    as shown in figures 1 and 2. The trees start with the actual words
    of the language (such as A, THE, DOG) which are called "terminal"
    symbols. The terminal words and their combinations are described by
    words such as "noun" or "verb phrase," which are not in the actual
    language but in what is called a "meta-language."

META-LANGUAGES are higher level languages used to describe a language.
    To distinguish between these two languages we will use capital
    letters within round boxes for the ordinary language; we will use
    small letters within square boxes for the meta-language. Notice in
    figure 1 that a verb phrase can consist of a verb followed by a noun
    phrase. In figure 2 a verb phrase is alternatively indicated as a
    verb followed by an adverb. In natural languages there are many
    such relationships.

SYNTAX DIAGRAMS are alternative ways of describing the form of languages
    as shown in figures 3, 4, 5, and 6. They show the proper sequence
    of symbols by lines joining the boxes. Any path that leads
    completely through a box is syntactically well formed; any path that
    stops within a box is not well formed. The syntax diagrams then
    describe all possible paths that are well formed. For example,
    "THE MAN ATE A MAN" is a well formed sentence, since it "flows"
    through the sentence box (which in turn calls on the other
    sub-boxes). The sequence "DOG ATE QUICKLY" or "A QUICKLY BIT THE
    DOG" or "MAN THE DOG ATE" are not proper sentences in this
    language.

SYNTAX EXAMPLES

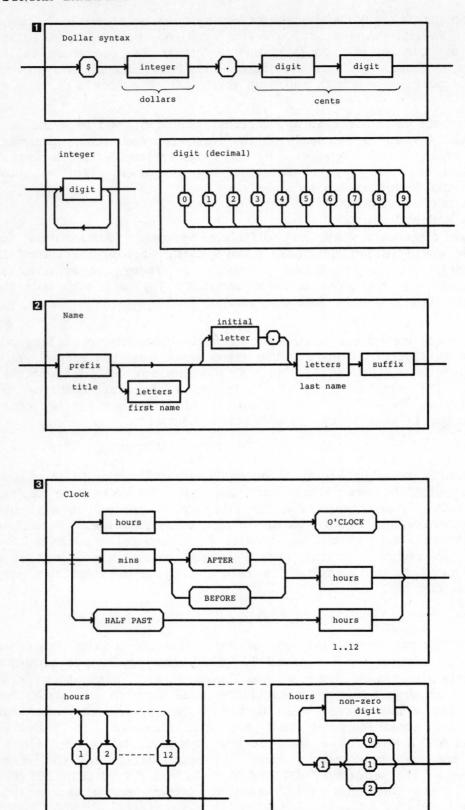

More Syntax, and Syntax Diagrams

Syntax diagrams are very helpful in showing the general form of
    sequences. Some simple examples follow, showing "mini-languages"
    involving money, names, and time.

DOLLAR syntax, of figure 1, shows the general form of money, with
    dollar amounts being integers, and cents being decimal digits. An
    integer is shown consisting of any number of decimal digits.
    Sequences having the proper dollar form include

    $1.26 $1234.56 $0.78

whereas sequences which are improper are

    $1.2 $12.345 $.12 $12 or 12$

Notice that the two words "dollars" and "cents" on the syntax
diagram describe semantics or meaning. These semantic comments are
positioned outside the inner boxes, so that they will not be confused
with the syntactic concepts within the boxes.

NAME syntax, of figure 2, is a way of showing the form of names. The
    prefix could be further defined (on another syntax diagram) as being
    MR, MRS, MS, or some other title (DR, PROF, or SIR). Similarly,
    the suffix could be defined as a degree (BS, MS, PhD, MD) or other
    (JR, II, III, or ESQ) or nothing at all. Blanks are assumed as
    separators, so are not shown on the syntax diagrams. This syntax
    describes names of the form

    MRS J. JONES or DR J. JONES MD or J. JONES III

CLOCK syntax, of figure 3, describes a common way of indicating time.
    Some properly formed times are:

    12 O'CLOCK   22 AFTER 2   HALF PAST 12

and some improperly formed times are

    49 O'CLOCK   77 BEFORE 0   2 HALF PAST 2

Notice that the form of the hours (from 1 to 12) is represented in
two ways. One method (at the left), is a complete listing of all 12
hours. Another method (at the right, involving non-zero digits) is
less exhaustive.

Notice also that some paths are encountered less often than other
paths. For example, the paths corresponding to H O'CLOCK and
HALF PAST H are encountered much less often than the other paths
(involving BEFORE and AFTER), and so these rare paths are marked
by a bar across them.

LANGUAGE LEVELS

1 'Tower of Babel'

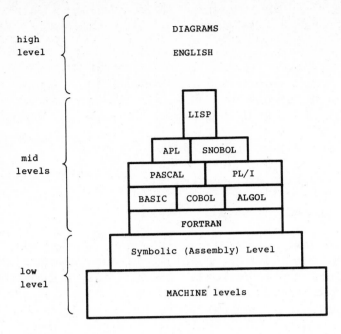

high level	DIAGRAMS ENGLISH
mid levels	LISP APL SNOBOL PASCAL PL/I BASIC COBOL ALGOL FORTRAN
low level	Symbolic (Assembly) Level MACHINE levels

2 HIGH LEVEL
(flow block diagram)
of LOAN

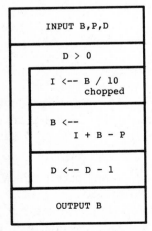

OBJECTS

```
BALANCE  B = [    ]
PAYMENT  P = [    ]
DURATION D = [    ]
INTEREST I = [    ]
```

ACTIONS

```
INPUT B,P,D

D > 0

I <-- B / 10
     chopped

B <--
     I + B - P

D <-- D - 1

OUTPUT B
```

3 MEDIUM LEVEL
(Pascal program)

```pascal
PROGRAM LOAN;
VAR
    BAL,
    PAYT,
    DURN,
    INT : INTEGER;
- - - - - - - - - - - - - - - - -
BEGIN
    READ(BAL,PAYT,DURN);
    WHILE DURN > 0 DO
        BEGIN
            INT:= BAL DIV 10;
            BAL:= INT + BAL
                 - PAYT;
            DURN:= DURN - 1;
        END;
    WRITE('BAL IS',BAL);
END.
```

4 LOW LEVEL
(Symbolic machine language)

```
0   TEN     INTEGER + 10
1   ONE     INTEGER + 1
2   BAL     INTEGER
3   PAYT    INTEGER
4   DURN    INTEGER
5   INT     INTEGER
- - - - - - - - - - - - - - - - -
6   BEGIN:  INPUT   BAL
7           INPUT   PAYT
8           INPUT   DURN
9   LOOP:   LOAD    DURN
10          BNEG    DONE
11          BZERO   DONE
12          LOAD    BAL
13          DIVIDE  TEN
14          STORE   INT
15          ADD     BAL
16          SUBT    PAYT
17          STORE   BAL
18          LOAD    DURN
19          SUBT    ONE
20          STORE   DURN
21          BRUN    LOOP
22  DONE:   OUTPUT  BAL
23          HALT
```

Levels of Programming Languages

Programming languages may be viewed in terms of levels, low levels
being close to the machines and high levels closer to humans. The
low level languages are often more efficient and fast, whereas the
higher level languages are usually more concise, natural, clear, and
portable (movable from machine to machine).

LOW level languages (assembly language or machine language), being
close to computers, are not natural for humans.

HIGH level languages (diagrams or graphs) are very convenient for
humans to understand, but are often inconvenient and time-consuming
to draw.

MEDIUM level languages are a compromise between the extreme levels.
The notation is similar to the human notation of algebra, symbolic
logic, and natural language, and yet it is in a simple linear form
of symbols which can be entered into a keyboard, and converted easily
to a machine language. Even with these medium level languages there
are some at a higher level (Lisp), and others at a lower level
(Fortran).

The TOWER OF BABEL, of figure 1, shows a number of levels of some real
languages. There are hundreds of such languages that are not shown
on this diagram. Additionally, hundreds of programming languages are
now "extinct"; some others are endangered.

LOAN, an algorithm previously discussed in Chapter 3 (page 3-33), is
done next in three levels.

Figure 2 shows LOAN done in the highest graphical level as a flow block
diagram. Notice that both objects and actions are shown.

Figure 3 shows LOAN done in a medium level language called Pascal.
The indentation attempts to capture some of the two-dimensional
quality of the graph.

Figure 4 shows LOAN done in a low symbolic level as one long sequence
of instructions very close to the machine. The next lower level
would be in terms of zeros and ones.

Notice that each successive level appears as a refinement of the
previous level.

PSEUDO-CODE REPRESENTATION OF ALGORITHMS

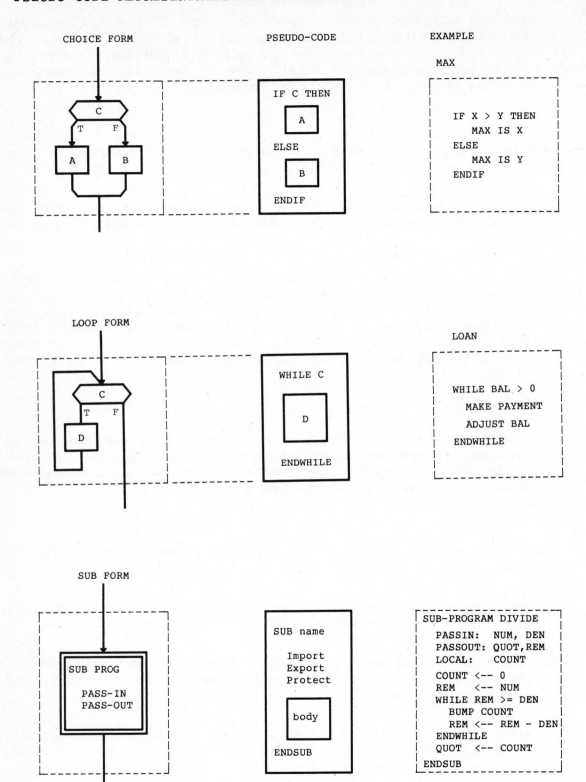

CHOICE FORM

PSEUDO-CODE

EXAMPLE

MAX

```
IF C THEN
    A
ELSE
    B
ENDIF
```

```
IF X > Y THEN
    MAX IS X
ELSE
    MAX IS Y
ENDIF
```

LOOP FORM

```
WHILE C
    D
ENDWHILE
```

LOAN

```
WHILE BAL > 0
    MAKE PAYMENT
    ADJUST BAL
ENDWHILE
```

SUB FORM

SUB PROG

PASS-IN
PASS-OUT

```
SUB name

Import
Export
Protect

    body

ENDSUB
```

```
SUB-PROGRAM DIVIDE
    PASSIN:  NUM, DEN
    PASSOUT: QUOT,REM
    LOCAL:   COUNT
    COUNT <-- 0
    REM   <-- NUM
    WHILE REM >= DEN
      BUMP COUNT
      REM <-- REM - DEN
    ENDWHILE
    QUOT <-- COUNT
ENDSUB
```

PSEUDO-LANGUAGES

Pseudo-language (or pseudo-code) is an informal language very often used to describe algorithms. It is a kind of "pidgin English", similar to programming languages but without the "dirty" details of these languages. It is very easy to convert pseudo-code into most high level languages.

CHOICE forms are illustrated in figure 1 with a flow chart, pseudo-code, and example.

The pseudo-code is written with the IF, ELSE, and ENDIF lined up and the actions indented. An alternative form for MAX may also be written horizontally as:

```
IF X > Y THEN MAX IS X ELSE MAX IS Y ENDIF
```

Alternatively the Choice form is sometimes laid out with the THEN and ELSE parts indented, and the FI (reversed IF) indicating the end of this IF form:

```
IF X > Y
    THEN MAX IS X
    ELSE MAX IS Y
FI
```

This form is often preferred because it conforms to the "sandwich" model, having a beginning and end (two slices of bread) with an indented body in between. An extreme vertical form is:

```
IF
    X > Y
THEN
    MAX IS X
ELSE
    MAX IS Y
ENDIF
```

LOOP forms have a pseudo-code as shown in figure 2. Note again the indentation of the body which is to be repeated. It can be alternately written in the DO-OD sandwich style as:

```
DO WHILE BALANCE > 0
    MAKE PAYMENT
    ADJUST BALANCE
OD
```

More complex examples, involving nesting, will be shown after the following digression on syntax of pseudo-code.

PSEUDO-CODE SYNTAX

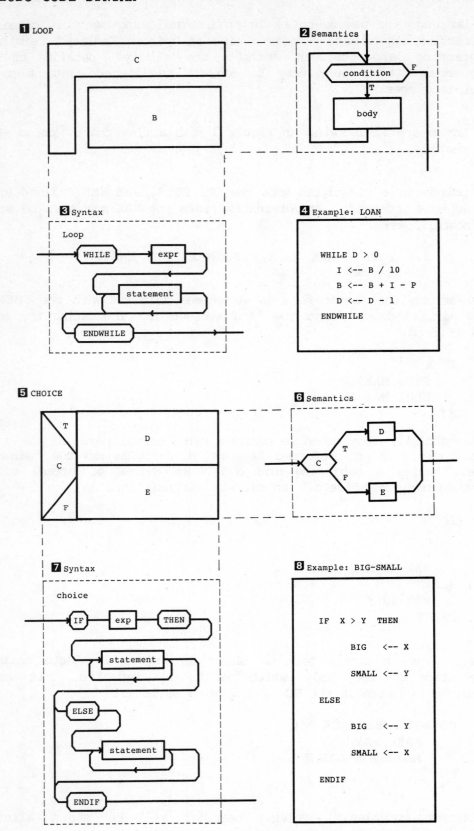

1 LOOP

C

B

2 Semantics

condition — F

T

body

3 Syntax

Loop

WHILE → expr

statement

ENDWHILE

4 Example: LOAN

```
WHILE D > 0
    I <-- B / 10
    B <-- B + I - P
    D <-- D - 1
ENDWHILE
```

5 CHOICE

T
C   D
F   E

6 Semantics

C   T   D
     F   E

7 Syntax

choice

IF → exp → THEN

statement

ELSE

statement

ENDIF

8 Example: BIG-SMALL

```
IF  X > Y  THEN

        BIG   <-- X

        SMALL <-- Y

ELSE

        BIG   <-- Y

        SMALL <-- X

ENDIF
```

Syntax of Pseudo-code

The syntax and semantics of pseudo-code are related in a simple way by the previous flow block diagram representation. From the flow block diagram, we can view both form and meaning, going from one to the other as necessary.

LOOP forms are drawn as L-shaped boxes in the flow block shape as shown in figure 1. The semantics (or behavior) of the loop is shown directly to the right of the L-shape, as a flowchart describing the condition and actions. The syntax, or form, of the loop is shown directly below the L-shaped form in figure 3. This syntax diagram shows that the pseudo-code for a loop consists of the word WHILE followed by an expression, followed by any number of statements, and finally ending with the word ENDWHILE. A sample example (LOAN) is shown in figure 4. Notice that the syntax diagram shows the physical two-dimensional layout, including the indentation of the body.

CHOICE forms also have a convenient relationship where the previous block diagram representation (drawn on its side) is related to the semantics (directly to the right) and the syntax (directly below). The syntax diagram shows two paths, one yielding a simple form:
    IF expr THEN statements ENDIF
and the other being more general of the form:
    IF expr THEN statements ELSE statements ENDIF
An example shows the pseudo-code notation, especially the indenting. The following two pages show more complex algorithms written in pseudo-code.

SUB-FORMS (or procedures) in this pseudo-code could also be represented syntactically. They could be defined (with formal parameters) in the form:

```
SUB name( PASSIN: params;  PASSOUT: params)
    statements
ENDSUB
```

Sub-forms could be used (or called) with actual parameters, in the form:
```
        name( params; params ).
```

For example, the division sub-program could be defined as

```
SUB  DIVIDE( PASSIN: NUM, DENOM;  PASSOUT: QUOT, REM )
    QUOT  <------ 0
    REM   <------ NUM
    WHILE REM > DENOM
        QUOT <--- QUOT + 1
        REM  <--- REM - DENOM
    ENDWHILE
ENDSUB
```

and it could be used in a simple change-making program as

```
        INPUT ( TENDERED,  COST )
        DIVIDE( TENDERED - COST, 25; QUARTERS, REST)
        DIVIDE( REST, 5; NICKELS, PENNIES)
```

PSEUDO-CODE OF NESTED CHOICES

PAY

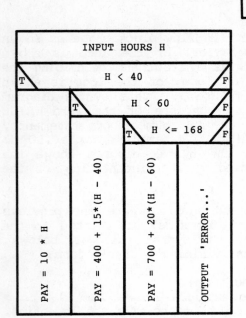

```
INPUT HOURS
IF  HOURS < 40  THEN
    PAY <-- 10 * HOURS
ELSE
    IF HOURS < 60 THEN
        PAY <-- 400 + 15*(HOURS - 40)
    ELSE
        IF HOURS <= 168 THEN
            PAY <-- 700 + 20*(HOURS - 60)
        ELSE
            OUTPUT 'ERR...'
        ENDIF
    ENDIF
ENDIF
```

'FAT' MAX3

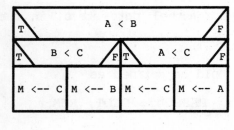

OR

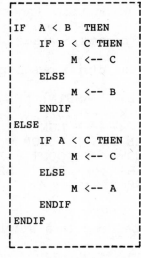

```
IF  A < B  THEN
    IF B < C THEN
        M <-- C
    ELSE
        M <-- B
    ENDIF
ELSE
    IF A < C THEN
        M <-- C
    ELSE
        M <-- A
    ENDIF
ENDIF
```

MORE COMPLEX ALGORITHMS & PSEUDO-CODE

1 GUESSING GAME

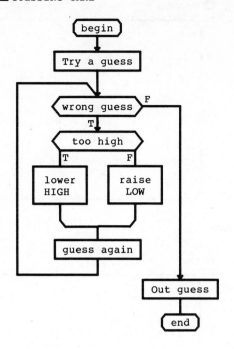

```
     TRY A GUESS(MID)
     WHILE GUESS IS WRONG
        IF GUESS IS HIGH THEN
           LOWER HI (TO MID)
        ELSE
           RAISE LOW (TO MID)
        ENDIF
        GUESS AGAIN (MID)
     ENDWHILE
     OUTPUT GUESS
```

2 CRAPS

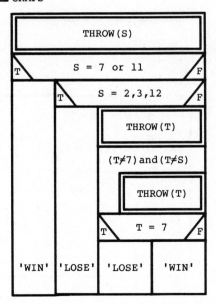

```
THROW(S)
IF (S = 7) OR (S = 11) THEN
   OUTPUT 'WIN'
ELSE
   IF (S=2)OR(S=3)OR(S=12) THEN
      OUTPUT 'LOSE'
   ELSE
      THROW(T)
      WHILE (T≠7) AND (T≠S)
         THROW(T)
      ENDWHILE
      IF T = 7 THEN
         OUTPUT 'LOSE'
      ELSE
         OUTPUT 'WIN'
      ENDIF
   ENDIF
ENDIF
```

PROGRAMMING LANGUAGES: Illustrated with LOAN

1 BASIC

```
100   REM LOAN IN BASIC
110   REM  B IS BALANCE
120   REM  P IS PAYMENT
130   REM  D IS DURATION
140   INPUT B,P,D
200   IF D <= 0 THEN 300
210      LET I = INT(B/10)
220      LET B = B + I - P
230      LET D = D - 1
240   GOTO 200
300   PRINT 'BAL IS'; D
500   END
```

4 SNOBOL

```
*     LOAN IN SNOBOL
        BAL = INPUT
        PAYT = INPUT
        DURN = INPUT
LOOP    LE(DURN,0)       :S(DONE)
            INT = BAL / 10
            BAL = BAL + INT - PAYT
            DURN = DURN - 1 :
            :(LOOP)
DONE    OUTPUT = 'BAL IS' BAL
END
```

2 FORTRAN IV

```
C        LOAN IN FORTRAN
         INTEGER  BAL,PAYT,DURN,I
         READ(60,10) BAL,PAYT,DURN
10       FORMAT(3I10)
20       IF(DURN.LE.0) GOTO 30
             I = BAL/10
             BAL = BAL + I - PAYT
             DURN = DURN - 1
             GOTO 20
30       CONTINUE
         WRITE(61,40) BAL
40       FORMAT(8H BAL IS ,I2)
         STOP
```

5 APL

```
           ∇LOAN
[1]   ⍝ LOAN IN APL
[2]   B←⎕
[3]   P←⎕
[4]   D←⎕
[5]   LOOP:→(D≤0)/10
[6]   I←⌊B÷10
[7]   B←B+I-P
[8]   D←D-1
[9]   →LOOP
[10]  'BAL IS';B
           ∇
```

3 PASCAL

```
(* LOAN IN PASCAL *)
PROGRAM LOAN(INPUT,OUTPUT);
VAR  BAL,PAYT,DURN,I: INTEGER;
BEGIN
  READ(BAL,PAYT,DURN);
  WHILE DURN > 0 DO
    BEGIN
      I := BAL DIV 10;
      BAL := BAL + I - PAYT;
      DURN := DURN - 1;
    END;
  WRITE('BAL IS ',BAL:2)
END.
```

6 LISP

```
      LOAN IN LISP
(LOAN  (LAMBDA (BAL PAYT DURN)
  (COND
    ((ZEROP DURN) BAL)
    ( T (LOAN
         (- (+ BAL(/ BAL 10)) PAYT)
          PAYT
          (SUB1 DURN)
       )
    )
  )
      )
)
(LOAN 100 20 5)
```

PROGRAMMING LANGUAGES: A Survey

Six different languages are shown on the facing page, all doing the same thing, the LOAN program. They were also shown in Chapter 0 doing the PAY algorithm. The semantics (meaning) is the same in all cases, but the syntax or form is very different. Let us observe the very general form, or overall layout, at the highest levels and resist getting into details.

LINE LAYOUT in some languages can be done freely, as sentences in ordinary English prose and poetry. In other programming languages, the layout is severely limited. For example, Pascal and Lisp have great freedom to continue over any number of lines. Fortran, however, requires one statement per line. Also, in Fortran the first five characters of every line can have only a number (or be blank), and the sixth position is sacred, used only to indicate whether the previous line was continued!

LINE LABELS are used to refer to lines. Basic has a line number associated with every line, whereas Fortran needs numbers only on the lines that will be referred to. Pascal requires no line numbers. Snobol allows non-numeric labels such as LOOP or DONE. Apl allows both numeric labels (such as 10, referred to in line 5) and non-numeric labels (such as LOOP, referred to in line 9). Lisp, different as usual, needs no labels.

COMMENTS, remarks, and notes may be included for human communication but are ignored by the computer. Again, each language indicates such comments differently. Basic precedes a remark by the word REM. Fortran precedes it with a symbol C in column 1. Pascal sandwiches comments between "(*" and "*)". Snobol has an asterisk in column 1, and Apl has a cap-null symbol (or lamp post) preceding the line. Lisp, ordinarily, has no provision for comments.

DECLARATIONS are specifications of the type of variables. The Pascal and Fortran examples here illustrate explicit declarations of all the variables, as integer type. In Snobol, the declarations are unnecessary because "everything" is viewed as a string type. In Apl, the types may change; the "boxes" can vary in size. Fortran and Basic use implicit declarations also, where the variable name also indicates the type (i.e., Fortran variables starting with letters I,J,K,L,M, or N are assumed integers, if not explicitly declared otherwise).

SYNTACTIC FEATURES: A COMPARISON

Language \ Feature	**1** COMMENTS	**2** LABELS	**3** ASSIGNMENT & INTEGER DIVISION **4**	
BASIC	REM preceeding	integer on all lines	LET I =	INT (B / 10)
FORTRAN	C in position 1	integer on some lines	I =	BAL / 10
PASCAL	(* sandwich *)	none necessary	I :=	BAL DIV 10
SNOBOL	* in position 1	names	I =	BAL / 10
APL	⍝ in position 1	integer and names	I <--	⌊B + 10
LISP	none	none	none	(/ BAL 10)
OTHER	/* in PL/I */	1.12 in Joss	COBOL DIVIDE BAL BY 10 GIVING I	

Language \ Feature	**5** NAMES	**6** CONDITIONS	**7** INPUT	**8** GOTO
BASIC	one character or char + digit	D <= 0	INPUT B,P,D	GO TO 200
FORTRAN	6 letters or digits	(DURN .LE. 0)	READ(60,10) BAL,PAYT,DURN 10 FORMAT(3I10)	GOTO 20
PASCAL	8 letters or digits	DURN <= 0	READ(BAL,PAYT,DURN)	not necessary
SNOBOL	16,000 + ?	LE(DURN,0)	BAL = INPUT PAYT = INPUT DURN = INPUT	:S(DONE) :(LOOP)
APL	?	(D≤0)	B←⎕ P←⎕ D←⎕	→LOOP
LISP	?	(ZEROP DURN)	(LOAN 100 20 5)	none (in PURE)
OTHERS		D IS NOT GREATER THAN 0 (in Cobol)		

Comparing Syntactic Features of Languages

We have considered semantics extensively when creating algorithms, structuring them, and tracing them. Now we will consider the syntactic form by comparing the six programs. This is often viewed as a fashionable "syntactic features" view of languages, with emphasis on the differences in dirty details. These syntactic features are always secondary to the semantics; they are only a means to an end.

COMMENTS, shown in figure 1 (column 1), were described earlier. Notice that only Pascal here sandwiches comments, so they can be inserted anywhere within a line; most other languages require an entire line for comments only.

LABELS, of column 2, also considered earlier, include integers, names and a "Dewey Decimal" number as found in a language called JOSS.

ASSIGNMENTS, shown in column 3, range from the key word LET in Basic, to a colon-equal combination in Pascal, to a left arrow in Apl, and finally to no such operation in "pure" Lisp.

INTEGER DIVISION, of column 4, is also done in many ways:
Basic uses a special function INT,
Fortran uses the slash operation, and the knowledge
    that BAL and 10 are integers,
Pascal uses a special integer divide operator DIV,
Apl uses both a divide symbol and a function
    (downstile) to chop the result,
Lisp uses a prefix operation (reading "Divide BAL by 10"),
Snobol uses the slash (with spaces required to surround it).

NAMES, or identifiers, shown in column 5, are of varying forms. Most names begin with a letter and can be followed by some other letters or digits. Basic allows at most one digit to follow the letter. Fortran allows only six characters (digit or letter). Pascal allows eight characters; more may be used, but only the first eight have meaning. Snobol allows thousands of characters (up to the memory limit of the computer). Apl allows long names, but usually only short ones are used, in keeping with the conciseness of the language.

CONDITIONS, as compared in column 6, show great differences also. The condition "less than or equal to" is represented by one symbol (or character) in Apl, two symbols in Basic, four symbols (including dots) in Fortran. It is also shown as a function in Snobol, and can be written out in Cobol.

INPUT, of column 7, is done for this example in three lines (Snobol and Apl), or two lines (Fortran), or one line (Basic, Pascal). The OUTPUT comparison is similar, but not shown here.

GOTO, the last and certainly least feature, is shown in column 8.

FORMS OF FORMULAS

1 Fully parenthesized form

((5/9) * (F - 32))		(((9/5) * C) + 32)

2 Precedence form

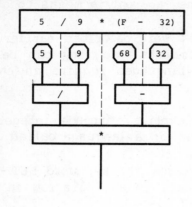 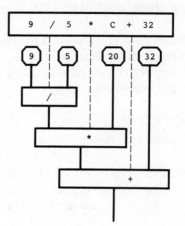

3 Right-to-Left (APL)

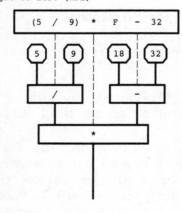 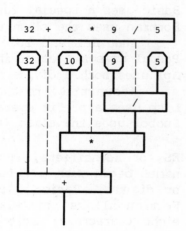

4 Postfix form (RPN)

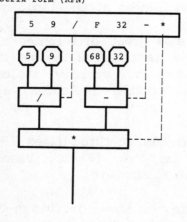 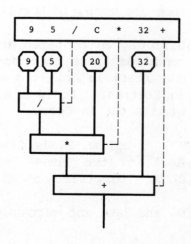

Forms of Formulas

Formulas representing expressions can be indicated algebraically in many ways. Each programming language has a particular form for representing them. Trees show the differences in the forms very quickly. As examples of formulas, we will consider the two expressions for converting temperatures.

FULLY PARENTHESIZED forms simply use parentheses to indicate all the groupings, as shown in figure 1. This method is very clear, for parentheses surround each pair of operands to be combined. This method, however, uses too many parentheses, sometimes hiding the basic simplicity of the formula.

PRECEDENCE forms involve conventions about operations at various levels; for example, some operations (multiplication and division) are at higher levels and therefore done before others at a lower level (addition and subtraction). This method results in fewer parentheses, as shown in figure 2, but the levels of precedence must be remembered. Additional conventions indicate that operations at the same levels (such as 9/5*C) are done in order from left to right (i.e., as (9/5)*C rather than 9/(5*C)). This precedence form is one of the most common forms for programming languages such as Fortran, Basic, PL/I, Algol, and Pascal.

RIGHT TO LEFT forms combine operands starting at the right and proceeding to the left. This is used in the language APL, which has many very different operators, whose many levels would be difficult to remember. Notice that some parentheses are still required, as shown in figure 3. For example, (5/9)*F-32 is evaluated as (5/9)*(F-32), and with all brackets removed would be evaluated as 5/(9*(F-32)).

POSTFIX form (or Reverse Polish Notation, RPN) is yet another representation of formulas often found on hand-held calculators. In the postfix form, operands are given first and then followed by operators. This is in contrast to all the previous "infix" forms, where operators were in between the operands. For example, the usual infix form (A + B) would be A B + in postfix form. Similarly, (A+B)*C is written A B +C *, and A + (B*C) is written A B C * +. This postfix form requires no parentheses.

Other forms of representing formulas are possible (left to right, and Polish prefix form), but the above examples are sufficient to show that differences exist.

1 FACTORIAL N

```
F <-- 1
I <-- 1

I <= N

    F <-- F * I
    I <-- I + 1
```

```
C       FACTORIAL N
        FACT = 1
        I = 1
C
100     IF(I .GT. N) GOTO 199
          FACT = FACT * I
          I = I + 1
          GOTO 100
199     CONTINUE
```

2 BIG and SMALL

```
      T    S <-- X
           B <-- Y
X<Y
           S <-- Y
      F    B <-- X
```

```
C       BIG AND SMALL
        IF(X .GE. Y) GOTO 100
          SMALL = X
          BIG   = Y
        GOTO 110
100       SMALL = Y
          BIG   = X
110     CONTINUE
```

ALTERNATE CODE

3 ODD SQUARE

```
S <-- 0
I <-- 1

While  I < N + N

    S <-- S + I
    I <-- I + 2
```

```
        S = 0
        I = 1
C
C       WHILE
11      IF(  I .LT. N + N ) GOTO 21
                              GOTO 31
21         S = S + I
           I = I + 2
                              GOTO 11
C       ENDWHILE
31                            CONTINUE
```

4 SORT2

```
  T      X > Y      F

B <-- X        B <-- Y
S <-- Y        S <-- X
```

```
C       IF
        IF(  X .GT. Y ) GOTO 15
C       THEN
                          GOTO 25
15         BIG   = X
           SMALL = Y
C       ELSE
C
25         BIG   = Y
           SMALL = X
35                        CONTINUE
C       ENDIF
```

Position 1

Coding into a Language

Coding is the process of converting an algorithm into a program in some programming language. It can be done simply in some languages (Pascal, PL/I) and not so simply in others (Fortran, Snobol, and assembly language). But coding in any language is a much easier process than the original creating of the algorithm.

Fortran will be the language used here to illustrate some concepts of coding. Fortran (actually Fortran IV) has no While form and no Choice form as we know it. It has instead a "logical IF," of the form

        IF (condition) GOTO lino

which transfers control to the given line number (lino) if the condition is true; otherwise, the following statement is performed next. Fortran also has a CONTINUE statement, which does no action. It serves as a place to go to, and is often paired with a corresponding IF or GOTO, as will be shown next.

WHILE forms may be created from this IF by the following equivalence (or transformation) which uses two line numbers (linos) and the reversed condition:

```
    WHILE condition        lino 1  IF (not condition) GOTO lino 2
        actions                        actions
    ENDWHILE                           GOTO lino 1
                           lino 2  CONTINUE
```

An example of this coding (or transformation) is shown in figure 1.

CHOICE forms can be created similarly from this IF by using the transformation:

```
    IF condition THEN              IF (not condition) GOTO lino 1
        actions                        actions
    ELSE                               GOTO lino 2
        actions            lino 1  CONTINUE
    ENDIF                              actions
                           lino 2  CONTINUE
```

An example of this (slightly modified) is shown in figure 2. Actually there is a newer dialect of Fortran (called Fortran 77) that includes an IF-THEN-ELSE which corresponds closely to our pseudo-code. But there is still no WHILE in Fortran.

Other methods are also possible to code these forms into Fortran. One interesting way is to write the codes as shown in figures 3 and 4, where the middle part (shown dotted) reads very clearly, like pseudo-code. However, to make it work properly, it requires various line numbers and comments at the left, and GOTOs and CONTINUEs at the right. This form may be harder to write, but is easier to read. These examples show that structuring is possible in any language, but it may involve some effort in some languages. More coding is done at a low level (Assembly language) in Appendix A, and is done at a high level (with Pascal) in Appendix B.

Objects and Actions of Languages

The LOAN problem was not a very fair example to indicate the power of any language. In fact, any one problem cannot be used for comparison of languages. This is because one language may be very much better than another for one problem, yet very much worse for another. In fact, languages in general have their preferred objects and actions, as we will survey (in reverse order, for fairness). This could be called the "theological" view of languages, for these preferred objects are often considered sacred!

Snobol views everything as strings, sequences of characters. Strings may include numbers, sentences, poems, or books. The operations on strings include searching a string for a given sub-string or pattern, and replacing one sub-string by another.

Apl views everything as arrays or tables, and its operations involve manipulation of tables (such as transposing, or exchanging rows for columns).

Lisp views everything as trees (or lists, or hierarchical structures). Its operations include tearing apart trees (removing heads and tails of lists), or combining them.

Fortran views everything as numbers, and its operations involve mainly numeric manipulations, including extra precision arithmetic operations, and operations on complex numbers.

Other general languages, including Pascal and Basic, do not have such an extreme view or preference to particular data objects. On the other hand, there are a number of very specialized languages that are severely limited to very few objects. For example, APT is for control of machines, ECAP and SPICE are for electrical circuits, and SPSS, SIMSCRIPT and SIMULA are for simulation.

Some newer languages (Simula, Pascal) allow a programmer to create any objects, and also to define operations or actions on these objects.

Languages affect greatly the way we think about problems. For this reason it is important to be selective in deciding on a language. If the only tool you give someone is a hammer, he (or she) may view everything as a nail!

Translation and Interpretation (Optional)

High level languages are far removed from low-level machines. This gap must be bridged, and the conversion is usually done by computers. There are two basic ways of converting between languages, very similar to converting natural languages such as French to English. Consider, for example, converting (and following) a French recipe into English.

TRANSLATORS take the recipe, first convert it all into English, and then follow (execute) it. Each time the translator again uses the recipe, the translated English version is used.

INTERPRETERS always work from the French version, converting and following (executing) instructions one at a time. Each time the interpreter uses the recipe, it must be re-converted.

In programming, some languages are translated (or compiled), and others are interpreted (or simulated). Pascal and Fortran are usually translated; Lisp, Apl, and Basic are usually interpreted; and Snobol is partly translated and partly interpreted.

A program translator (or compiler) can be faster, for, once it is converted, each subsequent execution requires no further translation; an interpreter (simulator) is slower because of its constant converting.

A program interpreter (simulator) is often more versatile or flexible, for it allows easier modifications without requiring entire reconversion for each change.

CONVERSION (Translation or Interpretation) is usually viewed in three stages. First (lexical analysis) is the recognition of tokens, or fundamental combinations of symbols (such as IF, THEN, WHILE). Then follows the syntactic stage which identifies the form or structure, and detects any improper sequences of symbols. Finally, the last stage is different, depending on the method of conversion. Translators ultimately generate code, whereas interpreters perform the actions directly.

There are many more interesting and significant concepts related to programming language conversion that are not treated here. They include the concepts of memory allocation, and binding (associating names with objects). Both of these may be static (done at compile time), or they may be dynamic (done at run time, during execution). Fortran does both statically, whereas Lisp does both dynamically. Algol allocates arrays dynamically, but binds statically. These behavioral aspects of languages are much more significant than the syntactic aspects.

LOGICAL LANGUAGE

1 LOGICAL ACTIONS

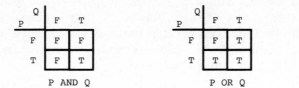

P \ Q	F	T
F	F	F
T	F	T

P AND Q

P \ Q	F	T
F	F	T
T	T	T

P OR Q

P	R
F	T
T	F

NOT(P)

2 LOGIC FLOW

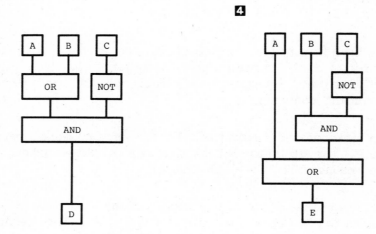

3 SYNTAX

4

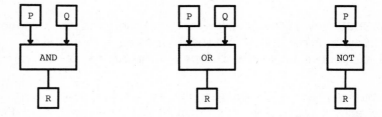

5 SEMANTICS

A B C	D
F F F	F
F F T	F
F T F	T
F T T	F
T F F	T
T F T	F
T T F	T
T T T	F

6

A B C	E
F F F	F
F F T	F
F T F	T
F T T	F
T F F	T
T F T	T
T T F	T
T T T	T

LOGIC AS A LANGUAGE   (Optional)

Logic is very useful in programming because the conditions within choice
    forms and loop forms are often formulas of logic. For example,
    some conditions are:
        (X < Y) AND (Y < Z)
        (A = B) OR (A = C)
        ((Inning <= 9) OR (S1 = S2)) AND NOT(rain)

SYMBOLIC LOGIC (also called propositional calculus) is an abstraction
    of such conditions. It is concerned with propositions (conditions or
    properties) that have only two values, True and False (sometimes
    written as 1 and 0). Propositions, labelled A, B, C, ... etc., are
    considered the basic "atoms" from which larger propositions are
    created using the operations (connectives) of AND, OR, and NOT.
    For example, the above mentioned "Play-ball" condition would be
    expressed symbolically as:
        (P OR Q) AND NOT(R)

SEMANTICS, or meaning of the operators, is given by truth tables as
    shown in figure 1. These can be viewed and used as small
    "multiplication" tables. If the truth value T (for True) is
    represented by the digit "1" and the value F is represented by digit
    "0", then the logical AND is actually multiplication. All the
    logical operations can be written as algebraic formulas in ordinary
    arithmetic as follows:
        P AND Q = P*Q
        P OR Q = P + Q - P*Q
        NOT P   = 1 - P

SYNTAX, or form, of compound formulas can be described by the
    definition:
        A formula is well formed if
        a. it is a simple formula of the form P
        b. it is of the form NOT(P), where P is well formed
        c. it is of the form (P OR Q) or (P AND Q) where both P
            and Q are well formed
        d. it is constructed of a finite number of operations of
            the above form.
        Examples of syntactically correct forms are:
        A,   (B OR NOT(C)),   NOT(D AND E),   ((F AND G) OR H)

Parentheses in the above formulas could be reduced by adopting the
    precedence convention that AND is at a higher level than OR (similar
    to the arithmetic convention that multiplication is done before
    addition). For example, the formula "P AND Q OR R" is interpreted
    as "(P AND Q) OR R"; it is not interpreted as "P AND (Q OR R)".

DATA FLOW DIAGRAMS are another way of describing the syntax of
    formulas. The logical operations are viewed as black boxes as shown
    in figure 2. Proper interconnection of these boxes occurs when the
    output of some box feeds into the input of one or more boxes, without
    causing "feedback" (i.e. without causing an output to affect the
    input of that box). Two properly interconnected flow diagrams are
    shown in figures 3 and 4.

SEMANTICS of logical formulas can be determined by indicating the
    output for all possible input combinations. Truth tables offer a
    systematic way of indicating the meaning, as shown in figures 5 and
    6. These tables correspond to the logical data flow diagrams of
    figure 3 and 4.

SYNTAX OF SYMBOLIC LOGIC

SYNTAX DIAGRAMS

SYNTAX TREES

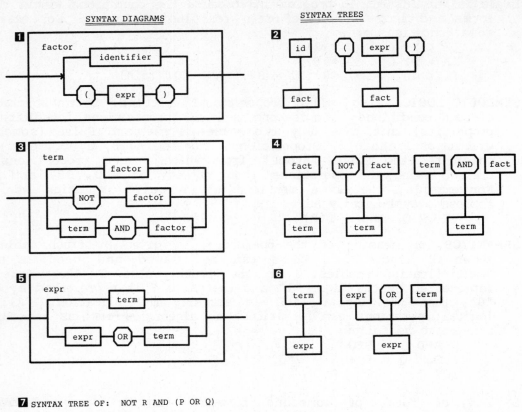

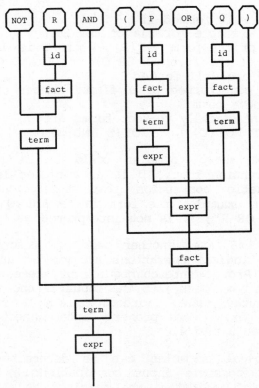

7 SYNTAX TREE OF: NOT R AND (P OR Q)

Syntax of Logical Formulas   (Optional)

SYNTAX of well-formed formulas in this logic can be described by syntax diagrams or syntax trees. The syntax for formulas having the operator precedence is shown in the the figures on the facing page. Examples of such well-formed formulas are:

A,   NOT(B),   C OR D,   E OR F AND G

(H OR I) AND J,   NOT K AND (L OR M)

FACTOR, shown in figure 1, is defined to be an identifier (such as A, B, C, ...) or an expression within brackets. An expression will be defined in a later syntax diagram. The two paths on the syntax diagram are shown as two separate syntax trees in figure 2.

TERM, shown in figures 3 and 4, is defined as either a factor or a NOT of a factor, or composed of a term followed by an AND followed by a factor. Some simple terms are:

A,   NOT B,   NOT C AND D,   NOT E AND NOT F

EXPRESSION, shown in figures 5 and 6, is defined as a term, or alternately as an expression followed by an OR followed by a term. Some examples of simple expressions are:

A, A OR B, B OR NOT C, A AND B OR C AND D

B OR C AND D, B OR C AND NOT D

Recall that a factor was also defined as an expression within parentheses, so more complex factors can be formed from the above expressions, leading to more complex terms and expressions such as:

(A OR B) AND (C OR NOT(D))

A OR B AND (C OR NOT(D))

SYNTAX TREES can be used to show the form of more complex formulas in this language, as shown in figure 7. Notice that each "sub-tree" has the form of a tree from figures 2, 4, and 6. Since most programming languages allow such compound expressions as conditions in both loop and choice forms, the syntax is significant. Algorithms have been developed to break down (or parse) such expressions.

BNF NOTATION   (Optional)

Languages can be described in many ways. For example, syntax has been
described by trees and syntax diagrams. Another common description
uses a notation called BNF (Backus-Naur Form). It was originally
used to define the Algol language. It is often preferable to trees
and syntax diagrams because no diagrams or graphs are required. This
BNF notation is however not as clear as the diagrammatic notations.

BNF notation is a "linear" description of syntax which has the form of a
formula. An example is:

     <noun phrase> ::= <article> <noun>

which reads "a noun phrase consists of an article followed by a
noun." The words describing the language are surrounded by angular
brackets, to distinguish them from the words within the language.
Here we also continue to capitalize the words in the language. These
formulas in the BNF notation are often called productions. As another
example, an article can be defined by a pair of productions as:

     <article> ::= A
     <article> ::= THE

These two descriptions can be combined into one by a vertical bar (or
exclamation point here) which reads "or" as in the examples:

     <article> ::= A ! THE

     <verb phrase> ::= <verb> <noun phrase> ! <verb> <adverb>

CLOCK, a language of telling time, from page 4-4 can be described in the
BNF form as:

     <clock> ::=   <hours> O'CLOCK ! HALF PAST <hours> !

                   <mins> AFTER <hours> ! <mins> BEFORE <hours>

SYMBOLIC LOGIC, described previously by syntax diagrams and trees, can
also be represented by the BNF notation as follows:

<expression> ::= <term> ! <expression> OR <term>

<term>   ::= <factor> ! NOT <factor> ! <term> AND <factor>

<factor>   ::= (<expression>) ! <identifier>

<identifier> ::= P! Q! R! S! T!

Programming Languages in BNF   (Optional)

Programming languages are often defined in the BNF notation. For example, the While form in pseudo-code can be described by the following sequence:

    <while form> ::= WHILE <expr> DO <statements> ENDWHILE

where the definitions of <expr> and <statements> are given elsewhere. For example, the list of statements (denoted <statements>) could be defined as a single statement, or a single statement followed by statements, as in the form:

    <statements> ::= <statement> ! <statement> <statements>

    <statement> ::= <assignment> ! <input> ! <output> !
                     <while form> ! <choice form> ! <sub form>

GENERATION of statements can be done from the BNF definitions. For example, the form

    <statements> ::= <statement> <statements>

generates (by substituting for <statement>)

    <statements> ::= <assignment> <statements>

Now again the second <statements> can be expanded by the original definition:

    <statements> ::= <assignment> <statement> <statements>

Again any statement, such as <output>, can be substituted, yielding:

    <statements> ::= <assignment> <output> <statements>

Finally, the last <statements> can be replaced by a single statement, which can be replaced by an assignment yielding

    <statements> ::= <assignment> <output> <assignment>

In this example, the BNF definition produced a sequence of three statements; in general, it produces all possible (infinite) sequences of statements. Notice that we were consistent in expanding the first "syntactic" variable at each step, so yielding a "leftmost" generation (or derivation).

PARSING, or breaking down programs in some language, is also done using such productions, but such methods are beyond this book.

REVIEW: of Chapter 4

LANGUAGES

Communicating Algorithms

Languages were introduced briefly in this chapter as a method for communicating algorithms.

Languages, in general, are sequences of symbols arranged in a linear stream. This includes natural languages, programming languages and many sequences we do not usually view as languages (dollars, names, clock times, parades).

Syntax describes the form, representation, grammar or structure of a language. It can be described by syntax diagrams, trees or the BNF notation.

Semantics describes the meaning, actions, function and behavior of a language.

Programming languages often have similar semantics, but differ greatly in their syntax.

Pseudo-code is an informal language to communicate algorithms. It is similar to most programming languages, and can be converted easily into any programming language.

Formulas expressing algebraic and logical statements can be represented in many forms (fully parenthesized, precedence, right-to-left, postfix), each having some advantages and some disadvantages.

Coding is the process of converting an algorithm into a program in some practical programming language. Here it is illustrated using Fortran. Coding in Pascal is simpler, and coding in an Assembly language is more difficult. Both are considered further in the appendices.

Symbolic Logic is viewed here as a language with simple syntax and semantics. It also illustrates different ways of defining the syntax (trees, syntax diagrams, and the definition of well formed) and semantics (truth tables, data flows, equivalent algebraic formulas).

PROBLEMS: on Chapter 4

1. SIMPLE SYNTAX
   Create syntax diagrams describing the following forms:
   a. Phone numbers
      (with area codes, prefix, suffix)
   b. License plate numbers
      (with three letters followed by three digits,
      and vice versa)
   c. Dates with year, month, day
      (such as 1984,Feb,28 or 28/2/84 or II-28-84)

2. IDENTIFIER
   An identifier in the standard Fortran language (as well as others)
   consists of one to six symbols, the first being a letter and the
   others being either letters or digits. Create a syntax diagram
   describing such identifiers, showing explicitly all possible paths.

3. ELEVATOR
   Create syntax diagrams describing the behavior of an elevator which
   travels between four floors. Typical sequences of travels (from the
   first to the fourth floor) are:

   1,2,3,4   1,2,3,2,3,4   1,2,1,2,3,4,3,2,3,4

4. WINNING LANGUAGE
   Create syntax diagrams describing all the winning sequences in a
   game of simple craps. Some typical sequences are:

   7   4,11,4   9,2,6,2,9   5,4,3,6,4,3,5

   Create other syntax diagrams of all losing sequences.

5. LANGUAGE OF PARADES
   Create syntax diagrams describing the "linear" structure of parades.
   For example, parade units could be: floats, animals, bands, etc.
   A band should not immediately follow another band, but animals
   could be clustered (followed by a sweeper).

6. ROLL YOUR OWN SYNTAX
   Find an example from everyday life which would have a structure that
   could be described by syntax diagrams. Examples could involve:
   addresses, ZIP codes, part numbers, card games, sports, trains,
   Robert's Rules of Order, etc.

7. ISBN SYNTAX
   Create a syntax diagram describing the International Standard Book
   Numbers (actually a simplified version of ISBN). Such a number
   consists of ten characters separated by hyphens. First there is a
   single digit (representing the language) followed by a publisher's
   number (of 2 to 6 digits), followed by a book number (of 6 to 2
   digits depending on the publisher number), finally followed by a
   check symbol (digit or "X").

8. BNF CONVERSION
   Convert into BNF form the three "unnatural" languages of page 4-4
   (Dollar, Name, and Clock).

MORE LANGUAGE PROBLEMS

8. ROMAN NUMBER SYNTAX
Create a syntax diagram describing the simple Roman numbers, which allow four identical symbols in a row, such as LXXXXIIII.
Do this only for numbers less than 100.
Extend the above diagram for the regular Roman numbers, which allow at most three identical symbols in a row.

9. CONVERT FORMS
Write the arithmetic expressions

S + 60*M + 3600*H   and   S + 60*(M + 60*H)

(which convert seconds, minutes and hours into seconds) in the following forms:
   a. fully parenthesized
   b. right to left
   c. left to right
   d. Polish postfix
   e. Polish prefix

10. POLISH SYNTAX
Create syntax diagrams describing formulas in the Postfix RPN notation.

11. PSEUDO-CODE
Put the following algorithms into pseudo-code:

   a. PAY algorithms of page 0-6.

   b. COMPARE and SERVICE of page 2-8.

   c. CHILI recipe of page 2-12.

   d. GRADES (all four) of page 3-18.

   e. CHANGE (many) of page 3-48.

   f. CARD TRICK of page 2-14.

   g. TRI of page 2-22.

   h. GUESS of page 2-18.

   i. MAJ of page 3-14.

   j. BISECT of page 3-52.

   k. SIGNED PRODUCT of page 3-46.

12. BINARY LANGUAGES
Create a syntax diagram describing each of the following sequences of zeros and ones.
   a. There is an even number of ones.
   b. There are no more than 3 ones.
   c. There are no adjacent ones.

Chapter 5

BIGGER BLOCKS:
  MORE, DIFFERENT,
  DEEPER CONCEPTS

MORE DATA

OTHER FORMS

DIFFERENT DATA TYPES

DEEPER NESTING

SUPER SUB-PROGRAMS

RECURSION

BIGGER BLOCKS:

MORE, DIFFERENT,
DEEPER CONCEPTS

    * Asterisks indicate the degree of importance *

Chapter 5

BIGGER BLOCKS

More, Different, Deeper Concepts

PREVIEW

In this chapter the concepts of the previous chapters are extended
to larger and often more convenient ones. There will be fewer
fundamental concepts, and more details or techniques. All of
these topics are not equally important; some are marked
optional, and others may be read quickly.

MORE DATA is considered first. The data previously encountered
was limited to a few fixed number of values, all of which were
internal to the computer. This will be extended to any number
of values, which could be external.

OTHER FORMS extend the previous CHOICE form to the more general
CASE form, where any number of choices can be made. Also the
LOOP form will be extended to a FOR loop (or loop-and-count).
An alternative loop form called the UNTIL is also briefly
considered.

The "bigger" structures given in this chapter are not always
better! For example, the FOR and CASE forms are sometimes
more convenient than the WHILE and CHOICE, but they are not as
general; they have limitations.

DIFFERENT DATA TYPES are also introduced, including characters,
logical truth values, strings, and programmer-defined types.

DEEPER NESTS of loops are developed by top-down refinement,
resulting in a number of stages, all of which are simple because
each stage involves only one loop.

SUPER SUB-PROGRAMS show how large programs can be broken into
small sub-programs from three viewpoints (control flow, data
flow, and data space), resulting in a simple relationship among
the parts. Passing of parameters (by value and reference) is
treated in detail. Recursion is also introduced here.

This chapter may be done at the same time as a language
(preferably parallel to Pascal of the appendix).

MORE DATA: INTERNAL AND EXTERNAL

1 AVERAGE PROGRAM

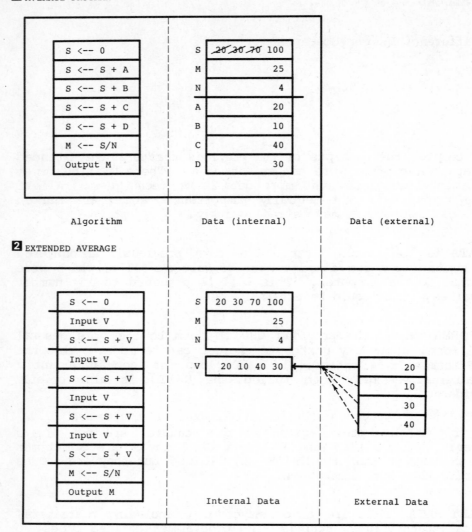

| Algorithm | Data (internal) | Data (external) |

2 EXTENDED AVERAGE

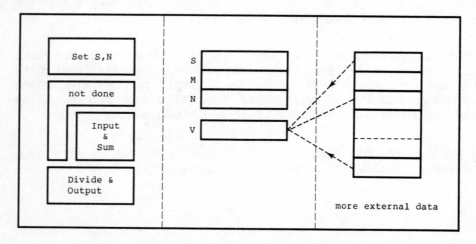

3 GENERALIZED AVERAGE

MORE DATA: External Data and Files

The data in all the examples so far has been viewed as values in
boxes, and all manipulations have involved boxes internal to
the program. Occasionally some data was input from outside,
but usually there were very few values. Often, however, there
are large quantities of data; the data can be external and
brought in only when necessary, one value at a time.

For example, consider the problem of computing some statistics,
such as the average (or mean) value. Previously, this was done
for four data values A, B, C, and D, all internal to the
program as shown in figure 1. First, the variable S is
initialized to a value of zero, then each value is accumulated
into this sum. Finally the sum is divided by the number of
values N, to determine the mean value M.

This method can be modified by keeping the data values external,
and reading in each of these external values one at a time into
a single internal variable V, which is accumulated into the sum
S. This method simplifies the internal data structure, but
makes the algorithm longer, as shown in figure 2.

A compromise such as this between complexity of algorithm and
complexity of data often occurs. If there are only a few
values, either method could be used, but if there are many
values, then finding the best method is crucial.

This program may be further generalized to average any number of
values, by replacing the series of input-accumulate actions by
a loop as shown in figure 3. This MEAN algorithm will be
refined further on the next page.

The external data can be input in many ways. One method is to
input from a keyboard, one value at a time. Another method is
to punch the data onto cards and read them in, following the
program. Yet another method uses files, described below.

FILES are a means of storing data on physical devices (such as
magnetic tapes and disks). These data values may easily be
retrieved, input to a program, modified, and output again to
update the file. So files can provide another source of input
to programs.

All these methods separate the data from the program, making the
program more general, applicable to many sets of data.

MORE REFINED MEAN PROGRAMS

1 MEAN with Counter

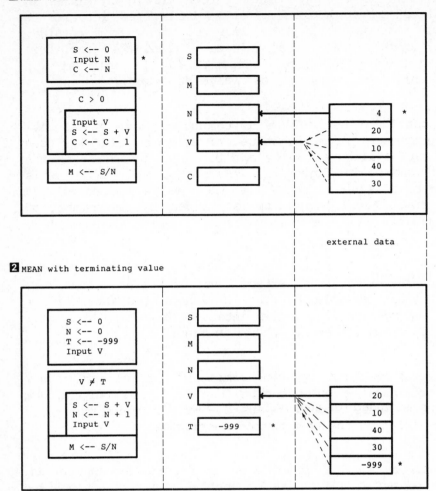

external data

2 MEAN with terminating value

3 MEAN with sandwich

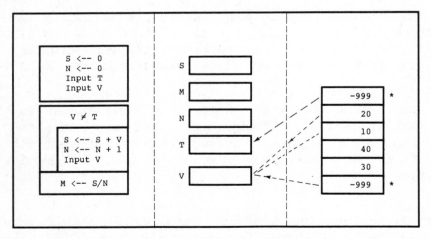

* stars indicate the main changes between versions.

Refining a MEAN Program

The MEAN algorithm can be further refined in a number of different ways. Three such refinements follow. They all involve different ways of indicating when all the data has been processed, so that the looping can be stopped.

One method of refining MEAN is to indicate the number of values it is to operate on. This value, say N, could be input as the first data value. The algorithm then includes a counter C which starts at N and is decreased once for each input value, until it reaches zero and stops the looping. This algorithm is shown in figure 1.

The problem with this method is that the value N must be determined externally before the computation begins. If the number of data values is large, and a human is to count them, there could easily be an error. Furthermore, humans should not need to do the mundane job of counting when a computer can do that better.

A second method of refining MEAN is to use the algorithm to count the number of values as they are input (figure 2). This can be done using a special "terminating" value, following the last input value. The terminating value (or sentinel, or trailer) is distinct from the data values, and when read it causes the looping to stop. Of course, this terminating value is not counted or included in the average. Such an algorithm is shown in figure 2.

The terminating value depends on the data, for it must be distinct from it. For example, if all values were percentages (ranging from 0 to 100), then a terminating value could be any number outside of this range (say 101 or 500). Similarly, if all values were positive numbers, then any negative number could be used as a terminating value. It is often useful to use an unusual value, such as -999, which is easy to recognize. Sometimes a computer supplies its own terminating value (often called EOD, or End of Data).

A third refinement of MEAN is a generalization of the second method. The second method used a terminator T which was a constant in the program. The program was not general, since it did not work for all kinds of values. If the nature of the data changed (say from averaging percentages to averaging days or dollars) the terminator would have to be changed within the program. To avoid modifying the program, method 3 provides the terminator as the first piece of data, and tests for its occurrence as the last piece as in figure 3. The terminator values "sandwich" the data. Now the program is finally general, averaging any kind of values.

MAXIMUM: Revisited and Extended

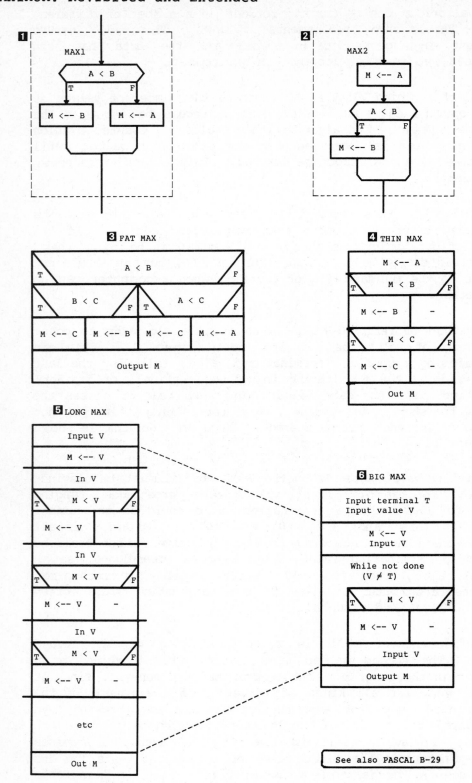

1 MAX1

A < B
T   F
M <-- B   M <-- A

2 MAX2

M <-- A
A < B
T   F
M <-- B

3 FAT MAX

	A < B	
T		F

| T | B < C | F | T | A < C | F |
| M <-- C | M <-- B | M <-- C | M <-- A |

Output M

4 THIN MAX

M <-- A
T   M < B   F
M <-- B   -
T   M < C   F
M <-- C   -
Out M

5 LONG MAX

Input V
M <-- V
In V
T   M < V   F
M <-- V   -
In V
T   M < V   F
M <-- V   -
In V
T   M < V   F
M <-- V   -
etc
Out M

6 BIG MAX

Input terminal T
Input value V
M <-- V
Input V
While not done
(V ≠ T)
T   M < V   F
M <-- V   -
Input V
Output M

See also PASCAL B-29

Big MAX From Little MAXes

There are often many algorithms that do the same thing, but some may be extended more easily than others. For example, there are two ways to find the maximum value of two variables A and B as shown in figures 1 and 2. The first method compares the two values directly and assigns the maximum value M immediately. The second method assigns one of the values to be the maximum, then checks this choice, and if the choice was wrong it changes the maximum to be the other value. Although this second method may seem more complex and unnatural, it will be easier to modify and extend.

The maximum value of three variables A, B, and C can also be done in two ways, by extending the above algorithms. One way involves a nesting of choices within a choice as shown in FATMAX of figure 3. Another way involves a series of choices, resulting in a thinner and longer form shown as THINMAX in figure 4.

The maximum value of four and more values could be done similarly. Then it becomes clear that the thinner max extends more easily than the fatter max.

The maximum of any number N of input values is also simply done as a long series shown in figure 5. This long series generalizes into a loop as shown in figure 6.

BIG MAX first inputs a terminal value; then it inputs the second value, assigning it to be the maximum. It successively inputs values and compares each to M, updating M if necessary, while the input value is not a terminating value. Finally the maximum is output.

Notice that this algorithm assumed that at least one value is given between the terminating values. If it is possible that no values are given (other than the two terminating values), then the algorithm must be modified by testing before assignment to M.

The BIG MAX algorithm can further be modified to find the number of values that are largest, and the second largest value. Try it.

CASE (SELECT): A Big Choice

1 Nested Choices

2 Actions Ai, selected by conditions Ci

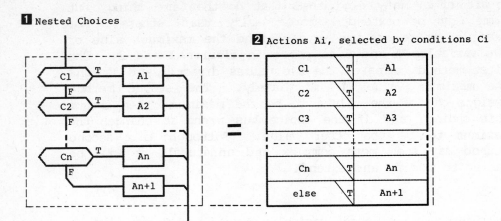

3 PRICE P: depends on QUANTITY Q

Q = 1	T	P <-- 99
Q = 2,3	T	P <-- 98
Q = 4,5,6	T	P <-- 95
Q = 7,8,9	T	P <-- 90
Q > 9	T	P <-- 85

4 GRADES G from percentages P

60 <= P < 80		G <-- 'C'
80 <= P < 90		G <-- 'B'
50 <= P < 60		G <-- 'D'
90 <= P <= 100		G <-- 'A'
P < 50		G <-- 'F'

5 IF C THEN D ELSE E

6 IF A THEN B

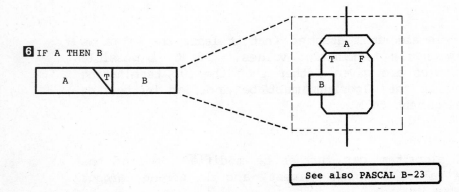

See also PASCAL B-23

OTHER FORMS: The CASE Form   (Optional)

The four fundamental forms (SERIES, CHOICE, LOOP and SUB) are sufficient to create all algorithms, but other forms may also be used. They include CASE, UNTIL and FOR forms.

THE CASE FORM (or Select form) is a natural extension of the CHOICE form, where instead of selecting from only two choices, there may be any number of choices, as shown in figure 1. Notice that the Choices are nested within one another. This form can also be represented conveniently in a rectangular notation as shown in figure 2. The conditions shown at the left are tested in the order (C1, C2, ..., Cn) until one condition Ci holds, in which case the corresponding action Ai is done, and the Case form is left. The dotted line to the right of the CASE box suggests the exit after the action is done.

PRICE, of figure 3, shows how the unit price P is selected by the quantity Q purchased.

GRADES, of figure 4, shows how the percentages P select the grades G. Notice the order of the output grades; the most common values are considered first, for greatest speed.

Binary Choice forms (IF...THEN...ELSE) could be drawn in this notation as shown in figure 5. This representation could be simpler to draw, and easier to extend to more choices. The simpler "one-sided" choice form, or IF...THEN form, can also be drawn in this new notation as shown in figure 6.

SIMPLE-PAY shows how some algorithms can be done as either nested choices or cascaded choices as shown in figures 7 and 8. A number of the simpler IF...THEN forms may be cascaded as in the following algorithm of figure 8. This series of choices differs from the nested choices of the CASE by not having any dotted line at the right. In the cascade CHOICE structure, every condition is tested.

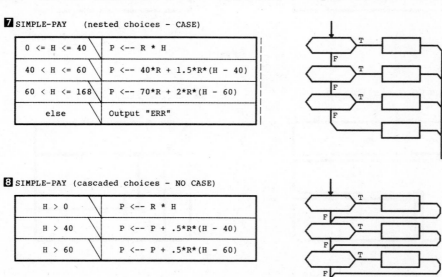

7 SIMPLE-PAY   (nested choices - CASE)

0 <= H <= 40	P <-- R * H
40 < H <= 60	P <-- 40*R + 1.5*R*(H - 40)
60 < H <= 168	P <-- 70*R + 2*R*(H - 60)
else	Output "ERR"

8 SIMPLE-PAY (cascaded choices - NO CASE)

H > 0	P <-- R * H
H > 40	P <-- P + .5*R*(H - 40)
H > 60	P <-- P + .5*R*(H - 60)

THE UNTIL LOOP

1

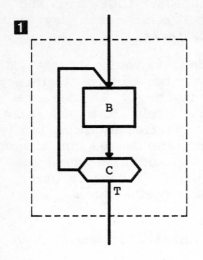

2

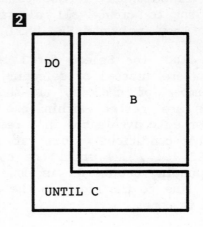

DO

B

UNTIL C

3 ODD SQUARE OF N

S <-- 0
I <-- 1

DO   S <-- S + I
      I <-- I + 2

UNTIL I > N + N

OUTPUT S

4 MEAN

S <-- 0
N <-- 0

DO   Input V
      S <-- S + V
      N <-- N + 1

UNTIL V = 0

M <-- S/(N - 1)

5 UNTIL from WHILE

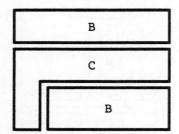

B

C

B

6 WHILE from UNTIL

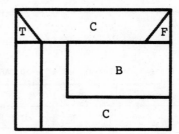

T   C   F

B

C

Other Loop Forms

The only loop form considered so far was the WHILE. It is the most fundamental form, and no other loop forms are necessary. However, some other loop forms may be useful or convenient at times. The two loop variations we will consider are the UNTIL loop and the FOR loop.

The UNTIL Loop (Optional)

The UNTIL loop (also called DO-UNTIL or REPEAT) is shown in figure 1, with a new notation in figure 2. Notice that the UNTIL does the action of the body first, and then later tests the condition. It repeats this body until the condition becomes true. This is sometimes called a post-test loop.

ODD-SQUARE, of figure 4, shows an example where the loop is repeated until the index I exceeds N+N.

MEAN, of figure 5, shows how input values V are accumulated and averaged until the terminal value of zero is input. Notice that the terminating value is first added into the sum S (and the count N bumped) before the test that determines it to be a terminating value. In this case (with zero as terminator) there is no problem, but if another terminating value is used, then it must be subtracted from the sum. Also, the terminating value gets added into N, so N must be reduced by 1. This type of "fix-up" is totally unnecessary when the WHILE loop is used.

Comparing the UNTIL loop with the WHILE loop shows the WHILE to be more fundamental. The UNTIL always does the action (body) first and then tests, when it may be too late to undo the action. Also, the UNTIL can be created from the WHILE as shown in figure 5, whereas the WHILE cannot be created directly from the UNTIL (for it needs an additional CHOICE form as shown in figure 6). So the WHILE is more powerful and universal (as well as less error-prone) compared to the UNTIL.

Pseudo-code of the UNTIL form could be written as shown by the following ODD-SQUARE program, with the body indented and sandwiched between a REPEAT and an UNTIL.

```
S <--- 0
I <--- 1
REPEAT
   S <--- S + I
   I <--- I + 2
UNTIL I > N + N
```

THE FOR LOOP: Loop and Count

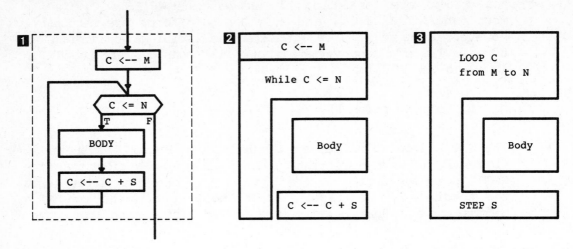

1
```
C <-- M

C <= N
  T        F

BODY

C <-- C + S
```

2
```
C <-- M

While C <= N

        Body

C <-- C + S
```

3
```
LOOP C
from M to N

        Body

STEP S
```

EXAMPLES

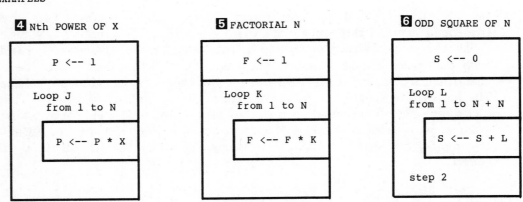

4 Nth POWER OF X
```
P <-- 1

Loop J
  from 1 to N

    P <-- P * X
```

5 FACTORIAL N
```
F <-- 1

Loop K
  from 1 to N

    F <-- F * K
```

6 ODD SQUARE OF N
```
S <-- 0

Loop L
  from 1 to N + N

    S <-- S + L

step 2
```

7 Trace of a 'super' loop

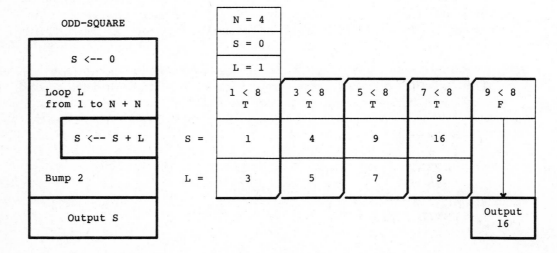

ODD-SQUARE
```
S <-- 0

Loop L
from 1 to N + N

    S <-- S + L

Bump 2

Output S
```

	N = 4				
	S = 0				
	L = 1				
	1 < 8 T	3 < 8 T	5 < 8 T	7 < 8 T	9 < 8 F
S =	1	4	9	16	
L =	3	5	7	9	
					Output 16

The FOR Loop

FOR forms (often called Super Loops, or Loop-and-count forms) are one of the most useful extensions of the four forms. A FOR loop consists of the usual WHILE loop with the condition involving a counter. The counter is initially set to some value, M, and is incremented during each loop, by any size step S, finally stopping when a given final value N is exceeded.

A flowchart of this form is shown in figure 1; the corresponding flow block diagram is in figure 2. By combining the initializing part, the "while" test part, and the incrementing part into one huge C-shaped block (surrounding the body), we arrive at a new notation, shown in figure 3. In most cases, the size of step S is one; if this step size is not indicated explicitly, it is assumed to be a value of one.

This new notation decreases the complexity of some algorithms (since it involves only one box instead of three surrounding the body). It allows us to think in terms of larger blocks, so making our algorithms look smaller and more intellectually manageable. Three examples of this new FOR form and notation are shown in the given figures.

POWER, of figure 4, computes the Nth (positive) power of a number X by successive multiplications.

FACTORIAL, of figure 5, now involves only three boxes compared to the previous 5 boxes.

ODD SQUARE, of figure 6, produces the square of an integer N by summing the first N odd integers (from 1 to N+N-1). This is done by starting the counter L at one, and looping with a step size of two, adding this odd counter value to S during each loop. A trace of this ODD square is shown in figure 7.

Pseudo-code for the FOR loop follows. The equivalent program (with four parts: SET, TEST, DO and BUMP) are shown to the right of the FOR form.

```
                                    C <---M
FOR C FROM M TO N STEP S            WHILE C <= N
    DO BODY                             DO BODY
ENDFOR                                  C <--- C + S
                                    ENDWHILE
```

This FOR form is so powerful that it is very often used. But it is too often also misused, for it introduces a counter where such a counter may not be necessary or natural!

LIMITATIONS of the FOR form are many, which may make this form unsuitable. For example, the beginning value M and final value N, which could be given as expressions, are evaluated only once on entry to this form; they should not be changed inside the loop. Also, the counter C should not be modified (or modifiable) by anything in the body of the loop. Additionally, in some languages (such as FORTRAN, where the FOR is called a DO), the values of M, N, C, and S may not be zero or negative or real. Finally, after the loop terminates, the value of the loop variable may be undefined!! The WHILE loop has no such restrictions, so it may always be used in such cases.

THE CHARACTER TYPE

1 CALCULATOR - 4 function

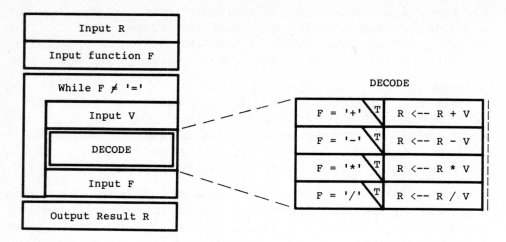

```
┌─────────────────────────┐
│        Input R          │
├─────────────────────────┤
│     Input function F    │
├─────────────────────────┤
│     While F ≠ '='       │
│  ┌──────────────────┐   │
│  │     Input V      │   │
│  ├──────────────────┤   │
│  │     DECODE       │   │
│  ├──────────────────┤   │
│  │     Input F      │   │
│  └──────────────────┘   │
├─────────────────────────┤
│    Output Result R      │
└─────────────────────────┘
```

DECODE

F = '+' ＼T	R <-- R + V
F = '-' ＼T	R <-- R - V
F = '*' ＼T	R <-- R * V
F = '/' ＼T	R <-- R / V

2 ISBN CODER

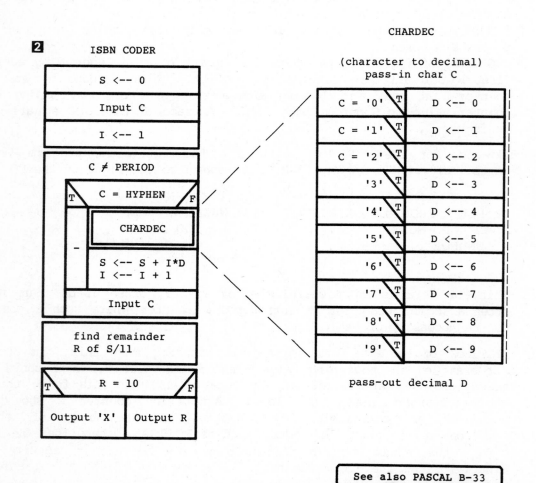

```
┌─────────────────────────┐
│        S <-- 0          │
├─────────────────────────┤
│        Input C          │
├─────────────────────────┤
│        I <-- 1          │
├─────────────────────────┤
│      C ≠ PERIOD         │
│ T  C = HYPHEN        F   │
│  ┌──────────────────┐   │
│  │     CHARDEC      │   │
│- ├──────────────────┤   │
│  │  S <-- S + I*D   │   │
│  │  I <-- I + 1     │   │
│  └──────────────────┘   │
│        Input C          │
├─────────────────────────┤
│    find remainder       │
│    R of S/11            │
├─────────────────────────┤
│ T    R = 10          F   │
│  Output 'X' │ Output R  │
└─────────────────────────┘
```

CHARDEC

(character to decimal)
pass-in char C

C = '0' ＼T	D <-- 0
C = '1' ＼T	D <-- 1
C = '2' ＼T	D <-- 2
'3' ＼T	D <-- 3
'4' ＼T	D <-- 4
'5' ＼T	D <-- 5
'6' ＼T	D <-- 6
'7' ＼T	D <-- 7
'8' ＼T	D <-- 8
'9' ＼T	D <-- 9

pass-out decimal D

See also PASCAL B-33

DIFFERENT DATA TYPES: The Character Type

Objects of our programs, until now, have been numbers which are of type integer or real. Other data types are also common including character, logical, string and complex types. In most languages, variables must be declared as being of one type. This declaration is usually given at the beginning of the program.

CHARACTER is a data type having values which include any single symbol on a keyboard. This includes all letters, digits, punctuation marks, brackets, and other miscellaneous symbols (%, $, etc.). The character values are put within quotation marks to distinguish them from variables. Some samples of character variables and their values are:

    GRADES   of 'A', 'B', 'C', 'D', 'F'
    REPLY   of 'Y' and 'N' (for yes and no)
    OPERATOR   of '+', '-', '*', '/'
    DIGIT   of '0', '1', '2', '3', '4', '5', ... '9'
    BRACKETS   of '(', ')', '[', ']'

OPERATIONS on characters include assignment, comparison, input and output.

Assignment of values to variables is done with the usual assignment operator, as for example:

    FAIL   <--- 'F'
    HYPHEN <--- '-'
    GRADE   <--- FAIL

Comparison of characters is done alphabetically (where 'A' is considered less than 'B'). For example the statement

    IF GRADE < 'C' THEN C <--- C + 1

bumps the counter C if the grade is the character 'A' or 'B'.

CALCULATOR, of figure 1, behaves as a four-function calculator. It accepts sequences of alternating numbers and operations. It recognizes (decodes) the operations and operates on the values until an equal sign is encountered, such as:

    1 + 2 * 3 =   (which returns 3*3 or 9)
    4 * 5 - 6 / 7 =   (which returns 14/7 or 2)
    9 / 5 * 100 + 32 = (which returns 212)

Notice the left-to-right order of operations, unlike normal precedence.

ISBN CODER (of figure 2) shows how to compute the checksum for the International Standard Book Number (ISBN) as described on page 1-3. This example illustrates the fact that a character such as '1' is not equal to the integer 1. A sub-program CHARDEC to convert these character digits to integer digits is useful. The algorithm accepts an input sequence of mixed hyphens and characters, ending with a period. It ignores the hyphens, and converts the numeric characters into their corresponding digits. It then weights the digits, accumulates them, and when completed divides the sum by eleven, obtaining the remainder R. If the remainder is 10, then the check symbol is 'X'; otherwise the check symbol is the remainder.

The Logical Type

The logical or Boolean type involves variables that have only two values, TRUE or FALSE (sometimes labelled T,F or 1,0). Logical variables occur often as conditions within Choice and Loop forms. Some examples of logical variables are:

FEMALE, DONE, OVER21, INCREASING, EQUILATERAL

Assignment is one operation on logical types which is very useful. Examples of some assignments are:

```
MALE <------- TRUE
OVER21 <----- (AGE > 21)
DANGER <----- (DENOMINATOR = 0)
DONE <------- (COUNTER = LAST)
TRIANGLE <--- (SMALL + MID > LARGE)
RIGHT <------ (X*X + Y*Y = H*H)
CLOSE <------ ( ABS(X-Y) < 0.001 )
```

Logical operations on such types include conjunction (AND), disjunction (OR) and negation (NOT).

CONJUNCTION is a logical operation often called AND. The conjunction "P AND Q" is true when P is true and Q is true. Some examples of the use of AND are:

```
INCREASING <---- ( (X < Y) AND (Y < Z) )
EQUILATERAL <--- ( (A = B) AND (A = C) )
ELIGIBLE <------ ( OVER21 AND EMPLOYED )
```

DISJUNCTION (often called OR) of two logical variables P,Q is written "P or Q" and is true when either P is true, or Q is true (or both are true). Some examples of the use of this "inclusive" OR are:

```
WIN <---------- (SUM = 7) OR (SUM = 11)
ERROR <-------- (AGE < 0) OR (AGE > 120)
ISOSCELES <--- (A=B) OR (B=C) OR (C=A)
```

NEGATION (also called NOT) simply reverses the truth values, changing TRUE values to FALSE and vice versa. Some examples of its use are:

```
FEMALE <---- NOT MALE
WHILE NOT DONE . . .
IF NOT INCREASING THEN . . .
```

IMPROPER FORMS of logical formulas are common when converting directly from English. Some improperly formed formulas follow, along with their corresponding correct versions.

```
A AND B = 5     should read (A = 5) AND (B = 5)
T = 7 OR 11     should read (T = 7) OR (T = 11)
A < B < C       should read (A < B) AND (B < C)
X OR Y > Z      should read (X > Z) OR  (Y > Z)
I = J AND K     should read (I = J) AND (I = K)
```

More Logic   (Optional)

Algorithms involving complex combinations of choices can often be
done simply, using logic only. For example, triangles can be
classified by the following series of logical assignments
(assuming angles A <= B <= C).

        TRI   <--- (A + B > C)

        ISOC   <--- (A=B) OR (B=C)

        ACUTE   <--- (A<90) AND (B<90) AND (C<90)

        OBTUSE <--- (C > 90)

        RIGHT   <--- (C = 90)

        EQUIL   <--- (A = C)

COMPARISON of truth values is possible, with the TRUE value
assumed greater than the FALSE value. Truth tables describing
some comparison operations follow.

		1	**2**	**3**	**4**
P	Q	P <= Q	P = Q	P ≠ Q	P > Q
F	F	T	T	F	F
F	T	T	F	T	F
T	F	F	F	T	T
T	T	T	T	F	F

Figure 1 shows the operator "P <= Q" (in logic, the Conditional
connective called implication, or "shoe"). It is read as "If
P then Q". This conditional connective is often used in
logical deduction.

Figure 2 shows the operator "P = Q" (the Biconditional
connective). It is read as "P if and only if Q."

Figure 3 shows the operator "P ≠ Q" (the "exclusive or); it is
true when only one and not the other value is true.

Figure 4 shows the operator "P > Q" (sometimes called the
inhibit-and); the value of P is inhibited by Q.

Other logical operations are also possible, including P < Q and
P >= Q.

More Types

1. STRINGS

    a) "STOP"
    b) "LEONARDO DA VINCI"
    c) "ONCE UPON A TIME........ LIVED HAPPILY EVER AFTER"

2. COMPLEX NUMBERS

    d) 1 + i1 (or 1.414 at 45 degrees, or (1,1))
    e) 3 + i4 (or 5.0 at 53.1 degrees, or (3,4))
    f) 4 + i3 (or 5.0 at 36.9 degrees, or (4,3))

3. PROGRAMMER-DEFINED TYPES (Simple Enumeration)

    g) GRADES (of Students)
        (A, B, C, D, F)

    h) RANKS (of Cards)
        (2,3,4,5,6,7,8,9,10,J,Q,K,A)

    i) SUITS (of Cards)
        (CLUBS, DIAMONDS, HEARTS, SPADES)

    j) DAYS (of the Week)
        (SUN, MON, TUE, WED, THUR, FRI, SAT)

    k) MONTHS (of the Year)
        (JAN,FEB,MAR,APR,MAY,JUNE,JULY,AUG,SEPT,OCT,NOV,DEC)

    l) LEVELS (of Students)
        (FRESHMAN, SOPHOMORE, JUNIOR, SENIOR, GRADUATE)

    m) DENOMINATIONS (of Money)
        (PENNY, NICKEL, DIME, QUARTER, HALF-DOLLAR, DOLLAR)

    n) RANK (of Teacher)
        (LECTURER, ASSISTANT, ASSOCIATE, FULL)

    o) RANK (of Military)
        (PRIVATE, CORPORAL, SERGEANT, LIEUTENANT, CAPTAIN)

    p) STATUS (of Marriage)
        (SINGLE, WIDOWED, MARRIED, DIVORCED)

    q) KINDS (of Device)
        (KEYBOARD, PRINTER, CONSOLE, CARDREADER)

    r) TRANSACTION (of Business)
        (BUY, SELL, RETURN, LOSE)

    s) SEASON (of the Year)
        (SPRING, SUMMER, FALL, WINTER)

See also PASCAL B-36

Other Data Types (Optional)

Most high level languages provide a number of pre-defined data types. Integers and real numbers are most common, but character and logical types are also given. Some languages additionally provide strings and complex numbers.

STRINGS are sequences of characters viewed as a unit (not in terms of the characters), as shown in figure 1. The strings may be of varying lengths, and operations include assignment, comparison, and pattern matching (searching for patterns and replacing sub-strings).

COMPLEX numbers are occasionally provided, especially in scientific languages (such as Fortran). They consist of pairs of numbers (with a real part and an imaginary part), which can be viewed as vectors (having a length and angle of direction), as shown in figure 2. Operations on complex numbers involve a kind of addition, subtraction, multiplication and division.

PROGRAMMER-DEFINED TYPES

In many of the modern languages, programmers can define their own data types. The simplest types (called enumerated types or scalar types) are defined by simply listing the values that a variable can have, as in figure 3 at the left. The order of listing indicates a ranking, in increasing order. Some operations on these types include selecting the next value (successor or predecessor), assignment, and comparison. One great advantage of such types is the resulting readability. For example:

```
DAY <--- MONDAY
WHILE DAY < FRIDAY ...
IF DAY = SATURDAY THEN ....
```

Readability, similar to this, can be accomplished in languages that do not have such programmer-defined types. It is done by making a correspondence between each value and an integer. For example, SUN could be assigned 0, MON assigned 1, TUE assigned 2, etc. and SAT assigned 6. Then these variables (SUN, MON, etc.) can be used and compared as if they were values, as in the above three statements.

An advantage of the programmer-defined data types over this correspondence is that the computer can check whether a variable is out of its range. For example, an error would be indicated if FRIDAY were compared to 9, or if a day of the week were compared to a rank of a professor.

More complex programmer-defined types (called records and arrays) are often possible and involve combinations of other simpler types. They will be considered later.

DOUBLY NESTED LOOPS: CHARGE

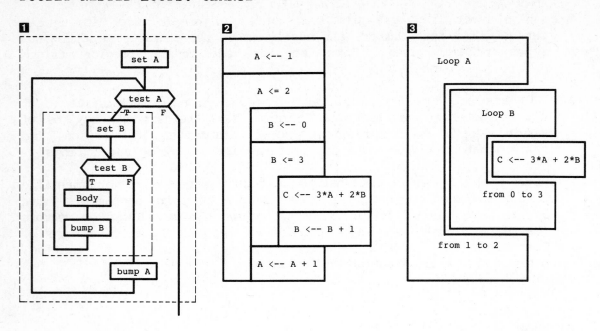

1

- set A
- test A — T / F
- set B
- test B — T / F
- Body
- bump B
- bump A

2

- A <-- 1
- A <= 2
- B <-- 0
- B <= 3
- C <-- 3*A + 2*B
- B <-- B + 1
- A <-- A + 1

3

- Loop A
- Loop B
- C <-- 3*A + 2*B
- from 0 to 3
- from 1 to 2

4 Detailed Trace

| A <-- 1 |
| A <= 2 |
| B <-- 0 |
| B <= 3 |
| C <-- 3A + 2B |
| B <-- B + 1 |
| A <-- A + 1 |

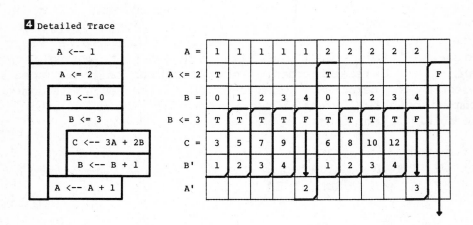

A =	1	1	1	1	1	2	2	2	2	2		
A <= 2	T					T						F
B =	0	1	2	3	4	0	1	2	3	4		
B <= 3	T	T	T	T	F	T	T	T	T	F		
C =	3	5	7	9		6	8	10	12			
B'	1	2	3	4		1	2	3	4			
A'					2					3		

5 Brief Trace

| Loop A |
| Loop B |
| C <-- 3*A + 2*B |
| from 0 to 3 |
| from 1 to 2 |

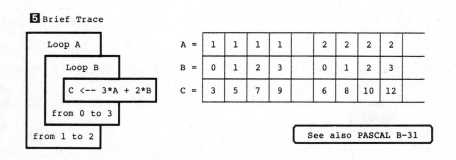

A =	1	1	1	1	2	2	2	2
B =	0	1	2	3	0	1	2	3
C =	3	5	7	9	6	8	10	12

See also PASCAL B-31

DEEPER NESTS OF LOOPS: Simple Nests

Loops nested within loops are very common and useful. They can, however, seem very confusing if the emphasis is on their details.

Figure 1 shows how complex a double nested algorithm can be, in general, involving seven boxes.

Figure 2 shows this drawn in a block form, but it still appears complex because the number of boxes have not changed.

Figure 3 shows the above redrawn in terms of the larger FOR loops. This notation hides most of the details. Notice that the nesting of loops corresponds to the nesting of these blocks, one nestled within the other. This figure, consisting of three components, is much simpler than the original one having seven components.

CHARGE is the algorithm given here. It computes the total admission charge C if adults A pay three dollars and babies B pay two dollars. The algorithm creates a table of charges for one to two adults, and zero to three babies.

This CHARGE algorithm could have been created top-down, in stages, as shown below.

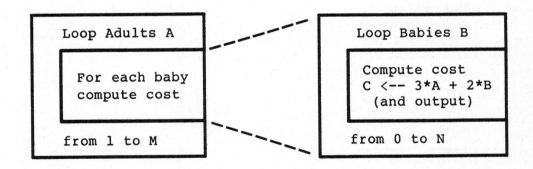

Figure 4 shows the trace of such a nested algorithm in detail. Such great detail is usually not necessary, for it can be done by a simpler trace, shown next. The detail is, however, important for understanding how the simpler trace works. It is also important as a last resort for tracing extremely complex nested algorithms. Most nesting of loops is, however, quite simple, even at three or four levels of nesting, if viewed properly.

Figure 5 shows a short and convenient trace. It simply lists all combinations of only the loop variables, with the inner loop variable B changing most rapidly compared to the outer loop variable A. The resulting charge C is then also listed, completing the entire table of CHARGE. The details are all hidden!

NICELY NESTED LOOPS

1 HOUR TIMER

Loop
minutes M

WAIT
A
MINUTE

from 0 to 59

Loop
seconds S

WAIT A
SECOND

OUTPUT M,S

from 0 to 59

2

Loop M

Loop S

M S

WAIT

OUTPUT M,S

3 DECIMAL COUNTER

Loop tens T

Loop units U

Output
T,U

from 0 to 9

from 0 to 9

tens
units

4 DICE 'COUNTER'

Loop die D1

Loop die D2

Output
D1,D2

1 to 6

1 to 6

5 BINARY COUNTER

Loop A

Loop B

Loop C

Output
A,B,C

0 to 1

0 to 1

0 to 1

6 ODOMETER

Loop hundreds A

Loop tens B

Loop units C

Loop tenths D

Output
A,B,C,D

A B C D

0 to 9

0 to 9

0 to 9

0 to 9

7 24 HOUR CLOCK

Loop forever

Loop hours H

Loop minutes M

Loop seconds S

Output H,M,S

wait a second

H M S

from 0 to 59

from 0 to 59

from 0 to 23

Nicely Nested Loops

Many algorithms involve loops directly nested within others, like the CHARGE algorithm of the previous page. Such algorithms have a similar behavior, of cycling through all combinations, like a big counter, or digital clock, or mileage odometer, as is illustrated in the following examples.

TIMER, of figure 1, shows how a one-hour timer can be created (top-down). First, the minutes loop from 0 to 59. For each minute, the seconds loop also from 0 to 59. Within the seconds loop, there is a delay of a second, and a display of minutes and seconds. Notice that the inner loop (seconds) changes faster than the outer loop (minutes). Figure 2 shows the nested loops in a single diagram; the dotted box shows the order of loops (first the minutes, then the seconds) as could be visualized on a digital clock. Many other such counters have this form.

DECIMAL COUNTER, of figure 3, shows how the TENS and UNITS of a base ten counter can be generated, putting out sequences:

    00, 01, 02, ... 10, 11, 12, ... 89, 90, ... 99.

DICE, of figure 4, shows similarly how all 36 possible dice combinations can be listed in order:

    11, 12, 13, 14, 15, 16, 21, 22, 23, 24, 25, 26,   31 ... 66.

BINARY COUNTER, of figure 5, shows how the binary numbers can be generated in increasing order:

    000, 001, 010, 011, 100, ... 111.

This could be used to generate all combinations to test algorithms such as the majority algorithm.

ODOMETER (or mileage meter), of figure 6, shows how four nested loops generate all decimal values from 000.0 to 999.9. The dotted box again shows the order of the variables A, B, C, D, the leftmost variable, A, changing the slowest and the rightmost one, D, changing fastest (like an actual automobile odometer).

CLOCK, of figure 7, shows a 24-hour clock which loops perpetually, using a while condition which is always true, such as $0 < 1$, or $H < 25$.

NASTY NESTED LOOPS

1 FAIR PAY

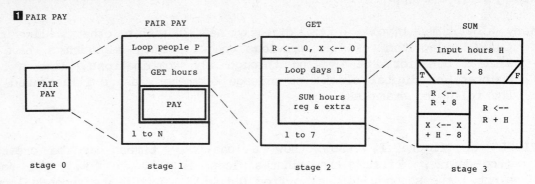

```
            FAIR PAY              GET                 SUM

FAIR      Loop people P     R <-- 0, X <-- 0     Input hours H
PAY                                           T     H > 8     F
          GET hours         Loop days D
                                             R <--        R <--
          PAY               SUM hours        R + 8        R + H
                            reg & extra
                                             X <-- X
          1 to N            1 to 7           + H - 8

stage 0   stage 1          stage 2           stage 3
```

2 PRODUCTION DATA

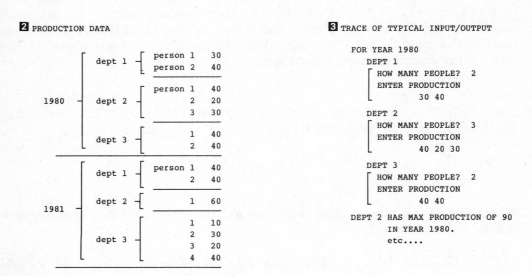

```
              dept 1  ┌ person 1   30
                      └ person 2   40

              dept 2  ┌ person 1   40
      1980            │        2   20
                      └        3   30

              dept 3  ┌        1   40
                      └        2   40
      ────────────────────────────────
              dept 1  ┌ person 1   40
                      └        2   40

      1981    dept 2  ─        1   60

                      ┌        1   10
              dept 3  │        2   30
                      │        3   20
                      └        4   40
```

3 TRACE OF TYPICAL INPUT/OUTPUT

```
FOR YEAR 1980
    DEPT 1
  ┌ HOW MANY PEOPLE?  2
  │ ENTER PRODUCTION
  └      30 40

    DEPT 2
  ┌ HOW MANY PEOPLE?  3
  │ ENTER PRODUCTION
  └      40 20 30

    DEPT 3
  ┌ HOW MANY PEOPLE?  2
  │ ENTER PRODUCTION
  └      40 40

DEPT 2 HAS MAX PRODUCTION OF 90
    IN YEAR 1980.
    etc....
```

4 PRODUCTION PROGRAM

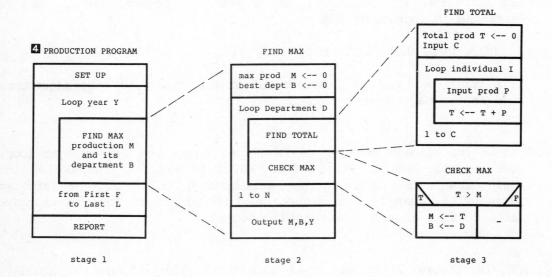

```
                                                            FIND TOTAL

                                                       Total prod T <-- 0
                                                       Input C

  PRODUCTION PROGRAM         FIND MAX                  Loop individual I
                                                           Input prod P
      SET UP            max prod  M <-- 0
                        best dept B <-- 0                   T <-- T + P
    Loop year Y
                        Loop Department D              1 to C
      FIND MAX
      production M          FIND TOTAL                       CHECK MAX
      and its
      department B          CHECK MAX               T      T > M      F

    from First F        1 to N                      M <-- T
    to Last  L                                      B <-- D        -
                        Output M,B,Y
      REPORT

    stage 1                stage 2                     stage 3
```

General (Nasty) Nested Loops

Most programs involving nested loops are not so simple as the previously nested loops. Now we will consider such general "nasty" loops. The understanding and creation of complex loop structures is simplest when done top-down in stages, so that each stage shows only one loop.

FAIR PAY, of figure 1, shows the nesting of two loops (and a choice) done in four stages. It describes a pay problem where overtime is paid for all hours over eight worked in a day. The first stage (or top level) consists of a single block which breaks out into a single loop at the next stage. This loop over each person P first must GET the hours and then compute the PAY. GET is then considered by itself, looping over the seven days of the week D, to accumulate the hours (both regular hours R and extra hours X). The accumulation of these two sums is then broken out at yet another stage as a choice form. Similarly PAY could be broken down further. If all of these stages were combined into one large stage, then the nesting would appear complex; but viewed as stages the whole seems more simple.

PRODUCTION is a program to analyse the manufacture (or sales) of items made by individuals in a company, over some years. The production (count of items, or dollar amount) is shown by the data of figure 2, involving two years and three departments with varying numbers of individuals. The main goal is to find the department with the maximum total sales each year. The typical trace of figure 3 shows the input of the data; notice its structured form (with indentation), which reflects the structure of the data. Actually such large amounts of data would not usually be input in the "conversational" mode, but from a data file stored on tapes or disks.

Stage 1 shows only a set-up, a looping from the first year F to the last year L, followed by a report of results. Within this first loop the maximum product is computed and further refined in stage two.

Stage 2 shows how the maximum total production M is computed by looping over all departments D from 1 to N. Within this loop it finds the total production T of each department, and then compares it to the maximum M (when necessary, replacing the maximum M and the best department B). After this it outputs the maximum production, and the best department of that year.

Stage 3 finds the total production T by looping and accumulating the production P of each individual I of the C individuals.

All these three stages could be "pushed together" into one big program, but this would hide the basic simplicity of the program. Also, when in the form of stages, it is simpler to modify. For example, we could find instead the maximum total production per person within each department by comparing the ratio T/C in the choice form. Similarly we could count the total number of people, accumulate the total production, and could compute the best production over all the years (not just for each year). Such modifications are often made after a program is written, so it helps to write it with this possible modification in mind.

Notice that this example involves four very different entities: time (in years), organizations (departments), individuals (people), and items (production). When four such diverse entities are mixed in a program, the result could be great confusion. Creating in stages (levels) minimizes this confusion.

MORE NESTS: PLOTS

1 PLOTTING

$Y = x^2/3$

2 PRINTER PAPER

direction of printing

3

	X	1	2	3	4	5
Sample values	Y	1/3	4/3	3	16/3	25/3
	Q	0	1	3	5	8

4

Loop X

Compute Y
Q is quantized Y

PRINT A LINE
corresponding
to Q

next line

from 0 to 5

5

Loop S 0 to 10

Print
appropriate
mark

6 SINGLE PLOT
of Y vs X

T   S = Q   F

Output "*"   Output " "

blank

7 Extended plot of two graphs

f[x]

$y = x^2$

$z = k*x$

X

8 DOUBLE PLOT
of Y and Z vs X

T   S = Q   F

T   S = Q2   F

Output "*"   Output "+"   Output " "

See also PASCAL B-30

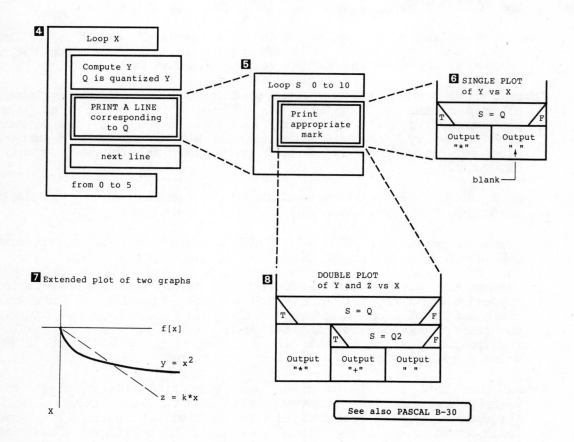
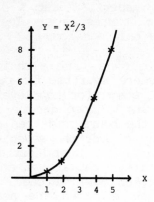
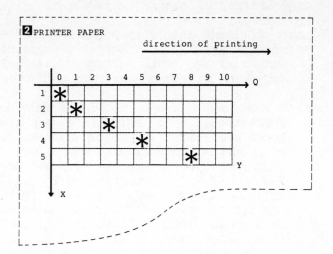

More Nests and Plots

Doubly nested loops are very convenient for two-dimensional output of tables, grids, calendars, graphs and plots.

SCAN, for example, shown below, is an algorithm to move and print in the pattern that humans usually use for reading or scanning: left to right along a row and proceeding downwards. The SCAN algorithm prints consecutive numbers as it scans this grid pattern for five rows and seven columns. This output can be viewed as a simple calendar.

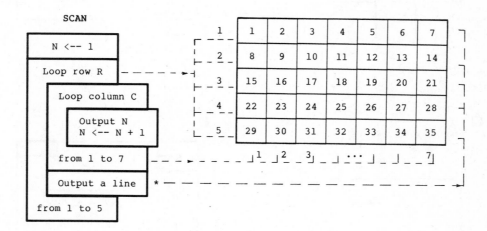

PLOT

Two-dimensional plots of formulas such as

$$Y = X^2/3$$

can be created by printing marks on a grid as shown in figure 1. Actually it is more convenient to plot this on its side as shown in figure 2. Then each row contains only one mark (a star * in this case). It will be convenient to view the printer head (or cursor) as "marching" row by row from top to bottom, and in each row from left to right.

The diagram of figure 3 shows how the values of the output Y are "quantized" or put into integers Q by the process of rounding.

The algorithm of figure 4 shows the top view of the plotting. It loops through the various values of X, first computing Y, then quantizing it to Q, and then printing a line corresponding to Q.

Figure 5 shows a refinement of the sub-algorithm which prints a line. The printing head marches, stepping S from 0 to 10. If S equals Q, then a mark is output; otherwise a blank is output.

Such a plot may be extended by printing headers, marking the axes, and even "scaling" any given values to fit onto a page. It can also be extended to plot another formula as shown in figure 7 by the slight modification shown in figure 8. Extensions to three or more formulas are done similarly.

SUB-PROGRAMS: Data Space View

1 Data flow diagram

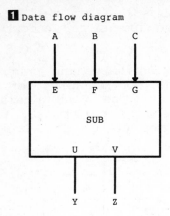

2 Data Space diagram

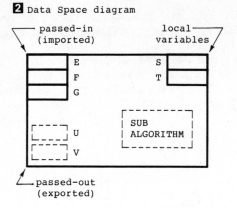

3

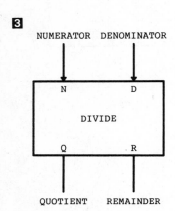

4 DIVIDE(N,D, Q,R)

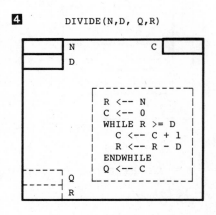

```
R <-- N
C <-- 0
WHILE R >= D
    C <-- C + 1
    R <-- R - D
ENDWHILE
Q <-- C
```

5

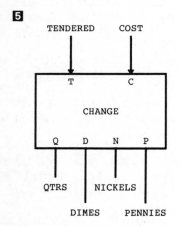

6 CHANGE(T,C, Q,D,N,P)

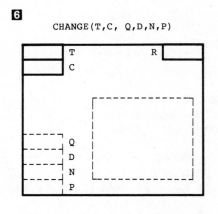

SUPER SUB-PROGRAMS: Data Space Diagrams

When considering sub-programs previously, we concentrated on the flow of
control and the flow of data. Now we will concentrate on the space
occupied by the data, and how the data values are communicated from
one space to another. As an example we will consider the DIVIDE
sub-program which is useful in many algorithms such as LEAP,
CHANGE, SECONDS, and DECBIN (decimal to binary conversion).

DATA SPACE DIAGRAMS show the variables associated with each
sub-program. A general algorithm is shown in figure 1 with its
corresponding data space diagram in figure 2. A particular sub-
program DIVIDE is shown in figures 3 and 4.

LOCAL variables are accessible only within a sub-program, and are drawn
at the upper right of the data space diagrams. The local variables
have no meaning (are undefined) outside the sub-program. This
serves to hide or protect any temporary variables which should not be
accessible from the outside. All communication between sub-programs
should be done by parameters.

PARAMETERS, or arguments, passed-in and passed-out of a sub-program
are drawn at the left of a data space diagram. Parameters passed-in
(imported) are drawn as boxes at the top left, and parameters
passed-out (exported) are shown as dotted boxes at the bottom left.

DIVIDE, for example, is a sub-program having a local variable C (the
loop counter), two input parameters N and D (Numerator and
Denominator), and two output parameters Q and R (Quotient and
Remainder), as shown in figure 4.

CHANGE, a sub-program of figures 5 and 6, has an amount tendered T
and a cost C which are passed-in, and the number of quarters Q,
dimes D, nickels N, and pennies P passed-out. There is also a
local variable R, representing the remaining money (at each stage).

Solid boxes (for local variables and input parameters) represent actual
locations where the values are stored. The dotted boxes for the
output parameters refer to actual locations outside of the
sub-program.

If CHANGE were a main program, then there would be no parameters passed
in or out of it; all the values would be local (and redrawn at the
right). The variables of a main program are called GLOBAL; they can
be accessed by any sub-programs.

PASSING parameters, using the notation of "pass-in" and "pass-out" is
often viewed as being too general. Instead we will use the notation
"pass by value" for pass-in, and "pass by reference" for pass-out.

MORE ON SUBS: Behavior

1 DATA FLOW DIAGRAM

```
   A + B      2
     |        |
     v        v
 +----------------+
 |  N        D    |
 |    DIVIDE      |
 |  Q        R    |
 +----------------+
     |        |
     C        D
```

2 ALGORITHM

```
+----------------------+
| R <-- N, C <-- 0     |
+----------------------+
|     R >= D           |
| +------------------+ |
| | C <-- C + 1      | |
| +------------------+ |
| | R <-- R - D      | |
| +------------------+ |
+----------------------+
|     Q <-- C          |
+----------------------+
```

3 DATA SPACE DIAGRAM

DIVIDE(N,D,Q,R)

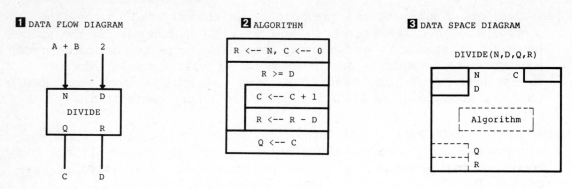

4 BEHAVIOR (SEMANTICS) OF SUB-CALL

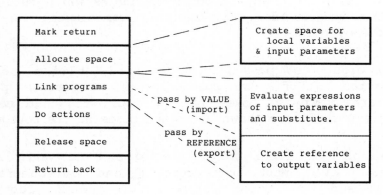

| Mark return |
| Allocate space |
| Link programs |
| Do actions |
| Release space |
| Return back |

Create space for local variables & input parameters

pass by VALUE (import)

Evaluate expressions of input parameters and substitute.

pass by REFERENCE (export)

Create reference to output variables

5 AVERAGE EXAMPLE

```
MEAN2              A  | 2 |
                   B  | 5 |
                   C  | 3 |
                   D  | 1 |

A <-- 2
B <-- 5

+------------------+
| DIVIDE(A+B,2,C,D)|
+------------------+

OUTPUT C
IF D=0 THEN
OUTPUT 'EXACTLY'
```

DIVIDE(A + B, 2, C, D)
      ‿
      7

DIVIDE(N , D, Q, R)

enter sub

6 DIVIDE(N,D, Q,R)

```
| 7 | N      C | 0123 |
| 2 | D

R <-- N
C <-- 0
WHILE R >= D
   C <-- C + 1
   R <-- R - D
ENDWHILE
Q <-- C

              Q
              R
```

return

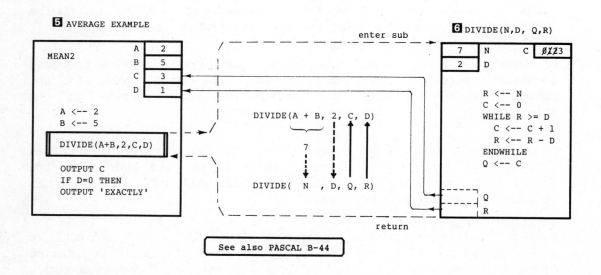

See also PASCAL B-44

Parameter Passing (by Value and Reference)

There are two main methods of passing parameters between programs: pass by Value (pass in) and pass by Reference (pass out). They will be illustrated by a simple program MEAN which uses the DIVIDE sub-program, and by a later program CHANGE, which also uses DIVIDE.

DIVIDE is repeated in figures 1, 2 and 3, in three different ways, all of which are useful. The MEAN main program of figure 4 simply inputs two values A and B, then calls DIVIDE to produce the average value C and a message "EXACTLY" only when the output is exactly a whole (integer) value.

General behavior of sub-programs is shown in figure 4. It will be illustrated with the AVERAGE example of figure 5.

First, when the sub-program is called, the point of return is marked. Then space is allocated for all the imported variables and local variables (N, D, and C), but not for the exported ones (Q and R). The two programs are linked by pairing the actual and formal parameters, as shown between figures 5 and 6. The expression A + B is evaluated to 7, and copied into N; the value 2 is substituted into variable D of the sub-program. Also, the formal output variable Q is made to refer to the actual variable C, and the remainder R is made to point to variable D of the main program.

Finally, the actions are performed. When the output variables Q and R are modified, they affect the corresponding actual variables C and D outside in the main program. When the actions are completed, the data sub-space is released (deallocated), and the control returns to the main or calling program. The values of the sub-space become completely inaccessible.

Notice that the variable name D occurs in both the main program and the sub-program. It refers to a different variable in each, and causes no problems, because of the "protective" nature of sub-programs.

PASS-BY-VALUE (pass in) is the method of passing parameters (expressions) by evaluating and copying the value into a temporary space in the sub-program. If this value is then changed in the sub-program, it does not affect the original corresponding variable in the calling program. This "protects" the variables.

PASS-BY-REFERENCE (pass out) describes the passing of variables (not expressions) where the variables of the called sub-program refer to the actual variables of the calling program. Whenever the formal variables of the sub-program are changed, they change the corresponding actual variables in the calling or main program.

Deciding on which way to pass parameters is usually clear from the data flow diagram. Variables which are input (with arrows into the box) should be passed by value; variables which are output should be passed by reference. Variables which are both input and output (passed through) should be passed by reference, so that they can be modified (passed out). Many examples will follow to illustrate this.

PASS-BY-NAME is yet another method where an un-evaluated expression is substituted literally, and re-evaluated each time it is encountered. This method is not often used now.

Many programming languages (like Pascal) allow passing by both value and reference. However, some allow only passing by value (Lisp). Algol 60 allows passing by name. Some unfortunately require passing by reference only (Fortran), so greater care must be taken in the programs to protect variables. Passing by reference is also known as passing by address (or location).

CHANGE AS SUB

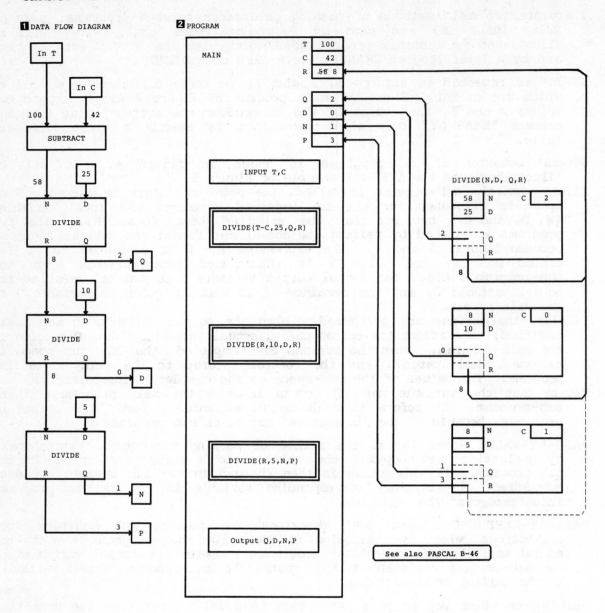

1 DATA FLOW DIAGRAM

2 PROGRAM

CHANGE Again with Sub-programs

Let us consider an algorithm CHANGE, which calls a sub-program a number of times. This algorithm inputs an amount tendered T and cost C, and outputs the number of quarters Q, dimes D, nickels N, and pennies P as shown in the data flow diagram of figure 1. The main algorithm calls the sub-program DIVIDE three different times.

The data space diagram of figure 2 shows snapshots of the sub-program calls. Notice that only one DIVIDE exists at any time. The first call of DIVIDE passes in the expression (T-C) and the constant 25 to be divided, and passes back the quotient Q, which is coincidentally called Q (for quarters) in the main program. It also passes back (returns) the remainder R of 8.

The second call to DIVIDE passes in the new remainder value R and the constant 10, returning a quotient of 0 as the number of dimes, and a remainder of 8. The correspondence between the actual parameters R, 10, D, R and the formal parameters N, D, Q, R is by their order of listing:

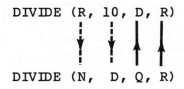

The third call passes in the remainder and the constant 5, and passes back the number of nickels N, and also the number of pennies P. Notice that in this last call, the R of the sub-program is not referring to the R of the main program (for the first time).

Note also that many of the same names refer to different data spaces. For example, C is the cost in the main program and is the counter in the sub-program. Also, D is the count of dimes in the main program, and also the denominator in the sub-program. Similarly, N represents nickels and numerator, and Q represents quarters and quotient. This extreme naming phenomenon could be very confusing for humans, but very meaningful for computers.

Usually such names are not chosen for confusion; but if they so happen to be chosen they cause no problem. In large programs where different people work on many parts, we need not insist that they know the names of all others' variables.

EXAMPLES OF PARAMETER PASSING

1 PASS IN ONLY

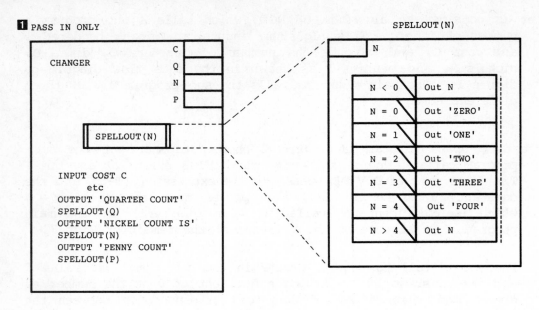

SPELLOUT(N)

```
CHANGER                    C
                           Q
                           N
                           P

              SPELLOUT(N)

    INPUT COST C
         etc
    OUTPUT 'QUARTER COUNT'
    SPELLOUT(Q)
    OUTPUT 'NICKEL COUNT IS'
    SPELLOUT(N)
    OUTPUT 'PENNY COUNT'
    SPELLOUT(P)
```

N	
N < 0	Out N
N = 0	Out 'ZERO'
N = 1	Out 'ONE'
N = 2	Out 'TWO'
N = 3	Out 'THREE'
N = 4	Out 'FOUR'
N > 4	Out N

2 PASS OUT ONLY

ENTERPOS(X)

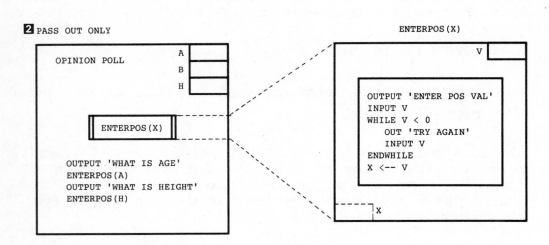

```
OPINION POLL               A
                           B
                           H

              ENTERPOS(X)

    OUTPUT 'WHAT IS AGE'
    ENTERPOS(A)
    OUTPUT 'WHAT IS HEIGHT'
    ENTERPOS(H)
```

```
                           V

    OUTPUT 'ENTER POS VAL'
    INPUT V
    WHILE V < 0
        OUT 'TRY AGAIN'
        INPUT V
    ENDWHILE
    X <-- V

                           X
```

3 PASS IN AND OUT

SORT2(P,Q,L,S)

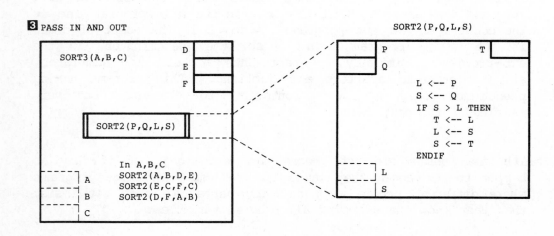

```
SORT3(A,B,C)               D
                           E
                           F

              SORT2(P,Q,L,S)

    In A,B,C
    SORT2(A,B,D,E)
A   SORT2(E,C,F,C)
    SORT2(D,F,A,B)
B

C
```

```
P                          T
Q

    L <-- P
    S <-- Q
    IF S > L THEN
        T <-- L
        L <-- S
        S <-- T
    ENDIF

                           L

                           S
```

More Parameter Passing

The various ways of passing parameters are shown in the four sub-programs that follow. One program (SPELLOUT) has only parameters that are passed in; another program (ENTERPOS) has only parameters that are passed out; a third (SORT3) has parameters that are passed through; SORT2 has some parameters that are passed in, and others that are passed out.

SPELLOUT(N) is a sub-program to output some small integer values, not as numbers but spelled out. Only numbers in the range 0 to 4 are spelled out in figure 1, but this could be extended easily. Here only one parameter, the number N, is passed into the program (by value). Nothing is passed out, but something is written out.

ENTERPOS(X) is a sub-program to enter a single positive value and assign it to variable X. The sub-program first prompts the user, inputs the value, and tests it, as shown in figure 2. While the value is not positive, the sub-program outputs a message and requests a new value. When a positive value is entered, the sub-program assigns it to the variable X of the calling program. Notice that the parameter X must be passed by reference, to affect the external variable. This allows the sub-program to be re-used to enter values into many different variables (such as Age, Height, etc.).

SORT3(A,B,C) is a sub-program to sort three values into non-decreasing order. It calls SORT2, and in turn it could be called by some other program. SORT3 has all parameters passed by reference; it takes the three values of A, B, and C and manipulates them so that they are in numerical order.

SORT2(P,Q, L,S) has two parameters P and Q passed in (by value), and two parameters L and S passed out (by reference), so that values of P and Q are not destroyed. It also has a local variable T, which is a temporary variable for swapping L and S when P and Q are out of order. Actually another sub-program SWAP could be used here for exchanging the values.

Here SORT2 could have been alternatively created, as SORT2(R,S), with only two parameters, both passed by reference (passed in and out). Similarly SORT3 could have been created with six parameters, as SORT3(A,B,C, L,M,S); the first three are passed in by value, and the last three are passed out by reference.

THREE VIEWS OF SUB-PROGRAMS

1 ACTIONS AND SUB-ACTIONS

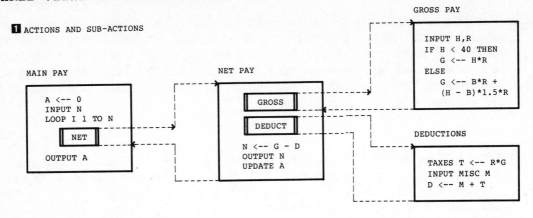

GROSS PAY

```
INPUT H,R
IF H < 40 THEN
    G <-- H*R
ELSE
    G <-- B*R +
    (H - B)*1.5*R
```

MAIN PAY

```
A <-- 0
INPUT N
LOOP I 1 TO N
    NET
OUTPUT A
```

NET PAY

```
GROSS
DEDUCT
N <-- G - D
OUTPUT N
UPDATE A
```

DEDUCTIONS

```
TAXES T <-- R*G
INPUT MISC M
D <-- M + T
```

2 DATA AND SUB-DATA SPACES

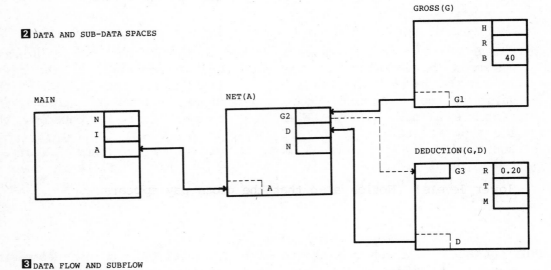

GROSS(G)

	H	
	R	
	B	40

| | G1 |

MAIN

	N	
	I	
	A	

NET(A)

G2		
D		
N		

| A |

DEDUCTION(G,D)

	G3	R	0.20
		T	
		M	

| | D |

3 DATA FLOW AND SUBFLOW

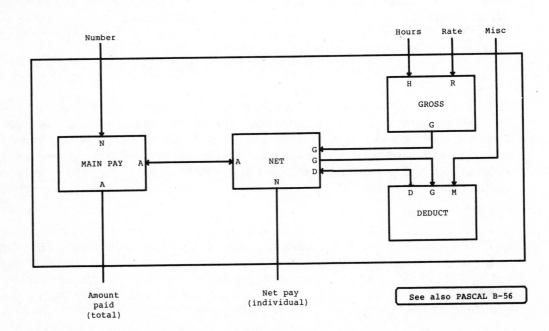

Number   Hours   Rate   Misc

GROSS

H   R

G

MAIN PAY   N   A

A   NET   A

N

DEDUCT

D   G   M

G
G
D

Amount
paid
(total)

Net pay
(individual)

See also PASCAL B-56

Bigger Subs: Three Views

Until now we have considered small programs and sub-programs, with little interaction among them. Now we will consider a more complex system to illustrate the inter-relations among actions, data spaces and data flows. The example used is BIGPAY, an extended payroll problem; it is sufficiently complex to suggest the power of sub-programs in large systems.

ACTIONS and sub-actions, of figure 1, are shown in a tree-like break-out with the dotted lines representing flow of control by calling of sub-programs. The MAIN program has input the number of employees N, and simply loops through all of them, calling the NETPAY algorithm, and ultimately outputs the total amount A paid out. The NETPAY program calls GROSS and DEDUCTIONS to get the Net Pay N, outputs it, and updates the amount A (of the MAIN). The GROSS program computes the gross pay G in the usual way. The DEDUCTION sub-program inputs the miscellaneous deduction M and adds this to the taxes T, which are a simple percentage rate R of the gross pay.

DATA SPACES and sub-spaces, of figure 2, show how data is distributed among the sub-programs. Notice particularly that the main program requires only three main variables (the count N, the loop variable I, and the amount A) and need not have access to other variables at lower levels! Notice also that the gross pay appears three times as G1, G2, and G3 (which could be referred to as simply G in all cases). The variable G1 is computed in GROSS and passed out to NET as G2. It is also passed into DEDUCT as G3 for use in computing the taxes.

It is important to see that DEDUCT did not directly get the gross pay from GROSS, but indirectly through NET at a higher level. This way, DEDUCT cannot modify the gross pay (G1 or G2), but only use it (copied as G3). This sub-dividing and hiding of data space is very significant in large systems.

DATA FLOWS and sub-flows, of figure 3, show how the external data values flow in and out, as well as how the parameters are passed in and out. The external inputs and outputs are shown by vertical arrows, the passage of parameters by horizontal arrows.

TREES essentially underlie the top-down structure of such interconnected sub-programs. Other representations of such forms are contours, considered next.

The boxes and sub-boxes (or modules) provide a unified and "modular" view of actions, data space, and data flow, which can reduce the complexity of large programs.

CONTOURS AND BINDING

1 Contour Diagram of PAY

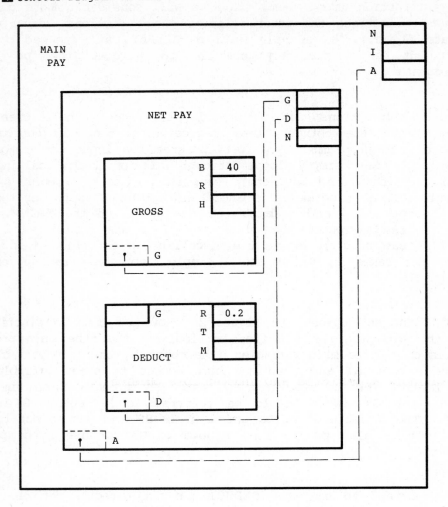

2 BINDING TABLE

Sub \ Name	describes "meaning" of Names in Sub-programs according to the "most closely nested" rule			
	GROSS PAY	DEDUCT	NET PAY	MAIN PAY
H	Hours	none	none	none
T	none	Taxes	none	none
G	Gross pay	Gross pay	Gross pay	none
R	Pay rate	Tax rate	none	none
N	Net pay	Net pay	Net pay	Number
A	Amount	Amount	Amount	Amount
I	Individual	Individual	Individual	Individual

Block Beauty (Binding and Contours)

BLOCKS are segments of programs that may have their own data space associated with them. Large programs consisting of sub-programs can be viewed as blocks arranged in contours as shown in figure 1 for the previous PAY program. The contours are nested sub-sets which form the outer limits of each sub-program and do not overlap, but enclose one another. The contours indicate variables, showing which names are associated with which objects. Binding is the term describing the association between names and objects.

BLOCK STRUCTURED languages (such as Algol, Pascal, PL/I) use blocks for sharing (communication of values) and also for privacy (hiding of values). In these languages, a name refers to the object (data space) in that block. If it does not have a space in that block, it "looks out" into the next bigger block until it finds it. This method of "reaching out" (never reaching in) is called the "most closely nested" binding rule. It is the most natural way of allowing access to only that data which a sub-program "needs to know." It is also simple to implement using stacks.

For example, the variable R when used in the GROSS sub-program refers to the rate of pay of a person; when used in the DEDUCT sub-program, it refers to the tax rate. If, however, R is accessed (say, output) in the NETPAY sub-program, then it would be undefined, for it does not appear in outer contours. This keeps the inner variable R protected and inaccessible outside.

Similarly, when variable N appears in the GROSS, DEDUCT, or NETPAY sub-programs, it refers to the Net pay; but when N is used in the main BIGPAY program, it refers to the number of people to be paid. If there were a variable B (for balance) in the main program, then it would have that meaning in the DEDUCT, NETPAY, and main BIGPAY, but B still would refer to the break-point value within the GROSS program.

BINDING TABLES show how names are associated with data spaces in various blocks. Figure 2 shows the binding table for the previous PAY program. Each entry shows the meaning (if any) of a name according to the "most closely nested rule" which usually corresponds to only the information that the block "needs to know." Other rules (such as "most recently called") are less common, but still used in some languages (such as APL).

GLOBAL variables are those defined in the MAIN program and since this is the outermost program, they can be accessed from all the sub-programs. This may seem useful; for example, the individual I could be accessed directly from the NETPAY program (without passing as a parameter) and actually output on the paycheck. However, this variable I could also be changed by an error in any of the sub-programs. Such an error could be very difficult to find. In general, global variables are too accessible to be used directly. It is considerably better programming practice to pass all variables as parameters.

DATES SUB-PROGRAMS

1 ELAPSED DAYS

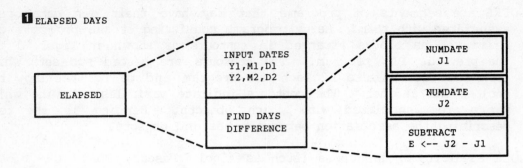

```
                          ┌──────────────────┐    ┌──────────────────────┐
                          │  INPUT DATES     │    │      NUMDATE         │
                          │  Y1,M1,D1        │    │      J1              │
   ┌──────────────┐       │  Y2,M2,D2        │    ├──────────────────────┤
   │              │       ├──────────────────┤    │      NUMDATE         │
   │   ELAPSED    │       │  FIND DAYS       │    │      J2              │
   │              │       │  DIFFERENCE      │    ├──────────────────────┤
   └──────────────┘       └──────────────────┘    │    SUBTRACT          │
                                                   │    E <-- J2 - J1     │
                                                   └──────────────────────┘
```

2 NUMDATE
(JULIAN)

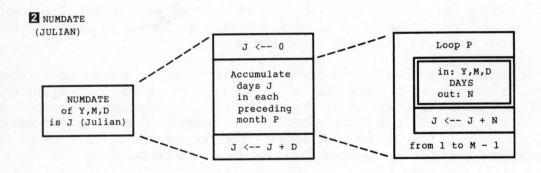

```
                          ┌──────────────────┐    ┌──────────────────────┐
                          │   J <-- 0        │    │      Loop P          │
                          ├──────────────────┤    │  ┌────────────────┐  │
   ┌──────────────┐       │  Accumulate      │    │  │ in: Y,M,D      │  │
   │  NUMDATE     │       │  days J          │    │  │    DAYS        │  │
   │  of Y,M,D    │       │  in each         │    │  │ out: N         │  │
   │  is J (Julian)│      │  preceding       │    │  ├────────────────┤  │
   └──────────────┘       │  month P         │    │  │  J <-- J + N   │  │
                          ├──────────────────┤    │  └────────────────┘  │
                          │   J <-- J + D    │    │  from 1 to M - 1     │
                          └──────────────────┘    └──────────────────────┘
```

3 UPDATE1

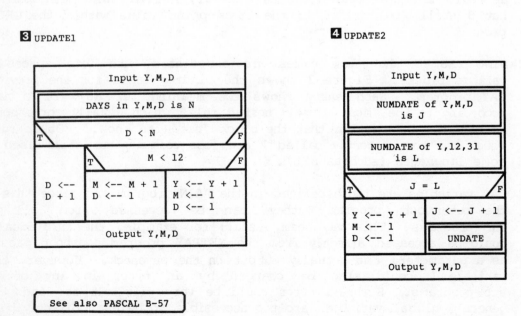

```
┌─────────────────────────────────────────────┐
│              Input Y,M,D                      │
├─────────────────────────────────────────────┤
│  ┌─────────────────────────────────────────┐ │
│  │       DAYS in Y,M,D is N                 │ │
│  └─────────────────────────────────────────┘ │
├──┬──────────────────────────────────────────┤
│ T│            D < N                         F│
│  ├──┬─────────────────────────────────────┬─┤
│  │ T│          M < 12                    F │ │
│ D<──│M <-- M + 1 │ Y <-- Y + 1            │ │
│ D+1 │D <-- 1     │ M <-- 1                │ │
│     │            │ D <-- 1                │ │
├─────┴────────────┴────────────────────────┤ │
│              Output Y,M,D                  │ │
└─────────────────────────────────────────────┘
```

4 UPDATE2

```
┌─────────────────────────────────────────────┐
│              Input Y,M,D                      │
├─────────────────────────────────────────────┤
│  ┌─────────────────────────────────────────┐ │
│  │       NUMDATE of Y,M,D                   │ │
│  │            is J                          │ │
│  └─────────────────────────────────────────┘ │
│  ┌─────────────────────────────────────────┐ │
│  │       NUMDATE of Y,12,31                 │ │
│  │            is L                          │ │
│  └─────────────────────────────────────────┘ │
├──────────────────────────────────────────────┤
│ T              J = L                        F │
│  Y <-- Y + 1        │  J <-- J + 1           │
│  M <-- 1            │  ┌──────────────┐       │
│  D <-- 1            │  │   UNDATE     │       │
│                     │  └──────────────┘       │
├──────────────────────────────────────────────┤
│              Output Y,M,D                      │
└──────────────────────────────────────────────┘
```

```
┌──────────────────────────┐
│  See also PASCAL B-57    │
└──────────────────────────┘
```

Building with Big Blocks: DATES

In programming there is often a temptation to create all algorithms from their smallest building blocks (starting from "scratch"). A significant alternative is to create algorithms out of larger "abstract" boxes which are not yet defined. Then later these boxes can be created, when we know what is expected of them.

DATES, consisting of a year Y, month M, and day D, are interesting objects that often must be manipulated.

ELAPSED is a sample algorithm we will create to determine the number of days between any two given dates (such as two birthdates) in a year. Proceeding top-down we would first input the two dates, indicating first the year, then the month and finally the day. The elapsed time between the dates could be determined easily if we knew the date as the number of days from the first of the year. We can assume that we have such a program, called NUMDATE, which converts a given date Y,M,D into the number J of days from January 1. This number of days from the first of the year is often called the Julian date. For example, March 15, 1984, has a Julian date J of 75, (31 + 29 + 15). So to find the elapsed time, we simply subtract the Julian dates of the two given days.

NUMDATE can now be created, for we know how it will be used. The top-down creation of it is shown in figure 2. It consists simply of a loop which accumulates the days in all the preceeding months P, and also the days D in month M. Notice that this requires knowing the number of days in any month, which is provided by the sub-program DAYS. DAYS, considered previously, has the simple form of a case statement. Notice also that DAYS may also call another sub-program LEAP to determine if February has 28 or 29 days.

UPDATE is another useful operation to change a particular date to its next date, one day later. Usually the day D is simply bumped, but sometimes the month and year must also be changed. Two algorithms for doing UPDATE are given in figures 3 and 4.

UPDATE1 starts with the details, first finding the number of days in the given month, and if necessary tests also if the month is the last.

UPDATE2 starts at the other end, determining first if the given date is the last day of the year, and if not then it just adds 1 to the Julian date, and calls UNDATE, which recreates the corresponding year, month, and day. This method again shows the use of another abstract box UNDATE, which is still to be created. Many such sub-algorithms involving dates are given in the set of problems following this chapter, and in the set of projects following the Pascal appendix.

ITERATION AND RECURSION

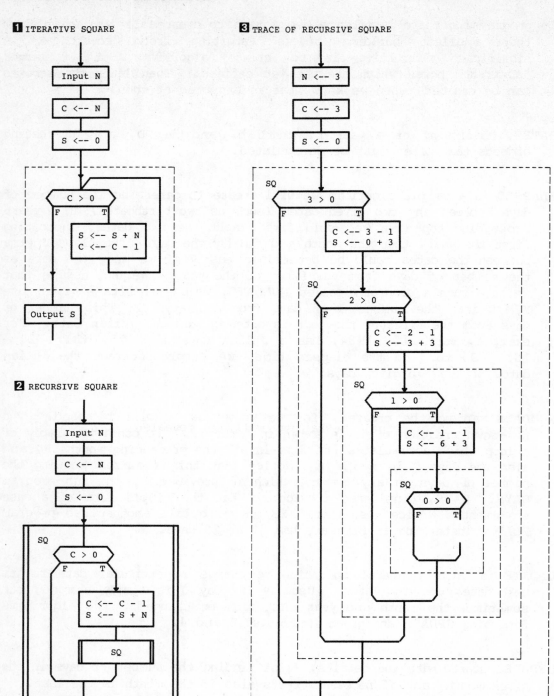

1 ITERATIVE SQUARE

Input N

C <-- N

S <-- 0

C > 0
F   T

S <-- S + N
C <-- C - 1

Output S

2 RECURSIVE SQUARE

Input N

C <-- N

S <-- 0

SQ

C > 0
F   T

C <-- C - 1
S <-- S + N

SQ

Output S

3 TRACE OF RECURSIVE SQUARE

N <-- 3

C <-- 3

S <-- 0

SQ

3 > 0
F   T

C <-- 3 - 1
S <-- 0 + 3

SQ

2 > 0
F   T

C <-- 2 - 1
S <-- 3 + 3

SQ

1 > 0
F   T

C <-- 1 - 1
S <-- 6 + 3

SQ

0 > 0
F   T

Output 9

RECURSION: Self-Referencing Sub-programs

Recursion is a process where a sub-program calls itself, or a
   sub-program is defined in terms of itself. Such a self-referring
   process may seem unusual initially, but many objects and algorithms
   are more naturally described recursively. Recursion is possible in
   most modern languages (such as Pascal, PL/I, and APL), but not
   Fortran or Basic. It is also available in many lower level assembly
   languages.

Recursion in its simplest form could be viewed as an alternative to the
   loop (or iterative) form. For example, the square of an integer N
   is done iteratively in figure 1. It could be done recursively by a
   choice and a sub-form (which calls itself) as in figure 2.

Tracing of this recursive square is shown in figure 3 for a value N = 3.
   The trace takes the form of a sub-program nested within itself many
   times. Each call of the sub form yields a contour (shown dotted),
   resembling levels on a map (stair-trace). On entry to a sub-program
   we step down a level, and then on exit we step up again. It is
   important to have a "lowest" level, a stopping point (a condition,
   such as C = 0), for otherwise the algorithm would be "bottomless" or
   unending.

The method or mechanism for doing recursion is not necessary to know at
   this time; it is only necessary to know that after a call (and
   subsequent detour), the control returns "to the sender". On the
   next page the actual mechanism will be revealed, but now it is
   important not to confuse what is being done (recursion) with how it
   is being done (mechanism).

Another example of a recursive sub-algorithm follows. It repeatedly
   outputs curses (re-curses?); the number of curses depends on the
   input value.

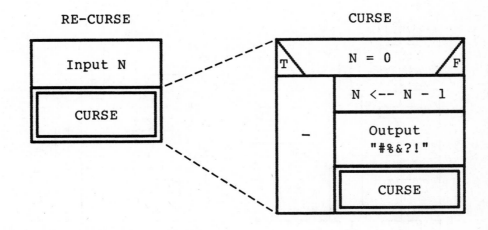

RE-CURSE   CURSE

RECURSIVE BEHAVIOR: Modified SQUARE

1 RECURSIVE SQUARE (Modified)

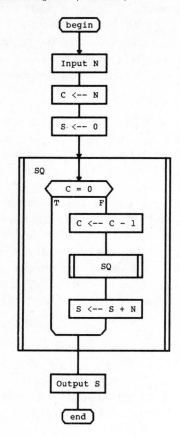

2 SQUARE PROGRAM

```
1   MAIN PROG
2   INPUT N
3   C <-- N
4   S <-- 0
5   CALL SQ
6   OUTPUT S
7   END MAIN
```

```
10   SUB SQ
11   IF C ≠ 0 THEN
12       C <-- C - 1
13       CALL SQ
14       S <-- S + N
15   ENDIF
16   ENDSUB
```

3 TRACE OF RECURSIVE SQUARE
with stack of return points

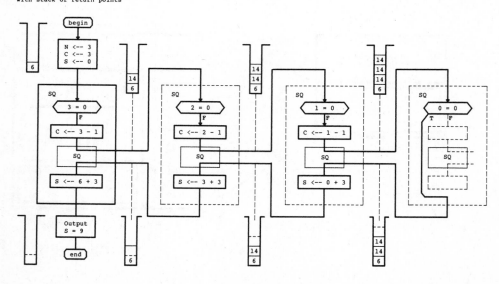

Recursive Behavior and Stacks

STACKS are the basic mechanisms involved in recursion. A stack can be viewed as simply a "top hat" where the first object put in (pushed) is the last one taken out (popped). Only the top object is accessible, and this happens to be the most recent item put on the stack. A sequence of pushes and pops are shown at the bottom of this page. Notice that this series of pushes followed by the series of pops simply serves to pop the values in the reverse order that they were pushed. More on stacks and their implementation is shown on page 6-35.

Sub-programs use stacks for saving return points (or addresses). Calling a sub-program causes a return address to be pushed onto a stack just before the "detour" to the sub-program. A return from the sub-program causes the return address to be popped off the stack to indicate where the control continues.

Recursion is illustrated by a flowchart of figure 1; its behavior is not very clear. It is also illustrated by pseudo-code in figure 2. This algorithm is a slight modification of the previous SQUARE algorithm. It is a generalization, with a computation performed both before and after the call to the sub-program.

Behavior of this SQUARE program can be seen from figure 2. When the square sub-program SQ is called from the main program (in line 5), it pushes the next line number (address 6) onto the stack, and then it jumps to the sub-program of line 10. It continues along this sub-program until it reaches another call (at line 13). It then saves the return point (14) on the stack, and jumps to itself again (at line 10). Additional calls cause additional stacking of the return points.

On reaching the return or end of the sub-program (on line 16), the control returns to the last return point, at the top of the stack (which is point 14). Then this top is popped off the stack. Further returns cause additional popping of the return points. The last return is to the first point (6), which returns to the main program.

Tracing of this entire algorithm for an input value N = 3 is shown in figure 3. It is drawn out as if each algorithm were calling a copy of the original algorithm. The status of the stack of return points is shown alongside each copy. It would be helpful now to read again the previous two paragraphs while referring to figure 3.

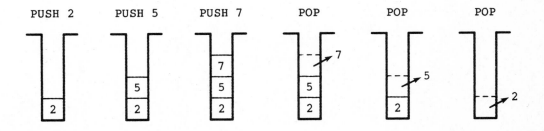

FACTORIAL: Structure and Definition

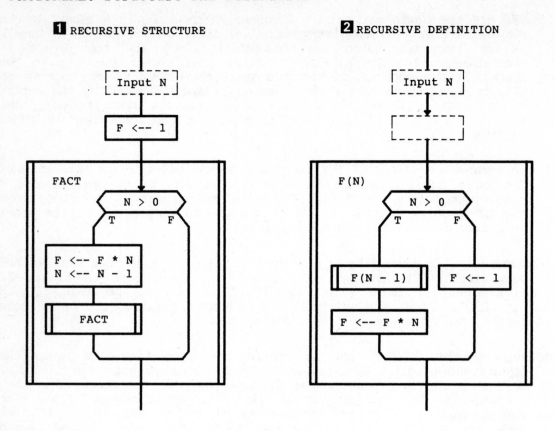

1 RECURSIVE STRUCTURE

Input N

F <-- 1

FACT

N > 0
T   F

F <-- F * N
N <-- N - 1

FACT

2 RECURSIVE DEFINITION

Input N

F(N)

N > 0
T   F

F(N - 1)   F <-- 1

F <-- F * N

3 Fibonacci Tree: evaluation of F(4)

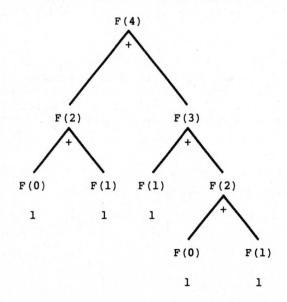

F(4)
+

F(2)   F(3)
+   +

F(0)   F(1)   F(1)   F(2)
1   1   1   +

F(0)   F(1)
1   1

Recursive Definition   (versus Recursive Structure)

Recursion has described a loop structure where a sub-form calls itself, but it can also be used for defining actions or objects. In a recursive definition, something is defined in terms of itself. It is a circular-looking definition, but it has a stopping condition to halt the "circulating." Some common examples of recursive definitions follow.

1. A descendant of a person is either the child of the person, or the descendant of a child of that person.

2. A queue is either a single object or a queue followed by a single object.

3. An integer is either a digit or an integer followed by a digit.

4. The factorial F(N) of a nonnegative integer N is either

$$F(N) = N * F(N-1) \quad \text{if } N > 0 \text{ or}$$
$$F(N) = 1 \qquad\qquad \text{if } N = 0.$$

Behavior of the recursive factorial function can be seen by applying it to some simple example, such as N = 4.

$$
\begin{aligned}
F(4) &= 4 * F(3) \\
&= 4 * 3 * F(2) \\
&= 4 * 3 * 2 * F(1) \\
&= 4 * 3 * 2 * 1 * F(0) \\
&= 4 * 3 * 2 * 1 * 1 \\
&= 24
\end{aligned}
$$

The diagrams of figures 1 and 2 contrast the flowcharts for factorial, first when given as a recursive structure and secondly as a recursive definition. Notice that the recursive definition is complete, including the initialization (F <-- 1).

In general, recursive definition involves a relation which generates a chain of stages, and a condition which stops this chain. This type of definition provides a brief way of describing an infinite set of objects, as will become clearer with more examples. It will also become a very natural way of defining many objects.

PRODUCT P(B,C) of two non-negative integers B and C can be defined recursively as:

$$P(B,C) = \begin{cases} 0 & \text{if } C = 0 \\ B + P(B,C-1) & \text{if } C > 0 \end{cases}$$

FIBONACCI'S Function F(X) can be defined recursively as:

$$F(X) = \begin{cases} 1 & \text{if } X = 0 \\ 1 & \text{if } X = 1 \\ F(X-2) + F(X-1) & \text{if } X > 1 \end{cases}$$

This could be evaluated for any value X (such as X = 4) by the previous method, or alternatively by a tree as shown in figure 3. Trees and recursion often go together. Notice that this sub-program calls itself twice within itself.

RECURSIVE SQUARE DEFINITION

1 Control view

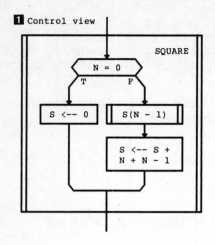

2 Data Space View

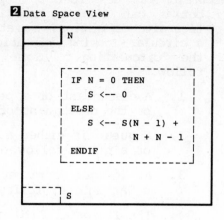

3 TRACE OF SQUARE

Inverted stacks show input parameters (& local variables)
Other stacks (of return addresses) are not shown.

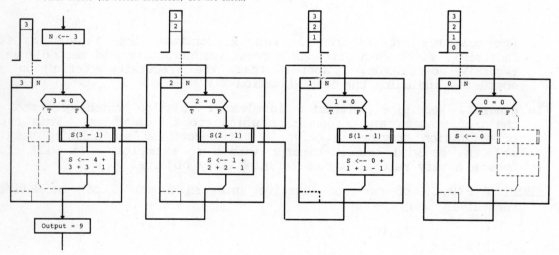

Creating Recursive Programs

Creating a recursive definition of a program, like creating an iterative program, is not always simple. It usually requires some thought, but sometimes simple algebraic methods help. For example, let us define the square S(N) of a positive integer N. We would want to find some relation between S(N) and S(N-1). Actually, it is easier to relate S(N+1) to S(N).

First recall that

$$S(N) = N^2,$$

$$\text{so } S(N+1) = (N + 1)^2$$

$$= N^2 + 2*N + 1$$

$$= S(N) + 2*N + 1 \quad \text{done!}$$

Now substituting N-1 for N yields

$$S(N-1+1) = S(N-1) + 2*(N-1) + 1$$

$$\text{or} \quad S(N) = S(N-1) + 2*N - 1$$

$$= S(N-1) + N + N - 1$$

(avoiding product)

This relation along with a stopping condition (value 0 at N = 0) defines another Square algorithm as shown in figures 1 and 2. Compare it to the previous two recursive squares; note that it does not have any intermediate variables!

SQUARE is shown from a control view in figure 1, and from a data space view in figure 2. Notice that the input parameter N is passed by value; in the previous examples, all variables were assumed global.

Tracing of this recursive square is shown in figure 3. Notice especially that the parameter N has a different value with each call. This is accomplished again by stacks (a stack of parameter values). The value required at any instant is that value at the top of the stack. The stack of return points is not shown in the figure.

In summary, recursively defined sub-programs involve stacks in two ways: one to save return points, and the other to save parameter values. What is important is that we (the programmers) do not need to be concerned with the stack mechanism. We need not confuse what is being done (recursion) with how it is being done (with stacks). Leave unto the computer what is the computer's ... .

In the next chapter recursion will be used to define objects.

REVIEW: of Chapter 5

BIGGER BLOCKS: More, Different, Deeper Concepts

Bigger blocks of many kinds were introduced in this chapter. Bigger is not always better.

Bigger data was in the form of external data, and could be very voluminous.

Bigger Maxes, Means, and other algorithms were simply extensions of the original algorithms. The concept of a terminating value is very common, but the terminating "sandwich" with terminator at the beginning as well as the end of the data is not common.

Bigger Choices, such as the CASE form, are possible either by nesting smaller choices or by cascading them.

Bigger Loop forms given by the FOR loop are convenient when counting is involved, but are also restrictive. An alternative UNTIL form is also possible.

Bigger nests of loops are potentially difficult to create and understand, but, when viewed one at a time on a proper top-down break-out diagram, they seem simpler.

Bigger choices of data types here include characters, logical truth values, and strings. Other data types may be created by the programmer.

Bigger sub-program blocks are perhaps the most important concepts introduced in this chapter. The sub-blocks are considered from the view of their data space along with their control flow and data flow. Recursion is also introduced here.

Bigger objects, including arrays and records, will be considered in the next chapter. Recursion will also be applied to these objects.

PROBLEMS: on Chapter 5

1. A CASE OF MAX, MID, and MAJ
    Create a case structure to compute M, which is:
    a. the maximum value of three variables A, B, and C.
    b. the middle value of three, A, B, and C (not the mean).
    c. the majority value of three binary variables A, B, and C,
        each having values 0 or 1.

2. SECOND MAX
    Modify the BIG MAX algorithm to find the second highest value S
        (if all values are different).

3. MANY MAX
    Modify the BIG MAX algorithm to find the number of values N
        which are maximum (when some values may be repeated).

4. MAXMIN
    Modify the MEAN program (with sandwich of page 5-5) to compute both
    the maximum and minimum values.

5. QUADRANT
    Create an algorithm which accepts the coordinates X and Y of some point
    and indicates which quadrant (1,2,3 or 4) the point falls into. If the
    point falls on an axis, the quadrant should be indicated as value zero.

6. BAD AVERAGE
    The given flowchart was created to compute the average of any number N
    of values. Analyse or criticize it from the following viewpoints:
    a) Logic...Does it do what it is to do? In all cases?
    b) Structure..Is it structured properly, in the 4 forms?
    c) Efficiency...Is it wasteful of time, instructions?
    d) Accuracy.....Is the output value precise, exact?
    e) Convenience....Would you like to use it?
    f) Others?

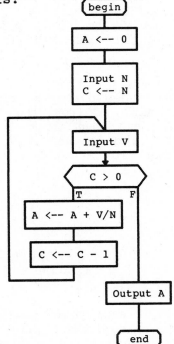

AVERAGE PROBLEMS

1. **BAT**

   The "batting average" of a baseball game or any other hit-or-miss activity is defined as the accumulated number of successes (hits, in baseball) divided by the total number of attempts (times at bat). Create an algorithm to compute the batting average for a sequence of pairs of values S,T (S representing successes, T representing times). A typical sequence follows (and ends for negative S).

INPUT		OUTPUT
S	T	B
1	4	.25
2	2	.50
1	4	.40
..	..	..

2. **GAS**

   Create an algorithm which inputs sequences of two values M and G representing the mileage M and gallons of gasoline G at a succession of refills. The algorithm is to compute and output the immediate average miles-per-gallon (labelled S for short range), and also the overall average mpg (since the beginning of the data) which is labelled L for long range. A typical input-output sequence follows (and ends with negative mileage).

INPUTS		OUTPUTS	
miles	gals	short	long
M	G	S	L
1000	20		
1200	10	20	20
1500	20	15	16.67
...	..	..	..

3. **GPA**

   The grade point average GPA of a student is computed from all the course grades G and units U. Corresponding to each grade is a numeric point P (where A has 4 points, B has 3 points, etc). The products of each grade point and its number of units are then summed. This sum is divided by the total number of units T, to yield the grade point average A. Create an algorithm to compute the grade point average for a sequence of pairs of values G,U (ending with negative values to signify the end).

4. **SPEED**

   Create an algorithm to analyse the speed during a trip of N stops. At each stop, the distance D and time T from the previous stop are recorded. These pairs of values are then input to a program which computes each velocity (V = D/T) and outputs it. It also ultimately indicates the maximum speed on the trip, and the overall average (total distance divided by total time).

   SAMPLE RUN (N = 5)

D	T	V	
45	1	45	
100	2	50	
55	1	55	
120	2	60	Avg = 380/8 = 47.5
60	2	30	Max = 60

5. **UNBIASED MEAN**

   In some sports, a number of judges each ranks performance on a scale from 1 to 10. To adjust for biases, both the highest and lowest values are eliminated before computing the average. Create a program to compute such an average for M judges on N performances.

PROBLEMS ON LOOPS

1. ONCE MORE
   What action is performed by the following program in pseudo-code?
   ```
   INPUT N
   S <--- 0
   LOOP I FROM 1 TO N
       LOOP J FROM 1 TO N
           S <--- S + 1
       ENDLOOP J
   ENDLOOP I
   OUTPUT S
   ```

2. DISPROOF
   Show that the following two programs are not equivalent.
   ```
   WHILE A              WHILE A AND B
       WHILE B              C
           C            ENDWHILE
       ENDWHILE
   ENDWHILE
   ```

3. EXPO
   The exponentiation function EXPO(X) can be computed from the first N terms of the series:

   $$EXPO(X) = 1 + X + X^2/2! + X^3/3! + X^4/4! + ...$$

   a) Create a program to compute this, assuming that FACTORIAL and POWER are available as sub-programs.
   b) Create another program procedure which does not call any other sub-programs, and also does not keep re-computing the factorial or power (but uses previously computed results, such as $5! = 5*4!$).

4. DOWN TIMER
   Create a timer to count down from a given number of hours, minutes and seconds to zero. At intervals of five seconds, it outputs the time (remaining to zero).

5. PYTHAGOREAN TRIPLETS
   Construct a Pascal program to produce all integers X, Y, and Z which satisfy the Pythagorean theorem (relating the sides of a right triangle):
   $$X*X + Y*Y = Z*Z \qquad (where\ X < Y < Z)$$
   Let X, Y, and Z be positive integers all less than some fixed input value M (say 100).

6. THANKS
   Create a general algorithm which outputs "THANK YOU" for a total of N times (where N is input). This greeting is printed three times per line (possibly less on the last line). There is a blank line between every dozen (twelve) greetings.

7. PLOT UP
   Create an algorithm to plot a formula right-side-up, where the Y-axis is vertical and the X is horizontal. Extend this plot by marking some numbers on the axes.

PROBLEMS ON TYPES

1. LOGICAL SWAP?
   Prove (or disprove) the fact that the following two algorithms swap the
   values of the logical variables, P and Q.

   ```
   P <--- NOT( P OR Q )          P <--- ( P = Q )
   Q <--- NOT( P OR Q )          Q <--- ( P = Q )
   P <--- NOT( P OR Q )          P <--- ( P = Q )
   ```

2. LOGICAL LESS
   If FALSE is defined as less than TRUE, draw a truth table for the
   operation P < Q. Draw also a table for P >= Q.

3. BINCON2
   Create a program to convert a sequence of binary input characters (not
   integers) into their corresponding decimal values. For example, 1101 is
   the decimal 13.
   a) Write the program if the input is read from left to right
      (ending with a period).
   b) Write the program if the input is read from right to left
      (ending with a blank).

4. WHEN IN ROME ...
   One method for converting an Arabic number into a Roman number is to
   separately convert each digit (the units, tens, hundreds, and thousands
   positions) as shown.

   ```
   1    9    8     4
   M    CM   LXXX  IV
   ```

   Write a program which accepts as inputs any values up to 3999, and
   outputs the corresponding Roman numbers.
   a) Do this if the number is entered digit by digit
      (least significant digits first, like 4 8 9 1).
   b) Do this if the number is entered digit by digit
      (most significant digits first, like 1 9 8 4).
   c) Do this if the number is entered as an integer, like 1984.

5. XOR-cise
   Prove (or disprove) the following cancellation property for the usual OR
   and the exclusive-or XOR.

   a) If (A OR B) = (A OR C) then B = C.

   b) If (A XOR B) = (A XOR C) then B = C.

6. TRANSLATE
   Convert the following conditions into logical statements (using ANDs,
   ORs and NOTs).
   a) Neither A nor B.
   b) Either A or else B.
   c) Exactly two of the three variables A,B,C are true.
   d) An odd number of the three variables A,B,C is false.

7. CALCULATOR SYNTAX
   Create a syntax diagram describing the input sequences to the
   CALCULATOR of page 5-14.

PROBLEMS ON SUB-PROGRAMS

1. DIVIDE-AND-CONQUER
    Use the previously defined DIVIDE sub-program to:
    a) convert pints to gallons, quarts and pints.
    b) convert a decimal number to binary.
    c) determine if a year is a leap year.
    d) convert 24-hour (military) time to civil time;
        indicate AM or PM.
    e) determine on what date Easter falls in any given year;
        check an encyclopedia.

2. SIGNED PRODUCT CONTOUR
    Create a contour diagram and a data space diagram for the previous
    signed product, of page 3-44.

3. DOUBLEALL
    What is output by the following program when it passes parameters by
    reference?

```
        MAIN PROGRAM              SUB-PROGRAM
          X <--- 2                  DOUBLE(A,B,C)
          DOUBLE(X,X,X)               A <--- A + A
          OUTPUT X                    B <--- B + B
        END MAIN                      C <--- C + C
                                    END SUB
```

4. DATES
    Use some of the previous algorithms (LEAP, DAYS) and create:
    a) VALID, an algorithm to test if a given date Y,M,D is a valid date.
    b) UNDATE, an algorithm to convert a Julian date J,Y back into the
        usual form Y,M,D.
    c) LIVED, an algorithm to determine the number of days a person has
        lived, from the birthdate to the present date.
    d) AGE, an algorithm to determine the (integer) age of a person.
    e) WEEKDATE, an algorithm to determine the weekday a given date falls
        on, when given that the first day of the year falls on the Wth day
        (where W = 0 for Sunday, W = 1 for Monday, ... and W = 6 for
        Saturday).
    f) FIRST DATE, an algorithm to determine the weekday of New Year's
        Day, given the year Y. Use the fact that January 1, 1901 was a
        Tuesday (W = 2). Notice that a year of 365 days has exactly 52
        weeks plus one day (i.e., 52*7=364).

5. BIND DATES
    Create a binding table and contour diagram for any of the above DATES
    programs.

6. RANGE
    Create an algorithm which reads in three values A,B,C and outputs the
    range R, which is the difference between the largest and smallest
    values. This is to be done using the following sub-programs, and
    providing the maximum hiding of variables and subs.

    The main program RANGE is to call a procedure BS3(I,J,K,L,S) which
    finds the largest L and smallest S of the formal parameters I,J,K.
    This procedure in turn calls two functions BIG(P,Q,R) and
    SMALL(P,Q,R), each of which must call a procedure SORT2(G,H) which
    takes G and H, and arranges them so G is largest and H is smallest.

MORE CHANGE CHANGE

The CHANGE algorithm can be modified to keep track of the number of coins of each denomination. For example, if Q is the number of quarters at any time, then part of the new algorithm (in pseudo-code) becomes:

```
WHILE (R >= 25) AND (Q > 0)
   OUTPUT 25
   R <--- R - 25
   Q <--- Q - 1
ENDWHILE
```

Indicate which of the following algorithms are equivalent to this part, or if not indicate why not.

```
a.  WHILE Q > 0
       IF R >= 25 THEN
          OUTPUT 25
          R <--- R - 25
          Q <--- Q - 1
       ENDIF
    ENDWHILE
```

```
b.  WHILE R >= 25
       IF Q > 0 THEN
          OUTPUT 25
          R <--- R - 25
          Q <--- Q - 1
       ENDIF
    ENDWHILE
```

```
c.  IF R >= 25 THEN
       WHILE Q > 0
          OUTPUT 25
          R <--- R - 25
          Q <--- Q - 1
       ENDWHILE
    ENDIF
```

```
d.  IF Q > 0 THEN
       WHILE R >= 25
          OUTPUT 25
          R <--- R - 25
          Q <--- Q - 1
       ENDWHILE
    ENDIF
```

```
e.  WHILE Q > 0
       WHILE R >= 25
          OUTPUT 25
          R <--- R - 25
          Q <--- Q - 1
       ENDWHILE
    ENDWHILE
```

```
f.  WHILE R >= 25
       WHILE Q > 0
          OUTPUT 25
          R <--- R - 25
          Q <--- Q - 1
       ENDWHILE
    ENDWHILE
```

PROBLEMS INVOLVING RECURSION

1. **REALLY**

   Indicate which of the following definitions are recursive, and if
   not then indicate why not.
   a) A human is a creature whose mother is a human.
   b) A chicken is an egg's way of creating more eggs.
   c) The ancestors of a person are that person's parents, or the
       ancestors of that person's parents.
   d) A multiple of 10 is 10 or any multiple of 10 multiplied by 10.

2. **COMB**

   Evaluate C(5,3) according to the definition

   $$C(n,k) = \begin{cases} 1 & \text{if } k = 0 \text{ or } k = n \\ n - (k-1) + C(n,k-1) & \text{otherwise} \end{cases}$$

   and also express C(n,k) in closed loop form (using factorial).

3. **RECURSIVE POWER**

   Create a recursive definition to compute the Nth (positive) power
   of X.

4. **REM (or MOD)**

   Create a recursive definition for R(A,B) describing the remainder
   after A divides B (use successive subtractions).

5. **ROLL YOUR OWN**

   Create a recursive definition of something you are familiar with
   (another square, number conversion, craps rules).

6. **TRACE** the following recursive algorithms.

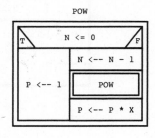

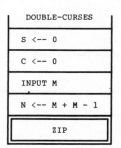

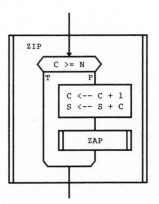

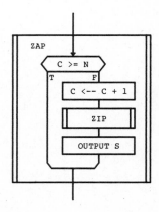

PROBLEMS ON PASSING PARAMETERS

Indicate the output of the following program if the input values are
    1,2,3.

Indicate the output if the sub-program call (in the main program)
    were changed in each of the following ways.

The input values are still 1,2,3 for each READ.

    a.   SUB(A,C)   (Answer: 6,2,5)

    b.   SUB(B,A)   (Answer: 8,2,3)

    c.   SUB(C,B)   (Answer: 7,6,3)

    d.   SUB(B,C)

    e.   SUB(C,A)

    f.   SUB(B,B)

MAIN

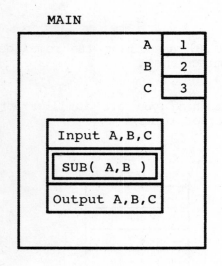

SUB(D,C)

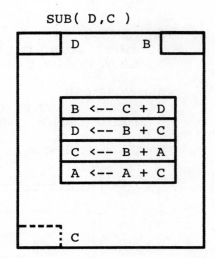

Chapter 6

OBJECTS:
    DATA STRUCTURES

SIMPLE ARRAYS

SORTING: 4 ways

SEARCHING: 3 ways

TABLES: 2D Arrays

RECORDS and fields

STACKS, QUEUES, etc.

TREES

OBJECTS:

DATA STRUCTURES

* Asterisks indicate the degree of importance *

Chapter 6

OBJECTS:

Data Structures

PREVIEW

In this chapter we group together smaller objects to form larger objects. If the smaller data objects (variables) are all of the same type they can be grouped into ARRAYS; if they are of different types they can be grouped into RECORDS. The data structures considered in this chapter will be mainly linear lists or rectangular tables.

ARRAYS (often called tables, matrices, n-dimensional lists, and subscripted variables) are groupings of objects all of the same type (all integer, or all real, etc.). The objects within the arrays are labelled (referenced, or accessed) by integers called indices.

LINEAR LISTS (often called vectors, or n-tuples, or one-dimensional arrays) are the simplest arrays. They can be viewed as values in a table, or as indexed variables.

OPERATIONS on linear lists include: finding the mean or maximum values, sorting (putting all values into order), and searching (retrieving a particular value). There will often be many ways to do any of these actions. For example, there are only four basic ways to sort an array, and dozens of variations of each of these ways. Only a few of the variations will be considered here.

TABLES, or arrays having two indices, are common, and will be considered here. Arrays of three and more indices are less common, so will be considered only briefly.

RECORDS are very significant data structures. They differ from arrays in that the objects grouped together need not be of the same type. Also, values are not accessed by integer indices, but by a dot notation.

LINEAR data structures include strings, stacks, queues, and files. These can be viewed as variations on arrays. For example, a stack could be viewed as a limited list accessible only at one end, and a file could be viewed as an extended list of arbitrary length.

FILES are linear data structures of indefinite length, which are useful for storing information. They are considered very briefly.

MORE complex data structures (involving recursion and trees) are considered briefly.

LINEAR ARRAYS

1 Hours as indexed variables

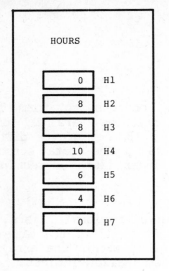

HOURS	
0	H1
8	H2
8	H3
10	H4
6	H5
4	H6
0	H7

2 Hours as a table of values

HOURS

D	H[D]
1	0
2	8
3	8
4	10
5	6
6	4
7	0

3 SCORE

I	S[I]
1	20
2	10
3	50
:	
N	:

(integer)

4 TEMPERATURE

H	T[H]	
1	98.6	
2	100.0	
3		
12		NOON
24		MIDNITE

(real)

5 GRADES

S	G[S]
1	'A'
2	'C'
3	'B'
	'B'
30	'D'

(char)

6 BELONGS

I	B[I]
100	T
101	T
102	F
199	T

(logical)

7 STORY

P	S[P]
1	'0'
2	'N'
3	'C'
	'E'
10000	'R'

(char)

8 NAME

D	N[D]
0	'SUN'
1	'MON'
2	'TUES'
6	'SAT'

(string)

SIMPLE ARRAYS: Linear Lists

The simplest arrays have only one index, and are called linear lists, vectors, n-tuples, or single dimensional arrays. An example of such a linear list is shown in figure 1. This array could represent the number of hours H worked on each day D of the week. Humans often write the index label as a subscript:

$$H_1 , H_2 , H_3 , \ldots H_7$$

but in most programming languages this is written within brackets as:

$$H[1], H[2], \ldots\ldots H[7]$$

Also, in most languages more meaningful names are chosen such as:

HOURS[MONDAY],   where MONDAY has an integer value of 2.

The index could be a constant, a variable, or an expression that ultimately evaluates to an integer.

Two Views

Arrays can be viewed in two ways as shown in figures 1 and 2. The first view is that of a number of indexed variables, all having the same name, but differing by their indices. A second view of an array is that of a table of values (entries) with a pointer D indicating the position of a value, as shown in figure 2. In both views the index serves as a selector. The index can be treated numerically as a constant, variable or any other expression as in:

$$H[6], \quad H[D], \quad H[I+1], \quad H[2*D-1]$$

Examples

Other examples of linear arrays are shown in the given figures. Notice that all components of each array are of the same type.

SCORE, of figure 3, shows the score S[I] of an individual I, with each score given as an integer.

TEMP, of figure 4, shows the temperature T[H] of some person at each hour H of the day. The temperatures are real values.

GRADE, of figure 5, shows a linear list of characters representing the grade G[S] of each student S.

BELONGS, of figure 6, consists of logical (Boolean) values (True or False) indicating whether a person P (numbered from 100 to 199) belongs to some organization or set.

STORY, of figure 7, shows a long sequence of characters, one in each position P from 1 to 10,000. Such long arrays of characters are often called strings.

NAME, of figure 8, shows the names of the days of the week as short strings of differing lengths. Not all languages allow such strings as components, and not all allow indices to be zero (or negative).

ARRAY OPERATIONS

1 SIMPLE INPUT

Input H[1]
Input H[2]
Input H[3]
Input H[4]
Input H[5]
Input H[6]
Input H[7]

2 INPUT LOOP

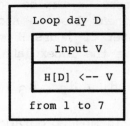

Loop day D

Input V

H[D] <-- V

from 1 to 7

3 INLIST
with terminator T

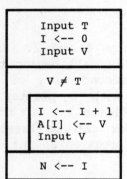

Input T
I <-- 0
Input V

V ≠ T

I <-- I + 1
A[I] <-- V
Input V

N <-- I

4 OUTLIST
when size N
is known

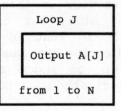

Loop J

Output A[J]

from 1 to N

5 MAXLIST
top down

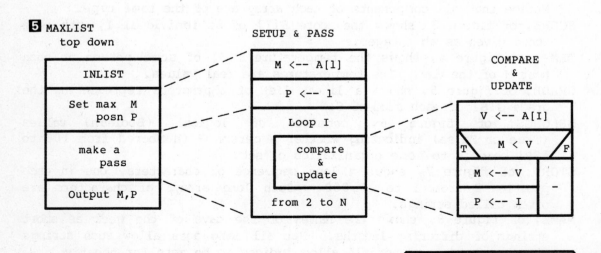

INLIST

Set max M
posn P

make a
pass

Output M,P

SETUP & PASS

M <-- A[1]

P <-- 1

Loop I

compare
&
update

from 2 to N

COMPARE
&
UPDATE

V <-- A[I]

T   M < V   F

M <-- V   -

P <-- I

See also PASCAL B-61

Operations on Arrays

Arrays are useful objects where the components (all of the same type) may be selected by giving the name followed by an index within square brackets. For example, we can put (store) a value X into position P of array A by the assignment:

    A[P] <--- X

Similarly, we can get (retrieve) a value from position P of array A and assign it to variable Y by:

    Y <--- A[P]

These indexed variables can be used anywhere a simple variable can be used as in the following (which is a "running" average).

    B[I] <--- (A[I-1] + A[I] + A[I+1])/3

These array accessing actions (put and get) are operations on components only; next we will consider actions on entire arrays.

INPUT of an entire array may be done in many ways. For example, let us input the seven hours-per-day worked in a week. One way is to use seven assignment statements as shown in figure 1. Another way is to use a loop as shown in figure 2. Such input methods are not general, however, for they require either a small number of entries or a known number of entries.

INLIST, of figure 3, is a general method for the input of a list where the number of entries is not known ahead of time (because it varies, or because it is large). It uses a terminating value to detect the end of the entries. It assigns the input values to consecutive entries of the array, counting them as they are input. After terminating, variable N is assigned to be the number of entries.

OUTLIST, of figure 4, is a simple loop because the number of entries is usually known. In the rare case that this number is not known, we would have to make use of a more complex loop with a terminator.

MAXLIST, of figure 5, is an algorithm to compute the maximum value of an array A having N values. It also indicates the (first) position P of the maximum value. The algorithm is shown developed top-down in three stages. The first stage shows the input, set-up of initial values, the "pass" and output.

The second stage shows more detail of initially setting the maximum as the first entry of the array. This is followed by a pass, where the index I ranges over all values from 2 to N, comparing and updating if necessary. The third stage shows the details of the comparison, the selection of a value V and the comparison of it to the present maximum.

MEAN AND VARIANCE

3

I	A[I]
1	30
2	20
3	40
4	10

MEAN M = (A[1] + A[2] + A[3] + A[4])/N
      = (30 + 20 + 40 + 10)/4 = 100/4 = 25

VAR1 V = ($(A[1] - M)^2$ + $(A[2] - M)^2$ + ... $(A[N] - M)^2$)/N
      = ($(30 - 25)^2$ + $(20 - 25)^2$ + $(40 - 25)^2$ + $(10 - 25)^2$)/4
      = (5^2 + 5^2 + 15^2 + 15^2)/4
      = 125

Flowchart:

```
INLIST A,N
S <-- 0
Loop I  1 to N
    S <-- S + A[I]
M <-- S / N
T <-- 0
Loop J  1 to N
    T <-- T +
          (A[J] - M)²
V <-- T / N
```

Trace — inlist:

	S <-- 0				
	I <-- 1 / 1 <= 4 / T	2 <= 4 / T	3 <= 4 / T	4 <= 4 / T	5 <= 4 / F
S =	30	50	90	100	
I =	I <-- 2	3	4	5	
				M <-- 25	
				T <-- 0	
	J <-- 1 / 1 <= 4 / T	2 <= 4 / T	3 <= 4 / T	4 <= 4 / T	5 <= 4 / F
T =	25	50	275	500	
J =	2	3	4	5	
					V <-- 125

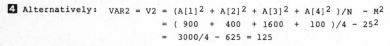

4 Alternatively: VAR2 = V2 = ($A[1]^2$ + $A[2]^2$ + $A[3]^2$ + $A[4]^2$)/N - M^2
      = (900 + 400 + 1600 + 100)/4 - 25^2
      = 3000/4 - 625 = 125

Flowchart:

```
INLIST A,N
S <-- 0
T <-- 0
Loop K  1 to N
    S <-- S + A[K]
    T <-- T + A[K]²
M <-- S / N
V <-- T/N - M²
```

Trace — as before:

	S <-- 0				
	T <-- 0				
	K <-- 1 / 1 <= 4 / T	2 <= 4 / T	3 <= 4 / T	4 <= 4 / T	5 <= 4 / F
S =	30	50	90	100	
T =	900	1300	2900	3000	
K =	2	3	4	5	
					M <-- 25
					V <-- 125

Other Ways with Arrays: CHANGE

CHANGE algorithm can be implemented very conveniently with an array. The previous CHANGE diagram (repeated in figure 1, below) involved many repetitions, with five similar loops. In the last chapter repetition was avoided by using a sub-program, DIVIDE. Here we make use of this repetition in another way -- with an array.

CHANGE, of figure 2 below, uses an array A which lists the denominations 50, 25, 10, 5 and 1 in order. As the variable I loops (from 1 to 5), the variable D is assigned the corresponding array values (first 50, then 25, 10, 5, 1), and the change for this D is computed and output.

The resulting algorithm is not only shorter than the previous versions, but it can be modified more easily. To extend it to apply to more denominations (such as 5 dollar bills, 10 dollars, 20 dollars, and even 2 dollars) requires only a slight change in the array values (and size of array). This algorithm could also be easily modified for making change of any foreign currencies.

MEAN, VARIANCE   (Optional)

Another use of arrays is to store data so that the values can be available for repeated access. For example, figure 3 shows the computation of the variance of some numbers. This algorithm first requires the mean of these numbers, so it makes two "passes" over the array, once to compute the mean and once to compute the variance. Actually, there is another method of computing the variance without requiring the mean to be computed first. This new method, as shown in figure 4, requires only one pass. So knowing equivalent algorithms can be quite useful.

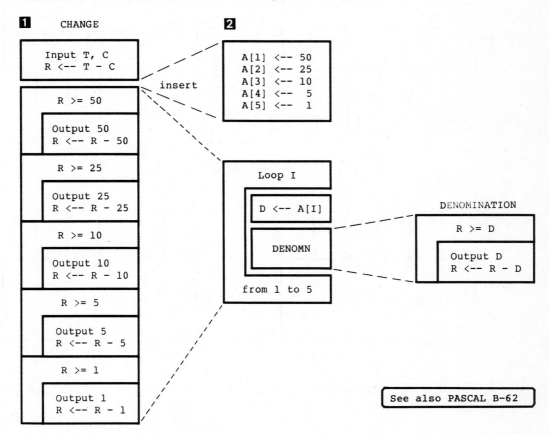

SORTING

general methods

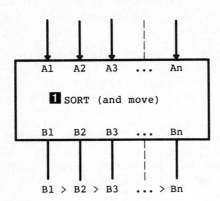

examples

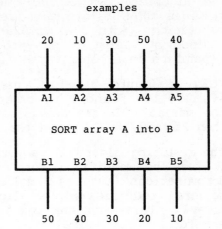

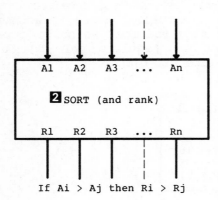

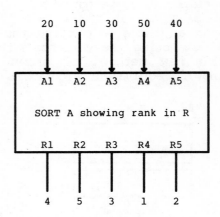

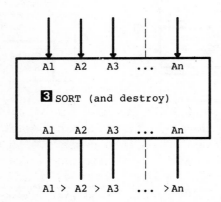

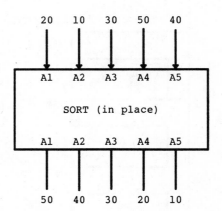

SORTING: All Sorts of Sorts

SORTING is an extremely common computing action. It is the process of
   putting items into an order. The items could be numbers or letters
   (or sometimes strings), and the order could be increasing or
   decreasing, numeric or alphabetic. The previous small sorts (SORT2,
   SORT3, etc.) sorted a fixed number of items, but now we want to
   sort any number N of items in an array.

OUTCOMES of any sorting process could be viewed in three general ways,
   as indicated in the given figures.

SORT (AND MOVE), of figure 1, shows that the items of array A could be
   sorted and copied in their proper order into a second array B. This
   method may be wasteful of space, since it involves two arrays, but
   the original order is preserved.

SORT (AND RANK), of figure 2, shows a second array R which provides
   ranking of the items in the original array A.

SORT (AND DESTROY), of figure 3, uses only one array A, with the final
   ordered values returned in A, having destroyed the original values.
   This sorting "in place" is, however, economical of space, requiring
   only one array.

SORTING: The Four Methods

   There are many different methods, or algorithms, for sorting, but all
   fall into one of the following four categories:

   1. COUNT SORT,
         involving enumerating and comparing,
   2. SWAP SORT,
         involving swapping of pairs of objects,
   3. SELECT SORT,
         involving selecting extreme values,
   4. INSERT SORT,
         involving moving and inserting of values.

These four basic sorting methods are illustrated with the following four
   algorithms. To simplify the algorithms, we first assume positive,
   non-equal integer values, which will be sorted into decreasing order.
   As an example, we will use the five values (in original order 20,
   10, 30, 50, 40). Later we will extend some of these algorithms to
   get more general and more efficient algorithms. Actually there are
   dozens of different sorts possible, but all of them fit into one of
   these four categories.

SORT BY COUNTING

1

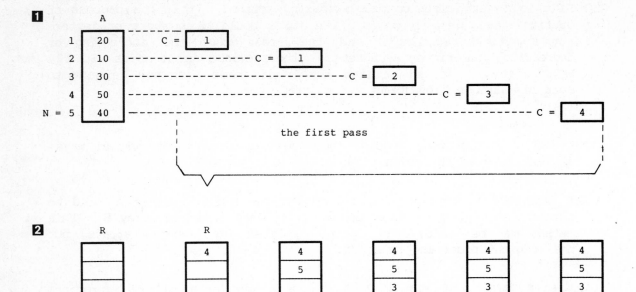

	A	
1	20	C = 1
2	10	C = 1
3	30	C = 2
4	50	C = 3
N = 5	40	C = 4

the first pass

2

R	R				
	4	4	4	4	4
		5	5	5	5
			3	3	3
				1	1
					2

After
pass =   1   2   3   4   5

3   COUNTSORT ALGORITHM

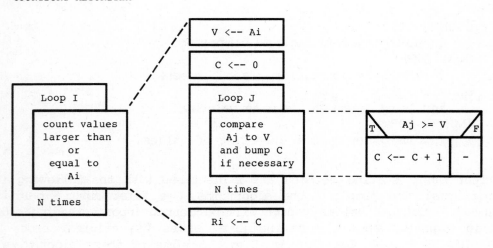

Loop I

count values
larger than
or
equal to
Ai

N times

V <-- Ai

C <-- 0

Loop J

compare
Aj to V
and bump C
if necessary

N times

Ri <-- C

	Aj >= V	
T		F
C <-- C + 1		-

COUNTSORT

COUNTSORT is one of the simplest sorts (but it is not always thought of first). It finds the rank of all values in an array, the largest having a rank of 1, the smallest having a rank of N (if all values are different). The rank of a value is found by comparing it to all the values in the array, and counting the number of the values which are larger than or equal to that value. The largest one has only one value (itself) equal to it, and so has rank 1. The second largest has two values greater than or equal to it, and so has rank 2. The smallest has all N values greater than (or equal to) it, and so has rank N.

Pass 1 of the array is shown in figure 1. It determines that the first value, 20, has rank four. Figure 2 shows the results of N such passes (where N = 5 in this example).

COUNTSORT is developed top-down in stages as shown in figure 3. In the first stage, I is looped for N passes. The next stage shows that during each pass a value V is selected, compared to all items of the array, and the resulting count put into another rank array R. The third stage shows the details of the comparison and counting.

Notice that all values shown here were different, and this method produced all ranks from 1 to N. If some values were repeated, then some ranks would be repeated, and some ranks would not correspond to any numbers. For example, if the value 10 was changed to 20, then there would be two items having rank five and none having rank four. Check that.

Analysis of COUNTSORT

Notice that for an array of N values the outer loop repeats N times, and for each of these N times the inner loop also repeats N times. Hence, the total number of repetitions (and therefore comparisons) is N*N or N squared. In this example, there are 5*5 = 25 comparisons. Doubling the size of an array (say from 5 to 10) does not simply double the number of comparisons, but quadruples this number (from 25 to 100). This quadratic growth results in a very slow sort, especially for larger sized arrays.

SORT BY SWAPPING

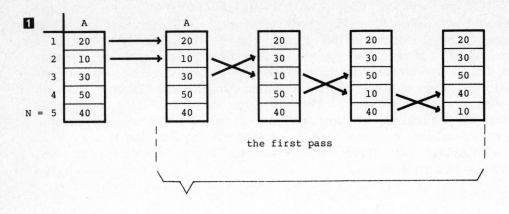

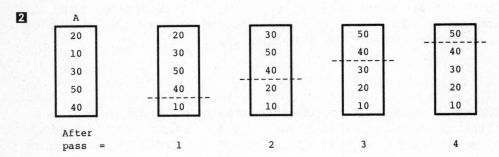

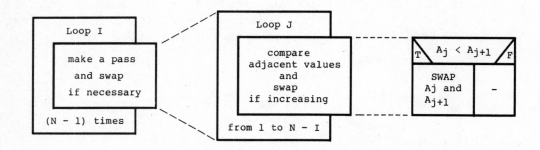

SWAPSORT: Bubble Sort

SWAPSORT involves the comparison of adjacent values, swapping them
if they are not in order. Figure 1 shows the first pass over
all the items of a typical array A, where all pairs of adjacent
items are compared. The result after this first pass is
summarized in figure 2. This result is followed by the results
of all the remaining passes. Notice that after pass one, the
smallest value (10) has dropped to its final position at the
bottom of the array. After pass two, the second smallest value
has "bubbled" down to the second last position. This
"bubbling" action of all values leads to its common name,
"Bubble Sort." In the worst case, the algorithm requires N-1
passes for all N values to bubble to their final positions.

The SWAPSORT algorithm is given in figure 3, developed top-down
in three stages. Stage one specifies simply that there are
(N-1) passes, where each pass involves a compare and
corresponding swap if necessary. Stage two describes an
individual pass through all pairs of adjacent items. Notice
the refinement of the action "swap if necessary" to "swap if
increasing." Stage three finally specifies the comparison in
all its detail.

Analysis of SWAPSORT   (Optional)

This SWAPSORT algorithm requires (N-1) passes. Each of these
(N-1) passes requires (N-1) comparisons, for a total of
(N-1)*(N-1) actions (comparisons). In this case there are
4*4 = 16 comparisons. This method is not much better than the
COUNTSORT, but it can be improved. Notice that each pass can
be one shorter than the previous pass (because one item has
bubbled to its final position at each pass), so that on the Ith
pass we need loop only (N-I) times. This results in an almost
unnoticeable change on the inner loop, changing it from (N-1)
to (N-I). With this change there are then (4 + 3 + 2 + 1) =
10 comparisons. In general for an array of N values the
number of comparisons is equal to the sum of the first (N-1)
integers, which can be shown to be equal to:

N*(N-1)/2

This number can be compared to N*N which is the number of
comparisons required by COUNTSORT. It shows that this
SWAPSORT is more than twice as fast as COUNTSORT.

Improving the speed of sorting algorithms is possible in many
ways. Some ways of improving SWAPSORT are considered on page
6-19.

SORT BY SELECTION

1

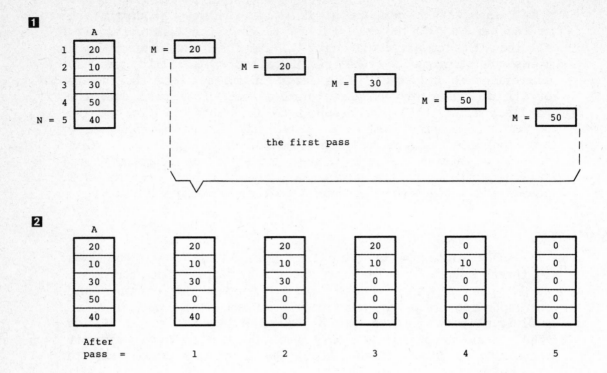

A

1	20
2	10
3	30
4	50
N = 5	40

M = 20

M = 20

M = 30

M = 50

M = 50

the first pass

2

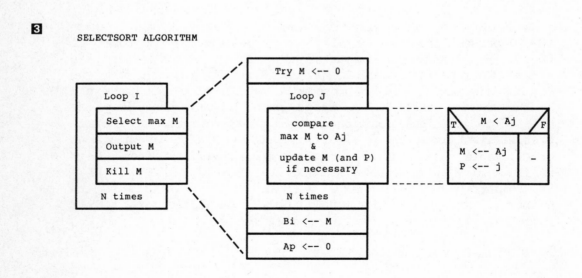

A

20	20	20	20	0	0
10	10	10	10	10	0
30	30	30	0	0	0
50	0	0	0	0	0
40	40	0	0	0	0

| After pass = | 1 | 2 | 3 | 4 | 5 |

3 SELECTSORT ALGORITHM

Loop I
Select max M
Output M
Kill M
N times

Try M <-- 0
Loop J
compare max M to Aj & update M (and P) if necessary
N times
Bi <-- M
Ap <-- 0

T	M < Aj	F
M <-- Aj P <-- j		-

SELECTSORT

SELECTSORT involves the selection of extreme values, either the maximum or minimum. For example, it could start by finding the maximum value of an array. This value is then noted (recorded, output, swapped, or put into another array) and eliminated from the array. Similarly, the maximum of the remaining array is selected, recorded and eliminated. This cycle continues for a total of N times.

Figure 1 shows the first pass over an array A of positive integers. The maximum value M is found to be 50, is output, and its value is replaced by zero.

Figure 2 shows snapshots of array A after each pass; notice that the array is slowly destroyed in the process, ultimately becoming an array of zeros.

The SELECTSORT algorithm is shown developed top-down in stages in figure 3. In the first stage, there is a loop of N passes, one for each value of the array. During each pass I, the maximum value M is found (as well as its position P), and is put into position I of a second array B. Then this Pth item is "killed" by setting it to zero. The third stage of the algorithm shows how the maximum value M is compared to each value A[J] and, if necessary, the value M and its position P are updated.

This method sorted positive integers only, for the "killing" was done by replacing the maximum by zero, the smallest positive integer. This algorithm could be modified to include negative values by substituting the lowest negative value to "kill" the maximum.

INSERTSORT

INSERTSORT involves entering a new item into an array by moving the existing items to make room for that item. The items are inserted one at a time into a growing array. This is the way we sort cards or spices on a rack. This algorithm is left as an exercise. It has a form very similar to all the other SORT algorithms, consisting of a choice nested within a loop which is nested within another loop.

IMPROVING SORTS

1 Swapsort with Finished Flag (DONE)

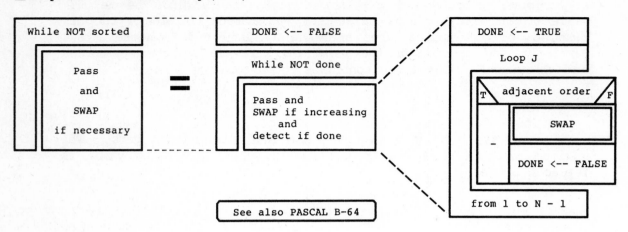

See also PASCAL B-64

2 Swapsort with directions alternating

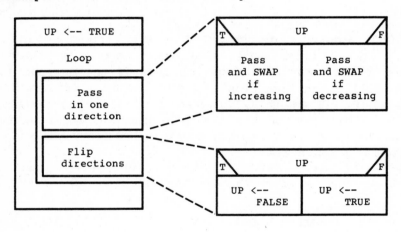

3 Swapsort with distant comparisons

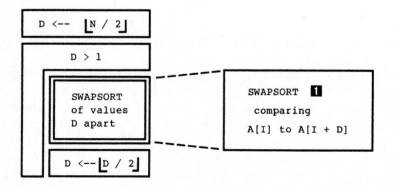

Improving Sorts   (Optional)

The four sorts we considered are the simplest forms of the four basic
methods. Many variations and improvements are possible on each of
these sorts. Here we will consider some ways of improving the
SWAPSORT algorithm.

The first improvement comes from noticing that SWAPSORT required (N-1)
passes. This is a worst case maximum; in many cases the values may
be sorted before all (N-1) passes are done, so this original method
was wasteful. It is possible to detect when the array is sorted and
so stop looping then. This is done using a logical variable DONE as
shown in figure 1. The outer loop continues while NOT DONE sorting.
Before each pass, the variable DONE is assigned True, and remains
True only if a swap is never made over an entire pass. As soon as a
swap is made, the variable is set to False, and after this complete
pass, another pass is to be made. So if an array is originally
sorted, then this method takes only one pass to verify that and stop.

Another improvement comes from alternating the direction of bubbling;
first the largest is bubbled down, then the smallest is bubbled up,
etc. This is also done with a logical variable UP, which flips from
True to False alternately after every pass as shown in figure 2.

A third improvement results when the comparison is not between adjacent
values but between values far apart. When two values that are a
distance D apart are swapped, this saves D individual swaps. Such a
method of sorting, shown in figure 3, is called Shell Sort. It
starts by comparing values which are a distance N/2 apart. On the
next pass it compares values which are N/4 apart. Then it continues
comparing values which are N/8 apart, and keeps reducing this
distance until finally it compares adjacent values (a distance D = 1
apart).

Other improvements are also possible on this SWAP SORT, and on the
other sorts. The improvements have lead to the creation of dozens of
sorts: Bucket-sort, Radix-sort, Heap-sort, and Quick-sort, to name
a few.

PERFORMANCE of algorithms is often measured by order statistics,
indicated by a function called O(f). For example, our four original
sorts required about n*n comparisons for sorting an array of n
items. These sorts are said to be of order n-squared, denoted
$O(n^2)$, read as "big-oh of n-squared". A worse (slower) sort would
have an order $O(n^3)$ and the best general sorts have order
O(n*log n), where the logarithm has base 2. If the sorts are
limited in some way, then computing times could be shorter, possibly
linear (of order O(n)) or even logarithmic (of order O(log n). If
a sort is limited to data having only 2 values (say 0 and 1) then it
can be sorted in just one pass (try it).

SEARCHING

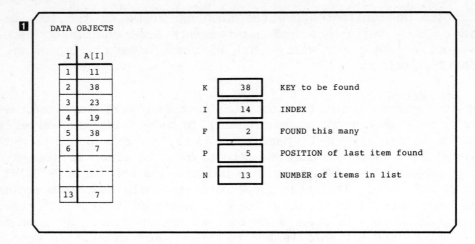

1 DATA OBJECTS

I	A[I]
1	11
2	38
3	23
4	19
5	38
6	7
- - -	- - -
13	7

K	38	KEY to be found
I	14	INDEX
F	2	FOUND this many
P	5	POSITION of last item found
N	13	NUMBER of items in list

2 SLOW SEARCH

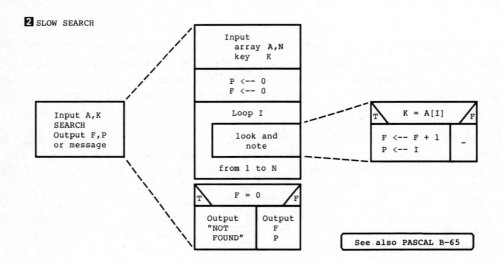

Input A,K
SEARCH
Output F,P
or message

Input
  array A,N
  key   K

P <-- 0
F <-- 0

Loop I

  look and
  note

from 1 to N

T   K = A[I]   F
F <-- F + 1   _
P <-- I

T   F = 0   F
Output   Output
"NOT   F
FOUND"   P

See also PASCAL B-65

3 FASTER SEARCH (still linear)

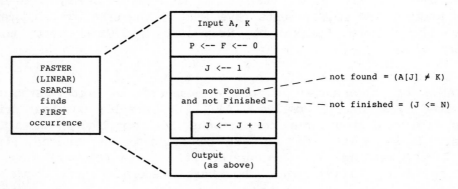

FASTER
(LINEAR)
SEARCH
finds
FIRST
occurrence

Input A, K

P <-- F <-- 0

J <-- 1

not Found
and not Finished

J <-- J + 1

Output
(as above)

not found = (A[J] ≠ K)

not finished = (J <= N)

SEARCHING: Three Ways

Search is a common action of looking into a table of items to find a
   particular item (sometimes called target or key). If the item
   occurs in the table, we would like its position; if it does not
   occur, we would like a message output. In some cases, we would
   want a count of the number of occurrences of the required item.

The data structure of figure 1 shows an array A of N = 13 items.
   The object is to search for the item K, counting the number of times
   it is found, in variable F, with the position of the last item found
   being in P.

Of the many ways to search, we will consider three: Linear search,
   Binary search, and Scattered search.

Linear Search

The simplest search, Linear search, involves one pass over an entire
   array. The slowest linear search, of figure 2, shows how the entire
   array is scanned once, with a found counter F bumped each time the
   item is found in the array. The position P indicates the position of
   the last occurrence. If instead the first occurrence is required,
   then the scan could be done in reverse order, from N down to 1. If
   the item is not found, the value of F remains at 0.

A faster linear search, shown in figure 3, proceeds step-by-step also,
   but as soon as the item is found, the loop exits with P indicating
   the position of the first occurrence. So sometimes the item is found
   early, and sometimes it is found late in the list, but on the average
   it goes halfway through the list.

Binary Search

The previous two linear searches were general, and made no
   assumptions about the data. But if the data values are sorted, say
   in increasing order, then we have a good idea where the item is
   located. This could be used to speed up the search.

We can use the previous method of Bisection to keep reducing the array
   until we find the item, or find that it is not there. The algorithm
   proceeds by halving the array at each stage. You may wish to create
   this Binary Search algorithm by modifying the Bisection algorithm of
   page 3-53.

The binary search method is considerably faster than the previous linear
   searches. For example, to search an array of N items requires N/2
   comparisons, on the average, for linear search. The method of
   bisection requires a number of comparison equal to

$$\log_2 N.$$

So, for an array of 1000 items, the linear search takes 500
   comparisons, whereas the binary search takes only 10 comparisons.
   Of course, the binary search also requires the array to be originally
   sorted, and this takes some additional comparisons. But if the
   array is searched often after each sort then the method is practical.

HASH SEARCH

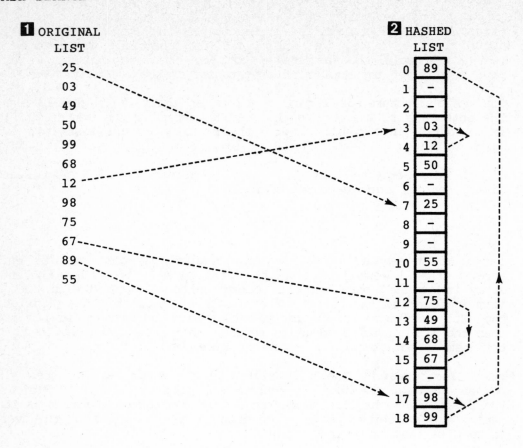

1 ORIGINAL LIST

25	
03	
49	
50	
99	
68	
12	
98	
75	
67	
89	
55	

2 HASHED LIST

0	89
1	–
2	–
3	03
4	12
5	50
6	–
7	25
8	–
9	–
10	55
11	–
12	75
13	49
14	68
15	67
16	–
17	98
18	99

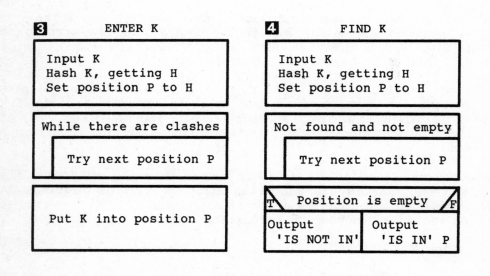

3 ENTER K

Input K
Hash K, getting H
Set position P to H

While there are clashes

    Try next position P

Put K into position P

4 FIND K

Input K
Hash K, getting H
Set position P to H

Not found and not empty

    Try next position P

T   Position is empty   F

Output 'IS NOT IN'	Output 'IS IN' P

Scattered Search (Hashing)

Scattered search, also called hashing, is a very fast method of searching. Whereas linear search may require N/2 comparisons or "probes" to complete a search, and binary search requires log N probes, hashing may require as few as one probe! This increase in speed comes with an increase in data space.

Hashing basically consists of taking some unique values (such as ID number, ISBN, phone number, or part number) and manipulating them in some way (by a hashing function) to determine a position in a table. Hashing functions could have many forms. One function could take the sum of all the digits in the ID. Another common hash function is the remainder when the ID is divided by some constant value.

For example, let us create a list of students in a class. A hashing function could be the last two digits of the student ID number. This number is used as an index into an array where the full ID number is stored. Such an array can hold at most 100 students. Unfortunately, two or more students may have the same last digits, a condition known as "hash clash." When the number of students is small (compared to the size of the table), this clash is less likely to occur. The clash may be resolved in a number of ways, one of which follows.

OPEN ADDRESSING is a simple way of resolving hash clashes. When a second value hashes to a position P already in the table, it is put into the next higher position that is free. This will be illustrated in detail with the following shorter example.

CLASSLIST is an example to show hashing. It involves only 12 students, too small to need hashing but sufficiently large to illustrate the main ideas. Here the hashing function can be chosen to be the sum of the last two digits of a student's ID number. This allows for up to 19 entries in the table (00 to 9+9). Suppose that the ID numbers (last two digits) are those given in figure 1. They are to be "hashed" into the array of figure 2.

ENTER, of figure 3, shows an algorithm which enters values into the hashed list. The first value, 25, is hashed into position 7 (because 2 + 5 = 7). The next few values also fit easily. Then the value 12 (hashed to 3) clashes in position 3, so is put into position 4. The next clash occurs with number 67 (hashed to 13), and it moves two positions to the next free position (with index of 15). Then 89 clashes with 98 in position 17, so it is put into the next position (wrapped around) at index 0, at the top of the array. Notice that if the values were entered in a different order, a slightly different table could result.

FIND (or HASH SEARCH), of figure 4, shows the algorithm for the hash search of this array. Notice that to find 67 in the array required three probes, and to find that 12 is not in the array takes four probes. In most cases, only one probe is required. On the average, the number of probes is only slightly larger than one. Notice that some "clustering" of values occurred here, and the clustering leads to slower searches. In general, a more random hashing function (such as ID MOD 19) would yield a better distribution, and minimize clustering.

TABLES (Arrays, Matrices)

1 General

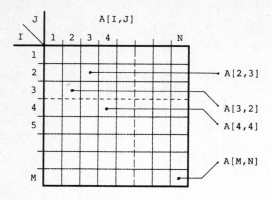

A[2,3]

A[3,2]

A[4,4]

A[M,N]

2 Particular - Grades

N = 3

Q P	1	2	3
1	40	60	80
2	70	30	80
3	100	100	100
4	80	60	40

G[P,Q]

M = 4

3 TIC-TAC-TABLE

T[R,C]

C R	1	2	3
1			
2		X	
3	O		

4 CHARGE TABLE

C[A,B]

B A	0	1	2	3
1	3.00	5.00	7.00	9.00
2	6.00	8.00	10.00	12.00
3	9.00	11.00	13.00	15.00

5 Traversing Array by ROWS

C[I,J]

J I	1	2	3
1	1	2	3
2	4	5	6
3	7	8	9
4	10	11	12

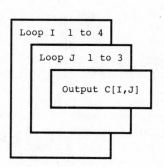

Loop I 1 to 4

Loop J 1 to 3

Output C[I,J]

7 INPUT ARRAY
(by Rows)

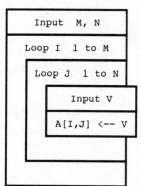

Input M, N

Loop I 1 to M

Loop J 1 to N

Input V

A[I,J] <-- V

6 TRACE OF ROW TRAVERSE

I =	1			2			3			4		
J =	1	2	3	1	2	3	1	2	3	1	2	3
IJ =	11,	12,	13	21,	22,	23	31,	32,	33	41,	42,	43

TABLES: Two-Dimensional Arrays

Tables, or matrices, are two-dimensional arrays involving two indices. Figure 1 shows a general array A with M rows and N columns. The value of element A[I,J] is found by moving horizontally along row I and vertically down column J until these two meet at a value.

For example, figure 2 shows a table of grades with indices P and Q. The grade of person P on quiz Q is denoted G[P,Q]. In this example, person P = 2 on quiz Q = 3 made a grade of 80 percent. This value G[2,3] is not to be confused with G[3,2], which is the grade of person 3 on exam 2 (of 100%). The order of the indices is important! This table has only four rows and three columns, but in general it could have M rows and N columns.

Examples of such two-dimensional tables include many games (such as chess or checkers) similar to the given Tic-tac-toe board of figure 3. Each entry T[R,C] corresponding to row R and column C has one of three character values: an 'X', an 'O' or a blank ' '. Another example is the table of admission charges C[A,B] for A adults and B babies given in figure 4. Notice that one index starts from 0 and another starts at 1, insisting on at least one adult and providing for no babies. A calendar could also be viewed as an array with the rows representing weeks W, and the seven columns representing the days D of the week. The value within the array is the day of the month. Another array H[W,D] could indicate the hours H worked on day D of week W. Notice again that the values within each array are of the same type; the grades were integers (percentages), the game positions were characters, the admission charges were real values.

The algorithm of figure 5 shows how the items in the array may be scanned, row by row. It loops through elements in order: C[1,1], C[1,2], horizontally, as shown in the trace of figure 6. A similar traverse could be done column by column. The algorithm of figure 7 inputs a sequence of values into an array, row by row.

As another example, to find the average grades of all people on all quizzes, we could sum all the 3*4 grades and divide this value by 12.

```
        S <--- 0
        LOOP P FROM 1 TO M
          LOOP Q FROM 1 TO N
             S <---- S + G[P,Q]
          END LOOP Q
        END LOOP P
        A <--- S/(M*N)
```

Other operations on arrays are shown on the following pages. They include averaging columns to find the average on each quiz, and weighted averaging of rows to find a student's grade. Other matrix operations shown include matrix addition and matrix multiplication.

OPERATIONS ON ONE ARRAY

1 AVERAGE of a Column

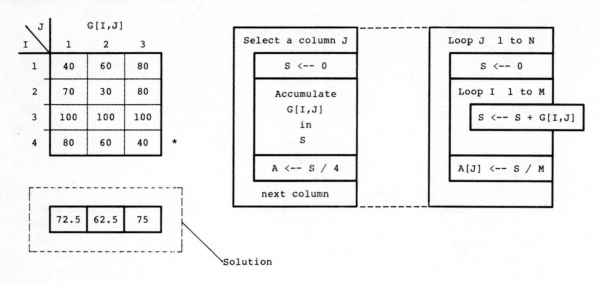

2 WEIGHTED AVERAGE OF A ROW

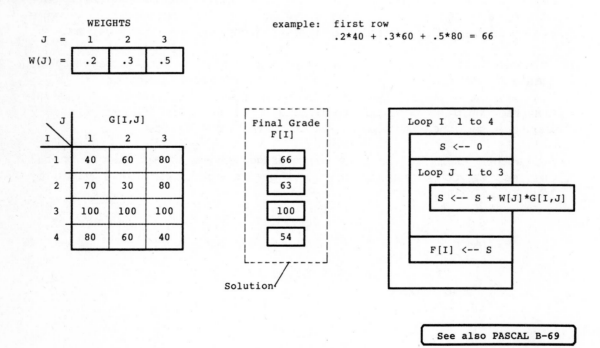

See also PASCAL B-69

OPERATIONS ON TWO ARRAYS

1 ARRAY ADDITION

A[I,J]

1	2
3	4

\+

B[I,J]

5	6
7	8

\=

C[I,J]

6	8
10	12

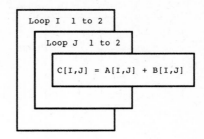

```
Loop I  1 to 2
  Loop J  1 to 2
    C[I,J] = A[I,J] + B[I,J]
```

2 ARRAY DIVISION

DISTANCE
D[I,J]

	1	2	3	4
1	0	150	100	180
2	150	0	60	80
3	100	60	0	30
4	180	80	30	0

VELOCITY
V[I,J]

	1	2	3	4
1	–	50	40	60
2	50	–	30	40
3	50	60	–	60
4	60	50	30	–

\=

TIME
T[I,J]

	1	2	3	4
1	0	3	2.5	3
2	3	0	2	2
3	2	1	0	0.5
4	3	1.6	1	0

3 MATRIX MULTIPLICATION

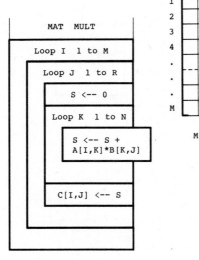

```
MAT  MULT
Loop I  1 to M
  Loop J  1 to R
    S <-- 0
    Loop K  1 to N
      S <-- S +
      A[I,K]*B[K,J]
    C[I,J] <-- S
```

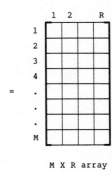

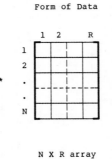

Form of Data

M X N array   *   N X R array   =   M X R array

Example

	1	2	3
	0	1	2
	3	4	5

M = 2

*

	1	2
	6	7
	8	9
	0	1

\=

8	11
50	62

RECORD EXAMPLES

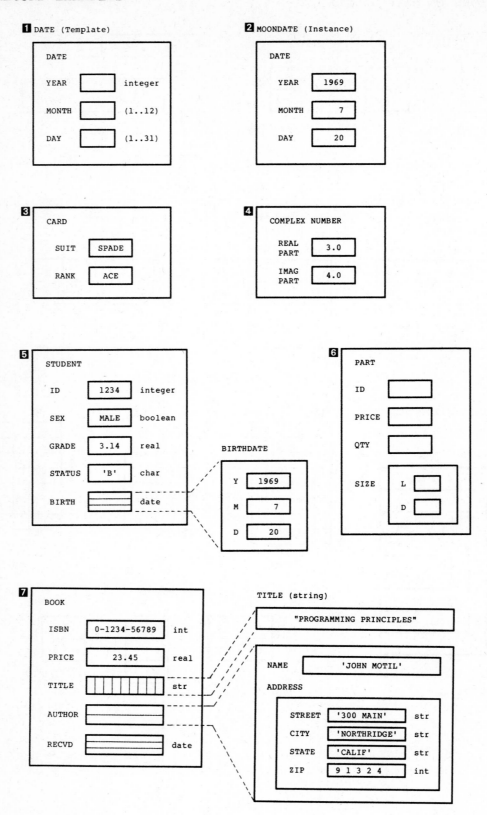

1 DATE (Template)

```
DATE

YEAR  [        ]  integer

MONTH [        ]  (1..12)

DAY   [        ]  (1..31)
```

2 MOONDATE (Instance)

```
DATE

YEAR  [ 1969 ]

MONTH [  7   ]

DAY   [  20  ]
```

3
```
CARD

SUIT  [ SPADE ]

RANK  [  ACE  ]
```

4
```
COMPLEX NUMBER

REAL
PART    [ 3.0 ]

IMAG
PART    [ 4.0 ]
```

5
```
STUDENT

ID     [ 1234 ]  integer

SEX    [ MALE ]  boolean

GRADE  [ 3.14 ]  real

STATUS [ 'B' ]   char

BIRTH  [======]  date
```

BIRTHDATE
```
Y  [ 1969 ]

M  [  7   ]

D  [  20  ]
```

6
```
PART

ID     [        ]

PRICE  [        ]

QTY    [        ]

SIZE       L [     ]

           D [     ]
```

7
```
BOOK

ISBN   [ 0-1234-56789 ]  int

PRICE  [   23.45   ]     real

TITLE  [|||||||]         str

AUTHOR [=======]

RECVD  [=======]         date
```

TITLE (string)
```
"PROGRAMMING PRINCIPLES"
```

```
NAME     [ 'JOHN MOTIL' ]

ADDRESS

     STREET [ '300 MAIN'   ]  str

     CITY   [ 'NORTHRIDGE' ]  str

     STATE  [ 'CALIF'      ]  str

     ZIP    [ 9 1 3 2 4    ]  int
```

RECORDS: And Sub-records

A record is a compound data structure consisting of a number of parts (called components, fields, properties, or attributes) which may be of different types. It can be viewed as a template (outline or skeleton), showing the form of an object. A record allows a collection of parts to be viewed as a whole object. With record types we can create our own objects and sub-objects as we did with programs and sub-programs. Some sample records follow. They are drawn as "record diagrams" which consist of nested boxes and sub-boxes representing objects.

DATE, of figure 1, shows how a date is described by three components, YEAR, MONTH, and DAY. Figure 2 shows a particular example or instance of this DATE type. It describes MOONDATE, the day humans first set foot on the moon.

CARD, of figure 3, similarly shows a typical playing card and its two main features, SUIT and RANK. With its four possible suits and 13 ranks, this form describes all 4*13 = 52 cards.

COMPLEX NUMBERS, of figure 4, often used in engineering and mathematics, consist of two parts, a Real part and an Imaginary part.

STUDENT, of figure 5, consists of an identification number (integer), sex (binary or Boolean), a grade average (real), and a status in the class (character). Notice that all of these are of different types.

A student also has a BIRTHDATE which is a sub-record within this record. This sub-record is described by the previous record called DATE.

PART, of figure 6, shows a typical part (perhaps in a warehouse) consisting of an ID number, a price, and a quantity. It also has a size, which is a sub-record of the two dimensions (length L and diameter D). Each of these parts could be of different types; for example, length could be an integer, and diameter could be real.

BOOK, of figure 7, shows a more complex record. It is described by a number (ISBN), by a price, a title, and author. The title could be described by a string (or array of characters). The author could be described by another sub-record consisting of two other sub-records (a name and an address). It could also be described by a sub-record DATERECEIVED of type DATE. More of such complex records will be considered later.

OTHER records could describe cars, clothes, catalog items, employees, loans, reservations, customers, bank accounts, schedules, patients, and many others.

MORE RECORDS AND ARRAYS

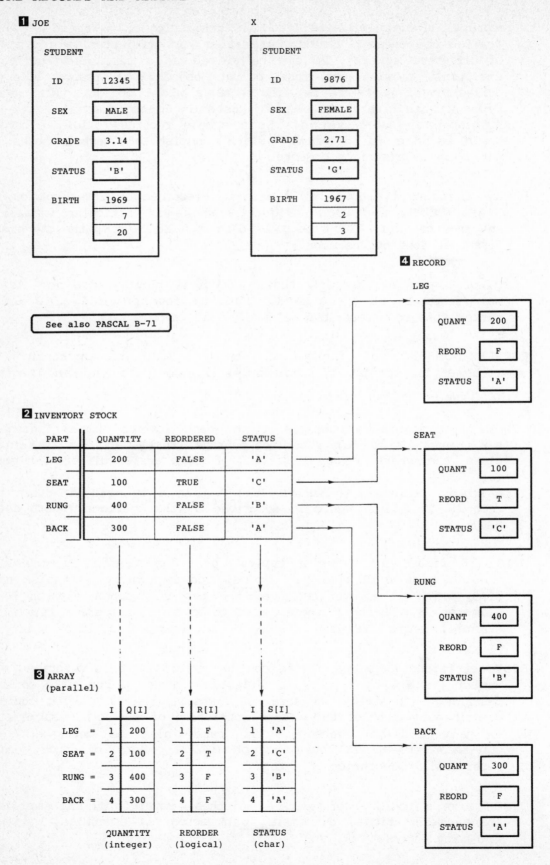

1 JOE

X

STUDENT

ID	12345
SEX	MALE
GRADE	3.14
STATUS	'B'
BIRTH	1969
	7
	20

STUDENT

ID	9876
SEX	FEMALE
GRADE	2.71
STATUS	'G'
BIRTH	1967
	2
	3

See also PASCAL B-71

4 RECORD

LEG

QUANT	200
REORD	F
STATUS	'A'

SEAT

QUANT	100
REORD	T
STATUS	'C'

RUNG

QUANT	400
REORD	F
STATUS	'B'

BACK

QUANT	300
REORD	F
STATUS	'A'

2 INVENTORY STOCK

PART	QUANTITY	REORDERED	STATUS
LEG	200	FALSE	'A'
SEAT	100	TRUE	'C'
RUNG	400	FALSE	'B'
BACK	300	FALSE	'A'

3 ARRAY
(parallel)

	I	Q[I]		I	R[I]		I	S[I]
LEG =	1	200		1	F		1	'A'
SEAT =	2	100		2	T		2	'C'
RUNG =	3	400		3	F		3	'B'
BACK =	4	300		4	F		4	'A'

| QUANTITY | REORDER | STATUS |
| (integer) | (logical) | (char) |

ACCESSING RECORDS: The DOT Notation

Records are accessed or selected by a notation involving dots. The component COMP of a record called NAME is indicated in the dot notation as:

    NAME.COMP

For example, consider the two students named JOE and X given by the record in figure 1. The identification number ID of student JOE is written JOE.ID and the grade of X is written X.GRADE. Such components are treated as any other variables, which can be assigned, input, output, compared, such as:

    JOE.ID <--- 12345
    G <--- JOE.GRADE
    IF X.GRADE < 2.5 THEN OUTPUT X.ID
    WHILE X.STATUS < 'C' ...
    X.GRADE <--- JOE.GRADE

Nested sub-records such as BIRTH, of type DATE, are also easily accessed by a series of dots, as for example:

    JOE.BIRTH.YEAR <--- 1969
    OUTPUT X.BIRTH.DAY

A more detailed description of a student, involving more levels, could yield longer dot forms such as:

    JOE.SPOUSE.BIRTH.YEAR
    JOE.ADDRESS.STREET.NUMBER

An entire sub-record may be assigned without assigning every component, by a simple statement such as:

    JOE.BIRTH <--- MOONDATE

RECORD CONSTRUCTORS are convenient operators for creating records simply by listing all components such as:

    MOONDATE <--- DATE(1969, 7, 20)
    JOE <--- STUDENT(1234, MALE, 3.14, 'B', DATE(1969, 7, 20))

Records vs Arrays: Two Views

Records and arrays are similar yet different, as will be shown with the given example STOCK of figure 2. It describes chair parts (leg, seat, rung, and back) in a warehouse and some data about each part (its quantity, whether it was reordered, and its status).

ARRAYS could describe this stock by three "parallel" arrays Q, R, S of figure 3, with a common index, I. Notice that the arrays are of different types (integer, logical, and character). If LEG was associated with index 1, and SEAT was associated with index 2, etc, then we could select components by the array bracket notation as in the following statements:

    QUANTITY[LEG] <--- 5
    INPUT STATUS[SEAT]
    IF REORDERED[RUNG] THEN . . .

RECORDS could describe this same stock system from a "horizontal" view by taking each row as a record. Figure 4 shows that each of the four items has three components Q, R, and S (of different types). Components could be selected by the dot notation as:

    LEG.QUANTITY <--- 5
    INPUT SEAT.STATUS
    IF RUNG.REORDERED THEN . . .

In this example, arrays and records are equally appropriate; in other examples, one may be preferable to another. Actually they will be intermixed, resulting in arrays of records and records of arrays, which are considered next.

COMBINATIONS OF RECORDS AND ARRAYS

1 RECORD OF ARRAYS

PUPIL

PROJECTS

I	P[I]
1	'C'
2	'B'
3	'A'
4	'A'
5	'B'
6	'A'

QUIZZES

J	Q[J]
1	87
2	66
3	92
4	70

2 ARRAY OF RECORDS

WORKER W[I]

W[1] = | 40 | HOURS |
       | 10 | RATE |

W[2] = | 10 | HOURS |
       | 40 | RATE |

W[3] = | 50 |
       | 5.50 |

W[N] = | | HOURS |
       | | RATE |

See also PASCAL B-72

SELECT (VARIANT) RECORDS

3
SALARIED
EMPLOYEE

ID   4567

SENIOR   10

MALE   T

etc

SALARY   700

Similar

Different

4
HOURLY
EMPLOYEE

ID   789

SENIOR   3

FEMALE   T

HOURS   50

RATE   10.00

5
EMPLOYEE

ID

SENIOR

SEX

T   SALARIED   F

SALARY

HOURS

RATE

Complexes of Arrays and Records

Arrays and records may be nested within one another in various combinations; some of the more common ones are shown here.

RECORDS OF ARRAYS are simply records whose components are arrays. For example, figure 1 shows a pupil's record consisting of two arrays, one with grades received on projects, and the other array with scores on quizzes. The score of JOE on quiz 2 is described by the mixed dot and bracket notation as

JOE.Q[2]

or more clearly, if the second quiz is the midterm:

JOE.QUIZ[MIDTERM]

ARRAYS OF RECORDS are arrays whose items are records. For example, figure 2 shows an array of workers W[I] where each worker I is specified by the number of HOURS worked and a RATE of pay. The time worked by the third person could be selected by the notation:

W[3].HOURS

More complex structures could be created from these above two. For example, the array of workers could be a component of a Department. This would involve a record of an array of records. The hours worked by the third person in the research department is denoted:

RESEARCH.WORKER[3].HOURS

Also, a classroom could be an array of pupils, making it an array of a record of arrays. Similarly, a school could be a record of classrooms; or (to be confusing) it is a record of an array of a record of arrays.

SELECT RECORDS (or Variant Records) are parts of records which may be selected depending on some condition. For example, employees who are paid differently (salaried or hourly) need not be described by two separate records as shown in figures 3 and 4, but may be described by a single record which has a part that can be selected as shown in figure 5.

TAGS are the names given to the variables which select the proper sub-record. In this case the tag is the logical variable SALARIED. In other records the tag may have many values. For example, a tag may be the marital STATUS having values: single, married, divorced, widowed, etc.

STRINGS

1 STRINGS: PATTERN MATCHING

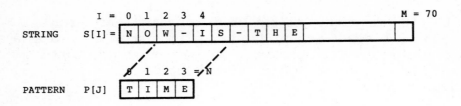

2 SEARCH a string S for a pattern P
(counting the number of matches C)

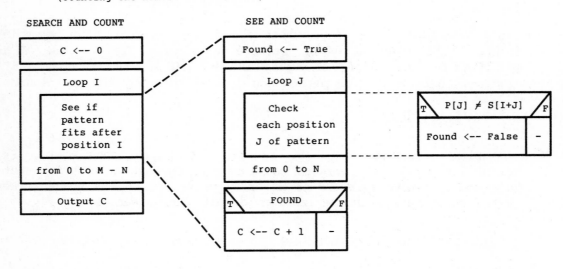

3 FIND-FIRST MATCH (fast)

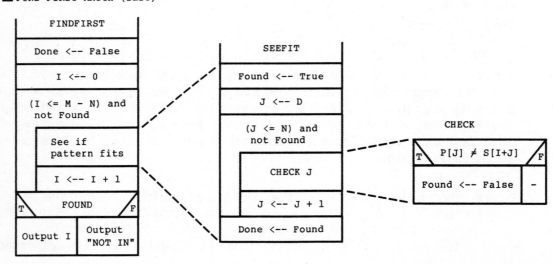

OTHER LINEAR STRUCTURES: Strings

STRINGS are simply sequences of symbols that are viewed as one single object. A symbol is any character of the keyboard, including the letters of the alphabet, decimal digits, punctuation marks, arithmetic operators, and the blank (space).

Programming languages differ greatly in their treatment of strings. Some languages have no strings available, others have strings of only a constant or limited length, and others allow strings of any variable length. Some languages, such as Snobol, are oriented mainly to string processing.

Representation and implementation of strings also differ among languages; some view strings as single entities, others view them as arrays of characters. But strings are usually represented within quotes (single or double) to avoid confusion with other sequences of symbols of the languages.

Examples of some typical strings follow.
```
    "F"         a string consisting of a single character
    'FAIL'      a short string of letters only
    "FEB 31/84" a string of mixed symbols
    "   "       a string of three blanks
    "LONG AGO.." a long story string.
```

OPERATIONS on strings are many, including assignment, input-output, comparison, join, and matching.

COMPARISON of two strings S and T is done alphabetically (called lexicographical order), where "Z" is considered greater than "A" so that ('YES' > 'YEA') is true.

JOIN (or concatenation or append) is the operation of putting together two strings, say S and T, to create a third new resulting string R. This operation is sometimes represented by the notation R <--- S + T, or alternately by a sub-program JOIN(S,T,R).

PATTERN MATCHING, to determine if a string pattern P is a substring completely within another string S, is a useful search operation. It can be done by moving the pattern P along the string as shown in figure 1. Two algorithms can be used to compare the strings.

SEARCH-AND-COUNT, of figure 2, passes P along S comparing all values and bumps a counter when all characters match. It is slow because it keeps comparing the characters of the pattern and string even after finding a difference. Also it passes along the entire string counting all matches.

FIND-FIRST MATCH, of figure 3, is a faster match because it only compares characters of the pattern to the string until it finds a mismatch, and then it moves the pattern over for another try. Also it stops when it finds the first match.

STACKS

1 OBJECT

2 ACTIONS

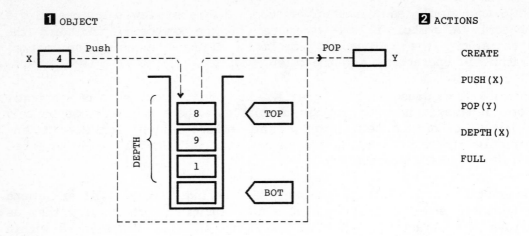

CREATE

PUSH(X)

POP(Y)

DEPTH(X)

FULL

3 An implementation (as an array)

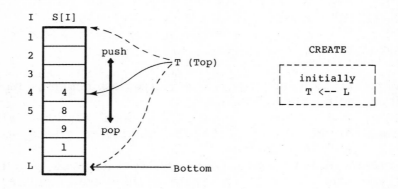

4 PUSH(X)

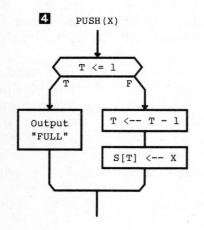

5 POP(Y)

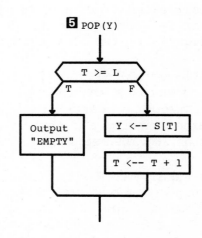

Stacks

A stack is a simple but very useful concept in computer science. It is
used both in a hardware sense (with stack machines) and in a software
sense (with sub-programs, as on page 5-45). A stack in general is
a linear list of objects with only the top object accessible. This
top object is the last one which was put onto the stack; the first
object put on is at the bottom of the stack.

Behavior of a stack is often described as "LIFO": last-in first-out.
This essentially provides for good simple data management, for
whatever is needed is immediately available at the top of a stack.
No addressing mechanism is required.

Operations on stacks are many, the most common being PUSH and POP.
Some stack operations are:

    PUSH   to insert an object on the top,
    POP   to delete the object on the top,
    CREATE   to set up the stack originally,
    DEPTH   to indicate the number of objects in the stack,
    TOP   to indicate the value of the top of the stack,
    FULL   to indicate whether the stack is full,
    EMPTY   to indicate whether the stack is empty,
    AVAIL   to indicate how many more objects can be held.

Implementation of a stack is possible in many ways, one of which is
shown in figure 3. It consists of an array, S, with the bottom at
position L and the variable T pointing to the top.

PUSHING an object X onto the stack is shown by the algorithm in
figure 4. First it tests to see if it is already full (i.e.,
T <= 1), and only if it is not full does the top pointer change
(decreasing by 1), and the value of X is put into this position.

POPPING an object off the top of the stack and into a variable Y is
similar but opposite to PUSH. First is a test for emptiness
(T >= L). Then if not empty the topmost value is assigned to Y,
and the top is changed to point to the next object on the stack.

CREATE is a single simple action of setting the top pointer to the last
object of the stack (the bottom).

DEPTH, indicating the number of objects in a stack, is a counter which
is increased by one for each PUSH and decreased by one for each POP.

Other implementations of stacks are possible. For example, the given
one has the bottom of the stack at the bottom (position L) of the
array. Another common method is to put the bottom of the stack at
the top of the array (position 1).

Two other methods involve the top of the stack being in position L and
at position 1. Stacks could also be implemented with records and
pointers.

QUEUES

1 General Object

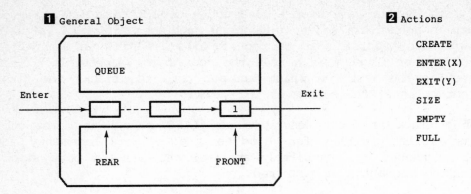

2 Actions

CREATE

ENTER(X)

EXIT(Y)

SIZE

EMPTY

FULL

3 An Implementation (circular list)

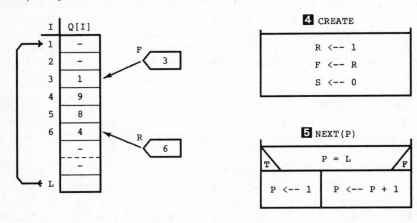

4 CREATE

R <-- 1

F <-- R

S <-- 0

5 NEXT(P)

T	P = L	F
P <-- 1		P <-- P + 1

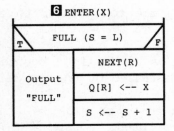

6 ENTER(X)

T	FULL (S = L)	F
	NEXT(R)	
Output	Q[R] <-- X	
"FULL"	S <-- S + 1	

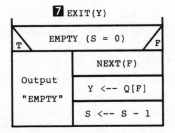

7 EXIT(Y)

T	EMPTY (S = 0)	F
	NEXT(F)	
Output	Y <-- Q[F]	
"EMPTY"	S <-- S - 1	

SEE ALSO PAGE 7-35

Queues

Queues occur very commonly in everyday life; they consist of lines of objects usually waiting to be served one at a time. Examples of queues include people lined up to get something, vehicles stopped at an intersection, and tasks waiting to be done. Queues are used as fair ways of serving objects in the order of their arrival ("first-come, first-served").

Queues in general consist of a channel where objects enter at one end (called the REAR) and ultimately exit at the other end (the FRONT) as shown in figure 1. There is no entry or exit in the middle of the queue. The first object into a queue is the first one out (called FIFO).

Operations on queues are many. The two most common are:
      ENTER(X) to put a value X onto the rear of the queue,
      EXIT(Y) to remove a value Y from the front.

Other queue operations (or attributes) include:
      CREATE   to set up the queue originally,
      SIZE   to indicate the number of objects in the queue,
      EMPTY   to indicate if the queue has no objects,
      FULL   to indicate if the queue is full to capacity.

Implementation of queues are many, one of which is shown in figure 3. It consists of an array Q, with a variable F (for FRONT) pointing to the first value, and a variable R (for REAR) pointing to the value following the last one.

CREATE puts both FRONT and REAR variables to the same index initially, and sets the size S of the queue to zero, as shown in figure 4. As objects (values) are entered, the rear pointer advances, and as they are removed (with EXIT) the front pointer also advances, leaving behind some "used" values. So the queue "snakes" through the array. As each pointer passes the last item of the array it continues to the first item, so creating a circular array.

NEXT(P) is a sub-program which bumps pointer P (either the FRONT or the REAR). Usually the pointer is increased by 1, but after reaching the end of the array it is reset to 1.

ENTER(X) first tests to see if the queue is full (size greater than the array length), and if not it moves the rear pointer to its next position, puts a value into it, and bumps the size counter S.

EXIT(Y) first checks if the queue is empty (size S is zero) and if not it moves the front pointer, puts the value into Y, and decreases the size count S.

Pascal programs implementing queues as both arrays and records are shown on pages 7-34 and 7-35.

FILES: Serial

1 OBJECT

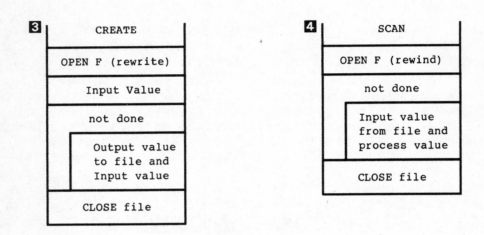

window

name F

begin   end of file

2 ACTIONS

OPEN FILE

CLOSE FILE

INPUT FROM FILE

OUTPUT TO FILE

END OF FILE

3 CREATE

| OPEN F (rewrite) |
| Input Value |
| not done |
| Output value to file and Input value |
| CLOSE file |

4 SCAN

| OPEN F (rewind) |
| not done |
| Input value from file and process value |
| CLOSE file |

5 WORD ANALYSIS

| OPEN file
Set: W <-- 0
      S <-- 0 |
| not terminal |
| SKIP over blanks |
| find length L of word and update |
| M <-- S / W |
| CLOSE file |

6

| Input C from file |
| C = blank |
| Input C |

| L <-- 0 |
| C not blank and not term |
| L <-- L + 1
Read CH |
| S <-- S + L
W <-- W + 1 |

Files

Files are ordered collections of data components, such as characters of a text, numbers of an inventory, or records of patients. They are often used to store large amounts of data on secondary storage devices (such as tapes or disks). They may be accessed by any number of programs. Files are often viewed as data structures consisting of records, which may in turn consist of fields.

Two common types of files are: serial and random-access. Serial files access records in sequence, so some records may take more time to access than others. Random-access files are viewed as arrays of records, usually of fixed size, where any record can be accessed in about the same length of time. So serial files are slower, but simpler than random-access files.

Simple Serial Files

A serial file can be viewed as a linear tape, as shown in figure 1. It is indefinitely long, and accessible at only one place, called the window.

Actions on a serial file are shown in figure 2. The operations of OPEN and CLOSE prepare a file to be available for input and output. Opening a file for reading is often called reset or rewind, and opening it for writing is often called rewrite. INPUT from a file and output to a file often resemble the usual Read and Write statements except that a file name must also be specified. Larger actions on files include CREATE, SCAN, and UPDATE, some of which are considered next.

CREATION of a file involves repeatedly appending records to it as shown in figure 3. First the window is positioned at the beginning of the file by a REWRITE command. Then each WRITE command causes a record to be appended to the file.

SCAN of a file, shown in figure 4, requires the window to be set at the beginning of the file by a RESET (or REWIND) command. Then each READ command moves the window (only in one direction) to access the next record. An EOF (End-of-File) variable can be tested to determine if the end is near.

WORD ANALYSIS, of figure 5, shows an algorithm which determines the average length of a word within a given file of characters. It first sets the word count W to zero, along with the accumulated sum S of characters in a word. It then loops, skipping over spaces, and finding the lengths L of words, which are accumulated into S. When finally the terminating symbol is input, the Mean Length of word is computed by dividing the accumulated sum S of the lengths by the number of words W.

RECURSIVE OBJECTS

1 RECURSIVE REVERSE

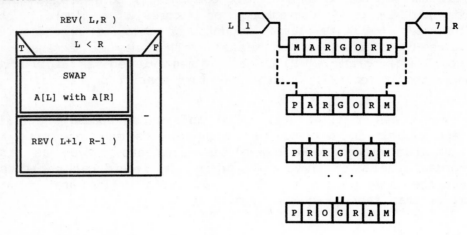

REV(L,R)

T	L < R	F
	SWAP A[L] with A[R]	–
	REV(L+1, R-1)	

2 RECURSIVE MERGE SORT

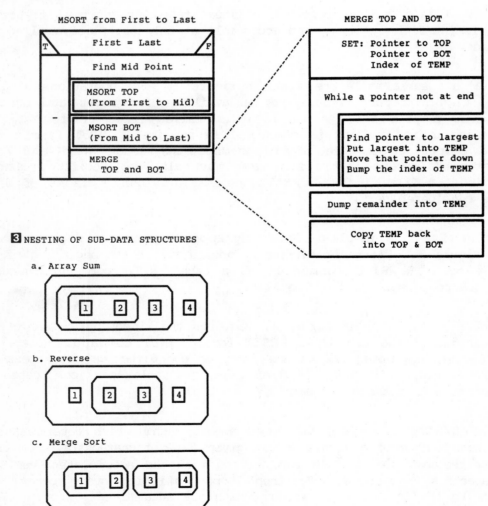

MSORT from First to Last

T	First = Last	F
	Find Mid Point	
–	MSORT TOP (From First to Mid)	
	MSORT BOT (From Mid to Last)	
	MERGE TOP and BOT	

MERGE TOP AND BOT

SET: Pointer to TOP
Pointer to BOT
Index of TEMP

While a pointer not at end

Find pointer to largest
Put largest into TEMP
Move that pointer down
Bump the index of TEMP

Dump remainder into TEMP

Copy TEMP back
into TOP & BOT

3 NESTING OF SUB-DATA STRUCTURES

a. Array Sum

b. Reverse

c. Merge Sort

RECURSION AND DATA STRUCTURES (Optional)

Recursion is often useful when applied to data structures. Here it will be used in three "linear" examples (involving simple arrays); later it will be applied to "nonlinear" structures such as trees.

Essentially, recursion can be viewed as a sub-program consisting of pieces, each of which is similar to the original sub-program. It is more of a description rather than a prescription, declarative rather than imperative.

SUMming of an array A of N items can be done by adding the last value A[N] to the sum of the remaining (N-1) values. This can be formally written as:

$$SUM(N) = A[N] + SUM(N-1)$$

An ending condition is obtained by realizing that the sum is zero when there are no more elements. The complete recursive definition is then:

$$SUM(N) = \begin{cases} 0 & \text{if } N = 0 \\ A[N] + SUM(N-1) & \text{otherwise} \end{cases}$$

REVERSE of an array A of N items can also be done recursively by first swapping the end points and then applying the same REVERSE to the remaining items, as shown in figure 1. The end points L and R (at the left and right, respectively) continue to move inward, and the recursion stops when they meet.

MSORT (Merge Sort) of an array A of N items can be done recursively by finding the midpoint and splitting it into two arrays called TOP and BOT. Then these two arrays are sorted (by calling this same MSORT!). The two sorted parts are finally merged together. This merging is done simply with a pointer "sliding down" each array, with the maximum value of the two put into the array TEMP, at the right of figure 2. Although this Merge Sort mechanism looks complex, this sort is considerably faster than all the sorts considered thus far.

These three recursive algorithms also illustrate three "nested" ways of breaking up the arrays, as shown in figure 3. SUM forms "concentric" nests, each excluding the rightmost item. REVERSE forms more symmetric concentric nests, each successive nest excluding both a left and a right item. MSORT proceeds by splitting each sub-array into two smaller sub-arrays. In all these cases, the sub-parts are similar to all other sub-parts.

TREES: Representing and Traversing

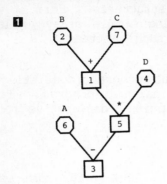

1

2

NODE N	PARENT P[N]
1	5
2	1
3	0
4	5
5	3
6	3
7	1

3

NODE N	LEFT L[N]	RIGHT R[N]
1	2	7
2	0	0
3	6	5
4	0	0
5	1	4
6	0	0
7	0	0

4 TRAVERSING

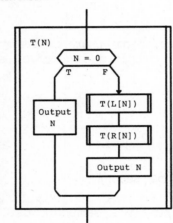

5 TRAVERSE(N)

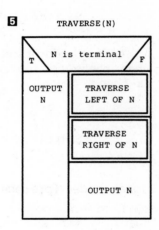

6 TRACE OF POST-ORDER TRAVERSE

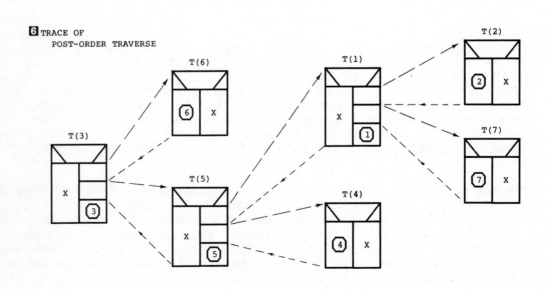

TREES: Tracing and Traversing (Optional)

Trees are extremely common objects in computing. We have already encountered many of them. For example:

>   Hierarchies of people in an organization were described by a BOSS-tree on page 1-8.

>   Structure of arithmetic expressions is also described by trees on page 1-8.

>   Levels of a job description were shown by the ORDER-TAKER of page 2-28.

>   Breakdown of problems and programs also has a tree-like form as shown in PROJECT and PAY of page 2-37.

>   Syntactic form of logical formulas is shown by syntax trees on page 4-26.

REPRESENTATION of trees is possible in many ways. A typical tree is shown in diagrammatic form in figure 1. This tree could represent the algebraic formula "A - (B + C)*D". Trees could also be represented as arrays in two different ways as shown in figures 2 and 3. The first form indicates for each node N which is the single next higher node (predecessor or parent). The second form indicates for each node its left and right branches. The first form emphasizes movement up the tree (from leaves to trunk); the second one emphasizes movement down the tree.

IMPLEMENTATION of trees could be done using arrays; the first form requires one array, the second requires two. Other implementations are possible, but beyond the scope of this book. The implementation chosen depends on the actions to be done on the tree.

ACTIONS or operations on trees include inserting nodes, deleting them, searching them, and traversing them.

TRAVERSING a tree is a most interesting action, previously done as the "spitting spider" tour of page 2-37. The traversing algorithm is shown in figure 4 as a flow chart, and in figure 5 as a flow block diagram. Notice that it is highly recursive, calling itself twice from within itself.

TRACING of the algorithm is shown in figure 6. Notice that the trace resembles a tree (lying on its side). The outputs are circled and appear in the order: 6,2,7,1,4,5,3. If the node numbers were re-labelled to correspond to the expression "A - (B + C)*D" then the resulting trace is "A B C + D * -". It converts the infix form to the postfix form.

REVIEW: Of Chapter 6

OBJECTS: Data Structures

Objects considered here are large, consisting of groupings of smaller objects. Arrays group objects which must be of the same type; records group objects which may be of different types.

Arrays group objects of the same type by a common name, and access the different components by indices, within brackets. Arrays having one index are very common. They can be sorted in four basic ways (by swapping, counting, selecting or inserting). Searching can also be done in a number of different ways.

Arrays of two dimensions (and more) are less common than those of one dimension, and so are treated in less detail. Also, many multi-dimensional objects are better done as records.

Records group objects by their individual names, and access their components by a dot notation. This method allows the structuring of data in a top-down form.

Records may consist of other records or arrays, and in turn may be part of other records or arrays. This leads to structures of arrays of records and records of arrays, and arrays of records of records of arrays, etc.

Other data structures included here are strings, stacks, queues, and trees. They are implemented here (and in Chapter 7) by arrays and records. Files are also introduced briefly. These objects are so important that usually a following course in data structures is devoted to them and their many implementations and uses.

General actions on most data objects are:

            Create   (set up, initialize)
            Insert   (put, push, enter, append)
            Remove   (get, pop, exit, delete)
            Arrange   (sort, shuffle, reverse)
            Combine   (merge, intersect, join)

More examples, implementations, and applications of these data structures are shown in Chapter 7. Some Pascal programs are also given there.

PROBLEMS: on Chapter 6

MANIPULATIONS OF LINEAR LISTS

1. REVERSE
    Create an algorithm to reverse the values in a linear list L.

2. NORMALIZE
    Create an algorithm to convert a list of numbers (frequencies) into a
    list of probabilities, by summing all the values and then dividing each
    by this sum.

3. WEED
    Create an algorithm to "weed out" or eliminate duplicate entries from a
    linear list V, creating a second list (or set) W.

4. K-BIG
    Create an algorithm to find the k-th largest value of an array A of N
    different values.

5. INTERSECTION
    Create an algorithm to compare the items of two sets (linear lists each
    having no repeated items) and to output those items which are common to
    both sets. Compute also the UNION, those items in either set or in both.

6. HILO-GRADE
    Create an algorithm that computes an average of grades, and then
    indicates for each grade whether it is above, at, or below the average.

7. SPEEDY-SORT
    Given an array B of N binary values (say 0s and 1s only) create an
    algorithm to sort this array in two passes. Can this array be sorted in
    one pass? Indicate how, or else why not.

8. MEDIAN
    Create some algorithms to find the MEDIAN value of a list; this is the
    middle value (for an odd-sized list), or the average of the two mid
    values (for an even-sized list).

9. A LA MODE
    The mode M of an array A of N values is the value which occurs most
    often. Show two general algorithms to determine the mode. Anticipate
    exceptional cases and handle them in any way you wish.

10. SLOW-SORT
    Given an array A of N integers (not necessarily different) ranging from 0
    to 1000, create an algorithm to sort the values by checking (in
    increasing order) if each of the 1000 integers is in the array (and if
    so, it outputs the value). Compute the number of comparisons required
    for this sort, and compare it to some of the other sorts.

PROBLEMS ON TABLES

1. SCALE TIME
   Given a table indicating the time T[I,J] to travel between points I and J in hours, create an algorithm to convert this time to minutes.

2. MORE-CHARGE
   Recall the previous CHARGE algorithm of Chapter 1, when drawn as a table (in figure B4, where the charge C[A,B] is three dollars for each adult A, and two dollars for each baby B). Create an algorithm to draw such a table for any given number of adults M and babies N.

3. FLIP-N-FLOP
   Trace the algorithm given below when operating on the given table. Then indicate verbally its behavior in general.

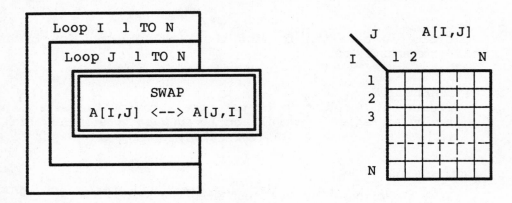

4. TRANSPOSE
   Create an algorithm to transpose an array (i.e., to convert all values A[I,J] to A[J,I]). This essentially "rotates" the array values about a diagonal.

5. MINIMAX
   Given an array of M rows and N columns, construct a flow block diagram which finds the smallest entry in the row having the greatest sum.

6. TIC-TAC-WIN
   The game of Tic-tac-toe (or Xs and Os, or naughts and crosses) is played on a table as shown in figure 3 of page 6-22. A game is won if there are three identical symbols in a row, in a column, or along a diagonal. Show two different algorithms to detect a win.

7. NORMALIZE FREQUENCIES
   Two dice are rolled N times, with outcomes D1 and D2 noted and put into a table F[D1,D2] of frequencies of occurrence. Create an algorithm to convert (normalize) this table of frequencies F into a table of probabilities P, by dividing each entry by N. Then use this P table to find the probability of all sums S from 2 to 11. For example, the probability of (S=11) is P[5,6] + P[6,5].

MORE PROBLEMS ON DATA STRUCTURES

1. UNIVERSITY RECORD
    Create a record of a university. It is described by a name, enrollment, age, ZIP code, and phone number (having three parts: Area code, Prefix, and Suffix). The university is also classified as being Private or Nonprivate.

    Write a program to search an array of such universities and output the names of all those within a given telephone area code.

2. PLAY RECORD
    Create a record describing a card game, such as Bridge or Poker.

3. QUICK QUEUE
    Create a queue and its operations ENTERQ and EXITQ, using the already created STACK and its operations.

4. DOUBLE STACKS
    Two stacks can be implemented by a single array, with the stacks "growing" toward each other as shown below. Create a general algorithm for pushing (PUSH1 and PUSH2) and popping (POP1 and POP2) the appropriate stacks.

5. MORE QUEUES
    The given diagrams show two more implementations of a queue, using arrays. The first queue Q1 always has its HEAD at position one of the array, and on EXITQ all values are moved up. The second queue Q2 moves "snakewise" down the queue (like the circular queue), but when the REAR hits the bottom of the array, then all entries are shifted up so that the FRONT is at the top again. Create programs to enter and EXIT these queues. Compare the two queue implementations briefly.

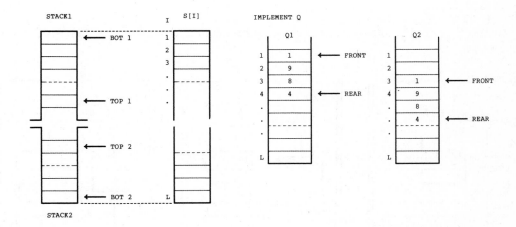

STILL MORE PROBLEMS ON OBJECTS

1. CONVOLUTION
   Trace the following algorithm when operating on the given linear lists.

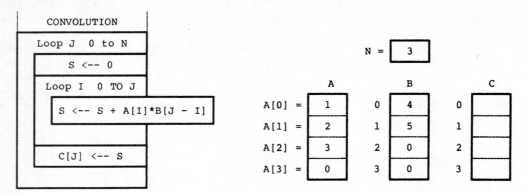

```
         CONVOLUTION
   Loop J   0 to N
        S <-- 0
   Loop I   0 TO J
      S <-- S + A[I]*B[J - I]

        C[J] <-- S
```

N = 3

	A		B		C
A[0] =	1	0	4	0	
A[1] =	2	1	5	1	
A[2] =	3	2	0	2	
A[3] =	0	3	0	3	

2. INSERT-SORT
   Create a sorting algorithm which enters new values into an array by moving existing values to make space for the new value.

3. MERGE-SORT
   Create an algorithm to merge two already sorted arrays into one larger sorted array. Do this in two ways.

4. RECURSIVE SEARCHES
   Given an array A of N items, create a recursive algorithm to search the array. Do this as a linear search and also as a binary search.

5. BAR PLOT
   Create an algorithm which draws a histogram (bar plot) where values are plotted in proportion to some values (given as an array). Do this first with the bars plotted horizontally, then again with the bars plotted vertically.

6. OTHER TREE TRAVERSES
   Using the following recursive algorithms, raverse the tree of page 6-42.

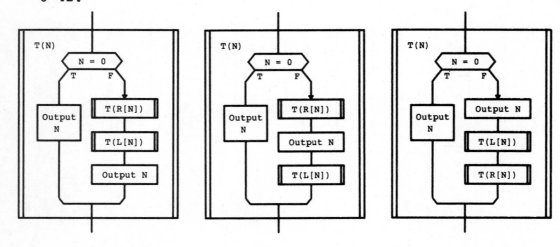

Chapter 7

APPLICATIONS:
    DESIGN, SYSTEMS

DESIGNING

SIMULATING

CALCULATING

GRAPHING

COMPUTING

SCHEDULING

APPLICATIONS:

DESIGN, SYSTEMS, EXAMPLES

*   Asterisks indicate the degree of importance   *

Chapter 7:

APPLICATIONS

Design, Systems, Examples

PREVIEW

This chapter is a mixture of applications, techniques, and design
    methods. Computers and programming have uses or applications in
    many areas including: engineering, business, mathematics, geography,
    art, psychology, biology, and education.

    Although the applications may seem different, they may use similar
    processes, data structures, and programming methods. Some of these
    will be illustrated here.

TECHNIQUES may be common to diverse areas. For example, techniques
    involving random numbers can be used in business to study markets,
    in biology to study wild life, and in mathematics to do integration.

DATA STRUCTURES of the same kind can also appear in different areas.
    For example, complex numbers (vectors) could represent alternating
    currents, distances, or forces.

DESIGN METHODS of various kinds will be illustrated, including bottom
    up as well as top down. There is no single general design method
    that works in all cases.

Applications considered here are:

        SST,   a simple sales terminal,
                      to show top-down design
        CRAPS,   a simulation of a dice game,
                      to show random number techniques
        BCT,   a big calculator tool, for large integers
                      to show design of a special purpose tool
        COMPLEX, a complex number calculator,
                      to show records and bottom-up design
        PLOT,   a graphical plotting program,
                      to show 2D arrays and graphics
        BIT,   a simulation of a digital computer,
                      to show simulation
        RROBIN,   a method (Round Robin) of scheduling jobs,
                      to show creation and use of objects (queues).

The applications considered here are usually developed from the top, and
    done only for a few levels. They are also shown in Pascal. Most
    are not completely finished; you may wish to continue developing some
    of them.

PROGRAM DESIGN: Top-down

SIMPLE SALES TERMINAL (SST)

1 DATA STRUCTURE

CASH Inventory		ITEM Inventory			
		ID I	PRICE P[I]	QUANT Q[I]	B[I]
PENNIES P =	50	1	10	100	
NICKELS N =	40	2	5	10	
DIMES D =	0	3	25	50	
QUARTERS Q =	30	4	39	200	
HALVES H =	0	5	14	43	
ONES O =	10				
FIVES F =	2	M	29	81	
WORTH W =	30	S =	0	SALES	

2 PROGRAM STRUCTURE

3 Level 2

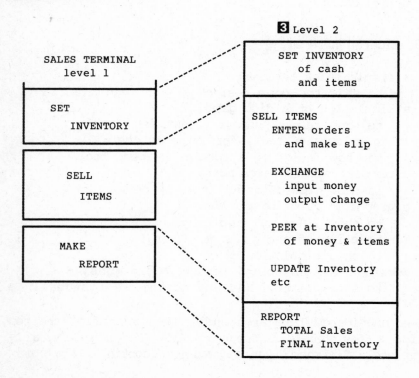

SALES TERMINAL
level 1

SET
    INVENTORY

SELL
    ITEMS

MAKE
    REPORT

SET INVENTORY
    of cash
    and items

SELL ITEMS
    ENTER orders
        and make slip

    EXCHANGE
        input money
        output change

    PEEK at Inventory
        of money & items

    UPDATE Inventory
    etc

REPORT
    TOTAL Sales
    FINAL Inventory

DESIGNING: Simple Sales Terminal (SST)

TOP-DOWN design will be illustrated by creating a small sales terminal, sufficiently complex to illustrate many design concepts, and yet sufficiently simple to be convenient. The sales terminal is to be used in a small shop which could sell tickets or tobacco, or donuts, or magazines, or films.

Goals of this system are to keep track of the sales (making sales slips, accumulating the total, making change) and also to keep track of the items (inventory of quantity, price, etc.). It is, however, not too extensive: it does not keep track of customers, nor does it provide for advance orders or credit. It is strictly a "cash and carry" business. It can later be extended to be more complete.

Structure of Data and Program

DATA structures describing this simple sales terminal are shown in figure 1. The cash inventory is given with its initial values at the beginning of the day. Many businesses provide such a fixed amount of cash initially. The total worth of this cash (30 dollars) is indicated in variable W.

Inventory of the items is given by two arrays, showing the price $P[I]$ and quantity $Q[I]$ of any item I. There could be other such arrays, including:

    B[I] showing the beginning inventory
    C[I] showing critical quantities
    D[I] showing a description (name)
    etc.

These arrays are of length M, providing for M items. The total sales amount is accumulated in variable S. This data structure of "parallel arrays" could instead be implemented as a record, in those languages allowing records.

If the business were more complex, involving credit, and advance orders, and customers' names, then the data structure of this sales terminal would be more complex.

PROGRAM structure of the sales terminal at the top level is shown in figure 2. First the inventory (of both cash and items) is set, then items are sold, and finally a report is generated.

Refinement of this algorithm, shown in figure 3, shows that SELL involves

    ENTERING   orders, making a slip, totalling it,
    EXCHANGING items and change for any amount tendered,
    PEEKING   at either inventory, at any time,
    UPDATING   the inventories by adding or deleting.

Other operations could be added here (perhaps later). They include a HELP operation, to offer hints when the user is not certain what other operations are available.

REFINEMENT: TOP LEVELS

1 SALES TERMINAL
level 3

```
┌─────────────────────────────┐
│      SET INVENTORY          │
├─────────────────────────────┤
│                             │
│    Request command          │
├─────────────────────────────┤
│  Input response C           │
├─────────────────────────────┤
│  While C ≠ "EXIT"           │
│   ┌──────────────────────────┐
│   │  case of commands C      │
│   │ ┌──────────────┬────────┐ │
│   │ │ C = "ENTER  T│ ENTER  │ │
│   │ │     ORDER"   │ STUB   │ │
│   │ ├──────────────┼────────┤ │
│   │ │              │EXCHANGE│ │
│   │ │ C ="EXCHANGE"│ STUB   │ │
│   │ ├──────────────┼────────┤ │
│   │ │ C = "PEEK"   │ STUB   │ │
│   │ ├──────────────┼────────┤ │
│   │ │ C = "UPDATE" │        │ │
│   │ ├──────────────┼────────┤ │
│   │ │ C = "HELP"   │ Output │ │
│   │ │              │message │ │
│   │ ├──────────────┼────────┤ │
│   │ │   else       │ Output │ │
│   │ │              │ "ERR"  │ │
│   │ └──────────────┴────────┘ │
│   ┌──────────────────────────┐
│   │   request command        │
│   ├──────────────────────────┤
│   │  Input response C        │
│   └──────────────────────────┘
├─────────────────────────────┤
│ REPORT                      │
└─────────────────────────────┘
```

2 BEHAVIOR (test)
of level 3
(with dummy stubs)

IT: WELCOME

ENTER COMMAND.

IF UNSURE, TYPE HELP

US: help

IT: POSSIBLE COMMANDS

ARE:

ENTER, EXCHANGE,

PEEK, UPDATE,

HELP, EXIT

NEXT COMMAND?

US: enter

IT: ENTERING

IT: NEXT COMMAND?

US: exchange

IT: EXCHANGING

IT: NEXT COMMAND

US: peek

IT: PEEKING

IT: NEXT COMMAND

US: update

IT: UPDATING

IT: NEXT COMMAND

US: stop

IT: NO SUCH COMMAND

NEXT COMMAND

US: exit

IT: REPORTING

IT: GOODBYE.

Refinement of SST

Structure of SST, at a high level, is given in figure 1. It could be viewed as a supervisor (dispatcher, executive, scheduler, or boss). First a command is requested, and the response input. While this response is not EXIT, the response is identified (or decoded) by the big case structure. If the response is one of the proper ones (ENTER, EXCHANGE, PEEK, UPDATE, etc.), then it performs the corresponding stub. A STUB (or phantom-sub) is simply a dummy block which shows where the corresponding sub-program is to be. It may be a single output message (such as ENTERING, EXCHANGING, PEEKING, etc.) to indicate what it should be doing. After so "doing" any command (including the detection of improper ones), it requests another command, and continues looping through the case structure similarly, until the command is EXIT.

Behavior of the program at this high level is shown to the right of the algorithm, in figure 2. It takes the form of a conversation between US and IT. This interaction essentially exercises the algorithm, trying all paths.

Coding the program (whenever it begins and in whatever language) should start at this top level. Then testing can be done on this top level, yielding a trace similar to the conversation in figure 2. It is very encouraging to be assured that this part works, independently of whatever part is to be added! We do not need to wait until all parts are done in order to test it.

Refinement can now proceed to lower levels, by replacing each stub by a sub-algorithm. The process continues in a tree-like growth as shown in the figure below. At the next level the subs SETUP and REPORT can first be created and then tested along with the SUPERVISOR.

Bottom up design would proceed in the opposite way: first creating all the sub-programs and then ultimately connecting them all into one large program. Each sub-program could also be tested (by a program called a driver), but this driver program does not become part of the main system after serving its test purpose. In comparison, the top-down system at the higher levels serves as the test program for the lower levels. The top-down method tests not only the sub-programs but also their interconnection. The interconnection between sub-programs is most significant, and if it is not done well it could lead to weird behavior.

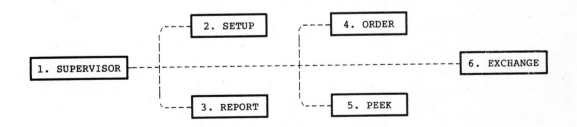

FURTHER REFINEMENT

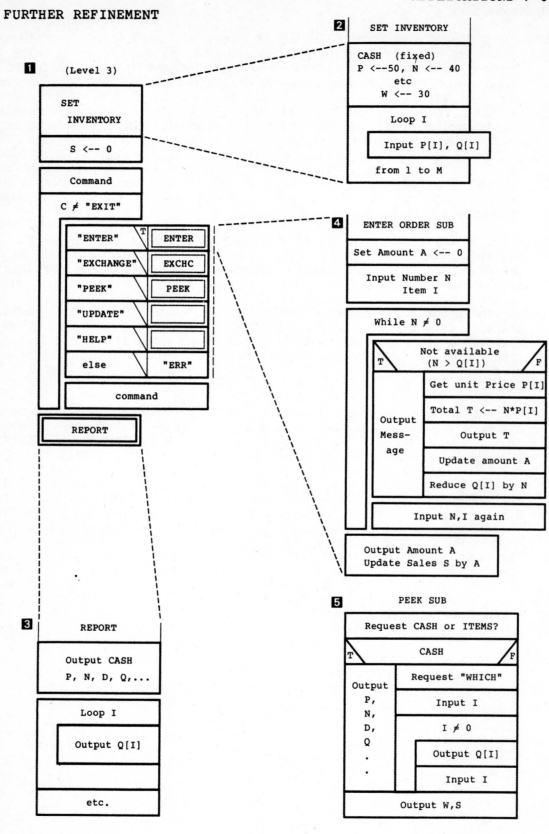

1 (Level 3)

| SET |
| INVENTORY |
| S <-- 0 |

| Command |
| C ≠ "EXIT" |

"ENTER"	T	ENTER
"EXCHANGE"		EXCHC
"PEEK"		PEEK
"UPDATE"		
"HELP"		
else		"ERR"
command		

| REPORT |

2 SET INVENTORY

| CASH (fixed) |
| P <--50, N <-- 40 |
| etc |
| W <-- 30 |

| Loop I |
| Input P[I], Q[I] |
| from 1 to M |

4 ENTER ORDER SUB

| Set Amount A <-- 0 |

| Input Number N |
| Item I |

| While N ≠ 0 |

	Not available	
T	(N > Q[I])	F
Output	Get unit Price P[I]
Mess-	Total T <-- N*P[I]
age	Output T
	Update amount A
	Reduce Q[I] by N

| Input N,I again |

| Output Amount A |
| Update Sales S by A |

5 PEEK SUB

| Request CASH or ITEMS? |
T	CASH	F
Output	Request "WHICH"
P,	Input I
N,	I ≠ 0
D,	Output Q[I]
Q	Input I
.
.
Output W,S

3 REPORT

| Output CASH |
| P, N, D, Q,... |

| Loop I |
| Output Q[I] |

| etc. |

Further Refinement Of SST

More refinement of SST is shown in the adjacent figures. The high
level supervisor is repeated again in figure 1. The remaining
stubs are expanded into sub-programs or modules.

SET, of figure 2, initializes the inventory of cash (which is fixed
each day) and inputs the Price P[I] and Quantity Q[I] of each
item I. Later this initializing input can be done from a data
file.

REPORT, of figure 3, at the end of the day just outputs some
inventory amounts. It first reports on the cash, the amount
of change, the total worth W of this change, and the total
amount of sales S. Then it outputs the quantities of all
items. If the beginning inventory B[I] of each item was input
in SET, it could be used to determine the amount of each item
sold by subtracting Q[I] from B[I].

ENTER, of figure 4, enters orders from customers, so creating a
sales slip. It first asks for the number N of any item I.
When this is entered, a check is made to determine if there are
that many of the item available. If not, it outputs a message
("Sorry, we are out of these" or "There are only 2 left").

Otherwise, it computes the total price T for these items,
outputs it, adds it to the customer's accumulating total A,
and decreases the inventory of quantity Q[I]. This looping
continues until a zero value is read in for N, at which time it
outputs the total amount A to be paid, and it increases the
total sales S by the amount A.

PEEKSUB, of figure 5, can indicate the inventory of cash or items
at any time.

Other modules are shown on the next page. A more extensive PEEK
is shown in the form of pseudo-code. Notice that this
pseudo-code appears much more complex than the flow block
diagram. A simple CHANGE algorithm is also shown expanded
into EXCHANGE, which keeps track of the numbers of coins of
each denomination. This new EXCHANGE outputs the appropriate
denominations if they are available.

Pascal programs also follow along with some typical test runs.
The last program of page 7-13 makes use of text files to store
the inventory (prices and quantities).

Yet More Refinement

Pseudo-code Specification of PEEK Sub-algorithm


```
    PURPOSE: to examine inventories

    Request from user a command, either
       ITEMS to display some or all items
       CASH  to display all denominations
       NONE  to get out of PEEK subprogram
    Enter the requested command.

    While command is not NONE

       If command is ITEMS then
          Request "ALL", "SOME" or "NONE"
          Enter the requested command
          While command is not NONE
             If command is "ALL" then
                Display entire inventory
             else
                if command is "SOME" then
                   Request item number
                   Enter item number
                   While item number is positive
                      If item number is valid then
                         Output price and quantity
                      else
                         Output error message
                      endif
                      Request item number again
                      Enter the item number
                   endwhile (* positive *)
                else
                   Output error message
                endif (* some *)
             endif (* all *)
          endwhile

       else (* command is not ITEMS *)
          if command is "CASH" then
             for each denomination
                Output denomination
                Output quantity
             endfor
             Output total value of cash
          else
             Output error in command
          endif (* cash *)
       endif

       Request new command
       Enter new command

    endwhile
```

CHANGE-MAKER MODIFICATION

EXCHANGE

Enter amount tendered T

R <-- T - A

SIMPLE CHANGE

C <-- 0
While R >= 25
C <-- C + 1
R <-- R - 25
Output C

C <-- 0
R >= 10
C <-- C + 1
R <-- R - 10
Output C

C <-- 0
R >= 5
C <-- C + 1
R <-- R - 5
Output C

C <-- 0
R >= 1
C <-- C + 1
R <-- R - 1
Output C

C <-- 0
R >= 25 and Q > 0
C <-- C + 1
R <-- R - 25
Q <-- Q - 1
Q1 <-- C

C <-- 0
R >= 10 and D > 0
C <-- C + 1
R <-- R - 10
D <-- D - 1
D1 <-- C

C <-- 0
R >= 5 and N > 0
C <-- C + 1
R <-- R - 5
N <-- N - 1
N1 <-- C

C <-- 0
R >= 1 and P > 0
C <-- C + 1
R <-- R - 1
P <-- P - 1
P1 <-- C

T	R > 0	F
Output "SORRY"	Output P1,N1,D1 etc	
	P <-- P - P1 N <-- N - N1 etc	

PASCAL PROGRAM: Of Top Level

```
1000    PROGRAM SST1( INPUT, OUTPUT );
1010      (* SIMPLE SALES TERMINAL *)
1020      (* TOP SUPERVISOR LEVEL  *)
1099
1500    VAR
1510      COMMAND: CHAR;
1999
9000    BEGIN (* MAIN *)
9090
9100      WRITELN(' SETTING INVENTORY ');
9110
9200      WRITELN(' ENTER  A  COMMAND ');
9210      WRITELN(' IF UNCERTAIN, TYPE HELP ');
9220      READLN; (* CLEAR *)  READ( COMMAND );
9230
9300      WHILE COMMAND <> 'E' DO
9310        BEGIN
9320
9400          IF COMMAND = 'O' THEN
9410            WRITELN('  ORDERING ')
9420          ELSE ——— ——— ——— ——— ———
9430          IF COMMAND = 'C' THEN
9440            WRITELN('  CHANGING ')
9450          ELSE ——— ——— ——— ——— ———
9460          IF COMMAND = 'P' THEN
9470            WRITELN('  PEEKING  ')
9480          ELSE ——— ——— ——— ——— ———
9490          IF COMMAND = 'U' THEN
9500            WRITELN('  UPDATING ')
9510          ELSE ——— ——— ——— ——— ———
9520          IF COMMAND = 'H' THEN
9530            BEGIN (* HELP *)
9540              WRITELN(' COMMANDS ARE:');
9550              WRITELN(' ORDER, CHANGE');
9560              WRITELN(' PEEK, UPDATE ');
9570              WRITELN(' HELP, & EXIT ');
9580            END (* HELP *)
9590          ELSE ——— ——— ——— ——— ———
9600            WRITELN(' NO SUCH COMMAND');
9610          ——— ——— ——— ——— ———
9700          WRITELN;
9710          WRITELN(' NEXT COMMAND ');
9720          READLN;   READ( COMMAND );
9730          ——————————————————————
9800        END (* COMMAND LOOP *);
9810
9820      WRITELN(' REPORTING ');
9830
9900    END (* MAIN *).
```

```
SETTING INVENTORY

ENTER  A  COMMAND
IF UNCERTAIN, TYPE HELP
? HELP

COMMANDS ARE:
ORDER, CHANGE
PEEK, UPDATE
HELP, & EXIT

NEXT COMMAND
? ORDER
   ORDERING

NEXT COMMAND
? CHANGE
   CHANGING

NEXT COMMAND
? PEEEK
   PEEKING

NEXT COMMAND
? P
   PEEKING

NEXT COMMAND
? U
   UPDATING

NEXT COMMAND
? KILL
NO SUCH COMMAND

NEXT COMMAND
? POKE
   PEEKING

NEXT COMMAND
? EXIT

REPORTING
```

PASCAL PROGRAM: With Setup and Report

```
1000   PROGRAM SST2( INPUT, OUTPUT );
1010     (* SIMPLE SALES TERMINAL *)
1020     (* WITH SETUP AND REPORT *)
1099
1200   CONST
1210     M = 6;   (* SIZE OF INVENTORY *)
1220
1500   VAR
1510     COMMAND: CHAR;
1520
1600     PRICE: ARRAY[1..M] OF REAL;
1610     QUANTITY: ARRAY[1..M] OF INTEGER;
1620     SALES: REAL;
1999
2000   PROCEDURE SETUP;
2010     (* INITIALIZES INVENTORIES *)
2020     VAR
2030       I: INTEGER;
2040     BEGIN
2500     (* INVENTORY OF ITEMS *)
2510       WRITELN(' ENTER PRICE (SPACE) QUANTITY ');
2520       WRITELN(' FOR EACH ID NUMBER GIVEN     ');
2530       FOR I := 1 TO M DO
2540         BEGIN
2550           WRITELN(' ITEM ', I:3);
2560           READ( PRICE[I], QUANTITY[I] );
2570         END;
2580
2600       SALES := 0.00;
2990   END (* SETUP *);
2999
3000   PROCEDURE REPORT;
3010     (* MAKES FINAL INVENTORY REPORT *)
3020     VAR I,T: INTEGER;
3030       BEGIN
3100         (* REPORT OF ITEM INVENTORY *)
3110         WRITELN(' INVENTORY OF ITEMS ');
3120         WRITELN(' ID PRICE QUANTITY  ');
3130         FOR I := 1 TO M DO
3140           WRITELN( I:3, PRICE[I]:6:2, QUANTITY[I]:8 );
3150         WRITELN;
3199
3200         T := 0;
3210         FOR I := 1 TO M DO
3220           T := T + QUANTITY[I];
3230         WRITELN(' TOTAL QUANTITY IS ', T:5 );
3240
3300         WRITELN(' SALES ARE ', SALES:6:2 );
3400
3900       END (* REPORT *);
3999
9000   BEGIN (* MAIN *)
9100     SETUP;
9200     WRITELN(' ENTER A COMMAND ');
9210     WRITELN(' IF UNCERTAIN, TYPE HELP ');
9220     READLN;   READ( COMMAND );
         ETC....
```

```
ENTER PRICE (SPACE) QUANTITY
FOR EACH ID NUMBER GIVEN
 ITEM   1
? 10.00 100
 ITEM   2
? 5.00  10
 ITEM   3
? 25 50
 ITEM   4
? 39 200
 ITEM   5
? 14 43
 ITEM   6
? 29 81

 ENTER A COMMAND
 IF UNCERTAIN, TYPE HELP
? O
 ORDERING

 NEXT COMMAND
? C
 CHANGING

 NEXT COMMAND
? PIKE
 PEEKING

 NEXT COMMAND
? U
 UPDATING

 NEXT COMMAND
? EXITE

 INVENTORY OF ITEMS
 ID PRICE QUANTITY
  1 10.00    100
  2  5.00     10
  3 25.00     50
  4 39.00    200
  5 14.00     43
  6 29.00     81

 TOTAL QUANTITY IS   484
 SALES ARE   0.00
```

PASCAL PROGRAM: Of Order Sub

```
4000   PROCEDURE ORDER;
4010     (* ENTERS ORDERS, TOTALS THEM, MODIFIES INVENTORY *)
4020
4100     VAR
4110       NUM, ID: INTEGER;
4120       COST, TOTAL: REAL;
4130
4200     BEGIN
4210       TOTAL := 0;
4220       WRITELN(' ENTER THE ORDER ');
4230       WRITELN(' FIRST, NUMBER REQUIRED ');
4240       WRITELN(' THEN, THE ID NUMBER ');
4250       WRITELN(' END ORDER WITH ZERO VALUES ');
4260       WRITELN;
4270
4300       READLN;  READ( NUM, ID );
4310       WHILE NUM <> 0 DO
4320         BEGIN
4330           IF NUM > QUANTITY[ID] THEN
4340               WRITELN(' SORRY, QUANTITY IS ', QUANTITY[ID]:3)
4350           ELSE
4360             BEGIN
4400               QUANTITY[ID] := QUANTITY[ID] - NUM;
4410               COST := NUM*PRICE[ID];
4420               WRITELN( COST:21:2 );
4430               TOTAL := TOTAL + COST;
4440             END;
4450           READLN; READ( NUM, ID );
4460         END (* WHILE *);
4500
4510           WRITELN(' TOTAL SALE IS ', TOTAL:6:2);
4520           SALES := SALES + TOTAL;
4900     END (* ORDER *);
4999
9000   BEGIN (* MAIN *)
9100     SETUP;
```

```
ENTER PRICE (SPACE) QUANTITY
FOR EACH ID NUMBER GIVEN
  ITEM    1
? 1 10
  ITEM    2
? 2 10
  ITEM    3
? 3 10
  ITEM    4
? 4 10
  ITEM    5
? 5 10
  ITEM    6
? 6 10


  NEXT COMMAND
? exit
  INVENTORY OF ITEMS
  ID PRICE QUANTITY
   1  1.00        0
   2  2.00        0
   3  3.00        5
   4  4.00       10
   5  5.00       10
   6  6.00       10

  TOTAL QUANTITY IS     35
  SALES ARE  45.00
```

```
  ENTER A COMMAND
  IF UNCERTAIN, TYPE HELP
? order
  ENTER THE ORDER
  FIRST, NUMBER REQUIRED
  THEN, THE ID NUMBER
  END ORDER WITH ZERO VALUES

? 12 1
  SORRY, QUANTITY IS  10
? 10 1
                 10.00
? 10 2
                 20.00
? 5 3
                 15.00
? 0 0
  TOTAL SALE IS  45.00
```

PASCAL PROGRAM: With Text Data File

```
1000    PROGRAM SST4( INPUT,OUTPUT, INV );
1010      (* SIMPLE SALES TERMINAL *)
1020      (* WITH TEXT DATA FILES  *)
1030      (* SEE ALSO PAGE B-74    *)
1099
1200    CONST
1210      M = 6;  (* SIZE OF INVENTORY *)
1220
1500    VAR
1510      COMMAND: CHAR;
1600      PRICE: ARRAY[1..M] OF REAL;
1610      QUANTITY: ARRAY[1..M] OF INTEGER;
1620      SALES: REAL;
1700      INV: TEXT;  (* INVENTORY FILE OF TYPE TEXT *)
1999
2000    PROCEDURE GETINV;
2010      (* EXTENDED SETUP PROGRAM *)
2012      (* GETS INVENTORY FROM    *)
2014      (* THE KEYBOARD OR A FILE *)
2020      VAR
2030        I: INTEGER;  REPLY: CHAR;
2040      BEGIN
2100        WRITELN(' GET DATA FROM WHERE ');
2110        WRITELN(' KEYBOARD OR FILE?    ');
2120        WRITELN(' ENTER K OR F ONLY    ');
2200        READLN;   READ( REPLY );
2210        IF REPLY = 'K' THEN
2220          BEGIN (* ENTER AS BEFORE *)
2510              WRITELN(' ENTER PRICE (SPACE) QUANTITY ');
2520              WRITELN(' FOR EACH ID NUMBER GIVEN     ');
2530              FOR I := 1 TO M DO
2540                BEGIN
2550                  WRITELN(' ITEM ', I:3);
2560                  READ( PRICE[I], QUANTITY[I] );
2570                END
2580          END (* ENTER AS DONE BEFORE *)
2590        ELSE
2600
2610          BEGIN (* ENTRY FROM INVENTORY FILE *)
2620            RESET( INV );
2630            FOR I := 1 TO M DO
2640              READLN( INV, PRICE[I], QUANTITY[I] );
2650          END  (* ENTRY FROM FILE *);
2699
2700        SALES := 0.00;
2710
2790      END (* GET INVENTORY *);
2795
2799
2800    PROCEDURE PUTINV;
2910      (* PUTS INVENTORY ONTO FILE INV *)
2920      VAR I: INTEGER;
2930      BEGIN
2940        REWRITE( INV );
2950        FOR I := 1 TO M DO
2960          WRITELN( INV, PRICE[I], QUANTITY[I] );
2970      END (* PUT INVENTORY *);
2999
```

RANDOM NUMBER GENERATORS (RNGs)

1 DATA FLOW DIAGRAM OF RNG

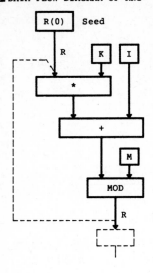

2 SAMPLE SEQUENCE

(for SEED = 3,000)

RANDOM NUMBER	RANDOM PROBABILITY
32521	.497
54806	.84...
46951	.72...
35148	.53...
58453	.88...
64993	.98
41934	.63...

3 SIMULATION OF COIN

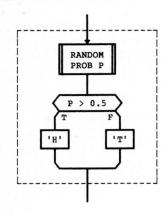

4 SIMULATION OF A DIE

GENERATE RANDOM PROB P		
P < 1/6	T	D <-- 1
P < 2/6	T	D <-- 2
P < 3/6	T	D <-- 3
P < 4/6	T	D <-- 4
P < 5/6	T	D <-- 5
else	T	D <-- 6

6 SIMULATION OF STOCHASTIC SOURCE

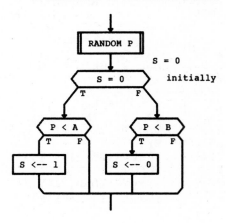

5 STOCHASTIC SOURCE

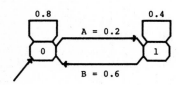

SIMULATING: Monte Carlo

Simulation is a common way of studying systems by modelling or imitating them. For example, the dice craps game could be programmed with the dice simulated by random numbers, and run for many games to determine the probability of winning. Similarly, vehicles can be simulated in a traffic system, customers can be simulated in a business system, and predators and preys can be simulated in a biological system. This method of simulation is often called the "Monte Carlo" method. Essentially this simulation consists of creating a "world" of individual units, and studying how the individuals interact together to create some overall effect.

Random Numbers

Random numbers are often useful for simulation. A sequence of random numbers $R(1)$, $R(2)$, $R(3)$,.... can be created from the formula

$$R(T+1) = (I + K*R(T)) \text{ MOD } M$$

where the three constants I,K and M must be carefully chosen. A data flow diagram of such a random number generator is shown in figure 1. Initially $R(0)$, called the "seed," is given a beginning value, and this generates a sequence of values as shown in figure 2. The numbers generated by such formulas are called "pseudo-random" numbers, for they repeat after M values (or less). Often these numbers are divided by the maximum value M, yielding random probabilities varying uniformly between 0 and 1, shown also in figure 2.

COIN flips can be simulated with a random probability generator by outputting "HEADS" for any probability less than 0.5, and outputting "TAILS" otherwise, as shown in figure 3.

DICE similarly can be simulated by splitting up the probabilities into six equal parts, each corresponding to an outcome of the die, as shown in figure 5. Another way to simulate a die is to take a random probability, multiply it by 6, chop the result (yielding an integer between 0 and 5), and finally add one to it. The sum of two such dice throws is obtained by doing the above algorithm twice and simply adding.

The simulation of vehicles at an intersection can be done similarly by selecting ranges depending on the portion of time the various activities (right turn, left turn, etc.) occur. Other physical systems may be modelled in the same way.

STOCHASTIC systems are those where the probability of one symbol depends on the previous symbol. Figure 5, for example, shows a binary sequence generated so that zeros often follow zeros (with probability 0.8), and ones seldom follow ones (with probability 0.4). This creates sequences with long "runs" of zeros and short runs of ones. The zeros could represent times of inactivity and the ones could represent the short bursts of activity. These two states could also represent brands (of soap, cigarettes, etc.) where consumers "stick" with brand 0 (with probability 0.8), and "switch" away from brand 1 (with probability 0.6). The algorithm for such a stochastic source is given in figure 6.

Pascal programs simulating a coin, error bursts and a crap game are shown on the following pages.

PASCAL PROGRAM: Coin Simulation

```
100    PROGRAM COIN(INPUT, OUTPUT);
110    (* SIMULATES COIN THROWS *)
115
120    VAR
130      TRIALS, RAND, I, HEADCOUNT: INTEGER;
140
200    BEGIN
210      RAND := 377;  (* SEED *)
220      WRITELN( 'ENTER NUMBER OF TRIALS' );
230      READ( TRIALS );
235      HEADCOUNT := 0;
240      FOR I := 1 TO TRIALS DO
250        BEGIN
300          RAND := 3141*RAND MOD 4096;
310          IF RAND > 4096 DIV 2 THEN
320            WRITE( 'T' )
330          ELSE
340            BEGIN
350            WRITE( 'H' );
360            HEADCOUNT := HEADCOUNT + 1;
370            END;
380        END;
390        WRITELN;
400        WRITELN( 'PROB  OF HEADS IS ' );
410        WRITELN( HEADCOUNT/TRIALS:5:3 );
420    END.
```

```
ENTER NUMBER OF TRIALS
? 60
HTTTTTHHTHTHTHTHHHTTHHTHHHHTHHTHTTTTHHTHHTHHTHHTHHHTHTTTTTTTTHH
PROB  OF HEADS IS
0.517
```

```
100    PROGRAM BURSTS( INPUT,OUTPUT );
110      (* SIMULATES ERROR BURSTS *)
115
120    VAR
130      I,A,B,R,S: INTEGER;
135      RNO: REAL;
140
200    FUNCTION RANDO: REAL;
210      BEGIN
220        R := 3141*R MOD 4096;
230        RANDO := R/4096;
240      END (* RANDO FUNCTION *);
250
300    BEGIN (* MAIN *)
310      R := 377;  (* SEED *)
320      S := 0;
330      FOR I := 1 TO 60 DO
340        BEGIN
345          RNO := RANDO;
350          IF S = 0 THEN
355            BEGIN
360              IF RNO < 0.1 THEN
370                S := 1
380            END
390          ELSE
395            BEGIN
400              IF RNO < 0.4 THEN
410                S := 0;
415            END;
417          WRITE( S:1 );
420        END;
500    END.
```

000000100110001111111001000001111101100001101100000000000000

PASCAL PROGRAM: Dice Simulation

```pascal
PROGRAM SIMULATE(INPUT,OUTPUT);
   (* SIMULATES  DICE  CRAPS *)

VAR
   GAMES, TOTAL, I: INTEGER;
   WINCOUNT: INTEGER;
   WIN: BOOLEAN;
   PROB: REAL;
   R: INTEGER;

   PROCEDURE RANDOM( VAR P: REAL );
      (* RETURNS RANDOM PROBABILITY *)
      (* R MUST BE DEFINED OUTSIDE  *)
      CONST
         M = 32767;    (* MODULUS     *)
         K = 12345;    (* COEFFICIENT *)
         I = 6789;     (* INCREMENT   *)
      BEGIN
         R := (K*R + I) MOD M;
         P := R/M;
      END (* RANDOM PROBABILITY *);


   PROCEDURE THROW( VAR SUM: INTEGER );
      (* SIMULATES THROW OF TWO DICE *)
      VAR D1, D2: INTEGER; P1,P2: REAL;
      BEGIN
         RANDOM( P1 );
         D1 := TRUNC( 6*P1 ) + 1;
         RANDOM( P2 );
         D2 := TRUNC( 6*P2 ) + 1;
         SUM := D1 + D2;
      END (* THROW *);


   PROCEDURE PLAY( VAR WIN: BOOLEAN );
      (* PLAYS ONE GAME OF CRAPS *)
      VAR P,S.T: INTEGER;
      BEGIN
         THROW( S );
         IF (S = 7) OR (S = 11) THEN
            WIN := TRUE
         ELSE
         IF (S=2) OR (S=3) OR (S=12) THEN
            WIN := FALSE
         ELSE
            BEGIN (* POINT PART *)
               P := S;
               THROW( T );
               WHILE (T<>7) AND (T<>P) DO
                  THROW( T );
               IF T = 7 THEN
                  WIN := FALSE
               ELSE
                  WIN := TRUE;
            END (* POINT PART *);
      END (* GAME *);


BEGIN (* MAIN *)
   WRITELN( 'ENTER SEED' );  READ(R);
   WRITELN( 'ENTER NUMBER OF GAMES');
   READ( TOTAL );
   WINCOUNT := 0;
   FOR GAMES := 1 TO TOTAL DO
      BEGIN
         PLAY( WIN );
         IF WIN THEN
            WINCOUNT := WINCOUNT + 1;
      END;
   PROB := WINCOUNT/TOTAL;
   WRITELN( 'WIN PROB IS ', PROB:5:3 );
END (* MAIN *).
```

CALCULATOR: OF LARGE OBJECTS

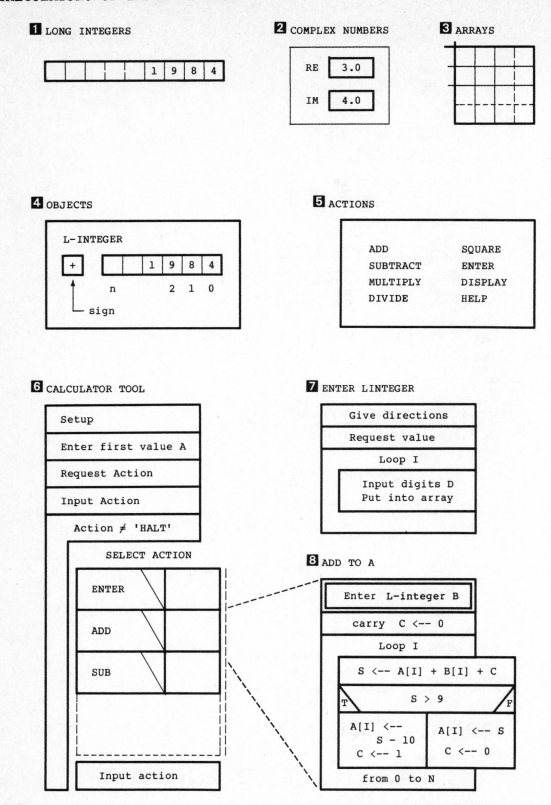

1 LONG INTEGERS

| | | | | 1 | 9 | 8 | 4 |

2 COMPLEX NUMBERS

RE 3.0

IM 4.0

3 ARRAYS

4 OBJECTS

L-INTEGER

+ | | | 1 | 9 | 8 | 4 |

n   2 1 0

— sign

5 ACTIONS

ADD   SQUARE
SUBTRACT   ENTER
MULTIPLY   DISPLAY
DIVIDE   HELP

6 CALCULATOR TOOL

Setup

Enter first value A

Request Action

Input Action

Action ≠ 'HALT'

SELECT ACTION

ENTER

ADD

SUB

Input action

7 ENTER LINTEGER

Give directions

Request value

Loop I

Input digits D
Put into array

8 ADD TO A

Enter L-integer B

carry C <-- 0

Loop I

S <-- A[I] + B[I] + C

T   S > 9   F

A[I] <--   A[I] <-- S
S - 10   C <-- 0
C <-- 1

from 0 to N

CALCULATING: Big Calculator Tool (BCT)

A hand calculator is a convenient tool that deals with numbers, allowing them to be entered, added, multiplied, etc. It could be convenient to have a similar tool that deals with larger objects such as complex numbers, matrices, or very large integers as in figures 1, 2 and 3. Here we will develop such a tool.

L-INTEGERS, or long integers, will be used to illustrate the design. They may be larger than the 8 digits of a calculator, and even the 10 to 20 digits available on a computer. We will manipulate integers of any number of digits N (say N = 200) by representing each digit of the number by an element of an array as shown in figure 4. The sign could be in the leftmost position of the array.

ACTIONS on L-integers are the usual arithmetic operations, along with Enter and Display operations, as shown in figure 5. Each of these actions could be described separately as a sub-program at this time; this bottom-up approach could be appropriate here.

BEHAVIOR of the calculator could be first described by a typical "conversation" between us (the user) and it:

```
IT: VALUE?
US: 12345678987654321
IT: ACTION?
US: ADD
IT: VALUE?
US: 98765432123456789
IT: ACTION?
US: DISPLAY
IT: 111111111111111110
IT: ACTION?
    etc.
```

STRUCTURE of the program can be specified, now that we know what it is to do. It acts on one object A (accumulator?) modifying it by operating on it with a binary operator (such as addition) or a unary operator (such as display, or square). An algorithm for this is shown in figure 6.

INPUT, or entering a value, could be simple for the programmer to create if the least significant values were entered first, but this would be awkward for the user because it reverses the number. Also, entering a number digit by digit (separated by blanks) could be convenient for programming but artificial for a user. There is often such a trade off, which is not a problem if the programmer is the user, but this should not be assumed.

ADDITION is shown as a typical action in figure 7. It is done stage by stage, with the resulting sum replacing the original value. A Pascal program, BIGCALCULATOR, follows on the next page.

COMPLEX NUMBERS, used in electrical engineering, could be manipulated similarly. The actions could be: add, subtract, multiply, divide, rotate, conjugate. A record, consisting of a real part and an imaginary part, would be the obvious data structure to use. This tool could be created bottom-up by first writing all the sub-programs separately and then putting them together as shown in the Pascal program, COMPLEXCALC, of page 7-21.

MATRICES, used in mathematics, also would be manipulated (added, multiplied, transposed, inverted) by a similar program.

PASCAL PROGRAM: Of Large Integer Calculator

```pascal
PROGRAM BIGCALCULATOR(INPUT,OUTPUT);
  (* MANIPULATES LARGE INTEGERS  *)

CONST
  N = 50;     (* NUMBER OF DIGITS *)

TYPE
  LINTEGER = ARRAY[0..N] OF INTEGER;

VAR
  A:  LINTEGER;
  ACTION: CHAR;
```

```pascal
PROCEDURE ENTER( VAR X: LINTEGER );
  (* INPUT A LARGE INTEGER *)
VAR
  I,DIGIT: INTEGER;
BEGIN
(* CLEAR *)
  FOR I := 0 TO N DO
    X[I] := 0;
  WRITELN;
(* INSTRUCT *)
  WRITELN( 'ENTER LONG INTEGER' );
  WRITELN( 'LEAST SIGNIF FIRST' );
  WRITELN( 'SEPARATED BY SPACE' );
  WRITELN( 'END WITH NEGATIVE ' );
(* INPUT *)
  I := 0;
  READ( DIGIT );
  WHILE DIGIT >= 0 DO
    BEGIN
      X[I] := DIGIT;
      I := I + 1;
      READ( DIGIT );
    END;
 END (* ENTER PROCEDURE *);
```

```pascal
PROCEDURE ADD( VAR A: LINTEGER );
  (* ADDS A LINTEGER TO A *)
VAR
  B: LINTEGER;
  I,SUM: INTEGER;
  CARRY: INTEGER;
BEGIN
  ENTER( B );
  CARRY := 0;
  FOR I := 0 TO N DO
    BEGIN
      SUM := A[I] + B[I] + CARRY;
      IF SUM <= 9 THEN
        BEGIN
          CARRY := 0;
          A[I]  := SUM;
        END
      ELSE (* SUM > 9 *)
        BEGIN
          CARRY := 1;
          A[I] := SUM - 10;
        END;
    END (* FOR *);
  WRITELN;  READLN;
END (* ADD PROCEDURE *);
```

```pascal
PROCEDURE DISPLAY( A: LINTEGER );
  (* DISPLAYS LINTEGER A *)
VAR
  I: INTEGER;
BEGIN
  WRITELN;
  FOR I := N DOWNTO 0 DO
    WRITE( A[I] );
  WRITELN;
END (* DISPLAY *);
```

```pascal
BEGIN (* MAIN *)
WRITELN( 'ENTER A VALUE'    );
ENTER( A );
WRITELN( 'ENTER AN ACTION' );
READLN; READ( ACTION );

WHILE ACTION <> 'H' DO
  BEGIN
    IF ACTION = 'E' THEN
        ENTER(A)
    ELSE
    IF ACTION = 'A' THEN
        ADD(A)
    ELSE
    IF ACTION = 'D' THEN
        DISPLAY(A)

    (* MORE ACTIONS CAN GO HERE *)

    ELSE
        WRITELN( 'NO SUCH ACTION' );

    WRITELN( 'ENTER ACTION' );
    READ( ACTION );
    WRITELN;
  END;

END (* MAIN *).
```

PASCAL PROGRAM: Of Complex Number Calculator

```
PROGRAM COMPLEXCALC( INPUT, OUTPUT );
   (* A COMPLEX NUMBER CALCULATOR *)
   (* SHOWS THE PASSING OF RECORDS*)
   (* DONE USING THE UCSD PASCAL  *)


CONST
   ENTER = 'E';  PRINT  = 'P';
   ADD   = 'A';  SUB    = 'S';
   MULT  = 'M';  DIVIDE = 'D';
   QUIT  = 'Q';  CONJUG = 'C';
   HELP  = 'H';


TYPE
   COMPLEX = RECORD
      RE: REAL;
      IM: REAL;
   END (* COMPLEX *);


VAR
   A,B: COMPLEX;
   ACTION: CHAR;


PROCEDURE
   ENTERSUB( VAR C: COMPLEX );
      BEGIN
         WRITELN( 'ENTER REAL PART' );
         READLN( C.RE );
         WRITELN( 'ENTER IMAGINARY PART' );
         READLN( C.IM );
      END (* ENTER SUB PROGRAM *);


PROCEDURE
   PRINTSUB( C: COMPLEX );
      BEGIN
         WRITELN( C.RE:6:3, ' ', C.IM:6:3 );
      END (* PRINT PROCEDURE *);


PROCEDURE
   ADDSUB( A,B: COMPLEX; VAR C: COMPLEX);
      BEGIN
         C.RE := A.RE + B.RE;
         C.IM := A.IM + B.IM;
      END (* ADD SUB PROGRAM *);


PROCEDURE
   MULTSUB( A,B: COMPLEX; VAR C: COMPLEX);
      BEGIN
         C.RE := A.RE*B.RE - A.IM*B.IM;
         C.IM := A.IM*B.RE + A.RE*B.IM;
      END (* MULTIPLICATION *);


PROCEDURE
   CONJUGATE( VAR C: COMPLEX );
      BEGIN
         C.IM := - C.IM;
      END (* CONJUGATE *);


BEGIN (* MAIN *)
   WRITELN( 'ENTER A VALUE' );
   ENTERSUB(A);
   WRITELN;
   WRITELN( 'ENTER AN ACTION' );
   READLN( ACTION );

   WHILE ACTION <> QUIT DO
      BEGIN
         IF ACTION = ENTER THEN
            ENTERSUB(A)
         ELSE
         IF ACTION = PRINT THEN
            PRINTSUB(A)
         ELSE
         IF ACTION = ADD   THEN
            BEGIN
               ENTERSUB(B);
               ADDSUB(A,B,A)
            END
         ELSE
         IF ACTION = MULT  THEN
            BEGIN
               ENTERSUB(B);
               MULTSUB(A,B,A)
            END
         ELSE
         IF ACTION = CONJUG THEN
            CONJUGATE( A )
         ELSE
            WRITELN( 'ERROR' );

         WRITELN;
         WRITELN( 'ENTER ACTION' );
         READLN( ACTION );
      END (* WHILE *);

END (* MAIN *).
```

```
ENTER A VALUE
ENTER REAL PART
 1.000
ENTER IMAGINARY PART
 2.000

ENTER AN ACTION
C

ENTER ACTION
P
 1.000 -2.000

ENTER ACTION
A
ENTER REAL PART
 3.000
ENTER IMAGINARY PART
 4.000

ENTER ACTION
P
 4.000  2.000

ENTER ACTION
Q
```

BLOCK PLOT

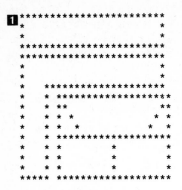

1
```
*************************
*                       *
*                       *
*************************
*************************
*                       *
*                       *
*    * ******************
*    * **               **
*    *                 *  *
*    * ******************
*    *  *        *        *
*    *  *        *        *
*****  **************     *
```

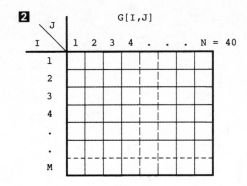

2 G[I,J]

3 MOVE(X,Y)

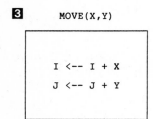

I <-- I + X
J <-- J + Y

4 RIGHT(D)

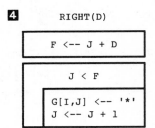

F <-- J + D

J < F

G[I,J] <-- '*'
J <-- J + 1

5 Output of BOX

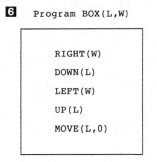

6 Program BOX(L,W)

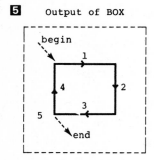

RIGHT(W)
DOWN(L)
LEFT(W)
UP(L)
MOVE(L,0)

7 LOOP(W,H,D)

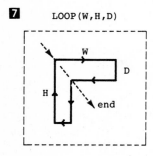

8 CHOICE(W,H,D,L)

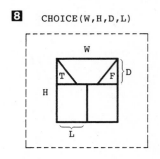

GRAPHING: Simple Block Plot

It is often convenient to use printers to draw figures, such as
    flow block diagrams, by plotting a sequence of asterisks as
    shown in figure 1. Actually, some printers allow much finer
    movement (one-sixtieth of an inch) so that adjacent periods
    form a thick line, and adjacent dashes form a thin line. Most
    of the graphics of this text were produced by such a method.
    Here, however, we will be limited to the use of ordinary
    printers.

The data structure of figure 2 shows a two-dimensional array of
    height M and width N (measured in asterisks). Initially this
    array is filled with blanks by a CLEAR procedure. Then
    various sub-programs are called to plot lines, boxes, loops,
    etc.

Initially, the pen "point" is located at the top left corner
    (position 0,0). This point can be moved by a MOVE(X,Y)
    sub-program, which moves it X units horizontally and Y
    vertically, without drawing any symbol.

RIGHT(D) is a sub-program which creates a line of asterisks D
    units to the the right. It does this by a simple loop as shown
    in figure 4. Other sub-programs, LEFT, UP, and DOWN,
    similarly draw lines in the given directions.

BOX(W,H) creates a box of width W and height H by simply calling
    the above subs. The box begins at the top left, and ends at
    the bottom left, in preparation for a box following it, as
    shown in figure 5.

LOOP(W,H,D) creates an L-shaped loop form of width W, height H,
    and depth D, as shown in figure 7. It starts at the upper
    corner of the L-shape and finishes at the inner corner of the
    L-shape, ready to draw a box within the body of the loop.

CHOICE(W,H,D,L) creates a choice box as shown in figure 8.

Other objects may be plotted, including sub-boxes, case boxes, and
    slanted lines (going any of four directions). Also, symbols
    other than the asterisk may be printed. Numbers and words may
    also be added to the plot.

The main program to draw any combination of boxes consists of a
    sequence of calls to the above sub-programs. Then finally a
    SHOW program is called to print out the array.

PLOTS is a Pascal program (on the following page) corresponding to
    the given algorithms. In that program the main part consists
    of a series of calls to sub programs. The program must be
    changed for each new plot. A better alternative is to create
    each plot on a file, and have the main program simply step
    through that file.

PASCAL PROGRAM: Of Plot

```
100   PROGRAM PLOTS(INPUT ,OUTPUT);
110     (* PLOTS FLOW BLOCKS *)
120
130   CONST
140     MARK = '*';
150     BLANK = ' ';
160     M = 60;
170     N = 40;
199
200   VAR
210     G: ARRAY[1..M, 1..N] OF CHAR;
220     I,J: INTEGER;
230     K,F: INTEGER;
299
300   PROCEDURE SETUP;
310     (* CLEARS THE DRAW SPACE *)
320     BEGIN
330       FOR I := 1 TO M DO
340         FOR J := 1 TO N DO
350           G[I,J] := BLANK;
360       I := 1;   J := 1;
370     END (* SETUP *);
399
400   PROCEDURE MOVE( I1, J1: INTEGER );
410     (* MOVES, BUT DOESN'T PRINT  *)
420     BEGIN
430       I := I + I1;   J := J + J1;
440     END (* MOVE *);
499
500   PROCEDURE RIGHT( DIST: INTEGER);
510     (* MOVES TO RIGHT A DISTANCE *)
520     BEGIN
530       F := J + DIST;
540       WHILE J < F DO
550         BEGIN
560           G[I,J] := MARK;
570           J := J + 1;
580         END;
590     END (* RIGHT *);
599
600   PROCEDURE LEFT( DIST: INTEGER );
620     BEGIN
630       F := J - DIST;
640       WHILE J > F DO
650         BEGIN
660           G[I,J] := MARK;
670           J := J - 1;
680         END;
690     END (* LEFT *);
699
700   PROCEDURE DOWN( DIST: INTEGER);
710     (* MOVES DOWN A DISTANCE *)
720     BEGIN
730       F := I + DIST;
740       WHILE I < F DO
750         BEGIN
760           G[I,J] := MARK;
770           I := I + 1;
780         END;
790     END (* DOWN *);
799
800   PROCEDURE UP( DIST: INTEGER );
820     BEGIN
830       F := I - DIST;
840       WHILE I> F DO
850         BEGIN
860           G[I,J] := MARK;
870           I := I - 1;
880         END;
890     END (* UP *);
899
```

```
*******************************
*                             *
*                             *
*                             *
*                             *
*                             *
*******************************
*******************************
*                             *
*                             *
*                             *
*                             *
*     *************************
*     * ***********************
*     * *                     *
*     * *                     *
*     * *                     *
*     * *     *****************
*     * *     * ***************
*     * *     * *             *
*     * *     * *             *
*     * *     * *             *
*     * *     * *             *
*     * *     * *             *
****** ****** ****************
*******************************
**                         **
*  *                     *  *
*   *                   *   *
*    *                 *    *
*******************************
*             *             *
*             *             *
*             *             *
*******************************
*******************************
*                             *
*                             *
*                             *
*******************************
```

PLOT PROGRAM (continued)

```
900     PROCEDURE SHOW;
910       BEGIN
920         FOR I := 1 TO M DO
930           BEGIN
940             FOR J := 1 TO N DO
950               WRITE( G[I,J] );
960             WRITELN;
970           END;
980       END (* SHOW *);
999
1000    PROCEDURE BOX( WIDTH, HEIGHT: INTEGER );
1010      (* CREATES A RECTANGULAR BOX *)
1020      BEGIN
1030        RIGHT( WIDTH );
1040        DOWN( HEIGHT );
1050        LEFT( WIDTH  );
1060        UP(   HEIGHT );
1070       MOVE( HEIGHT + 1, 0);
1080      END (* BOX *);
1099
2000    PROCEDURE LOOP( WIDTH, HEIGHT, DEPTH: INTEGER);
2020      BEGIN
2030        RIGHT( WIDTH );
2040        DOWN( DEPTH );
2050        LEFT( WIDTH - DEPTH);
2060        DOWN( HEIGHT - DEPTH);
2070        LEFT( DEPTH );
2080        UP( HEIGHT );
2085        I := I + DEPTH + 1;
2086        J := J + DEPTH + 2;
2090      END (* LOOP *);
2099
3000    PROCEDURE CHOICE( WID, HT, DEP, LBAR: INTEGER);
3020      BEGIN
3030        RIGHT( WID );
3040        DOWN(HT);
3050        LEFT(WID);
3060        UP( HT );
3070        FOR K := 1 TO DEP DO
3100          BEGIN
3110            RIGHT(1);
3120            MOVE(1,0);
3130          END;
3140        LEFT(DEP);
3150        RIGHT(WID);
3160        UP( DEP );
3170        FOR K := 1 TO DEP DO
3180          BEGIN
3190            LEFT(1);
3200            MOVE(1,0);
3220          END;
3230        MOVE(0,DEP + LBAR - WID);
3240        DOWN(HT - DEP);
3250        MOVE(0, -LBAR);
3260        MOVE(1,0);
3500      END (* CHOICE *);
3999
9000    BEGIN (* MAIN *)
9010      SETUP;
9020      BOX(30,5);
9030      LOOP( 30, 20, 5);
9040      LOOP( 25, 14, 5);
9050      BOX(20,8);
9060      MOVE(0, -14);
9070      CHOICE(30,10,5,20);
9080      BOX(30,4);
9900      SHOW;
9999    END (* MAIN *).
```

SIMULATION OF THE BIT COMPUTER

1 A typical program
(in octal)
to swap contents
of locations 7 and 10

location		Content					
0	0	0	3	0	0	0	7
0	1	0	4	0	0	1	1
0	2	0	3	0	0	1	0
0	3	0	4	0	0	0	7
0	4	0	3	0	0	1	1
0	5	0	4	0	0	1	0
0	6	0	7	0	0	0	0
0	7	0	0	0	0	1	0
1	0	1	0	0	0	0	5
1	1	0	0	0	0	0	0

(See the MACHINE
appendix for more
detail on this program)

The BIT computer structure

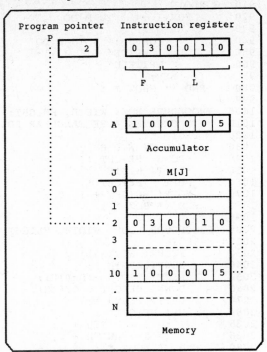

3 Behavior of Computer
(top down)

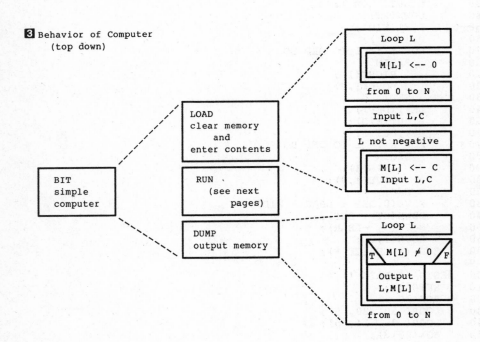

COMPUTING: Simulation of a Computer

One interesting application of computers is to simulate or imitate other
computers. For example, let us create a simple low level computer,
called BIT, described in the appendix. This simulated computer
could then later be used to gain some experience in programming such
machines.

The goal of this project is to take a program, as in figure 1 (in
octal), load it into the computer, run it, and then "dump" a listing
of its final memory contents.

STRUCTURE of the computer is shown in figure 2. It is typical of most
single-address computers. It has a single accumulator A, program
pointer P, and an instruction register I. The instruction in
register I is broken into an operation part (or function) F, and a
location part L. The location L points to an address in the memory
M[L] where the contents will be operated on.

Simulation of the structure could also be done in other ways. For
example, the memory could be viewed as a two-dimensional array
M[L,P], where L indicates the location (row), and P indicates the
position of the octal digit within that location. This choice for the
simulation (model) would become very detailed quickly; but it could
be more realistic. Another alternative simulation would be to
represent the contents completely in binary. This would be even more
detailed, but for some purposes may be better. We will continue
with our simple original model, using a linear array M[L].

BEHAVIOR of the computer is shown in figure 3. It consists of loading
the memory, running the program, and finally dumping the contents of
memory.

LOAD of the program first clears all the memory registers, and then
inputs pairs of values representing a location L and its contents C.
The loading process stops when a negative location is input as a
terminator.

RUN of the program is described on the following pages.

DUMP of the program simply outputs the contents of the locations as
shown in the lower right of the figure. In this case, only the
non-empty registers are output.

Modification of this system is possible in many ways. Notice first the
simple series of operations, first load, then run, finally dump; that
is a very batch oriented view. This could be modified at the top
level by having a supervisor (executive, dispatcher) to allow
interactive operation (of edit as well as load, run, etc.)
repeatedly in any order.

Another modification for learning and debugging purposes is to allow
"single stepping" of the run. This halts the run at every cycle,
displays the contents of a few selected registers (accumulator,
instruction pointer, etc.) and proceeds to the next step only after
some time duration (or until the user hits some key).

SIMULATION OF COMPUTER RUN

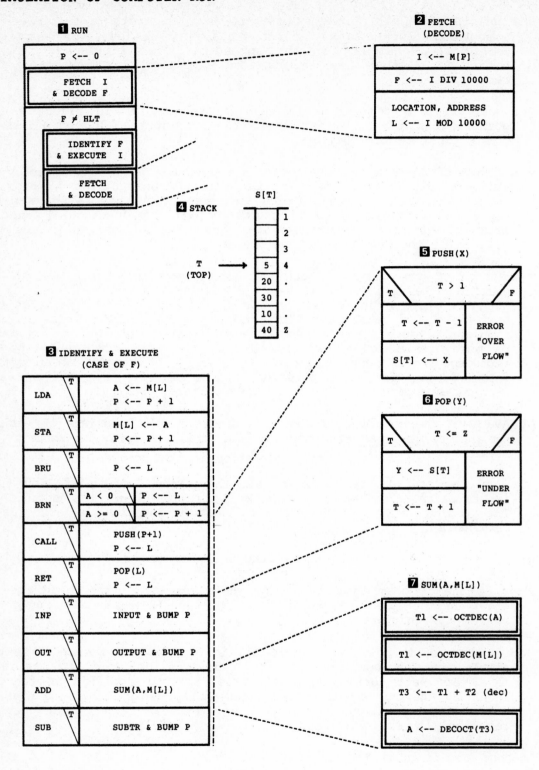

Refinement of the Simulated Computer

RUN, of figure 1, describes the behavior of the computer. First the program counter P is initialized and an instruction I is fetched and decoded into an operation part F and a location part L. Then, while the operation is not a halt, the instructions are repeatedly executed and new instructions fetched.

FETCH, of figure 2, shows the process of decoding an instruction. First the instruction specified by the program counter is put into the instruction register I. Then I is divided by 10000 yielding as quotient the leftmost two digits of I, representing the operation part F. Similarly, "I MOD 10000" produces the remaining four rightmost digits of I, which represent the location part L.

EXECUTE, of figure 3, is a large CASE form; depending on the operation F, different actions are done.

LDA L, the load accumulator instruction, causes the contents of memory location L to be put into the accumulator A, and the program counter advanced by one to point to the next instruction.

BRN L (or branch-on-negative to L) first tests the sign of the accumulator ; if it is negative the program counter is set to point to the instruction in location L; otherwise, it points to the next location P + 1.

Arithmetic instructions (of ADD, SUBtract, MULTiply, and DIVide) could be done by converting the numbers into either decimal values or binary values, doing the arithmetic operation in that convenient base, and then re-converting the result back into octal. Of course, all this could also be done in octal.

If the octal contents were converted into binary, then it would be possible also to include logical operations such as AND, OR, and NOT.

CALL and RETurn instructions of sub-programs are shown using stacks, so recursive algorithms could be run on this machine. The "CALL L" instruction causes the return address R (which is P + 1) to be pushed onto the stack, and the program counter P then points at the entry location L of the sub-program. It continues executing the sub-program until a return instruction RETurn is met.

RET, the return instruction, causes the return address to be popped off the stack and the program counter is made to point at the location following this return address, so continuing in the main program after the sub-program "detour."

Pascal programs simulating such a computer follow. The first program has very few instructions (LOAD, STORE, I/O, BRU, BRP). The second program is a further refinement of the first.

PASCAL PROGRAM: OF THE COMPUTER

```
00001    PROGRAM COMPUTER( INPUT, OUTPUT );
00002    (*SIMPLE SINGLE ADDRESS MACHINE*)
00003
00004    CONST    (* OP CODES *)
00005      ADD=01; SUB=02; LDA=03; STA=04; BRU=05;
00006      BRN=06; BRP=07; BRZ=10; INN=11; OUT=12;
00007      CAL=13; RET=14; MPY=15; DVA=16; HLT=17;
00008
00009      N = 100;  (* SIZE OF MEMORY*)
00010
00011    VAR
00012      LOCN, CONT, INSTR : INTEGER;
00013      ACC, POINT, OPERN : INTEGER;
00014      MEM: ARRAY[0..N] OF INTEGER;
00015
00016    BEGIN
00017
00018      (* LOAD PROGRAM *)
00019        FOR LOCN := 0 TO N DO
00020            MEM[LOCN] := 000000;
00021        WRITELN( 'ENTER LOCN & CONTENT' );
00022        READLN; READ(LOCN, CONT);
00023        WHILE LOCN >= 0 DO
00024          BEGIN
00025            MEM[ LOCN ] := CONT;
00026            READLN; READ(LOCN,CONT);
00027          END;
00028
00029      (* RUN PROGRAM *)
00030        POINT := 0;
00031        INSTR := MEM[ POINT ];
00032        OPERN := INSTR DIV 10000;
00033        LOCN  := INSTR MOD 10000;
00034
00035        WHILE OPERN <> HLT DO
00036          BEGIN (* CASE OF OPERATIONS *)
00037
00038            IF OPERN = LDA THEN
00039                BEGIN
00040                ACC := MEM[LOCN];
00041                POINT := POINT + 1;
00042                END
00043            ELSE
00044            IF OPERN = STA THEN
00045                BEGIN
00046                MEM[LOCN] := ACC;
00047                POINT := POINT + 1;
00048                END
00049            ELSE
00050            IF OPERN = INN THEN
00051                BEGIN
00052                READ( MEM[LOCN] );
00053                POINT := POINT + 1;
00054                END
00055            ELSE
00056            IF OPERN = OUT THEN
00057                BEGIN
00058                WRITELN( MEM[LOCN] );
00059                POINT := POINT + 1;
00060                END
00061            ELSE
00062            IF OPERN = BRU THEN
00063                POINT := LOCN
00064            ELSE
00065            IF OPERN = BRN THEN
00066                IF ACC < 0 THEN
00067                    POINT := LOCN
00068                ELSE
00069                    POINT := POINT + 1
00070
00071            (* OTHER OPERATIONS GO HERE *)
00072
00073            ELSE
00074              BEGIN
00075              WRITELN('ERROR IN OPERATION');
00076              POINT := POINT + 1;
00077              END;
00078
00079            INSTR := MEM[POINT];
00080            OPERN := INSTR DIV 10000;
00081            LOCN  := INSTR MOD 10000;
00082          END (* WHILE *);
00083
00084      (* DUMP PROGRAM *)
00085        WRITELN;
00086        WRITELN( 'PROGRAM DUMP' );
00087        FOR LOCN := 0 TO N DO
00088            IF MEM[LOCN] <> 0 THEN
00089                WRITELN( LOCN:4, MEM[LOCN]:7);
00090
00091    END.
```

```
ENTER LOCN & CONTENT
? 00 030007
? 01 040011
? 02 030010
? 03 040007
? 05 040010
? 06 170000
? 07 000007
? 10 000011
? 11 000000
? 04 030011
? -1 -1

PROGRAM DUMP
   0   30007
   1   40011
   2   30010
   3   40007
   4   30011
   5   40010
   6  170000
   7      11
  10       7
  11       7
```

PASCAL PROGRAM: THE COMPUTER (continued)

```pascal
PROGRAM COMPUTER( INPUT, OUTPUT );
(*SIMPLE SINGLE ADDRESS MACHINE*)
(*  WITH SUB PROGRAM ADDED       *)

CONST    (* OP CODES *)
    ADD=01; SUB=02; LDA=03; STA=04; BRU=05;
    BRN=06; BRP=07; BRZ=10; INN=11; OUT=12;
    CAL=13; RET=14; MPY=15; DVA=16; HLT=17;

    N = 100;  (* SIZE OF MEMORY *)
    Z = 20;   (* SIZE OF STACK  *)

VAR
    LOCN, CONT, INSTR : INTEGER;
    ACC, POINT, OPERN : INTEGER;
    MEM: ARRAY[0..N] OF INTEGER;
    STACK: ARRAY[0..Z] OF INTEGER;
    TOP: 0..Z;

PROCEDURE PUSH( X: INTEGER );
  BEGIN
    IF TOP > 1 THEN
       BEGIN
       TOP := TOP - 1;
       STACK[TOP] := X;
       END
    ELSE
       WRITELN( 'OVERFLOW' );
  END (* PUSH *);

PROCEDURE POP( VAR Y: INTEGER );
  BEGIN
    IF TOP <= Z THEN
       BEGIN
       Y := STACK[TOP];
       TOP := TOP + 1;
       END
    ELSE
       WRITELN( 'UNDERFLOW' );
  END (* POP *);

BEGIN
    (* LOAD PROGRAM *)
       FOR LOCN := 0 TO N DO
           MEM[LOCN] := 000000;
       WRITELN( 'ENTER LOCN & CONTENT' );
       READLN; READ(LOCN, CONT);
       WHILE LOCN >= 0 DO
         BEGIN
         MEM[ LOCN ] := CONT;
         READLN; READ(LOCN,CONT);
         END;

    (* RUN PROGRAM *)
       TOP   := Z;
       POINT := 0;
       INSTR := MEM[ POINT ];
       OPERN := INSTR DIV 10000;
       LOCN  := INSTR MOD 10000;

       WHILE OPERN <> HLT DO
         BEGIN (* CASE OF OPERATIONS *)

           IF OPERN = CAL THEN
              BEGIN
              PUSH( POINT + 1 );
              POINT := LOCN;
              END
           ELSE
           IF OPERN = RET THEN
              POP( POINT )
           ELSE
           IF OPERN = LDA THEN
              BEGIN
              ACC := MEM[LOCN];
              POINT := POINT + 1;
              END
           ELSE

              etc...etc
```

```
ENTER LOCN & CONTENT
? 00 110050
? 01 130020
? 02 130020
? 03 170000
? 20 120050
? 21 120050
? 22 120050
? 23 140000
? -1 -1
? 7
               7
               7
               7
               7
               7
               7

PROGRAM DUMP
   0  110050
   1  130020
   2  130020
   3  170000
  20  120050
  21  120050
  22  120050
  23  140000
  50       7
```

SCHEDULING OF JOBS

1 ROUNDROBIN

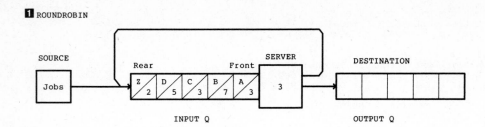

SOURCE

INPUT Q

SERVER

DESTINATION

OUTPUT Q

2 TRACE OF ROUNDROBIN

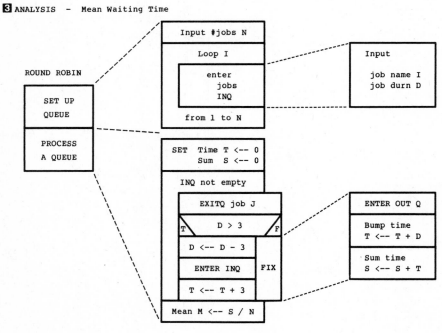

3 ANALYSIS - Mean Waiting Time

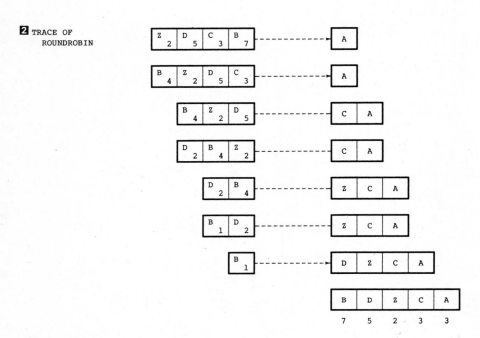

SCHEDULING: Round Robin Method of Queuing

QUEUES, or waiting lines, are often encountered in everyday life and also in computing. A particularly useful application in computer science is that of scheduling jobs in a time-shared system.

Jobs, or tasks, require different amounts of computing time. If they are served on a first-come, first-served basis, then the longer jobs may hold up the shorter ones. If short jobs are let ahead of the longer ones, then the longer ones may be unfairly delayed. A good compromise between these two scheduling methods is the Round Robin Schedule.

ROUND ROBIN scheduling makes use of an input queue where jobs are entered in the order that they arrive. The server (computer) gives each job a fixed duration of time (say, a 3 unit time slice). If the job is finished in this time, it goes into an output queue; otherwise, it gets reentered at the end of the input queue, but requiring 3 less units of time. Figure 1 shows this scheduling system with a Source of jobs, a Server, and a Destination. At the given instant, it shows five jobs (labelled A,B,C,...) and the time to complete each.

TRACING the dynamic behavior of this system is done in figure 2. The final snapshot of the output queue shows that the jobs were output approximately in the order of their original size; the shorter ones get out faster, the longer ones remain longer.

PERFORMANCE of this system could be indicated by the average waiting time. The analysis of the waiting time is shown in figure 3. It sets up a typical input queue with some random jobs, then follows them through the system. When each job enters the output queue, the time is recorded, and these processing times are finally averaged. As a simple test example consider 5 jobs all requiring a time duration of one unit. The first job waits 1 unit, the second one requires 2 units, the third requires 3, etc., for a total of

$$1 + 2 + 3 + 4 + 5 = 15 \text{ time units.}$$

The average waiting time is then 15/5 = 3.0 time units. More realistic examples would be more complex to compute.

Pascal programs involving queues are shown on the following pages. The first program shows the algorithms of page 6-37 implementing a queue as an array. Notice that each operation (CREATE, ENTERQ, EXITQ, EMPTY) is created as a sub-program. This representation is not very general, because if another queue is needed, then a separate set of operations is required.

Another implementation of queues involves records as shown on page 7-35. This representation is more general, defining a "class" of queues so that individual queues (such as INQ and OUTQ) may be declared. This program then uses the queues to analyse the Round Robin scheduler.

PASCAL PROGRAM: Of Simple Queue

```pascal
PROGRAM SQUEUE(INPUT,OUTPUT);
   (* SIMPLE QUEUE SYSTEM  *)
   (* SEE ALSO   PAGE 6-36  *)
   (* ANOTHER ONE FOLLOWS  *)

CONST
   LENGTH = 30;

VAR
   QUEUE: ARRAY[1..LENGTH] OF CHAR;
   FRONT, REAR, SIZE: INTEGER;
   A,B: CHAR;
```

```pascal
PROCEDURE CREATE;
   BEGIN
     REAR := 1;
     FRONT:= REAR;
     SIZE := 0;
   END (* CREATE *);
```

```pascal
PROCEDURE NEXT
 (VAR POINT: INTEGER );
   BEGIN
     IF POINT = LENGTH THEN
        POINT := 1
     ELSE
        POINT := POINT + 1;
   END (* NEXT POINT *);
```

```pascal
FUNCTION EMPTY: BOOLEAN;
   BEGIN
     IF SIZE  = 0 THEN
        EMPTY :=   TRUE
     ELSE
        EMPTY := FALSE;
   END (* EMPTY *);
```

```
(* CREATE  FUNCTION FULL *)
```

```pascal
PROCEDURE ENTERQ( X: CHAR );
   BEGIN
     IF SIZE = LENGTH THEN
        WRITELN( 'FULL' )
     ELSE
        BEGIN
          NEXT(  REAR );
          QUEUE[ REAR ] := X;
          SIZE := SIZE + 1;
        END
   END (* ENTER QUEUE *);
```

```pascal
PROCEDURE EXITQ( VAR Y: CHAR );
   BEGIN
     IF EMPTY THEN
        WRITELN( 'EMPTY' )
     ELSE
        BEGIN
          NEXT( FRONT );
          Y := QUEUE[ FRONT ];
          SIZE := SIZE - 1;
        END
   END (* EXITQ *);
```

```pascal
BEGIN (* MAIN *)
     CREATE;
  (* INPUT CHARACTER VALUES *)
     WRITELN( 'ENTER LETTERS');
     WRITELN( 'END WITH '$'  );
     READ( A );
     WHILE A <> '$' DO
        BEGIN
          ENTERQ(A);
          READ( A );
        END;

  (* ECHO VALUES  IN ORDER *)
     WHILE NOT EMPTY DO
        BEGIN
          EXITQ(B);
          WRITE(B);
        END;
END (* MAIN *).
```

PASCAL PROGRAM: Of Queues

```
PROGRAM ROUNDROBIN(INPUT, OUTPUT);
  (* EVALUATES SCHEDULING *)
  (* DEMONSTRATES QUEUES  *)

CONST
  LENGTH = 10;

TYPE

  QITEM = RECORD
    NAME: CHAR;
    NUMR: INTEGER;
    NEED: INTEGER;
  END (* Q ITEM *);

  QLIST = ARRAY[1..LENGTH] OF QITEM;

  QUEUE = RECORD
    ITEM : QLIST;
    REAR : 1..LENGTH;
    FRONT: 1..LENGTH;
    SIZE : 0..LENGTH;
  END (* QUEUE *);

VAR
      A,JOB : QITEM;
   INQ,OUTQ : QUEUE;
  I,N,T,SUM : INTEGER;
      SLICE : INTEGER;
       MEAN : REAL;

PROCEDURE CREATEQ( VAR  Q: QUEUE );
  BEGIN
    Q.REAR := 1;
    Q.FRONT:= 1;
    Q.SIZE := 0;
  END (* CREATEQ *);

PROCEDURE NEXT( VAR P: INTEGER);
  BEGIN
    IF P = LENGTH THEN
        P := 1
    ELSE
        P := P + 1;
  END (* NEXT *);

PROCEDURE ENTERQ( VAR Q:QUEUE;
                      X:QITEM );
  BEGIN
    IF Q.SIZE = LENGTH THEN
        WRITELN( 'FULL' )
    ELSE
        BEGIN
          Q.ITEM[ Q.REAR ] := X;
          NEXT( Q.REAR );
          Q.SIZE := Q.SIZE + 1;
        END;
  END (* ENTERQ *);

PROCEDURE EXITQ( VAR Q:QUEUE;
                     VAR Y: QITEM );
  BEGIN
    IF Q.SIZE = 0 THEN
        WRITELN( 'EMPTY')
    ELSE
     BEGIN
       Y := Q.ITEM[ Q.FRONT ];
       NEXT( Q.FRONT );
       Q.SIZE := Q.SIZE - 1;
     END;
  END (* EXITQ *);
```

```
BEGIN (* MAIN  Q-TEST *)

  CREATEQ( INQ );  CREATEQ( OUTQ );

  WRITELN( 'ENTER NUMBER OF JOBS' );
  READ( N );

  WRITELN( 'ENTER TIME SLICE' );
  READ( SLICE );

  WRITELN('ENTER NAME-NUMBER PAIRS');
  WRITELN('CHAR, RET, INTEGER, RET');

  READLN;
  FOR I := 1 TO N DO
    BEGIN
      READLN( A.NAME );
      READLN( A.NUMR );
      A.NEED := A.NUMR;
      ENTERQ( INQ, A );
      WRITELN( 'NEXT');
    END;

  SUM := 0;  T := 0;
  WHILE INQ.SIZE <> 0 DO
    BEGIN
      EXITQ( INQ, JOB );
      IF JOB.NEED > SLICE THEN
        BEGIN
          JOB.NEED := JOB.NEED - SLICE;
          ENTERQ( INQ, JOB );
          T := T + SLICE;
        END
      ELSE
        BEGIN
          ENTERQ( OUTQ, JOB );
          T := T + JOB.NEED;
          SUM := SUM + T;
        END;
    END;

  MEAN := SUM/N;
  WRITELN( 'MEAN WAIT = ', MEAN:6:2 );

END (* MAIN *).
```

```
ENTER NUMBER OF JOBS
5
ENTER TIME SLICE
3
ENTER NAME-NUMBER PAIRS
CHAR, RET, INTEGER, RET
A
3
NEXT
B
7
NEXT
C
3
NEXT
D
5
NEXT
Z
2
NEXT
MEAN WAIT =  13.00
```

REVIEW: of Chapter 7

APPLICATIONS: Design, Systems, Examples

Applications of computers can be found in very many fields. In fact, there are very few areas that cannot be touched by computers. This chapter considers some typical applications, along with their design. Most practical applications are rather large, and so are only begun here.

Despite the diversity of application areas, there are often many techniques and data structures that are common to different areas.

Techniques, such as simulation, are particularly general, and can be used in most areas.

Data structures, also, may be the same for very different application areas. Sometimes it is possible to trade off data structures for program structures. Sub-programs are used extensively to manage this complexity of size. Sub-data, in the form of records and other data structures, also helps to break down the complexity.

Design methods for large systems are many; there is no unique method for the design of all kinds of systems. Some typical design "methodologies" follow briefly. They are organized according to what activity is done first.

TOP-DOWN emphasizes the "systems" view, first creating the "supervisor", and then proceeding with stubs, stepwise-refining them.

BOTTOM-UP emphasizes first the creation of sub-programs, and then later is concerned with interconnecting these "building blocks."

OUTSIDE-IN emphasizes the view of the user (or client), whereas INSIDE-OUT emphasizes the easiest way for the programmer.

EASY-TO-HARD starts with the simpler, more familiar parts, whereas HARD-TO-EASY starts with the harder parts.

Many more advanced design methods are possible, but cannot be described as simply as the above methods. A course on program design would be appropriate following this one.

PROBLEMS: on Chapter 7

1. SYM-SQUARE
Create an algorithm to find all integers from 1 to N whose squares read the same backward and forward. For example, the number 11 when squared yields 121, which is a symmetric square. To show the various data structures, do this
    a) using two arrays
    b) using one array
    c) using no arrays.

2. COIN PLOT
Simulate the throwing of a coin for at least 100 flips, and plot the proportion of "heads" against the number of flips. Notice at what point the proportion is within 10 percent of 0.5.

3. DRILL
Create an algorithm and corresponding conversational program to drill students in mathematics. Notice the structured nature of the following specification.

A total of N questions on multiplication are asked.
For each question P and Q are selected randomly.
The product of P and Q is requested.
While the response R is not correct
    (for up to three trials),
    it provides a hint
    indicating if the response is too high or low.
Ultimately it indicates a response
either "correct" or the solution.
It also counts the correct responses.
Finally it indicates the percentage correct.

4. DATA ANALYSER USING MENU
Create a system of programs which analyses any quantity of data as given by the following menu.

SELECT ACTION BELOW
    1. To enter items and count them
    2. To list out the items in order
    3. To select extreme MAX and MIN
    4. To compute average and variance
    5. To indicate ranks of all values
    6. To sort into increasing order
    7. To plot a horizontal bar graph
    8. To modify items: add, delete
    0. To end all actions and exit
ENTER A DIGIT (0..9)

5. MATCH MAKER
Create an algorithm to match individuals I for compatibility or agreement on preferences P. Each individual I is asked M questions for a preference P, which is shown on a table as C[I,P], with entries ranging from 0 to 5 as a degree of preference. The compatibility between two individuals is measured by finding the differences between each preference (in absolute value) and adding them up (so a value of zero indicates two perfectly compatible people). The program is to find the pairs of individuals who are most compatible.

MORE APPLICATIONS

1. SMALL ACCOUNT SYSTEM: SAS

You are required to create a system for a small business or club to manage some accounts. The data structure consists of a linear array of balances B[A] corresponding to accounts A (numbered from 100 to 199). The system repeatedly requests and performs any of the following actions (transactions) which are selected by their first characters:

'D'   DEPOSIT, increases the balance in the given account A by the given amount X.

'W'   WITHDRAWAL, decreases the balance (if possible) in a given account A by a given amount X, or else it gives a message.

'M'   MOVE, transfers a given amount from one account A (if possible) to another account B.

'E'   EXIT, causes these transactions to stop, and produces a report which indicates the balance in every account, and also the total sum of all balances.

Create this entire program first generally, and then in Pascal.

2. RESERVATION

A reservation system for a daily tour (by boat, bus or plane) is described by a two-dimensional array R[D,S]. Each day D of a month is represented by a row, and each seat S is represented by a column. The value within the array indicates the ID number of the person making the reservation for day D and seat S.

Create a top-down design of a system having the following operations (actions):

MAKE   to arrange for a reservation (if possible).

BREAK   to arrange to cancell the reservation.

VERIFY   to check which reservations were made by person with ID number I.

AVAIL   to indicate the number of available seats on a given tour D.

Alternately, implement this system by using records.

3. TINY TEXT PROCESSOR: TTP

Plan a program (data structure and algorithm) which takes a long sequence of characters (representing a one-page letter) and formats it onto a page into lines of any given length of L characters. The characters are made to extend to the right margin by inserting blanks between words. The input sequence may also have control characters embedded within it. For example, % causes a start of a new line, and # causes an indentation of three spaces. Also, the symbol & followed by a two-digit number specifies the line length. A typical input sequence and corresponding formatted output of length 20 is shown below.

```
&20
DEAR MOM
%# HI.                          DEAR MOM
HOW ARE YOU?  I AM FINE.           HI.  HOW ARE YOU?
HAVING A GREAT TIME.            I AM FINE.  HAVING A
WISH YOU WERE HERE.             GREAT TIME. WISH YOU
%#                              WERE HERE.
PLEASE SEND SOME MONEY.            PLEASE SEND  SOME
I LOVE YOU.                     MONEY.  I  LOVE YOU.
DID THE LAUNDRY GET THERE?      DID THE LAUNDRY  GET
BEST WISHES.                    THERE?  BEST WISHES.
%%
SINCERELY                       SINCERELY
%                               CHARLIE
CHARLIE
```

MORE PROBLEMS

1. INTEGRATE

The integral of a function F(X) corresponds to the area under the curve of this function. The area can be computed by slicing the X-axis into pieces X(1), X(2), X(3), ... X(n), so forming many smaller areas with varying heights F(X(i)) and constant width W.

Create an algorithm to compute the integral if each small piece is approximated by a rectangle (with height being the average midpoint) having area

    A = W*(F(X(i)) + F(X(i+1)))/2

Create another algorithm to compute the integral if each piece is approximated by a trapezoid having area

    A = W*F((X(i) + X(i+1))/2)

Compare the above two algorithms by computing the integral of the sine function from zero to 90 degrees.

2. MORE INTEGRATION WITH RANDOM NUMBERS

The area under a curve may be found using random numbers by randomly selecting many points X,Y on an area A (usually rectangular) which includes the required curve. The proportion of the points that fall under the curve approximates the fraction of A that is the required integral.

Create an algorithm to do this integration and compare it to the above two methods.

3. IMPROVE BIG CALCULATOR

The Big Calculator program developed in this chapter can be modified and improved in many different ways. Make some of the following improvements:

a. Check for proper input values as they are entered.
b. Test for overflow of a value, on entry and after add.
c. Suppress the output of leading zeros.
d. Use the Pascal subrange type DECIMALDIGIT = 0..9.
e. Simplify input by entering most significant digits first.
f. Simplify Entry by not requiring spaces between digits.
g. Provide user instructions, as Menu or with Help action.
h. Extend the actions to Multiply, Divide, find Root, etc.
i. Extend the objects to include negative values.
j. Generalize the objects and actions to real values.
k. Speed up some operations, by not pre-loading zeros.
l. Make your own improvements.

LARGE DESIGN PROJECTS

Imagine some large system (like SST) that you might want to create.
Then do the "top" design of that system. Continue the top-down
design for two or three levels only. Do the algorithm, data
structures, and some typical "runs" generally (as in the text).

Some sample projects follow:

    RESERVATION of rooms, transportation, or meal table, etc.
        (with actions of MAKE, BREAK, VERIFY, etc.)

    MATCH of people to homes, pets, entertainment, other people
        (with actions of ENTER, BEST, RANKED, etc.)

    MANAGE of accounts for clubs, business, personal
        (with actions of DEPOSIT, TRANSFER, BALANCE, etc.)

    EVALUATE of sports, diets, exercise plans, etc.
        (with actions of INPUT, AVERAGE, PLOT, PLAN, etc.)

    TEACH of some subject matter: math, history, computing, etc.
        (with actions of DRILL, TEST, EVALUATE, etc.)

    PLOT of various graphs, X vs Y, bar graphs, etc.
        (with actions of INPUT, SPECIFY, MODIFY, etc.)

    PAY of money for work, services, etc.
        (with actions of INPUT, OUTCHECK, REPORT, etc.)

    MANIPULATE of some objects like arrays, or very large integers
        (with actions of GET, ADD, MULTIPLY, PUT, etc.)

    POLL of people for opinions about events, states, others
        (with actions of TAKE, TABULATE, PLOT, etc.)

    or other such projects
        (like MAINTAIN, DECIDE, EXPERIMENT, PLAY, PROVE,
               SCHEDULE, TEST, etc.)

```
Appendix A

COMPUTERS:
  LOW-LEVEL MACHINE VIEW
```

```
UNITS AND LEVELS

REGISTERS AND TRANSFER

STRUCTURE AND BEHAVIOR

PROGRAMMING AND CODING
```

Appendix A   Table of Contents

COMPUTERS:

A LOW LEVEL MACHINE VIEW

* Asterisks indicate degree of importance *

Appendix A:

COMPUTERS

A Low-Level Machine View

PREVIEW

This is a very brief introduction to computers, providing a low level view of the inner details and hardware of computers. It may be studied at any time, but preferably after Chapter 3.

Computers, like automobiles and other machines, have varying sizes, shapes, powers, accessories and characteristics. But computers also have much in common, making it possible and useful to study the basic concepts that are common.

For example, virtually all computers are composed of electronic devices, operating at two electrical levels (the binary values 0 and 1). Most computers also have a very similar structure within them. Once the similar and general structures are understood, they are portable and apply to other machines which may differ in particular details. However, some knowledge of the basic inner system is useful. This appendix aims at providing such a basis.

Computers are more general than their name suggests; they can be used for control and communication as well as computation. Perhaps a more meaningful name for such a machine is "information transformer." In fact, we shall call our simple model IT, for such a reason. We will consider two versions of IT; first BIT (Binary Information Transformer) at the lowest binary and octal levels, and then SIT (Symbolic Instruction Translator) at a higher symbolic level.

Structure of computers will be considered at a number of levels, from the highest Units to the lower Registers. A common single-address machine will be used. A simulation of this computer can be found in chapter 7; it includes a Pascal program of the simulation.

Behavior of computers is illustrated by considering a small subset of instructions (such as ADD, STORE, CALL) which are then combined to create the four fundamental forms.

A COMPUTER...In Levels

1 Unit level

PROCESSING UNIT	MEMORY UNIT	INPUT-OUTPUT UNIT

2 Sub-unit level

Processing unit	Memory unit	I/O unit
CONTROL UNIT	PROGRAM SPACE	Input units CARD READER KEYBOARD
ARITH & LOGIC UNIT	VALUE SPACE	Output units LINE PRINTER GRAPHIC DISPLAY

3 Basic Register level

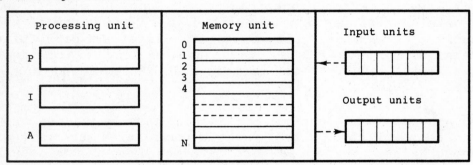

4 Detailed register transfer level

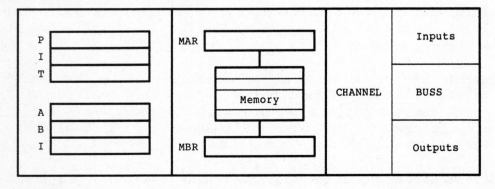

5 Gate & electronic level

COMPUTERS: Units in Levels

Computers may be viewed in many levels, the top level being very
general, and the bottom level being very detailed. The given
figures show five levels and their relation. The first two
levels are too broad, and the last two are too narrow. We will
be mainly concerned with the middle level, but it is useful to
see how this mid level is related to the other levels above and
below it.

LEVEL 1, at the top, shows a computer composed of three units: a
processing unit, a memory unit, and an input-output unit.
These units are not always physically separate, but it is
useful to view them functionally this way.

LEVEL 2 shows each above unit split into sub-units.

Processing units consist of a control unit for supervising the
behavior, and an arithmetic-and-logical unit (ALU, or
operation unit) for carrying out the required operations.

Memory units are also broken into two parts; one contains a
program, and the other contains the values that the program
is to operate on. This concept of a "stored program" is
very significant, for it makes possible a general purpose
machine; changing the program in memory changes the
behavior of the machine.

Input-output units serve either to input information (with
switches, card readers, keyboards), or to output
information (with lights, printers, or graphic displays).

LEVEL 3, the register level, shows how sub-units are made up of
registers which are viewed as general boxes having names,
addresses, and contents.

Processing units have a few registers: a program counter P
(which points to the instruction being performed) and an
instruction register, labelled I, (which holds the present
instruction).

Operation units, or ALUs, contain working registers that hold
intermediate results of the operations. The most common
working register is called an Accumulator, or simply the A
register.

Memory units consist of very many registers, each with a
number (address, or location) to be accessed by.

LEVEL 4, the register transfer level, shows a detailed level
involving more registers (T for timing, B for buffering, X for
indexing, MAR for memory addressing, and MBR for memory
buffering). These and other registers are needed for timing,
for matching devices operating at different speeds, and for
more elaborate microprogramming operations. These details are
not necessary for us at this time; they will be hidden or
transparent to us now.

LEVEL 5 involves logical gates and ultimately electronic
components. This level is too detailed for our purposes of
programming, but is important if we wished to create, modify,
or repair computers.

BASIC BUILDING BLOCKS OF MACHINES: REGISTERS

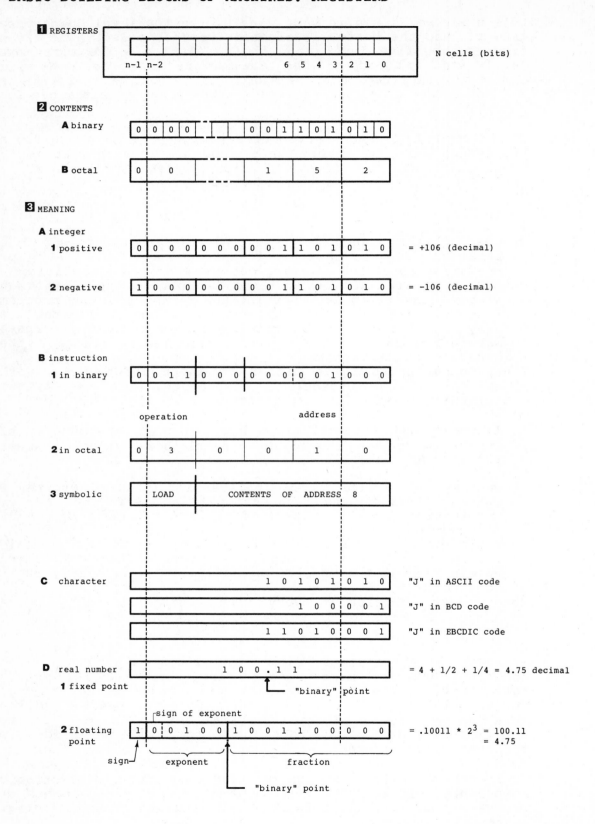

REGISTERS: and Register Transfer

Registers are the basic building blocks of computers. They consist of many small cells, each containing a binary digit (or bit) having the value of either 0 or 1, as shown in figure 1. Computers may have as few as eight such bits in each register, with typical sizes being 12, 16, 18, 24, 32, and 60 bits.

In our computer, IT, we will use 16-bit registers as shown in figure 2. In the 16 bits we can arrange 2^{16} or 65,536 different combinations of bits. In general, n bits can provide 2^n different arrangements.

Since long sequences of 16 zeros and ones may be difficult and error-prone to read and write, we often represent the binary combinations as much shorter octal (base 8) numbers. This is done by grouping the zeros and ones of a binary number in threes (from the right) and reading (from the left) the corresponding octal equivalents of each group. For example, as shown in figure 2, the binary sequence:

0 000 000 001 101 010 in octal is 0 0 0 1 5 2

INTERPRETATION or meaning of register contents is most important; the bit patterns can represent numbers, characters or instructions.

Integers can be represented in a sign-and-magnitude notation, with the leftmost digit indicating the sign (0 for positive, 1 for negative), and the rest indicating the usual positional notation. In our 16-bit machine, we can represent integers from -32,767 to +32,767. For example, the previous sequence

0000000001101010 represents $2^6 + 2^5 + 2^3 + 2^1 = +106$

and, similarly, the negative of this number, -106, is

1000000001101010.

Notice also that the octal equivalent of the above number

$152 = 1 \times 8^2 + 5 \times 8^1 + 2 \times 8^0 = 106$

yields the same value 106.

Instructions can also be coded as digits within registers. A "single address" instruction, for example, has an operation part and an address part, as shown in figure 3b. In our computer, the first four bits will represent operations (such as ADD or SUBtract), and the last nine bits will represent addresses of registers containing the values to be operated on. The four bits of the operation part allow 2^4 or 16 different operations, and the nine bits of the address part allow 2^9 or 512 possible addresses. The remaining three bits between these two parts will not be used as yet, but can extend either the number of operations (to 128) or the number of operands (to 4096). Also, the meaning and use of the above operations will be considered later.

Characters, such as letters of the alphabet, are shown represented by three different codes called ASCII, BCD, and EBCDIC in figure 3c. Real numbers, involving decimals, can also be coded as binary digits in many ways, a few of which are shown for completeness in figure 3d.

READING AND WRITING OF REGISTERS

The content of a register may be "read" from one register and "written" into another. The electronic process of reading from a register does not destroy the content of that register; it simply copies the content. However, the process of writing into a register destroys the previous content of that register. So reading is non-destructive, and writing is destructive.

STRUCTURE AND BEHAVIOR OF COMPUTERS

1 STRUCTURE OF IT

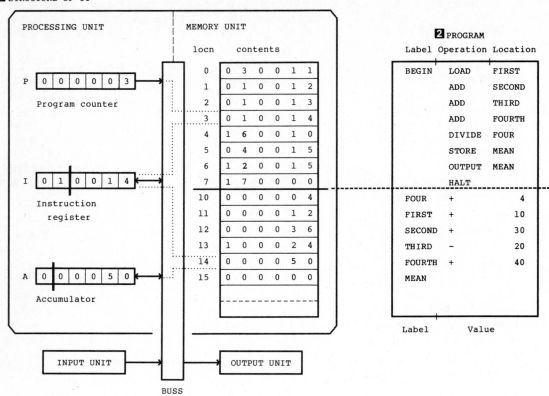

locn	contents
0	0 3 0 0 1 1
1	0 1 0 0 1 2
2	0 1 0 0 1 3
3	0 1 0 0 1 4
4	1 6 0 0 1 0
5	0 4 0 0 1 5
6	1 2 0 0 1 5
7	1 7 0 0 0 0
10	0 0 0 0 0 4
11	0 0 0 0 1 2
12	0 0 0 0 3 6
13	1 0 0 0 2 4
14	0 0 0 0 5 0
15	0 0 0 0 0 0

P: 0 0 0 0 0 3 — Program counter

I: 0 1 0 0 1 4 — Instruction register

A: 0 0 0 0 5 0 — Accumulator

2 PROGRAM

Label	Operation	Location
BEGIN	LOAD	FIRST
	ADD	SECOND
	ADD	THIRD
	ADD	FOURTH
	DIVIDE	FOUR
	STORE	MEAN
	OUTPUT	MEAN
	HALT	
FOUR	+	4
FIRST	+	10
SECOND	+	30
THIRD	−	20
FOURTH	+	40
MEAN		

Label	Value

3 BEHAVIOR OF IT

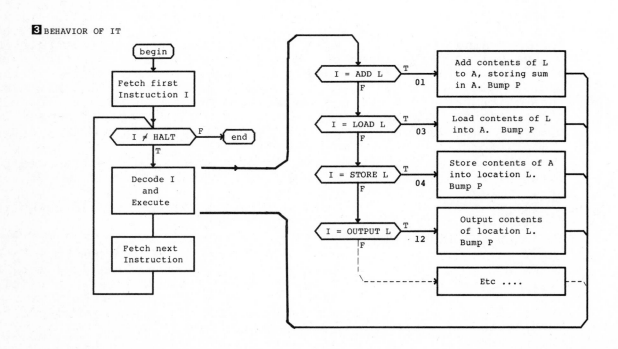

Structure and Behavior

STRUCTURE of a simple computer is shown in figure 1. The registers are connected together by a BUSS, for the flow of both data and instructions. This diagram represents a snapshot, showing the values at one instant in the middle of a computation (described later in step 3).

The program in memory is obscure because it is shown in octal. A more symbolic form of this program is directly to the right of the octal version for comparison.

The first eight memory locations contain instructions. Each instruction consists of an operation and an operand. For example, the first instruction has a LOAD operation (with octal op code of 03) which operates on the operand called FIRST (which is in location 0011).

Opcodes for some common operations are:

01 for ADD, 03 for LOAD, 04 for STORE,

12 for OUTPUT, 16 for DIVIDE and 17 for HALT.

The last six memory locations contain values. For example, the memory location labelled THIRD has the octal location 13 (decimal 11), and has the octal content -24 (which is decimal -20).

BEHAVIOR of a computer is shown by the algorithm of figure 2. The program pointer is first set to the beginning instruction. While this instruction is not HALT, the computer executes it, then fetches the next instruction, and keeps looping in this fetch-execute cycle. The behavior of the LOAD, STORE, ADD, and OUTPUT instructions are shown in the flow chart. After each of these instructions, the program pointer simply advances to the next instruction in the sequence. Later, with branching instructions, this will not be so; the pointer will change, depending on various conditions.

AVERAGE, the program shown in memory, sums four values, divides by 4, and outputs the resulting MEAN value of the four. The step-by-step behavior of this program follows.

0. 030011 Loads the content of FIRST location 11 (value 10) into the accumulator, destroying anything there.

1. 010012 Adds the content of SECOND location (value 30) into the accumulator (yielding 10 + 30 = 40 decimal).

2. 010013 Adds the content of THIRD location (value -20) into the accumulator (yielding 40 - 20 = 20).

3. 010014 Adds the content of FOURTH location (value 40) into the accumulator (yielding 40 + 20 =60).

4. 160011 Divides the content of the accumulator (60) by the content of location 10 (value 4), yielding 15.

5. 040015 Stores the content of the accumulator (now 15) into location 15, which is called MEAN.

6. 120015 Outputs the mean value (of 15) from location 15 to a printer or display screen.

7. 170000 Halts.

MORE BEHAVIOR

```
┌──┬──────────────────────────────────────────┬──┐
│  │ BEHAVIOR OF COMPUTER                      │  │
│  ├──────────────────────────────────────────┤  │
│  │    Set Program counter P                  │  │
│  │        to initial value                   │  │
│  │          P <-- 0                          │  │
│  ├──────────────────────────────────────────┤  │
│  │ Fetch                                     │  │
│  │        the instruction I                  │  │
│  │        that P points to                   │  │
│  │          I <-- M[P]                       │  │
│  ├──────────────────────────────────────────┤  │
│  │ While I ≠ HALT                            │  │
│  ├──┬─────────────────────────────────────┐ │  │
│  │  │ ┌──────────────┬─────────────────┐  │ │  │
│  │  │ │ I = LOAD L  \T│ A <-- M[L]      │  │ │  │
│  │  │ │              │ P <-- P + 1      │  │ │  │
│  │  │ ├──────────────┼─────────────────┤  │ │  │
│  │  │ │ I = STORE L \│ M[L] <-- A       │  │ │  │
│  │  │ │              │ P <-- P + 1      │  │ │  │
│  │  │ ├──────────────┼─────────────────┤  │ │  │
│  │  │ │ I = ADD L   \│ A <-- A + M[L]   │  │ │  │
│  │  │ │              │ P <-- P + 1      │  │ │  │
│  │  │ ├──────────────┼─────────────────┤  │ │  │
│  │  │ │ I = SUB L   \│ A <-- A - M[L]   │  │ │  │
│  │  │ │              │ P <-- P + 1      │  │ │  │
│  │  │ ├──────────────┼─────────────────┤  │ │  │
│  │  │ │ I = INPUT L \│ Read input into L│  │ │  │
│  │  │ │              │ P <-- P + 1      │  │ │  │
│  │  │ ├──────────────┼─────────────────┤  │ │  │
│  │  │ │ I = OUTPUT L\│ Write output of L│  │ │  │
│  │  │ │              │ P <-- P + 1      │  │ │  │
│  │  │ ├──────────────┼─────────────────┤  │ │  │
│  │  │ │ I = BRU L   \│ P <-- L          │  │ │  │
│  │  │ ├──────────────┼────────┬────────┤  │ │  │
│  │  │ │ I = BRN L    │ A >= 0\│P <-- P+1│  │ │  │
│  │  │ │              ├────────┼────────┤  │ │  │
│  │  │ │              │ A < 0 \│ P <-- L │  │ │  │
│  │  │ ├──────────────┴────────┴────────┤  │ │  │
│  │  │ │              etc                │  │ │  │
│  │  │ ├─────────────────────────────────┤  │ │  │
│  │  │ │ Fetch    instruction I           │  │ │  │
│  │  │ │        I <-- M[P]                │  │ │  │
│  │  │ └─────────────────────────────────┘  │ │  │
│  └──┴─────────────────────────────────────┘ │  │
└──┴──────────────────────────────────────────┴──┘
```

Instructions

A detailed description of the behavior of a computer is given in figure
1. It shows the simplest but most common and fundamental
instructions involving the operations of moving, arithmetic, input,
output, and branching.

LOAD L, is the load-accumulator instruction, which acts on the operand
(location L). It copies the content of L into the accumulator, and
bumps the program pointer.

STORE L, is the store-accumulator instruction, which copies the
content of the A-register into location L. It also bumps the
program pointer.

ADD L, is the instruction which adds the content of the operand L to
that of the A-register, and puts the resulting sum into the
A-register. It again bumps the program pointer.

SUBT and MULT are arithmetic operations similar to the ADD. For
example, SUBT L subtracts the contents of a given location L from
the contents of A, and puts this difference back into A.

DIVD L is an instruction which divides the contents of A by the
contents of location L, and puts the quotient (chopped result) back
into A.

INPUT L, is an instruction which inputs a value into a specified
location L.

OUTPUT L, similarly outputs a value from a location L to a printer or
other output device.

After each of the above instructions, the program pointer simply
advances to the next instruction in sequence. However, in the
following branch instructions the program pointer behaves
differently.

BRUN L, the branch-unconditional instruction causes the program
pointer to branch to the address L given by the operand, taking the
next instruction from that address. This unconditional branch,
sometimes denoted BRU, is also called a JUMP.

BRNEG L, the branch-on-negative instruction, first tests the value of
the A-register. If it is negative, then the program pointer gets a
new value L, and the next instruction is taken from this new point.
If the value is not negative, the program pointer is simply bumped
to the next instruction in sequence.

BRPOS L, or more briefly BRP L, branches to L when the A-register is
positive. Similarily BRZRO L (or BRZ L) branches to L when A is
negative.

CALL L (not shown in the figure) is the sub-program call. It first
saves the program pointer value (to return to) and then branches to
the given location L. It continues execution there until it meets a
RETN (return instruction), which causes the program pointer to
receive the saved return location, and continues from there.

Other instructions are also possible (including logical and character
operations), but are not considered here. Each of these operations
has a corresponding op-code which is given in the simulated version
of this computer on page 7-30.

THE FOUR FUNDAMENTAL FORMS: Low Level

1 Series Form

```
                        SWAP:    LOAD   FIRST    100   LDA   200
TEMP    <--- FIRST               STORE  TEMP     101   STA   202
                                 LOAD   SECOND   102   LDA   201
FIRST   <--- SECOND              STORE  FIRST    103   STA   200
                                 LOAD   TEMP     104   LDA   202
SECOND  <--- TEMP                STORE  SECOND   105   STA   201
                                 HALT            106   HLT
                       FIRST:    7               200      000007
                      SECOND:    11              201      000011
                        TEMP:    7               202      000007
```

2 Choice Form

```
IF                   MAXIMUM:    LOAD   THIS     300   LDA   400
   THIS > THAT                   SUBT   THAT     301   SBT   401
                                 BRNEG  THERE    302   BRN   306
THEN                    HERE:    LOAD   THIS     303   LDA   400
   MAX <--- THIS                 STORE  MAX      304   STA   402
                                 BRUN   OUT      305   BRU   308
ELSE                   THERE:    LOAD   THAT     306   LDA   401
   MAX <--- THAT                 STORE  MAX      307   STA   402
ENDIF                    OUT:    NOOP            308   NOP
                        THIS:    2               400      000002
                        THAT:    4               401      000004
                         MAX:    4               402      000004
```

3 Loop Form

```
                       BEGIN:    LOAD   NUM      500   LDA   600
REM <---NUM                      STORE  REM      501   STA   602
                        BACK:    LOAD   REM      502   LDA   602
WHILE                            SUBT   DEN      503   SBT   601
   REM >= DEN                    BRNEG  NEXT     504   BRN   509
DO                               LOAD   REM      505   LDA   602
   REM <---                      SUBT   DEN      506   SBT   601
        REM - DEN                STORE  REM      507   STA   602
ENDWHILE                         BRUN   BACK     508   BRU   502
                        NEXT:    NOOP            509   NOP
                         NUM:    14              600      000014
                         DEN:    4               601      000004
                         REM:    2               602      000002
```

4 Sub Form

```
                        MAIN:    LOAD   VAL      700   LDA   800
CALL ABS                         CALL   ABSUB    701   CAL   900
   IMPORT: VAL                   STORE  MAG      702   STA   801
   EXPORT: MAG                   HALT            703   HLT
                         VAL:    -7              800      100007
                         MAG:    7               801      000007

SUBPROGRAM ABSUB       ABSUB:    LOAD   VAL      900   LDA   800
   MAG <--- VAL                  STORE  MAG      901   STA   801
   IF VAL < 0 THEN               BRPOS  FINIS    902   BRP   906
                                 LOAD   ZERO     903   LDA   907
      MAG <--- 0 - VAL           SUBT   VAL      904   SBT   800
   ENDIF                         STORE  MAG      905   STA   801
END-SUB                FINIS:    RETN            906   RET   702
                        ZERO:    0               907      000000
```

PROGRAMMING: Coding the Four Forms

The four fundamental forms may be easily implemented in this low
   level language. An example of each of the four forms follows.
   These are only segments of a program; they do not involve
   inputs or outputs. Notice the refinement of each program.
   First, at the left, the program is written in pseudo-code. To
   the right of the pseudo-code it is written in a lower form,
   where the labels, operations, and operands are symbolic.
   Finally, at the far right of each program, there is a very low
   version with labels and operands indicated by their location;
   only the operations are symbolic (and shortened).

SERIES is illustrated by the SWAP of two registers labelled FIRST
   and SECOND, using a temporary register TEMP.

CHOICE is illustrated by the MAX algorithm, which finds the
   larger of two values THIS and THAT. The condition
   (THIS > THAT) is changed to (THIS - THAT > 0) by simply
   subtracting THAT from both sides; this is necessary because
   decisions on branching are done by comparing to zero.

LOOP is illustrated by the REMainder algorithm, which computes
   the remainder REM when numerator NUM is divided by denominator
   DEN. This is done by successively subtracting away the
   denominator from the numerator until the remainder is less
   than the denominator. Notice again that the loop condition
   involves a comparison to zero.

SUB forms are illustrated by the absolute value algorithm ABS.
   The main program simply puts some value into the accumulator,
   calls the ABS sub-program to operate on this value, and
   finally stores the resulting absolute value into MAG.

The ABS sub-program computes the absolute value of this number
   in the accumulator by subtracting its value from zero (if
   necessary). To do this, it uses a temporary variable TEMP and
   a constant ZERO. Finally, when it encounters the return
   instruction RETN, it returns to the program that called it.
   The absolute value has been "passed back" to the calling (or
   main) program through the accumulator.

Other examples of program pieces are shown on the following
   pages. Complete programs are also shown in this low level
   language. Some of the examples are done in a higher level
   symbolic language resembling Pascal (and could be called
   PASQUAL: baby brother of Pascal). In this following version
   of the language the data values (constants and variables)
   precede the instructions; in other such languages the data
   part follows the instruction part. Notice also, on page A-13,
   that the comments are in the form of pseudo-code.

BIGGER FORMS

1 The FOR form - with FACTORIAL

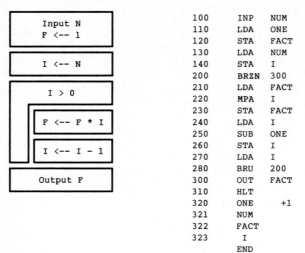

Input N F <-- 1		
I <-- N		
I > 0		
F <-- F * I		
I <-- I - 1		
Output F		

```
100    INP    NUM
110    LDA    ONE
120    STA    FACT
130    LDA    NUM
140    STA    I
200    BRZN   300
210    LDA    FACT
220    MPA    I
230    STA    FACT
240    LDA    I
250    SUB    ONE
260    STA    I
270    LDA    I
280    BRU    200
300    OUT    FACT
310    HLT
320    ONE       +1
321    NUM
322    FACT
323    I
       END
```

```
          FACTORIAL

      Input Num
      FACT <-- 1

      Loop I

        FACT <-- FACT*I

      from N to 1

      Output FACT
```

2 The CASE form - with GRADES

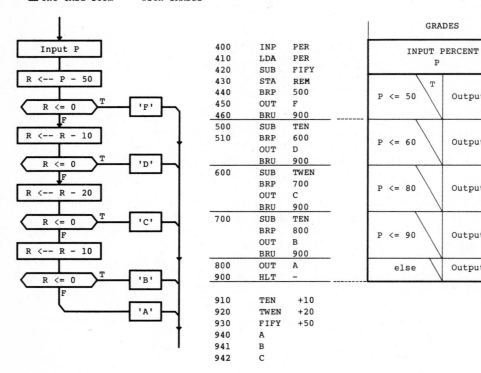

```
400    INP    PER
410    LDA    PER
420    SUB    FIFY
430    STA    REM
440    BRP    500
450    OUT    F
460    BRU    900
500    SUB    TEN
510    BRP    600
       OUT    D
       BRU    900
600    SUB    TWEN
       BRP    700
       OUT    C
       BRU    900
700    SUB    TEN
       BRP    800
       OUT    B
       BRU    900
800    OUT    A
900    HLT    -

910    TEN    +10
920    TWEN   +20
930    FIFY   +50
940    A
941    B
942    C
```

		GRADES	
	INPUT PERCENT P		
P <= 50		Output 'F'	
P <= 60		Output 'D'	
P <= 80		Output 'C'	
P <= 90		Output 'B'	
else		Output 'A'	

A COMPLETE LOW-LEVEL PROGRAM

```
PROGRAM  MAX-AND-COUNT;

  (* SEARCHES  FOR MAXIMUM *)
  (* AND COUNTS THE VALUES *)


CONSTANTS
  ZERO = 0;
  ONE  = 1;

VARIABLES
  TERM  : INTEGER;
  VALUE : INTEGER;
  MAX   : INTEGER;
  COUNT : INTEGER;


BEGIN: (* MAIN *)       (********MAX AND COUNT*********)

        INPUT   TERM;   (*  READ( TERM, VALUE )        *)
        INPUT   VALUE;
        LOAD    VALUE;  (*  MAX <-- VALUE              *)
        STORE   MAX;
        LOAD    ZERO;   (*  COUNT <-- 0                *)
        STORE   COUNT;
        INPUT   VALUE;  (*  READ( VALUE )              *)

AGAIN:  SUBT    TERM;
        BRZRO   NEXT;   (*  WHILE VALUE <> TERM DO     *)

        LOAD    COUNT;
        ADD     ONE;    (*      BUMP COUNT             *)
        STORE   COUNT;

        LOAD    MAX;    (*      IF MAX < VALUE THEN    *)
        SUBT    VALUE;
        BRPOS   THERE;  (*          MAX <-- VALUE      *)
        LOAD    VALUE;
        STORE   MAX;    (*      ENDIF                  *)
THERE:  NOOP;
        READ    VALUE;  (*      READ VALUE             *)
        BRUN    AGAIN;
                        (*  ENDWHILE                   *)
NEXT:   OUTPUT MAX;
        OUTPUT COUNT;   (*  WRITE( MAX, COUNT )        *)

END   (* MAIN *).       (*****************************)
```

REAL COMPUTERS

Actual computers are similar to the machine described here, and yet also different. Some of these differences and similarities will be illustrated by considering briefly three different sized machines: a micro, a mini, and a maxi (or monster) machine.

Micro computers typically have short word lengths (4, 8, 12, 16 bits). They are inexpensive, but slow. Monster computers usually have long word lengths (16, 24, 32, or 60 bits). They are expensive and fast. Mini computers (having word lengths of 12, 16, or 18 bits) are usually a good compromise between speed and cost.

Monster machines are illustrated by the Cyber computer made by Control Data Corporation. It has very long registers of 60 bits. Each register may hold four instructions, which may be executed at the same time. Operations are performed among 32 general-purpose registers (or accumulators). Transfers among these general-purpose registers are much faster than transfers among memory registers because of the "bottleneck" of getting in and out of memory.

Mini computers are illustrated by the PDP-11 computer made by Digital Equipment Corporation. It has registers consisting of 16 bits. An instruction of this computer may consist of one, two, or three of these words. There are eight "working registers" (or accumulators), two of which have special purposes (one serving also as the instruction pointer).

Micro computers are illustrated by the 8080 computer made by the Intel Corporation. It has registers of 8 bits, and each instruction may take one, two, or three of these registers.

Some non-typical machines are the Burroughs B1700 having a word length of arbitrary size, and the Burroughs B6700, a stack machine.

Other unusual machine structures involve such concepts as pipelining, reconfigurability, parallelism, and data flow. Other concepts will undoubtably continue to develop in the future.

REVIEW: of Appendix A

COMPUTERS: A Low-level Machine View

Computers are viewed very briefly in this appendix. This description is sufficiently short to convey some basic insight into machines, but not sufficiently long to master programming at such a low level.

Registers are the basic building blocks of computers. They consist of many bits (from 4 to 60 or more). Contents of registers can represent numbers, characters, or instructions.

Units (memory units, processing units, and input-output units) are constructed out of registers. Of the various levels for viewing computers, this appendix emphasizes the register-transfer level.

Structure and behavior is shown for a typical single-address computer. Instructions are of the form "OPERN ADDR", where an operation OPERN (such as ADD, SUBT, STORE) acts on a single address, ADDR. Other computers may have two addresses (such as ADD B,C, which means add contents of B to the contents of C). A three-address machine could have instructions like ADD A B C, which means add contents of A to that of B and put the result into C. There are also four-address machines and even zero-address machines (stack machines).

Programming at a low machine level can be structured; the low-level instructions can be organized into the four fundamental forms. Structured programming is harder at such low levels, but it can be done.

Typical real computers (micro, mini, and maxi) have been briefly introduced, to show the differences and similarities among different computers.

Many aspects of low-level machines have not been covered in this brief introduction. One particularly important concept is that of addressing. Some typical modes include direct addressing, indirect (or deferred) addressing, and indexed addressing.

PROBLEMS: on Appendix A

Convert the following algorithms into programs in the low level
language of this chapter. Do this at the higher symbolic
level, rather than at the lower binary or octal levels.

SERIES
1. CHARGE of figure 1, page 1-4
2. TEMPERATURE CONVERSION of page 1-4
3. TIME algorithms of page 1-4   (Compare them!)
4. BASE conversion of an 8-bit number, as on page 1-4
5. ISBN checksum test of page 1-2

CHOICE
6. PAY algorithms of page 0-6
7. CHANGE algorithm of page 2-30
8. TRIANGLE algorithms of page 2-22
9. MAX algorithms of page 3-16
10. MAJority algorithms of page 3-14
11. LEAP algorithms of page 2-20
12. BIG-SMALL algorithms of page 3-10

LOOPS
13. SQUARE algorithm of page 3-26
14. PRODUCT algorithm of figure 2c, page 3-30
15. LOAN algorithm of page 3-32
16. CUBE algorithm of problem 4, page 3-63
17. POWER algorithm of problem 2, page 3-61

SUBS
18. MAX3 and MAX4 of page 3-34, using MAX2
19. SECONDS algorithm of page 3-36, using DIVIDE
20. SORT3 algorithm of page 3-38, using SORT2
21. MIN DIFFERENCE algorithm of figure 2, page 3-41

MIXED FORMS
22. GCD algorithm of page 3-46
23. CONVERT (decimal to binary) algorithm, page 3-46
24. CONVERT (decimal to binary, again), page 2-15
25. CHANGE algorithms of page 3-48, figures 2 and 4
26. BISECTION algorithm of page 3-52

```
Appendix B

PASCAL:
   PROGRAMMING
   PRACTICE
```

```
     PROGRAMS
     OBJECTS
     ACTIONS
     SERIES FORM
     CHOICE FORM
     LOOP FORM
     TYPES
     STYLE
     PROCEDURES
     FUNCTIONS
     ARRAYS
     RECORDS
     FILES
```

Appendix B   Table of Contents
PASCAL
PROGRAMMING PRACTICE

* Asterisks indicate degree of importance *

Appendix B

PASCAL

Programming Practice

PREVIEW

Pascal is a programming language developed by Niklaus Wirth around
1970. The language was named after Blaise Pascal (1623-1662), a
very early pioneer in computing (as well as a significant
contributor to physics, mathematics, literature, religion, and
philosophy).

Pascal is similar to many of the popular languages such as Basic,
Fortran, PL/I, and Algol. It is a rather simple language
(purposefully) of moderate size and complexity, but powerful,
compact, reliable, and efficient. Its clarity, simplicity, and
structure make it most suitable as the first language to be
learned.

Because Pascal was created by one person, it has a unity, integrity,
and beauty which is not usually found in anything which was put
together by many people (all adding their own favorite
features).

Here we will not consider the entire Pascal language, but a large
subset of it. How much we have is not as important as what we do
with what we have.

This appendix is best used after Chapter 3 of this book has been
studied. It can be used without this book if the reader is
already familiar with the basic concepts. But it is not a good
idea to learn the language first, for as good as Pascal is, it is
restrictive to think in terms of it (or any other programming
language).

Dialects of Pascal

There are a number of versions of Pascal which differ slightly in
some details. These details are usually very minor. The
version used here is the CDC (Control Data Corporation) version
on their Network Operating System (NOS). A sub-appendix
following this appendix shows the methods for accessing and
using this Pascal. All programs given here have been run on the
CDC Cyber system. Many of these programs have also been run,
usually with no modification, on the Apple micro computer with
the UCSD (University of California at San Diego) Pascal system.
Another sub-appendix shows how the UCSD system is used.

The programs written here were intended for interactive use
(conversational mode, using a keyboard and display), but the
text has also been used in a batch mode (with punched cards).
Runs of most programs are shown enclosed in dotted boxes. Solid
boxes are drawn around sub-programs and parts of programs which
could be used in creating larger programs.

PROGRAMS: A Top View of Pascal

Before getting into the details of the Pascal language, it is very important to get a view from a higher level to see where the details will fit in. This top view can be achieved by looking at some small but complete programs. The emphasis here will be on the syntax or form that is common to all Pascal programs.

First, it is important to realize that the line numbers at the left of each program are NOT a part of Pascal. These line numbers are mainly for our convenience, for referring to lines to discuss them. On some versions of Pascal line numbers are used for editing; then line numbers have gaps between them so that other lines can be inserted if necessary.

Programs consist of statements (declarative and imperative) which are separated by semi-colons. The first statement, called a header, is similar on all programs, differing only in the program name. The header is followed by statements declaring all the constants and variables (in that order), indicating their types. Finally, the main body is sandwiched between a BEGIN and END, and the program ends with a period. The indentation and spacing in a program are strictly for the convenience of humans; computers view the entire program as one long line! Comments, which have no meaning to the computer, may appear sandwiched between curly brackets (if available on a keyboard) or between "(*" and "*)" combinations of symbols.

CONVERT is a program which simply converts temperatures from degrees Fahrenheit to degrees Celsius (or Centigrade). A typical "conversational" run is shown in the dotted box at its right; the human's part of the conversation is underlined. First, an input is requested with the prompt "ENTER F". The value of F is read, the C computed, and its (rounded) value is output. A typical run of this program is shown in the dotted box, converting 98.6 degrees to 37 degrees. A WRITELN (write-line) statement, as shown on line 4, first writes and then advances to the beginning of the next line. A WRITE statement simply writes; it does not move onto the next line.

GRADES is a simple-minded grading program to illustrate the Choice form in Pascal. When run interactively, this program first prompts the user to input a value with "ENTER SCORE". The score is then read, a comparison is made to a constant limit (or cutoff value), and the appropriate message (PASS or FAIL) is output. Notice the indenting of each of the alternative sub-actions of the choice. Notice also that the cutoff grade, called LIMIT, has been declared as a constant, so that if it should change, it need be changed only at this one point at the top of the program, rather than everywhere it appears within the program. This method of allowing easy change of a "constant" is very convenient when there are many occurrences of the constant within a program.

TEMPTABLE is a program to illustrate the Loop form in Pascal. It outputs a table of Celsius temperatures and the corresponding Fahrenheit temperatures. The temperature C starts at 0 degrees, and "loops" to 100 degrees. Within the loop (which is indented) it computes F, writes both C and F (rounded off), then bumps C by 10 to get the next temperature. The run (or execution) of this program is shown in the dotted box at the right of the program. There the two columns of temperatures are shown separated slightly. Actually the amount of separation differs in different versions of Pascal. In the CDC version there is much separation; on the UCSD version there is no separation. The amount of separation can be specified by methods given on page B-12.

SOME SMALL PASCAL PROGRAMS

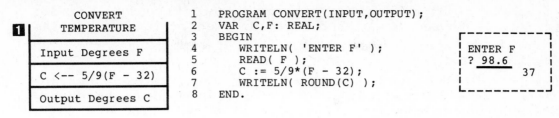

1 CONVERT TEMPERATURE

| Input Degrees F |
| C <-- 5/9(F - 32) |
| Output Degrees C |

```
1    PROGRAM CONVERT(INPUT,OUTPUT);
2    VAR  C,F: REAL;
3    BEGIN
4        WRITELN( 'ENTER F' );
5        READ( F );
6        C := 5/9*(F - 32);
7        WRITELN( ROUND(C) );
8    END.
```

```
ENTER F
? 98.6
                37
```

2 SIMPLE GRADER

| Limit L = 50 |
| Input score S |
| T   S < L   F |
| Output 'FAIL' | Output 'PASS' |

```
10   PROGRAM GRADES(INPUT,OUTPUT);
15     (* SHOWS CHOICE FORM *)
20   CONST
25     LIMIT = 50;   (* CUT-OFF *)
30   VAR
35     SCORE: INTEGER;
40
50   BEGIN
55     WRITELN( 'ENTER SCORE' );
60     READ( SCORE );
65     IF SCORE < LIMIT THEN
70         WRITELN( 'FAIL' )
75     ELSE
80         WRITELN( 'PASS' );
85   END.
```

```
ENTER SCORE
? 49
FAIL
```

```
ENTER SCORE
? 50
PASS
```

3 TEMPERATURE TABLE

| C <-- 0 |
| C <= 100 |
| F <-- 9/5C + 32
Output C,F
C <-- C + 10 |

```
100    PROGRAM  TEMPTABLE(INPUT,OUTPUT);
110      (* ILLUSTRATES THE LOOP FORM *)
120
130    VAR
140      C: INTEGER;
150      F: REAL;
160
200    BEGIN
210      C := 0;
220      WHILE C <= 100 DO
230        BEGIN
240          F := 9/5*C + 32;
250          WRITELN( C, ROUND(F) );
260          C := C + 10;
270        END;
280    END.
```

```
    0   32
   10   50
   20   68
   30   86
   40  104
   50  122
   60  140
   70  158
   80  176
   90  194
  100  212
```

Layout of Programs

Let us consider one more slightly larger complete program from a high level, to see its layout or arrangement. It is a program to make change for a dollar when purchasing something costing C cents.

The top-down plan is briefly sketched out in figure 1 to illustrate the structure. This plan does not always need to be drawn, because proper indentation and gaps show the structure as in figure 2. Notice that comments are freely interspersed, usually preceding a group of actions. These comments taken alone form a description of the program.

A typical run is shown in the dotted box. Notice the prompting of the input, and the identification of the output.

CHANGE2, a second version of this program, is shown below to illustrate an alternative layout -- short and fat. It behaves exactly the same as the above CHANGE1, but it is usually not preferred. It appears less readable, for it hides the structure. It is also less modifiable, for inserting a segment may require significant moving of the text, which may also result in errors.

Layout, or format, of a program is quite arbitrary; one statement may extend over many lines (as in CHANGE1), or one line may have many statements (as in CHANGE2). Our choice of layout determines a style of program.

MODIFICATIONS and improvements are always possible. For example, both programs above could use more descriptive names; variable Q could be renamed QTRS or QUARTERS, or even COUNTOFQUARTERS. This may not seem too important in a small program, but it makes a large program much more readable. Another version of this program, with longer variable names, is shown on page B-87.

The programs could also be modified to allow the input of any amount T (tendered), and to test for proper input values (anticipating negative values). The input cost could also be "echoed" and the amount of change printed. Output could also be fancier, for example printing numbers as ONE PENNY, or with plural denominations such as THREE PENNIES.

Notice also that programs here are written with all letters in upper case. On some systems, lower case (or mixed upper and lower case) is possible. In fact, the lower case could be more readable, but for learning purposes we wish to make a distinction between the language of Pascal and the English language (meta-language) we use to talk about Pascal.

In general, a Pascal program has a top part (declarations) indicating WHAT (objects, names, types), and a bottom part (actions) indicating HOW the objects are to be acted on. Documentation, in the form of comments, indicates WHY something is done.

A CHANGE MAKING
PROGRAM

2
```
100    PROGRAM CHANGE1(INPUT,OUTPUT);
110       (* CHANGE FOR A DOLLAR *)
115       (* SEE ALSO PAGE  3-48 *)
120
200    VAR
210       C,R,  Q,N,P: INTEGER;
220
300    BEGIN
310       (* INPUT THE COST *)
320          WRITELN( 'ENTER THE COST' );
330          WRITELN( 'IN CENTS' );
340          READ( C );
350          R := 100 - C;
360
400       (* MAKE THE CHANGE *)
410          Q := 0;
420          WHILE R >= 25 DO
430             BEGIN
440                Q := Q + 1;
450                R := R - 25;
460             END;
470
500          N := 0;
510          WHILE R >= 5 DO
520             BEGIN
530                N := N + 1;
540                R := R - 5;
550             END;
560
600          P := R;
610
700       (* OUTPUT THE COIN COUNT *)
710          WRITELN( 'THE CHANGE IS' );
720          WRITELN(Q,' QUARTERS');
730          WRITELN(N,' NICKELS');
740          WRITELN(P,' PENNIES');
900    END.
```

1

```
MAKE
CHANGE
for a
dollar
```

```
Input C
find R

QUARTERS
PART

NICKELS
PART

PENNIES

OUTPUT
```

3 A Typical Run

```
ENTER THE COST
IN CENTS
? 12
THE CHANGE IS
        3 QUARTERS
        2 NICKELS
        3 PENNIES
```

See also PASCAL B-87

4
```
1000    PROGRAM CHANGE2(INPUT,OUTPUT);
1100       (* SHORT CHANGE FOR A DOLLAR *)
2000    VAR  C,R,  Q,N,P: INTEGER;
3000    BEGIN
3100       WRITELN( 'ENTER THE COST' );  WRITELN( 'IN CENTS' );
3200       READ(C);  R := 100 - C;
4000       Q := 0;   WHILE R >= 25 DO BEGIN Q := Q + 1; R := R - 25; END;
5000       N := 0;   WHILE R >=  5 DO BEGIN N := N + 1; R := R - 5 ; END;
6000       P := R;
7000       WRITELN( 'THE CHANGE IS' );
8000       WRITELN(Q,' QUARTERS');WRITELN(N,' NICKELS');WRITELN(P,' PENNIES');
9999    END.
```

Syntax Diagrams: From the Top

The syntax, or form, of a Pascal program and all its parts can be described by syntax diagrams. They consist of various shaped boxes joined by arrows. Rounded boxes (such as the ones shown containing a period, or the word BEGIN) contain actual symbols written out in the program exactly as shown. Square boxes (such as the ones containing "series form" and "integer") refer to other syntax diagrams shown elsewhere. Arrows show all possible proper flows of the symbols. Let us consider some syntax diagrams at various levels (from high to low) as shown in the figures.

PROGRAMS are defined by the first syntax diagram as consisting of a header, followed by a semi-colon, then declarations, a semi-colon, followed by a series form, and finally ending with a period.

SERIES forms are defined at a lower level as the MID view of figure 2. It consists of a word BEGIN followed by any number of statements separated by semi-colons, and ending with the word END. This series form refers to a "statement" box which will be defined later (as either a loop, choice, series, I/O, or assignment form). The dotted line shows an alternate path.

CONVERT, the previous temperature program, is shown in figure 3 illustrating the proper syntax. The essential idea is that any path of symbols that leads through a syntax diagram is of proper form, and all others have improper form.

INTEGERS, defined in figure 4, provide another example at a lower level. An integer consists of a digit followed by any number of digits. A (decimal) digit is one of the ten values 0, 1, 2, ... 9. This is the general form of an integer, but actually there is a limit to the size of an integer depending on the particular computer used.

REAL numbers are defined by the syntax diagram of figure 5. Notice that the sequence 0.5 is a real number, for it corresponds to a path through this syntax diagram, whereas .5 is not a real number, for it does not go through the diagram. Similarly, 5.0 is a proper real number, but 5. is not.

Scientific notation is an alternative notation for real numbers, especially very large or small ones. A number such as 1.23E4 means $1.23*10$ or 12,300. Similarly, 0.000123 is equivalent to 1.23E-4. In other words, the number after the E indicates how many places the decimal point is to be moved; the sign of the number indicates whether it moves left (if negative) or moves right otherwise.

Headers are different on various implementations of Pascal. The shortest headers (on the UCSD Pascal) consist of the word "PROGRAM" followed by the name of the program. The Standard Pascal has in addition the program name followed by "(INPUT,OUTPUT)". Additionally, on the CDC version, a slash is required between the "INPUT" and the ",OUTPUT" to make it interactive (conversational).

SYNTAX DIAGRAMS

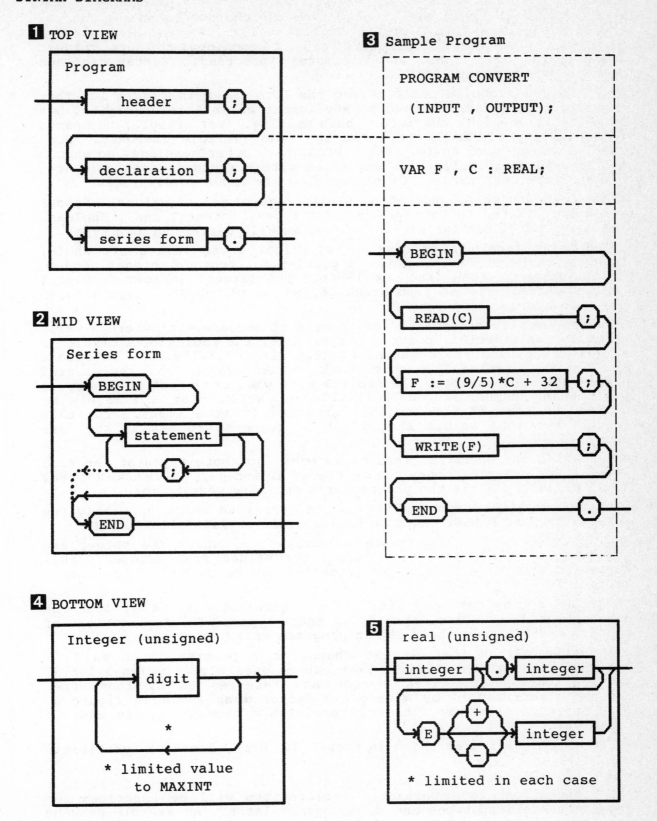

1 TOP VIEW

Program

header ;

declaration ;

series form .

2 MID VIEW

Series form

BEGIN

statement

;

END

3 Sample Program

PROGRAM CONVERT

(INPUT , OUTPUT);

VAR F , C : REAL;

BEGIN

READ(C) ;

F := (9/5)*C + 32 ;

WRITE(F) ;

END .

4 BOTTOM VIEW

Integer (unsigned)

digit

*

* limited value
to MAXINT

5 real (unsigned)

integer . integer

E + integer

-

* limited in each case

OBJECTS: Simple Types

All the objects in Pascal are created from the characters on a keyboard, including letters (A,B,C,...Z), digits (0,1,2,..9) and others (such as : ; + $). These characters can be combined to form values, identifiers, operations, and ultimately programs. Syntax diagrams describe these forms.

IDENTIFIERS are symbolic names having the form shown in figure 1. They consist of a letter followed by any number of letters or digits, but only the first eight characters have meaning. For example, the names TEMPORARY and TEMPORARX refer to the same variable TEMPORAR. Some special words, such as IF, BEGIN, REAL, have other meanings, so should not be used as identifiers. Any names within rounded boxes on syntax diagrams are unsuitable. Other examples are shown in figure 2.

TYPES describe objects, indicating their range or set of values. Pascal types are limited to four pre-defined types: integer, real, Boolean, and character (CHAR for short). Later we will define our own types.

INTEGERS arise from the process of counting, where values are whole, integral numbers. For example, a population count is integer, and so is the variable YEAR (such as 1984). The largest integer in Pascal (called MAXINT) ranges from about 16,000 to 16,000,000, depending on the computer used.

REAL values usually arise from the process of measurement, where a value normally has a decimal point. For example, the radius of a circle is a real value, and the constant PI (equalling 3.14159...) is also a real value. Actually, some real values cannot be represented precisely. For example, the decimal 0.20 when converted to binary is a repeating number (0.001100110011...) which must ultimately be chopped to some finite length, resulting in some error. For this reason, two real values should not be compared to see if they are equal.

Some variables may be either real or integer (not both types at the same time). For example, money can be viewed as integer (25 cents) or real (0.25 dollars). It's the programmer's decision what to make it.

BOOLEAN values arise from conditions and decisions which have only two values, TRUE or FALSE. More on Boolean values will follow later.

CHARACTER values arise from human communication, where the values are the symbols of the keyboard. Character values are enclosed within quotes so that a value such as grade 'C' can be distinguished from a variable C.

DECLARATIONS define data objects. In the simplest cases they list the constants and variables, specifying their types. The declarations of objects must precede their use in programs or sub-programs.

CONSTANTS are values that do not change in a program (such as PI = 3.14159 or the YEAR = 1984). They can be used directly (as 3.14159) within programs, or given a name and referred to by that name. Constants represented by a name are declared as shown in figure 3. This representation by a name is preferable because of its ease of modification.

VARIABLES are declared as shown in figure 4. Here, lists of identifiers can be given a type.

Declarations in general are shown in figure 5. The order of the four sub-declarations is important. Declarations will be described for programmer-defined types and sub-programs later. An example showing many typical declarations is given in figure 6.

1 Identifier (id)

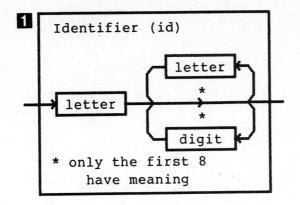

* only the first 8
   have meaning

2 Examples of Identifiers

Proper	Improper
A	7
AGE	2PIE
R2D2	2TQT
OVER21	OVER21
MAXAGE	MAX AGE
TEMPORARY	WHILE

3 Constant declaration

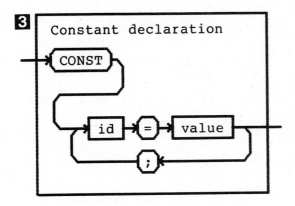

4 Variable declaration

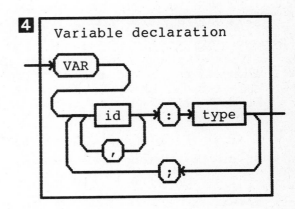

5 Declarations

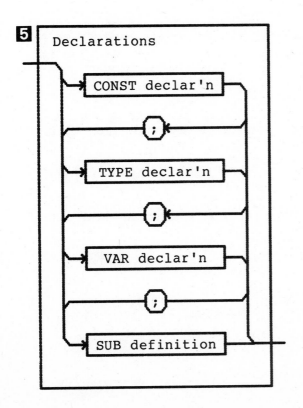

CONST declar'n

TYPE declar'n

VAR declar'n

SUB definition

6 Example declarations

```
CONST
  PI  = 3.14159;
  YEAR= 1984;
  DOT = '.';
  T   = TRUE;

VAR
  AGE  : INTEGER;
  B,C,D: REAL;
  MALE : BOOLEAN;
  GRADE: CHAR;

  COUNT,
  ISBN, ZIP: INTEGER;

  RADIUS, RATE,
  RATIO : REAL;
```

Actions: Operations

Actions performed on Pascal objects are many; some of the simpler actions are considered here.

ARITHMETIC operations of addition, subtraction, and multiplication are very similar for integers and real values. Division, however, differs between reals and integers. Division of two real values X and Y is indicated by "X/Y", and yields a resulting real number. Division of two integers I and J is indicated by "I DIV J", and it yields another integer by chopping the result. For example

 5/9 yields 0.55555, but 5 DIV 9 yields 0.

MOD (or modulo) is a useful operation on integers. The operation "X MOD Y" yields the remainder when X is divided by Y. For example, 5 MOD 3 yields 2. Some interesting properties of MOD follow.

 If (X MOD Y = 0), then Y divides X evenly; 1948 MOD 4 yields 0.
 X MOD 10 yields the rightmost digit of X; 123 MOD 10 yields 3.
 X MOD 2 yields 0 if X is even, 1 if X is odd; 5 MOD 2 yields 1.

EXPONENTIATION, or taking any number to some power, is one operator that Pascal does not have, but other languages do have. There are a number of alternatives to the use of exponentiation. One method is to create a sub-program, using functions or procedures (which will be given later). Another method is to avoid exponentiation as follows. Consider the polynomial

 P := A + B*Q + C*Q*Q + D*Q*Q*Q

It can be rearranged algebraically by factoring into

 P := A + Q*(B + Q*(C + Q*D))

Notice that it requires no exponentiation, and it also requires half as many multiplications, so is more efficient.

EXPRESSIONS in Pascal have the same form as in ordinary algebra. For example, in arithmetic expressions the multiply and divide operators have precedence over add and subtract operators. If operators are of the same precedence, then they are done from left to right. Parentheses would be used if there is any possibility of confusion about the order of doing the operations. For example, the formula

 9/5*C + 32 could be written as (9/5)*C + 32.

ASSIGNMENT is the action of copying a value, of any of the four types, into a box of the same type. The assignment operator is a combination of two symbols: a colon followed by an equal sign. An assignment statement has the form:

 identifier := expression

where an expression (formally defined on page B-35) may be a constant, variable, or a combination of these. Some sample assignment statements are:

 I := 0   AREA := PI*RADIUS*RADIUS
 F := M*A   C := 5/9*(F-32)

Mixed types (integers and reals) may appear in an expression. In such cases, whenever either operand is real then the result is real. For example, in the above temperature conversion formulas, the real division results in the entire expression evaluating to a real result.

Pre-Defined Functions

PRE-DEFINED FUNCTIONS (or built-in functions) are often-used actions which are made available in a language for convenience. In Pascal, these functions accept a single input argument (which may be an expression) and yield (or return) a single value of a given type. In the following examples variable R is of type real, I is of type integer, and variable E is of either type. Each of these functions can be viewed as a black box with a single input and a single output as shown below.

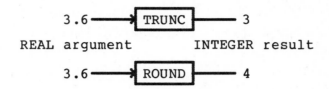

TRUNC and ROUND are two ways of getting an integer from a real number. TRUNC(R) simply chops off the decimal part of the real number R, whereas ROUND(R) provides the nearest integer to R. The input argument is real in both cases, and the output returned is of type integer.

SQR(E) computes the square of either a real or integer value E, and returns a result which is of the same type as E. SQRT(E) computes the square root of either a real or integer E, and always returns a value of type real.

ABS(E) computes the absolute value (value without sign) of any value E, returning a value of the same type as E.

Functions can be used anywhere a variable of that type may be used, for example within a statement such as:

```
HYPOTENUSE := SQRT( SQR(BASE) + SQR(HEIGHT) )
```

OTHER PRE-DEFINED FUNCTIONS (Optional)

TRIGONOMETRIC functions SIN(E) and COS(E) compute the sine and cosine of any value E, and return the result having the same type as E. The argument E must be in radians; to convert degrees to radians, multiply by PI and divide by 180.

LN(E) computes the natural logarithm of E (to base e = 2.71 ...). Similarly, EXP(E) computes the value of e raised to the power E. These two are useful for many scientific applications. They can be used to compute the Nth power of X by:

```
XTOPOWERN := EXP( N*LN(X) )
```

SUCC(E) returns the successor or following value of either an integer or character value E (as well as other types considered later). For example SUCC('A') is 'B'. Similarly PRED(E) returns the predecessor or preceding value of E.

ODD(I) is a Boolean function which determines whether an integer I is odd, and if so returns a value of TRUE; otherwise, FALSE. It then could be used to make some decision.

Other actions, such as MAXIMUM, MAJORITY and SORT, can be defined in Pascal (see pages B-51 and B-55), and used now as "black boxes." Later we will learn to define such actions.

Input/Output

Input and output can be done as simply as you wish, or formatted as elaborately as you wish. Input of the simplest kind involves numbers, and has the form:

READ(list of variable names)

where the variable names are separated by commas. The input values are entered and separated by spaces (any number of blanks). Syntax diagrams of input-output statements are shown in figures 1 and 2 at the bottom of the facing page.

OUTPUT of the simplest kind involves numbers and quotations (strings) in the form:

WRITELN(list of quotations or expressions)

where WRITELN means write-line (write and then move down to the beginning of the next line). The quotations are surrounded by single quotes, and the items of this list are separated by commas. The expressions may be constants, variables, or formulas. Everything between quotes is printed exactly as quoted, but the output format of numbers depends on the Pascal dialect (The CDC version allows a field of 10 print positions for integers, so printing most values far apart, whereas the UCSD version allows no spaces between values). Real values printed by this simple method are also awkward, for they are written in scientific notation.

INTEGER input and output are shown below in the program INOUT. A PROMPT, shown in line 210, indicates to the user which value is required. An ECHO, shown in line 230, simply repeats what the user puts in. The echo allows users to check what they thought they put in. The lonely WRITELN of line 240 simply skips to the next line, so leaving a gap on the output page.

REAL VALUE input and output examples are shown on lines 300 to 330. Notice that the output is in scientific notation, which is unnatural for business and some other purposes.

CHARACTERS can be input and output as shown in lines 400 to 430. More complex input of characters is shown on page B-32.

More output, involving expressions, is shown on line 500. First the expressions are evaluated, then the values are output. The last lines show how any number of variables may be input. The values are accepted (either all on one line, or all on separate lines, or combinations of these), and assigned to the variables in the given order, until all variables have been assigned.

```
100   PROGRAM INOUT( INPUT, OUTPUT );
110   (* SHOWS READING AND WRITING *)
120
130   CONST
140     NOW = 1984;
150   VAR
160     AGE: INTEGER;    WAGE: REAL;
170     GRADE: CHAR;     A,B,C,D: INTEGER;
180
200   BEGIN
210     WRITELN( 'ENTER AGE' );            ENTER AGE
220     READ( AGE );                       ? 21
230     WRITELN( 'AGE IS', AGE );          AGE IS         21
240     WRITELN;
300     WRITELN( 'ENTER WAGE' );           ENTER WAGE
310     READ( WAGE );                      ? 1234.56
320     WRITELN( 'WAGE IS', WAGE);         WAGE IS  1.2345600000000E+003
330     WRITELN;
400     WRITELN( 'ENTER GRADE' );          ENTER GRADE
410     READ( GRADE );                     ? A
420     WRITELN( 'GRADE IS ', GRADE );     GRADE IS A
430     WRITELN;
500     WRITELN( 'BORN ABOUT', NOW - AGE); BORN ABOUT       1963
510     WRITELN;
520     WRITELN( 'ENTER FOUR VALUES ' );   ENTER FOUR VALUES
530     READ( A,B,C,D );                   ? 2 0 -7 13
540     WRITELN(A,B,C,D);                           2         0        -7        13
600   END.
```

More Input/Output

General input and output statements in Pascal allow much more useful actions than the previous simple ones. Syntax diagrams showing these statements are given below. Notice that Boolean values may not be input; they also cannot be output. The WRITE command simply writes; it does not move to the next line as does WRITELN.

INTEGER OUTPUT can be placed, or formatted, within a given fixed space, called a field width, by a notation involving colons. For example, the statement

    WRITELN('YEAR ', NOW:4)

would print the word YEAR and a space, followed immediately by the four digits of the integer NOW. Without the colon and width 4, a "default" width (of about 10, on the Cyber) would have been used, so causing much greater separation between the quotation and the number. Similarly, the statement

    WRITELN('YOU ARE ', AGE:3, ' YEARS OLD.')

prints out the age in a field width of 3 as:

    YOU ARE   6 YEARS OLD.

The field width need not be a constant value, but may be any expression. For example, the previous output could be spaced very exactly by the following:

    IF AGE < 9 THEN WIDTH := 1 ELSE
    IF AGE < 99 THEN WIDTH := 2 ELSE
                     WIDTH := 3;
    WRITELN('YOU ARE ', AGE:WIDTH, ' YEARS OLD.')

REAL OUTPUT may also be formatted, but involves two colons, as in WRITELN(PAY:W:D), where the value W after the first colon indicates the field width (as before), and the value D after the second colon indicates the number of decimal places. For example, the statement

    WRITELN('PAY THE AMOUNT OF $', PAY:7:2)

could print out the following, depending on the value of PAY:

    PAY THE AMOUNT OF $1234.56
    PAY THE AMOUNT OF $ 78.90

Notice that the decimal point is counted as one of the seven symbols in the field. Notice also that the numbers fill the field from the right, with spaces added to the left. In the last example the space between the dollar sign and the dollar amount is especially dangerous for digits may be put into it dishonestly. This "gap" could be prevented by a method similar to the above method which found the exact width of AGE.

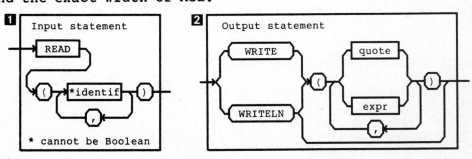

SERIES FORM

The Series form or compound statement is the simplest form in Pascal. The flow block diagram is given in figure 1, with a flow chart showing its meaning (semantics) in figure 2.

Syntax showing the structure of the Series form is described in figure 3. The Series consists of any number of statements separated by semi-colons, and sandwiched between a BEGIN and END. An example of such a series form is shown in figure 4.

SWAP is shown in figure 5; notice that there is no semi-colon following the last statement (just before the END), because semi-colons separate statements; they do not terminate them.

Alternatively, it is possible to insert a semi-colon after the last statement in a Series form (as shown by dotted lines on the syntax diagram and on the SWAP of figure 6). This allows insertion of other statements at the end of the Series form, without having to go back to the previous one to add the semi-colon. Actually, using this semi-colon causes creation of a "null" statement. Other statements which may be in a Series form are shown in figure 7. Some Series examples follow, showing short programs which may be useful.

SALE is a typical example of a simple series of statements showing a sales transaction involving computation of sales tax.

```
BEGIN (* SALE *)
  READ( QUANTITY, PRICE );
  COST  := QUANTITY*PRICE;
  TAX   := TAXRATE*COST;
  TOTAL := COST + TAX;
  WRITELN( TOTAL:5:2 );
END (* SALE *)
```

DEMILITARIZE TIME is a program showing how military time (given as an integer such as 2345) can be split into hours and minutes (such as 23 hours and 45 minutes). The integer DIVide operation (by 100) yields the hours directly. The MOD operation produces the remainder (minutes, or MINS) when TIME is divided by 100. An alternative to using the MOD operation is:

MINS := TIME - (TIME DIV 100)*100

```
BEGIN (* DEMILITARIZE TIME *)
  READ( TIME );
  HOURS := TIME DIV 100;
  MINS  := TIME MOD 100;
  WRITELN( HOURS, MINS )
END (* DEMILITARIZE TIME *)
```

POWER shows one way of raising any value X to the Nth power. It uses both the exponential and the logarithmic functions. Since Pascal does not have an exponentiation operator, this method could be particularly useful.

```
BEGIN (* POWER *)
  READ( X,N );
  P := EXP( N*LN(X) );
  WRITELN( P );
END (* POWER *)
```

TANGENT is a trigonometric function that is sometimes useful but not directly available in Pascal. First the degrees are converted into radians, and then the sine of the angle is divided by the cosine to yield the tangent.

```
BEGIN (* TANGENT *)
  WRITELN('ENTER DEGREES');
  READ( DEGREES );
  RAD  := (PI/180)*DEGREES;
  TAND := SIN(RAD)/COS(RAD);
  WRITELN( TAND )
END (* TANGENT *)
```

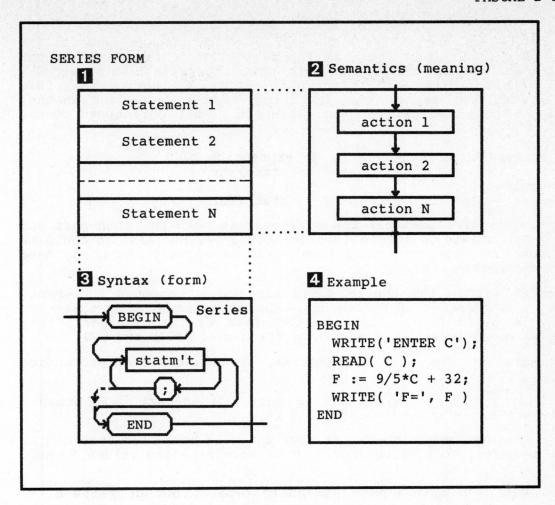

SERIES FORM

1

| Statement 1 |
| Statement 2 |
| - - - - - - |
| Statement N |

2 Semantics (meaning)

action 1

action 2

action N

3 Syntax (form)

Series

BEGIN

statm't

;

END

4 Example

```
BEGIN
  WRITE('ENTER C');
  READ( C );
  F := 9/5*C + 32;
  WRITE( 'F=', F )
END
```

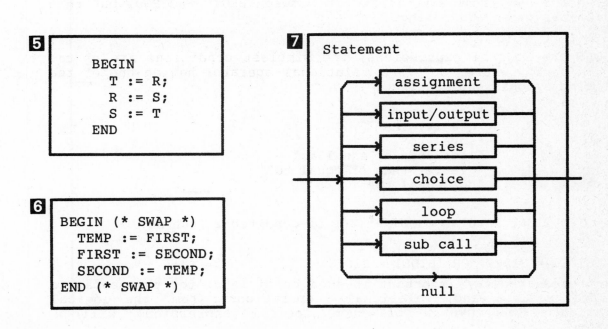

5

```
    BEGIN
      T := R;
      R := S;
      S := T
    END
```

6

```
BEGIN (* SWAP *)
  TEMP := FIRST;
  FIRST := SECOND;
  SECOND := TEMP;
END (* SWAP *)
```

7 Statement

assignment

input/output

series

choice

loop

sub call

null

CHOICE FORM

The choice form is shown in figure 1 as a flow block diagram drawn on its
side. The semantics is shown in the flowchart of figure 2; if the
condition is true then the action D is done, otherwise E is done. The
syntax of this choice form is shown in figure 3. Notice that this
diagram shows two paths, one involving a then-part, and another
involving both a then-part and an else-part. They correspond to the
following:

```
     IF expression THEN           IF expression THEN
                                      statement
          statement               ELSE
                                      statement
```

It is important to realize that the statement in both the then-part and
the else-part could be simple (assignment, I/O), but also it could be
another choice form, or a loop form, each of which in turn may have
other forms within them.

A statement within the choice could also be a compound statement,
consisting of a series of statements. In other words, when there are
two or more statements within the then-part or the else-part, they
must be combined into a series form by the use of BEGIN and END.

Sample segments are shown in the diagrams, to illustrate simple choice
forms.

Figure 5 is a simple choice having only a then-part. It bumps a
counter each time the age is less than 18.

Figure 6 also has only a then-part, but since it has three statements,
it must be made into a series form. This segment sorts values P and Q
into decreasing order.

Figure 7 has both a then-part and an else-part, but only the else-
part is compounded into a series form. The then-part could also be
made into a series by sandwiching it between BEGIN and END, but this
is unnecessary and confusing.

CONDITIONS are logical expressions; the simplest conditions are of the
form "X op Y", where "op" is a relational operator having one of the
following symbols and meanings:

```
     <     meaning   "less than"
     >        "      "greater than"
     =        "      "equal to"
     <=       "      "less than or equal to"
     >=       "      "greater than or equal to"
     <>       "      "not equal to"
```

COMPLEX CONDITIONS involve combinations of conditions such as

     (X < Y) AND (Y < Z)

     (SIDE1 = SIDE2) OR (SIDE1 = SIDE3)

Parentheses are very important in such conditions, for they separate
the arithmetic (and relational) operations from the logical
operations. The syntax of such logical expressions will be
considered later.

CHOICE FORM

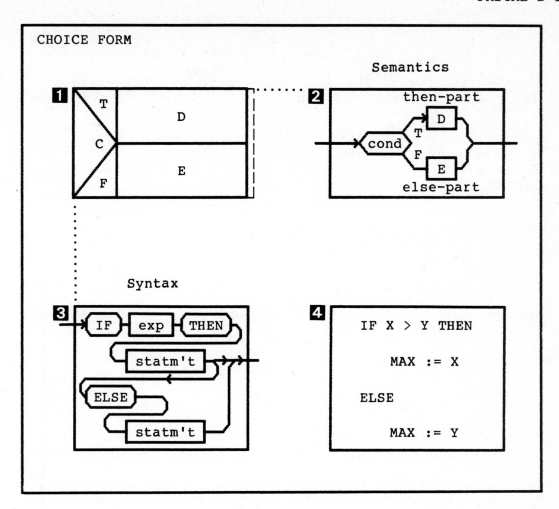

Semantics

1 T
C D
F E

2 then-part
cond T D
F E
else-part

Syntax

3 IF exp THEN
statm't
ELSE
statm't

4
```
IF X > Y THEN

    MAX := X

ELSE

    MAX := Y
```

5
```
IF AGE < 18 THEN
    MINORS := MINORS + 1
```

6
```
IF P < Q THEN
  BEGIN (* SWAP *)
    T := P;
    P := Q;
    Q := T;
  END (* SWAP *)
```

7
```
(* PROCESS THE AGE *)
IF AGE < 0 THEN
   WRITELN( 'ERR' )
ELSE
   BEGIN
     WRITE( AGE );
     SUM := SUM + AGE;
     COUNT := COUNT + 1;
   END
```

Choice Segments

Four other choice forms are shown in the following figures, along with their corresponding flow block diagrams.

BIG-SMALL illustrates the case where both the then-part and the else-part are compounded.

MAX3 shows two equivalent ways of finding the maximum of three values, by nesting choices and then by cascading them. Notice that laying the flow block diagram on its side makes for a better correspondence.

TRIANGLE shows an example where some choices are nested, and others are cascaded.

CONFUSION could possibly arise in only one nest of Choices, where an IF follows an IF without an intervening ELSE, as in the following:

        IF A THEN IF B THEN C ELSE D

Humans could unfortunately read and interpret this in two different ways:

```
    (* PROPER FORM *)          (* IMPROPER FORM *)
      IF A THEN                   IF A THEN
        IF B THEN                   IF B THEN
          C                           C
        ELSE                        ELSE
          D                           D
```

The first version associates the ELSE with the second IF; the second version associates the ELSE with the first IF. Pascal associates the lonely ELSE with the nearest preceding IF, as shown in the first example. If the second form (called improper) is intended, then a BEGIN and END must be inserted as follows:

```
      IF A THEN
        BEGIN
          IF B THEN
            C
        END
      ELSE
        D
```

CHOICE PROBLEMS

Write the following Choice algorithms as pieces of programs in Pascal:
1. The BIG-SMALL algorithm of figure 7 on page 3-10.
2. The CLASSIFIER algorithm of figures 1, 2 on page 3-12.
3. The MAJORITY algorithms on page 3-14.
4. The PAY algorithms of figures 3, 4 on page 0-6.
5. The COMPARE algorithm on page 2-8.
6. The LEAP algorithms on page 2-20.
7. The TRIANGLE algorithm of figure 3 on page 2-22.
8. The GRADES algorithms on page 3-18.

CODING CHOICES IN PASCAL

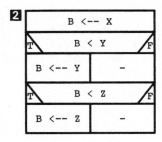

```
(* BIG-SMALL OF PAGE 3-10 *)

   IF X > Y THEN
      BEGIN
         BIG   := X;
         SMALL := Y;
      END
   ELSE
      BEGIN
         BIG   := Y;
         SMALL := X;
      END;
```

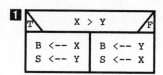

```
(* MAX3..LONG AND THIN OF PAGE 3-16 *)

   B := X;
   IF B < Y THEN
      B := Y;
   IF B < Z THEN
      B := Z;
```

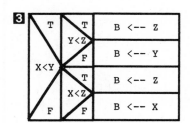

```
(* MAX3..SHORT AND FAT OF PAGE 3-16 *)

   IF X < Y THEN
      IF Y < Z THEN
         B := Z
      ELSE
         B := Y
   ELSE
      IF X < Z THEN
         B := Z
      ELSE
         B := X;
```

```
(* TRIANGLE CLASSIFICATION OF PAGE 2-22 *)
(* ASSUMING SIDES RELATED BY: A < B < C *)

   IF A + B <= C THEN
      WRITELN(' NOT A TRIANGLE ')
   ELSE
      IF A = C THEN
         WRITELN(' EQUILATERAL TRIANGLE ')
      ELSE
         BEGIN
            IF (A = B) OR (B = C) THEN
               WRITELN(' ISOSCELES ');
            IF (A*A + B*B = C*C) THEN
               WRITELN(' RIGHT TRIANGLE ')
            ELSE
               WRITELN(' TRIANGLE ');
         END;
```

Nested Choices

The previous choices involved selection between only two
    alternatives, but often more alternatives are required.
    The Choice form easily extends to more selections by simply
    nesting choices within choices. This is shown in the given
    three examples, where the indentation (or lack of it) does
    not reflect nesting, but instead reflects the selections.

GRADES shows how a grade G may be assigned, depending on a
    percentage P. The successive then-parts could be indented,
    but are not.

PRICES shows an algorithm to determine the price P of an item,
    depending on the quantity being sold. Notice that the
    conditions here are logical combinations.

LEAP indicates whether a given year is a leap year. It uses
    the fact that if a year Y is divisible by an integer N, then
    Y MOD N has value zero. This is because Y MOD N is the
    remainder of Y when divided by N.

Notice the conditions in each above example:

        grades were compared to see if they were within some
            range,
        quantities were compared to see if they were equal to
            constants,
        years were compared to see if they were divisible by
            values.

    If the comparison is that of a value to a constant, as in
    the middle PRICES example, then Pascal has another form,
    the CASE form, which can be used. It will be considered
    next, but it is limited to comparing for constant values --
    more limited than this general select form of nested
    choices.

The conditions need not all involve numbers, as in the
    following example, where GRADE is a character.

```
            (* MESSAGE DEPENDS ON GRADE *)
              READ( GRADE );
              IF GRADE = 'A' THEN
                WRITE( 'VERY GOOD' )
              ELSE
              IF GRADE = 'B' THEN
                WRITE( 'GOOD' )
              ELSE
              IF GRADE = 'C' THEN
                WRITE( 'OK' )
              ELSE
                WRITE( 'NOT GOOD' );
```

1

```
(* GRADES *)
   WRITELN(' ENTER PERCENTAGE ');
   READ (P);
   WRITE(' GRADE IS ');

   (* SELECT THE GRADE
      DEPENDING ON PERCENT *)
   IF P >= 90 THEN
       WRITE('A')
   ELSE
   IF P >= 80 THEN
       WRITE('B')
   ELSE
   IF P >= 60 THEN
       WRITE('C')
   ELSE
   IF P >= 50 THEN
       WRITE('D')
   ELSE
       WRITE('F');
```

2

```
(* PRICES *)
   WRITELN(' ENTER QUANTITY ');
   READ (Q);

   (* SELECT THE UNIT PRICE *)
   (* DEPENDING ON QUANTITY *)
   IF (Q = 1) THEN
       PRICE := 39
   ELSE
   IF (Q = 2) OR (Q = 3) THEN
       PRICE := 35
   ELSE
   IF (Q > 3) AND (Q < 7) THEN
       PRICE := 30
   ELSE
       PRICE := 25
   (* END OF SELECTION *);

   WRITE(' TOTAL IS ', PRICE*Q );
```

3

```
(* LEAP *)
   WRITELN(' ENTER THE YEAR ');   READ(Y);
   IF Y MOD 400 = 0 THEN WRITE(' LEAP ')     ELSE
   IF Y MOD 100 = 0 THEN WRITE(' NOT LEAP ') ELSE
   IF Y MOD   4 = 0 THEN WRITE(' LEAP ')     ELSE
                         WRITE(' NOT LEAP ');
```

Case Form (Optional)

The CASE statement is a multiple choice (or select) form. It
   has the general structure:

```
CASE  expression  OF

     list-of-values  :  statement  ;
     list-of-values  :  statement  ;
       .   .   .              .
       .   .   .              .
     list-of-values  :  statement

   END
```

The CASE form selects a statement depending on the value of the
   expression. This is illustrated in the given examples.
   The first two examples determine the number of days in any
   given month. The first program segment lists all the
   months systematically in order.

The second segment groups all months having the same number
   of days, so it results in a more compact form. This segment
   is also more "robust" or fail-safe, for it first checks if
   the input value is within limits. The first segment does
   not have such a check, so if an improper value is entered,
   the program would fail (in many versions of Pascal).

Notice that the number of days in February is defined as a
   constant DAYSINFEB. This "constant" is changed (twice)
   every four years.

The third segment shows that character values may also be
   used in the CASE form.

The Pascal Case statement is less general than the original
   Case or Select form of Chapter 5; it requires constant
   values, whereas the previous select form allowed selection
   based on a range of values.

The Case form can be created from (simulated by) Choice forms.
   For example, the days in a month can be given by:

```
(* CASE SIMULATED BY NESTED CHOICES *)

    IF (M=9) OR (M=4) OR (M=6) OR (M=11) THEN
      NUM := 30
    ELSE
    IF (M=2) THEN
      NUM := DAYSINFEB
    ELSE
    IF (M > 0) AND (M <= 12) THEN
      NUM := 31;
    ELSE
      WRITELN( 'MONTH IS OUT OF LIMITS' );
```

```
PROGRAM CASES(INPUT, OUTPUT);
   (* ILLUSTRATES CASE FORM*)

CONST
   DAYSINFEB = 28;

VAR
   MONTH, DAY, NUM: INTEGER;
   GRADE: CHAR;

BEGIN

(**************************************************)

(* SIMPLE LISTING OF CASES *)
   WRITELN(' ENTER MONTH '); READ(MONTH);

   CASE MONTH OF
     1: NUM := 31;
     2: NUM := DAYSINFEB;
     3: NUM := 31;
     4: NUM := 30;
     5: NUM := 31;
     6: NUM := 30;
     7: NUM := 31;
     8: NUM := 31;
     9: NUM := 30;
    10: NUM := 31;
    11: NUM := 30;
    12: NUM := 31
   END;

   WRITELN(' NUMBER OF DAYS IS ', NUM:2);

(**************************************************)

(* ROBUST COMPOUNDING OF CASES *)
   WRITELN(' ENTER MONTH '); READ(MONTH);
   WRITE('DAYS = ');

   IF (1 <= MONTH) AND (MONTH <= 12) THEN
     CASE MONTH OF
        9, 4, 6, 11  : WRITELN('30');
        1,3,5,7,8,10,12 : WRITELN('31');
                    2  : WRITELN(DAYSINFEB);
     END (*CASE*)
   ELSE
     WRITELN(' MONTH IS OUT OF LIMITS ');

(**************************************************)

(* CASES OF CHARACTERS *)
   WRITELN('ENTER GRADE'); READLN; READ(GRADE);

   CASE GRADE OF
        'A' : WRITELN(' EXCELLENT ');
        'D' : WRITELN(' BARELY PASSING');
        'F' : WRITELN(' FAILING ');
    'B', 'C' : WRITELN(' PASSING ');
   END (* CASE OF GRADES *);

(**************************************************)

END.
```

LOOP FORMS: While

The WHILE loop form is shown in figure 1 as an L-shaped flow block diagram. Figure 2 shows the semantics as a flowchart; while the condition C is true the body B is repeated. The syntax is shown in figure 3, consisting of a simple sequence: the word WHILE, followed by an expression, then the word DO, and finally a single statement. Usually, the body involves more than one statement, so the many statements are made into one series statement, with a BEGIN and END sandwiching the statements.

Examples of loops are very common. First, figure 4 shows one of the simplest possible loops with only one action within the body. This example shows one way of computing the remainder R, when A is divided by B.

FACTORIAL, of figure 5, is another typical example of a loop; notice the indentation of the body, which indicates the scope or range of the loop.

SQUARE, of figure 6, shows how the square of any variable N can be determined by summing the first N odd integers. Notice the bump by 2.

REINPUT, shown below, indicates a very useful method of entering data in the conversational mode. First, it prompts the user to enter the age. While the age is out of range, it indicates a message and asks for another entry. When a proper value is entered, it is repeated (or echoed) to check whether the intended value was actually received.

INORDER similarly enters three values, but does not continue further unless the values are in order.

```
(* REINPUT SEGMENT *)              (* INORDER SEGMENT *)
   WRITELN(' ENTER AGE ');            WRITELN('ENTER A,B,C INCREASING');
   READ( AGE );                       READ( A,B,C );
   WHILE AGE < 0 DO                   WHILE (A > B) OR (B > C) DO
     BEGIN                              BEGIN
       WRITELN('RE-ENTER');               WRITELN('ORDER THEM');
       READ( AGE );                       READ(A,B,C);
     END;                               END;
   WRITELN('AGE IS', AGE);            WRITELN('VALUES ARE',A,B,C);
(* END OF REINPUT *)               (* END OF INORDER *)
```

REPEAT-UNTIL is another loop form in Pascal. It first performs an action and then tests the condition. The form of this loop is:

```
REPEAT
   statements
UNTIL condition
```

WHILE LOOP

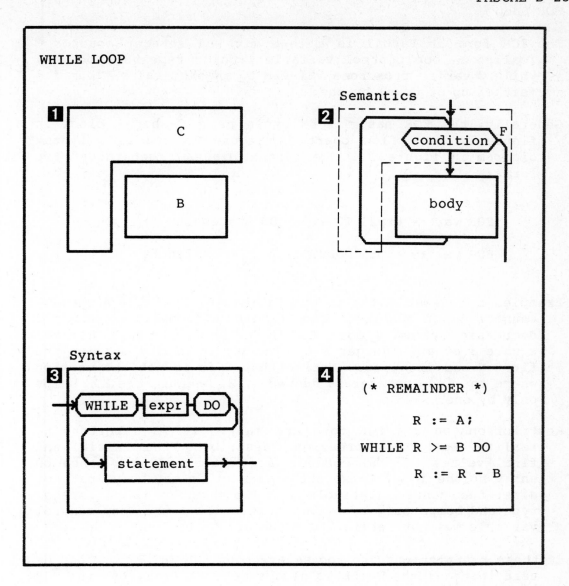

1

C

B

2 Semantics

condition F

body

3 Syntax

WHILE — expr — DO

statement

4
```
(* REMAINDER *)

        R := A;

WHILE R >= B DO

        R := R - B
```

5
```
(* FACTORIAL N *)

   F := 1;
   C := 2;

   WHILE C <= N DO
     BEGIN
        F := F * C;
        C := C + 1;
     END ;
```

6
```
(* ODD SQUARE *)

   S := 0;
   I := 1;

   WHILE I < N + N DO
     BEGIN
        S := S + I;
        I := I + 2;
     END ;
```

FOR Loop

The FOR form in Pascal is a loop with an integer counter C (called a loop control variable), which repeats a body B, while C varies from some value M to another value N bumping (either up or down) by one.

Generally, the FOR has a form shown as a C-shaped block in figure 1, as a flow chart in figure 2, and as a syntax diagram in figure 3. The syntax diagram "generates" two forms:

        FOR var := expr1 TO expr2 DO statement

        FOR var := expr1 DOWNTO expr2 DO statement

Examples are shown in the given figures, with figure 4 showing counter I increasing, and figure 5 showing counter J decreasing (from N down to 2). Figure 6 shows how the square S of any integer N can be determined by summing the first N odd integers. Notice that this is not the version where the loop counter is bumped by 2, because the FOR bumps only by one.

Restrictions on the FOR form are many. It is important to realize that the expressions describing the initial and final values of the counter are evaluated only once on entry to the loop. Also the statement in the body must not alter the control variable C. The counter is of integer type and bumps only by one. Additionally, the loop control variable may not retain its value after the loop is done.

If these restrictions are too severe then the WHILE form can be used instead; the WHILE is always more general, but the FOR is often convenient.

EQUIVALENCE between a FOR and a WHILE loop is shown below; the FOR is shorter, but the WHILE is more general and easily extended to bump by any value (including real values).

```
                                    C := M;
        FOR C := M TO N DO          WHILE C <= N DO
            (* Statement *)             BEGIN
            (* or SERIES *)                 (* Statement *)
                                            (* or SERIES *)
                                            C := C + 1;
                                        END
```

FOR LOOP

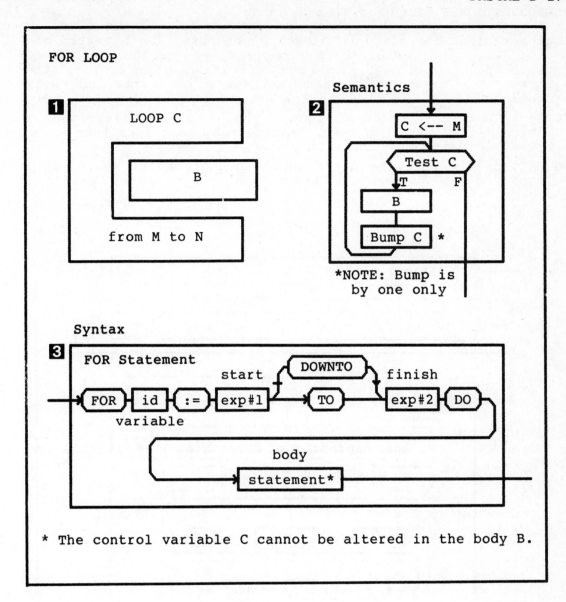

1 LOOP C

B

from M to N

Semantics

2 C <-- M

Test C

T   F

B

Bump C *

*NOTE: Bump is
by one only

Syntax

3 FOR Statement

```
                   start         DOWNTO      finish
FOR  id  :=  exp#1        TO            exp#2  DO
     variable

                        body
                   statement*
```

* The control variable C cannot be altered in the body B.

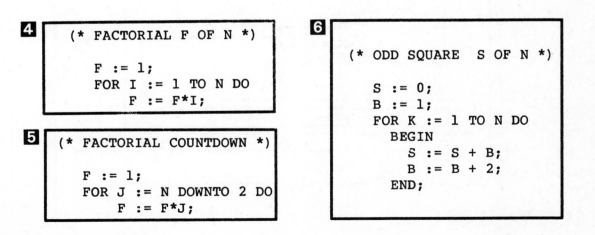

4
```
(* FACTORIAL F OF N *)

F := 1;
FOR I := 1 TO N DO
    F := F*I;
```

5
```
(* FACTORIAL COUNTDOWN *)

F := 1;
FOR J := N DOWNTO 2 DO
    F := F*J;
```

6
```
(* ODD SQUARE  S OF N *)

S := 0;
B := 1;
FOR K := 1 TO N DO
  BEGIN
    S := S + B;
    B := B + 2;
  END;
```

CONGLOMERATIONS: Mixed and Nested Forms

Conglomerations are mixed combinations of forms, both nested and cascaded. In Pascal such combinations cannot be viewed statement by statement, but must be considered in terms of the forms. The given examples illustrate mixed forms and their nesting.

GCD (the Greatest Common Divisor), shown below, illustrates a choice nested within a loop. Notice the break-down into three boxes, nested within one another.

BIG MAX, on the opposite page, shows another choice nested in a loop, and SIGNED PRODUCT shows two loops nested within a choice.

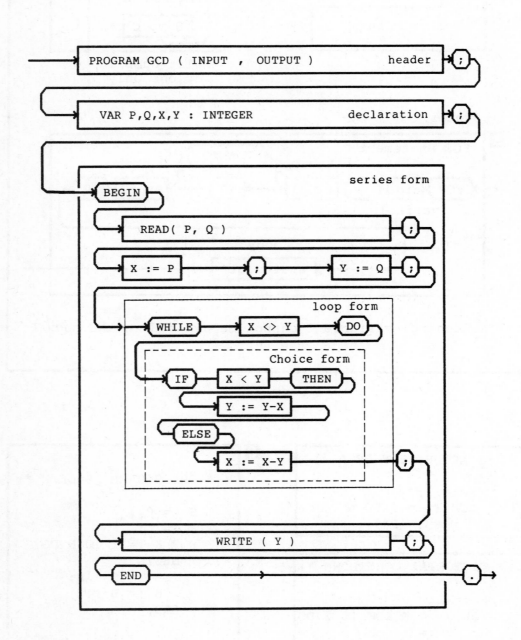

```
100   PROGRAM  BIGMAX(INPUT, OUTPUT);
110     (* SHOWS CHOICE IN A LOOP *)
120     (* SEE ALSO PAGES 5-4,5-6 *)
130
200   VAR
210     TERM, VAL, MAX: INTEGER;
220
300   BEGIN
320     WRITELN( 'ENTER TERMINAL VALUE' );
330     READ( TERM );
340     WRITELN( 'ENTER VALUES' );
350     READ( VAL );
360     MAX:= VAL;
370     READ( VAL );
380
400     WHILE VAL <> TERM DO
410       BEGIN
500         IF MAX <  VAL THEN
510             MAX := VAL;
600         READ( VAL );
610       END;
620
700     WRITELN( 'MAX IS ', MAX );
900   END.
```

```
ENTER TERMINAL VALUE
? -999
ENTER VALUES
? 20
? 10
? 40
? 30
? -999
MAX IS        40
```

```
100   PROGRAM SIGNEDPRODUCT( INPUT, OUTPUT );
110     (* SHOWS LOOPS NESTED IN A CHOICE *)
120     (* SEE ADDITIONALLY PAGES 3-46,47 *)
130
200   VAR
210     C,D,  X,Y, P: INTEGER;
220
300   BEGIN
310     WRITELN( 'ENTER TWO VALUES' );
320     READ( X,Y );  C := X;  D := Y;
325     P := 0;
330     IF C > 0 THEN
340        WHILE C > 0 DO
350          BEGIN
360            P := P + D;
370            C := C - 1;
380          END
400     ELSE
410        WHILE C < 0 DO
420          BEGIN
430            P := P - D;
440            C := C + 1;
450          END;
500     WRITELN( 'PRODUCT IS ', P);
600   END.
```

Nested Loops

Nested loops are very common in programs. Some of the more convenient "nicely" nested forms are shown here. They are easily created using FOR statements.

CHARGE, shown at the right, illustrates a doubly nested loop; a loop within a loop. It computes a table of amounts C to charge groups consisting of A adults and B babies (or children) if each adult pays 3 dollars, and each baby pays only 2 dollars.

MORECHARGE is a modification of the above to output the table in two dimensional form. It is also more general because it allows any costs to be input (not just the 2 and 3 dollars).

MAJORITY, shown also in the given figure, has three nested loops. Notice the indentation of the FOR statements. This program computes a table of all combinations of binary values A,B, and C, indicating the majority M of these values. It also includes a labelling of the columns.

PLOT, given below, shows a FOR loop nested within a WHILE loop. The outer loop steps through values of X vertically, and for each such value the inner loop steps over horizontally a distance proportional to the square of X and marks an asterisk there. The top-down design of this is done in Chapter 5.

```
100   PROGRAM PLOTXY( INPUT, OUTPUT );
110     (* PLOT OF FUNCTION Y VS X *)
120     (*   PRINTED ON ITS SIDE   *)
130     (*   SEE ALSO PAGE 5-26    *)
140
200   VAR
210     X,Y: REAL;
220     Q,S: INTEGER;
230
300   BEGIN
310     X := 0.0;
320     WHILE X <= 5 DO
330       BEGIN
340         Y := X*X;
350         Q := ROUND(Y);
360         FOR S := 0 TO 30 DO
370           IF S = Q THEN
380             WRITE( '*' )
390           ELSE
400             WRITE( ' ' );
410         WRITELN;
420         X := X + 0.25;
430       END;
440   END.
```

```
100   PROGRAM CHARGELIST( INPUT,OUTPUT );
110     (* COMPUTES A LIST OF CHARGES *)
120     (* IF A COSTS 3 AND B COSTS 2 *)
130     (* SHOWS NESTED LOOPS OF 5-20 *)
200   VAR  A,B,C: INTEGER;
210   BEGIN
220     FOR A := 1 TO 3 DO
230       FOR B := 0 TO 3 DO
240         BEGIN
250           C := 3*A + 2*B;
260           WRITELN(A:6, B:6, C:9);
270         END;
280   END.
```

```
 1      0         3
 1      1         5
 1      2         7
 1      3         9
 2      0         6
 2      1         8
 2      2        10
 2      3        12
 3      0         9
 3      1        11
 3      2        13
 3      3        15
```

```
100   PROGRAM  CHARGETABLE( INPUT,OUTPUT );
110     (* COMPUTES 2D TABLE OF CHARGES *)
120     (* WITH COSTS AND NUMBERS INPUT *)
130
200   VAR
210     A,B, NA, NB: INTEGER;
220     C, PA, PB  : REAL;
230
300   BEGIN
310     WRITELN( 'ENTER ADULTS AND BABIES');
320     WRITELN( 'PRICES' ); READ( PA, PB );
330     WRITELN( 'NUMBERS'); READ( NA, NB );
340
400     FOR A := 1 TO NA DO
410       BEGIN
420         FOR B := 0 TO NB DO
430           BEGIN
440             C := A*PA + B*PB;
450             WRITE( C:6:2 );
460           END;
470         WRITELN;
480         WRITELN;
490       END;
500   END.
```

```
ENTER ADULTS AND BABIES
PRICES
? 3 2
NUMBERS
? 4 3
 3.00  5.00  7.00  9.00

 6.00  8.00 10.00 12.00

 9.00 11.00 13.00 15.00

12.00 14.00 16.00 18.00
```

```
100   PROGRAM MAJORITY( INPUT,OUTPUT );
110   (* MAJORITY OF 3 VOTERS A,B,C *)
120   (* SHOWS TRIPLE NESTED LOOPS  *)
130
200   VAR
210     A,B,C,M: INTEGER;
220
300   BEGIN
310     WRITELN( '    A    B    C    M ');
320     WRITELN( ' ---------------------- ');
330
400     FOR A := 0 TO 1 DO
410       FOR B := 0 TO 1 DO
420         FOR C := 0 TO 1 DO
500           BEGIN
510             IF A + B + C < 2 THEN
520               M := 0
530             ELSE
540               M := 1;
550             WRITELN( A:5, B:5, C:5, M:7 );
560             WRITELN;
570           END;
600   END.
```

A	B	C	M
0	0	0	0
0	0	1	0
0	1	0	0
0	1	1	1
1	0	0	0
1	0	1	1
1	1	0	1
1	1	1	1

Character Type

Characters are the single printable symbols of a keyboard; they are not sequences of symbols, but are "lonely" symbols. Characters can be declared, assigned, compared, input and output much like integer and real values, but there are differences.

VALUES of characters must be distinguished from variables, so single quotes surround characters within programs (but not on input; more on that later).

DECLARATIONS show the distinction between constants and variables as in:

```
CONST  PERIOD = '.';   FAIL = 'F';   NO = 'N';
       BLANK  = ' ';   MAIL = 'M';    F = 'F';
VAR    C, CH, GRADE, REPLY, SEX, STATUS:  CHAR;
```

ASSIGNMENT can be made of a character to any variable of type CHAR such as:

```
REPLY := 'Y';  SEX := 'F';  GRADE := FAIL;
```

COMPARISON of character values can be made for equality as well as order; character 'A' is the lowest letter and 'Z' is highest. The character digit '0' is lowest and '9' is highest. Character digits are not equal to integer digits (so '1' does not equal 1). Other characters may be ordered differently on different systems. Some examples involving comparisons are:

```
IF GRADE < 'C' THEN WRITELN( 'GOOD' );
IF REPLY = 'Y' THEN COUNT := COUNT + 1;
IF (SEX = MALE) OR (SEX = 'F') THEN STATUS := 'G';
```

INPUT of a single character is done with a READ statement. When READ(C) is executed, whatever character is entered (without quotes) gets stored into character variable C. A sample segment which bumps a counter Y on receiving the character 'Y' follows.

```
READ(R);  IF R = 'Y' THEN Y := Y+1 ELSE N := N+1;
```

A robust program to enter sex follows:

```
(* INSEX *)
WRITELN( 'ENTER SEX' );  READ( S );
WHILE (S <> 'M') AND (S <> 'F') DO
  BEGIN
    WRITELN( 'ENTER M OR F ONLY' );
    READ( S );
  END;
```

MORE characters can be read from a stream or line of characters, by successive READs. Each READ inputs the new character in the line. For example, a program segment to input the day of the week and distinguish SUNDAY from SATURDAY is:

```
READ( CH1, CH2 );
IF(CH1 = 'S') AND (CH2 = 'U') THEN WEEKDAY := 1  ELSE
IF(CH1 = 'S') AND (CH2 = 'A') THEN WEEKDAY := 7  ELSE ...
```

Here only the first two characters are read; the remaining characters could be input but are ignored.

READLN (Read-line) is similar to the READ statement, but it begins reading a new line of data, and expects a return to indicate the end of the input. On the CDC version of Pascal a simple "READLN;" could be used to "clear the line" before a READ statement, so purging some of the unread characters (as in the above example).

LONGER sequences of characters can be read using a loop. For example, the following piece of program reads a sentence, counting the blanks in it. Notice the READLN which clears out the line before any input.

```
(* BLANK COUNTER *)
READLN;  READ( CH );
BLANKS := 0;
WHILE CH <> PERIOD DO
  BEGIN
    IF CH = BLANK THEN
      BLANKS := BLANKS + 1;
    READ( CH );
  END
```

CALCULATOR, the following program, illustrates the use of character input mixed with integer input. In such "mixtures" integers are separated by spaces, whereas characters have no separators. Notice the formulas input are not in precedence form, but left to right.

```
100   PROGRAM CALCULATOR( INPUT, OUTPUT );
110      (* A SIMPLE 4-FUNCTION CALCULATOR *)
120      (* SPACES MUST SURROUND OPERATORS *)
130
200   VAR
210      R, V: REAL;
220      F: CHAR;
230      BLANK: CHAR;
240
300   BEGIN
310      WRITELN(' ENTER SEQUENCE ');
320      READLN; READ( R, BLANK, F );
330      WHILE F <> '=' DO
340        BEGIN
400          READ(V);
410
500          IF F =  '+' THEN
510            R := R + V
520          ELSE
530          IF F =  '-' THEN
540            R := R - V
550          ELSE
560          IF F =  '*' THEN
570            R := R * V
580          ELSE
590          IF F =  '/' THEN
600            R := R / V
610          ELSE
620             WRITELN( 'ERROR' );
700          READ(BLANK); READ(F);
710        END;
720      WRITELN( R: 8: 3 );
800   END.
```

```
ENTER SEQUENCE
? 3 + 4 * 5 =
  35.000
```

Boolean Type

The Boolean type is very useful in Pascal. Objects or variables of type Boolean can have one of only two values: TRUE or FALSE.

Boolean variables and their declarations are illustrated in the example:

```
VAR
    OVER18, TALL, MALE, DONE:  BOOLEAN;
    WIN, TRIANG, INCREASING:   BOOLEAN;
```

Assignment is also useful, as, for example:

```
MALE    := TRUE;
DONE    := FALSE;
OVER18  := (AGE > 18);
AGED    := OVER18;
TALL    := (HEIGHT > 72);
TRIANG  := (SMALL + MID > LARGE);
```

Operators on Boolean variables are the three logical "connectives" AND, OR, and NOT, illustrated below.

```
EQUILATERAL := (A = B) AND (A = C );
WIN         := (S = 7) OR  (S = 11);
FEMALE      := NOT MALE;
```

Input/Output of Boolean values is not possible directly in Pascal. Input can be done indirectly by entering the characters "T" and "F" as follows:

```
(* BOOLIN *)
    WRITELN( 'ENTER TRUTH VALUE' );
    WRITELN( 'PRINT T OR F ONLY' );
    READ( REPLY );
    WHILE (REPLY <> 'T') AND
          (REPLY <> 'F') DO
          BEGIN
            WRITELN( 'T OR F ONLY' );
            READ( REPLY );
          END;
    IF REPLY = 'T' THEN
        TRUTH := TRUE
    ELSE
        TRUTH := FALSE;
```

Boolean expressions, consisting of complex combinations of variables and operations, are very common as conditions in both While and Choice forms. For clarity, parentheses should be used widely, especially around mixed Boolean and arithmetic expressions such as:

```
( (I <= 9) OR (S1=S2) ) AND NOT RAIN
```

EXPRESSIONS in general are described by the syntax diagrams on the next page.

More on Boolean (or logical) types can be found around pages 3-21, 4-25, and especially 5-17.

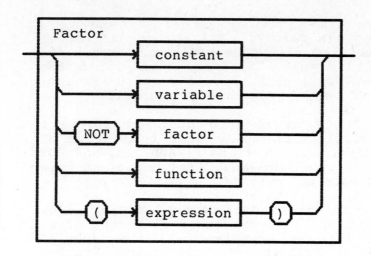

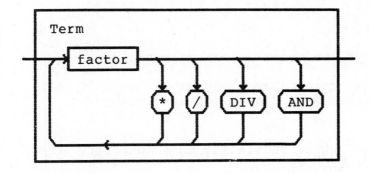

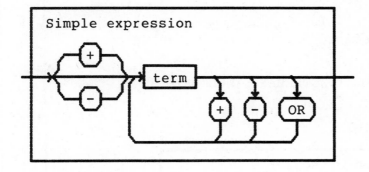

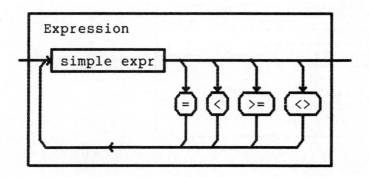

Programmer-Defined Types

TYPE is an important concept in Pascal. All objects in Pascal have a unique type associated with them. Standard types (or primitive or pre-defined types) already built into the language are the four: INTEGER, REAL, BOOLEAN, and CHARacter. Other types can be defined by the programmer in Pascal.

OPERATIONS depend on the types of objects operated on. For example, addition and subtraction apply only to objects of type Real or Integer. Also the operations of AND, OR, and NOT apply only to variables of type Boolean. Assignment and test for equality apply to objects of every data type.

PROGRAMMER-DEFINED types (also called user-defined types) allow any programmer to create types in a number of different ways. The simplest way is to list or enumerate all the "atomic" values. Other ways involve building of types using existing types. This second way leads to more complex types (arrays and records) known as structured types, considered later.

SIMPLE DEFINED TYPES (sometimes called scalar types or enumerated types) are lists of all the values of the type. They are listed in increasing order, so comparisons are possible.

DECLARATIONS of the simple types are defined in the syntax diagram given below. Examples of simple defined types are:

```
TYPE
    WEEKDAY = (SUN, MON, TUE, WED, THUR, FRI, SAT);
    SEASON  = (SPRING, SUMMER, FALL, WINTER);
    LEVELS  = (FRESH, SOPH, JR, SENIOR, GRAD);
    DENOMIN = (PENNY, NICKEL, DIME, QUARTER);
    GRADES  = (F, D, C, B, A);
```

Declaration of variables of these user-defined types is similar to declaration of pre-defined ones, as for example:

```
VAR
    DAY, D, TODAY, NOW, YESTERDAY:  WEEKDAY;
```

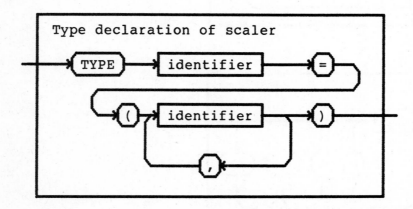

Type declaration of scaler

SUB-RANGE TYPES describe simple defined types which are sub-types of other types. For example, the digits 0 to 9 are a sub-range of the integers. Similarly, the days MON to FRI are within a WEEKDAY type. The sub-range types are declared in the form:

        TYPE typename = minvalue .. maxvalue

Examples of declarations of such sub-range types are:

```
        TYPE
            DIGIT   = 0..9;
            MIDWEEK = MON..FRI;
            YEAR    = 1900..2001;
            GRADE   = 'A'..'F';
```

OPERATIONS on simple defined types include comparison, assignment and the pre-defined functions PRED, SUCC, and ORD.
PRED(X) returns the value which precedes or comes before X.
SUCC(X) returns the value which succeeds or follows X.
    For example, PRED(FRI) is THUR and SUCC(FRI) is SAT. PRED(SUN) is not defined; it causes an error.
ORD(X) indicates the order or position of a scalar value X as an integer (with the first value being 0). So ORD(SUN) returns 0, and ORD(SAT) returns 6.

Program pieces involving these simple defined types follow; notice particularly how readable they are:

```
        IF DAY = FRI THEN WRITELN( 'FINALLY!' )
        IF LEVEL = SENIOR THEN READ( ID )
        WHILE DAY < THUR DO HOURS := HOURS + 24
        FOR DAY := MON TO FRI DO WORKSUB
        IF LABSCORE > LIMIT THEN GRADE := SUCC( GRADE )
        IF DAY <> SUN THEN YESTERDAY :=PRED( TODAY )
        IF DAY = SAT THEN NEXTDAY := SUN
```

INPUT and OUTPUT of such defined types is not directly possible. It can usually be done indirectly by entering characters. For example, WEEKIN is a segment of a program to enter weekdays.

```
    (* WEEKIN *)
    READLN (* TO CLEAR *);  READ( CH1, CH2 );
    IF (CH1 = 'S') AND( CH2 = 'U') THEN DAY := SUN   ELSE
    IF  CH1 = 'M'                  THEN DAY := MON   ELSE
    IF (CH1 = 'T') AND (CH2 = 'U') THEN DAY := TUE   ELSE
    IF  CH1 = 'W'                  THEN DAY := WED   ELSE
    IF (CH1 = 'T') AND (CH2 = 'H') THEN DAY := THUR  ELSE
    IF  CH1 = 'F'                  THEN DAY := FRI   ELSE
    IF (CH1 = 'S') AND (CH2 = 'A') THEN DAY := SAT   ELSE
                                        WRITELN( 'ERROR' );
```

OUTPUT of such defined types could similarly be done by using a Case form, and actually spelling out each weekday completely.

PROGRAMMING STYLE: Modification and Documentation

Modification of programs is very common. For example, the Bisection algorithm could be modified in two very different ways. One version, ROOT, finds the square root of any real number; another version, GUESS, plays a guessing game involving only integers. Both versions shown at the right are based on the general Bisection algorithm of pages 3-52, 2-8 and 2-18.

Extension of the GUESS program is also possible. For example, it could be generalized to guess within any number of trials N (not just the 7 trials of the range 0 to 127). The value of N could be defined as a constant, or could be entered by the user. The program could also be made robust by providing more detailed instructions (if requested), and by testing the input responses.

Documentation, or description, of a program is shown by GUESS2 on the next page. At the beginning of the program (in a starred box) is a brief statement of the goal of the program, the author and time of creation. Other relevant information could also be put here, including a list of inputs and outputs, special limitations, and warnings.

Constants (YES and NO) are created for the convenience of reading, even though Y and N are not too unreadable. The number of trials N and the high value H are also made into constants for the flexibility of changing the game to other ranges. This method of allowing easy change of "constants" is called parameterization, and is very important in large production programs, where there may be many occurrences of a constant. The relationship between the paramenters N and H is also given for convenience of modification.

The main program has gaps which break it up into "blocks" (fragments or pieces). Each block is preceded by a comment describing what is done in the block (not how it is done). These comments alone form a high-level algorithm:

```
        (* OFFER INSTRUCTIONS *)
        (* INITIALIZE VALUES  *)
        (* LOOP FOR N TRIALS   *)
            (* PROMPT INPUT  *)
            (* TEST INPUT    *)
            (* ADJUST MID    *)
        (* OUTPUT FINAL GUESS *)
```

Output, showing the run of this program, is given on the page facing the program. Notice the "friendly" nature of the dialogue:

    it offers to help with instructions,
    it tells the trial number,
    it prompts the user,
    it separates the trials,
    it forgives bad inputs.

Moderation in documentation is important; too much documentation may be overwhelming, and too little may be useless.

```
100   PROGRAM SQUAREROOT(INPUT,OUTPUT);
110     (* SQUARE ROOT BY BISECTION *)
120     (* SEE ALSO PAGE 3-52 *)
130
200   VAR
210     X, HIGH, LOW, MID, ERR: REAL;
220
300   BEGIN
310     ERR := 0.01;
320     WRITELN( 'ENTER A VALUE' );
330     READ( X );
340     LOW := 0.0;
350     HIGH:= X;
360     MID := (LOW + HIGH)/2;
370
400     WHILE ABS(MID*MID - X) > ERR DO
410       BEGIN
420         IF MID*MID > X THEN
430             HIGH := MID
440         ELSE
450             LOW  := MID;
460         (*ENDIF*)
470         MID := (LOW + HIGH)/2;
480       END (* WHILE *);
490
500     WRITELN( 'THE SQUARE ROOT IS', MID:10:5);
900   END.
```

```
+-----------------------------------+
| ENTER A VALUE                     |
| ? 2.0                             |
| THE SQUARE ROOT IS    1.41406     |
+-----------------------------------+
```

```
100   PROGRAM GUESS( INPUT, OUTPUT );
110   (* GUESSING USING BISECTION *)
120   (* SEE ALSO PAGE 2-18, 3-52 *)
130
200   VAR
210     LOW, HIGH, MID, TRIAL: INTEGER;
220     REPLY: CHAR;
230
300   BEGIN
310     WRITELN( 'PICK AN INTEGER' );
320     WRITELN( 'FROM 0 TO 1023 ' );
330
400     LOW := 0;
410     HIGH:= 1024;
420     MID := (LOW + HIGH) DIV 2;
430     TRIAL := 1;
440     WHILE TRIAL <= 10 DO
450       BEGIN
500         WRITELN( 'IS IT LESS THAN ', MID:4 );
510         READLN;  READ( REPLY );
600         IF REPLY = 'Y' THEN
610             HIGH := MID
620         ELSE
630             LOW  := MID;
700         MID := (LOW + HIGH) DIV 2;
710         TRIAL := TRIAL + 1;
720         WRITELN;
800       END (* WHILE *);
810
900     WRITELN( 'YOUR NUMBER WAS ', MID:4 );
999   END.
```

```
+-----------------------------+
| PICK AN INTEGER             |
| FROM 0 TO 1023              |
| IS IT LESS THAN   512       |
| ? Y                         |
|                             |
| IS IT LESS THAN   256       |
| ? Y                         |
|                             |
| IS IT LESS THAN   128       |
| ? N                         |
|                             |
| IS IT LESS THAN   192       |
| ? N                         |
|                             |
| IS IT LESS THAN   224       |
| ? Y                         |
|                             |
| IS IT LESS THAN   208       |
| ? Y                         |
|                             |
| IS IT LESS THAN   200       |
| ? N                         |
|                             |
| IS IT LESS THAN   204       |
| ? Y                         |
|                             |
| IS IT LESS THAN   202       |
| ? Y                         |
|                             |
| IS IT LESS THAN   201       |
| ? Y                         |
|                             |
| YOUR NUMBER WAS  200        |
+-----------------------------+
```

```
100    PROGRAM GUESS( INPUT, OUTPUT );
110
120      (****************************************)
130      (* SIMPLE GUESSING GAME USING BISECTION *)
140      (* SHOWS FANCY LAYOUT AND DOCUMENTATION *)
150      (* BY A. NONYMOUS  ON FEBRUARY 31/1984  *)
160      (*                                      *)
170      (****************************************)
180
200    CONST
210      YES ='Y';    NO = 'N';
220      N = 10;      (* NUMBER OF TRIES *)
230      H = 1024;    (* HIGHEST   VALUE  *)
240      (* H IS TO BE 2 TO THE POWER N *)
250
300    VAR
310      LOW, HIGH, MID, TRIAL: INTEGER;
320      REPLY: CHAR;
330
400    BEGIN
410    (* OFFER INSTRUCTIONS *)
412      WRITELN( 'DO YOU WANT ANY INSTRUCTIONS ?' );
414      WRITELN( 'ENTER ONLY YES OR NO....Y OR N' );
416      WRITELN( 'FOLLOWED BY HITTING RETURN KEY' );
418      READLN;   READ( REPLY );
420      IF REPLY = YES THEN
422         BEGIN
424            WRITELN;
426            WRITELN( 'THIS IS A GUESSING GAME ' );
428            WRITELN( 'YOU PICK ANY INTEGER     ' );
430            WRITELN( 'FROM 0 TO ', (H-1): 4      );
432            WRITELN( 'I WILL GUESS IT IN ', N:2, ' TRIES' );
434            WRITELN;
436         END (* INSTRUCTIONS *);
438      WRITELN;
440
500    (* INITIALIZE VALUES *)
510      LOW := 0;     HIGH := H;
520      MID := (LOW + HIGH) DIV 2;
530
540    (* LOOP FOR N TRIES *)
550      FOR TRIAL := 1 TO N DO
560         BEGIN
565            WRITELN( 'TRY', TRIAL:3 );
570            WRITELN( 'IS IT LESS THAN', MID:4 );
575            READLN; READ( REPLY );
600         (* TEST FOR CORRECT INPUT *)
610            WHILE (REPLY <> YES) AND (REPLY <> NO ) DO
620              BEGIN
630                 WRITELN( 'ENTER Y OR N ONLY' );
640                 READLN; READ( REPLY );
650              END (* TEST OF INPUT *);
700         (* ADJUST MID VALUE *)
710            IF REPLY = YES THEN
720               HIGH := MID
730            ELSE
740               LOW  := MID;
750            MID := (LOW + HIGH) DIV 2;
760            WRITELN; (* GAP BETWEEN TRIES *)
770         END (* FOR LOOP *);
780
800    (* OUTPUT GUESS *)
810      WRITELN( 'YOUR NUMBER WAS', MID:4 );
820      WRITELN;
830
900    END.
```

Some typical runs of GUESS

1 DO YOU WANT ANY INSTRUCTIONS ?
ENTER ONLY YES OR NO....Y OR N
FOLLOWED BY HITTING RETURN KEY
* ? Y

THIS IS A GUESSING GAME
YOU PICK ANY INTEGER
FROM 0 TO 1023
I WILL GUESS IT IN 10 TRIES

TRY 1
IS IT LESS THAN 512
? Y

TRY 2
IS IT LESS THAN 256
? Y

TRY 3
IS IT LESS THAN 128
? Y

TRY 4
IS IT LESS THAN 64
? N

TRY 5
IS IT LESS THAN 96
? N

TRY 6
IS IT LESS THAN 112
? Y

TRY 7
IS IT LESS THAN 104
? Y

TRY 8
IS IT LESS THAN 100
? N

TRY 9
IS IT LESS THAN 102
? Y

TRY 10
IS IT LESS THAN 101
? Y

YOUR NUMBER WAS 100

2 DO YOU WANT ANY INSTRUCTIONS ?
ENTER ONLY YES OR NO....Y OR N
FOLLOWED BY HITTING RETURN KEY
* ? N

TRY 1
IS IT LESS THAN 512
? Y

TRY 2
IS IT LESS THAN 256
? Y

TRY 3
IS IT LESS THAN 128
? N

TRY 4
IS IT LESS THAN 192
? N

TRY 5
IS IT LESS THAN 224
? Y

TRY 6
IS IT LESS THAN 208
? Y

TRY 7
* IS IT LESS THAN 200
? THAT'S IT
ENTER Y OR N ONLY
? N

TRY 8
IS IT LESS THAN 204
? Y

TRY 9
IS IT LESS THAN 202
? Y

TRY 10
IS IT LESS THAN 201
? Y

YOUR NUMBER WAS 200

Errors in Programming

In every complex creative activity, there are possibilities of making errors. In programming, the errors are often called "bugs" and the process of finding them is called "debugging." Unfortunately, even the smallest bug can cause a serious failure.

There are a number of different sources of errors, often classified as:

        Syntactic   (compile-time errors)
        Semantic   (execution or run-time errors)
        Logical   (performance errors)

SYNTACTIC ERRORS arise from improper forms in a language involving:

        Spelling   (INTERGER vs INTEGER)
        Punctuation   (semicolon following an ELSE)
        Typography   (letter O versus number 0)
        Order   (declaring VAR before CONST)
        Spacing   (space between : and = in assignment)
        Mismatch   (of types, or BEGIN-END pairs)
        Omission   (of declarations or parentheses)
        Misuse   (using BEGIN, DO, etc. as a variable)

Most of the syntactic errors are detected by the language compiler, so they are not very serious.

EXECUTION ERRORS are not found by the compiler, but do appear during a run. Some examples of these "run-time" errors involve:

        Undefined variables   (not initialized)
        Unexpected value   (value out of range)
        Invalid operations   (divide by zero)
        Infinite loop   (non-halting program)

LOGICAL ERRORS are those which do not prevent a program from running, but do produce wrong results and may go undetected. Some such errors include:

        Off by one   (looping one too many or few times)
        Wrong comparison   (less than instead of greater than)
        Wrong operation   (increasing instead of decreasing)
        Reversed operation   (equal vs not equal)
        Side effect   (inadvertent change of variable)

OTHER ERRORS may also be encountered, including:

        Misunderstanding of functions,
        Misuse of operating system, and
        Misbehavior of the computer.

Debugging, Testing, Proving

DEBUGGING is the process of finding and "exterminating" bugs. This could be very time-consuming. One method of debugging is to trace the program, by hand, using some simple values. Another useful tool is a well placed output instruction in the running program. A Write statement can be inserted at various points to indicate some information.

WHERE the action flows can be indicated by writing a trail of comments such as:

"INITIALIZING" "ENTERING FIRST LOOP" "LEAVING SWAP SUB"

WHAT values a program has at any intermediate points could also be output, yielding a computer-generated trace with outputs like:

"A = 2" or "X IS 5 AND Y IS 7"

HOW variables are related could be shown by checking and writing a loop invariant such as:

"S + B = I*I"   or   "4 + 5 = 3*3"

WHEN a particular condition occurs can be asserted by a statement such as:

"X IS EVEN" or "Y IS POSITIVE"

OTHER outputs could be created with a conditional Write operation. For example, a Write within a loop could produce much output, so it may be useful to limit the output by a conditional write statement as:

IF I = 3 THEN WRITE(I,J)

After the debugging Write statements have served their purpose, they can be removed. Also, a record should be kept of the bugs encountered; it is often instructive (and humbling). But even after the program starts working, it should be tested for different values.

TESTING is the process of checking or verifying to determine proper performance. It is a means for gaining confidence in a result. The fact that a program works for one set of input data does not necessarily mean that it will work for another set; one path through a program is not typical of all other paths.

One method of testing a program is to try all possible sets of data (checking all paths), but this is often impractical because too many combinations are necessary. For example, if there are 20 logical conditions (either in Choices or Loops), then there may be over a million different paths.

Another method is to test using random values, but such values may be too typical, and may not include critical values. Yet another method is to carefully select data values. Some data should be simple and easy to verify by hand computation. Some data should test for extreme, boundary values (such as zero, very large and very small values). Some data should be faulty or wrong, to check whether the program is robust and fails "softly." It also would be helpful if the test values were unique, each value testing and isolating one part at a time.

Unfortunately, testing can reveal the presence of bugs, but only in the simplest cases can it reveal their absence.

PROVING the correctness of programs is yet another way of verifying programs. Such a method is very new, rather complex, and beyond this book.

SUB-FORMS: PROCEDURES

Procedures are very convenient and powerful sub-forms. A general procedure is shown in figure 1 with a name, a list of objects that are imported (passed-in, by value), and a list of those to be exported (passed-out, by reference). It is often convenient to list the imported variables first, but it is not necessary. DIVIDE is an example of a procedure having numerator NUM and denominator DEN passed-in, and remainder R and quotient Q passed-out.

SEMANTICS of a procedure is shown in figure 2. This is covered in more detail on page 5-31. It is important to remember that the procedure allocates space only to imported parameters (NUM and DEN) and also local (or temporary) variables. The exported parameters refer to the actual variables in the calling (or main) program. The imported objects are protected; the exported ones are not!

SYNTAX of a procedure is shown in figure 3. Notice that this syntax of a sub-program is similar to that of a program, consisting of a heading, declaration, and a body. The parameter list of figure 5 specifies the imported and exported variables and indicates their type. The exported variables must be preceded by the word VAR. The VAR applies to the list of variables of one type that follow it. If variables of different types are passed out, each type would require its own VAR preceding each such list. Imported variables have no symbol such as VAR preceding them, although we could use a comment, such as (* IN *) or (*PASS-IN*) or (*IMPORTED*). The declarations following the parameter list describe only the local variables and their type.

DEFINITION of a procedure DIVIDE is shown in figure 4. The first line simply lists the name, the second line lists the imported variables NUM and DEN, and the third line specifies exported variables Q and R (following the VAR). The next VAR, outside of the header, specifies the local variable C, which counts the quotient in the division. Finally, the body of the procedure follows as a series of actions. Such a definition must be placed after the variable declarations, and before any programs or sub-programs that may refer to it, (as shown in figure 5, page B-9).

USE (calling or invoking) of a procedure is done by giving the name and the parameters which are to be passed. A procedure can be used wherever a statement is used. An example of the use of DIVIDE follows. The expression "FIRST + SECOND" is passed-in along with the constant 2. This sum is evaluated and divided by 2 yielding AVERAGE and REMAINDER, which are passed-out. Then the AVERAGE is output, along with the word "EXACTLY" only when the remainder has value 0.

```
READ( FIRST, SECOND );
DIVIDE( FIRST + SECOND, 2,  AVERAGE, REMAINDER);
WRITE( AVERAGE:4 );
IF REMAINDER = 0 THEN
    WRITELN( 'EXACTLY' );
```

sub-form - procedure

1
```
pass-in: A B C
         : : :
         : : :
   name ( E,F,G, S,T )
         : : :
         : : :
pass-out    C  D E
```

Semantics

2

mark the return point
allocate space
link parameters
perform actions
deallocate space
return to calling program

Syntax

3

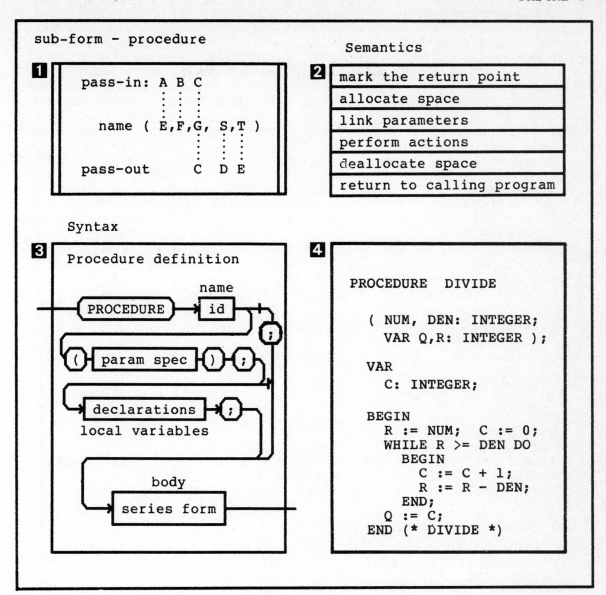

Procedure definition

name

PROCEDURE → id

(param spec) ;

declarations → ;
local variables

body
series form

4

```
PROCEDURE   DIVIDE

  ( NUM, DEN: INTEGER;
    VAR Q,R: INTEGER );

VAR
   C: INTEGER;

BEGIN
   R := NUM;  C := 0;
   WHILE R >= DEN DO
     BEGIN
       C := C + 1;
       R := R - DEN;
     END;
   Q := C;
END (* DIVIDE *)
```

5

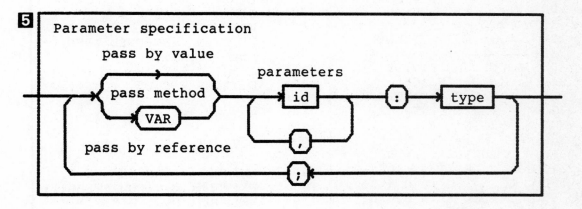

Parameter specification

pass by value

pass method

VAR

pass by reference

parameters

id : type

,

;

More Sub-programs

A complete main program CHANGER with a sub-program DIVIDE is shown below. The main program makes change, using a series of calls to a DIVIDE procedure. Notice that the procedure is declared before the main program; all things should be defined before they are used. This example is fully developed on page 5-33.

HIDING of variables within procedures is also shown in this program. The same variable names may appear in different programs with different meanings; they are isolated or hidden from one another. For example, notice the two different meanings of Q (quarters and quotient), and C (cost and counter), and D (dimes and denominator), and N (nickels and numerator). There are even two different variables called remainder R.

SHORTSORT, given on the opposite page, is an example of a main program with two procedures. The main program calls SORT3, which in turn calls SORT2 three times. Notice that SORT2 is defined before SORT3, because it is used (called) in SORT3.

SWAP is a third procedure which could be called within SORT2. In this case, the same variables are passed into and out of (passed through) the procedure, so must be declared (passed) by reference. Such a SWAP procedure is defined below.

```
PROCEDURE SWAP(VAR R,S: INTEGER);
    VAR T: INTEGER;
    BEGIN
        T := R;  R := S;  S := T;
    END (* SWAP *);
```

This SWAP procedure may be in series with the other two, ahead of SORT2. It could also be defined within SORT3. More on such nested procedures will be considered next.

```
100   PROGRAM CHANGER( INPUT, OUTPUT );
110      (* THAT MONEY CHANGER AGAIN *)
120      (* NOW DONE WITH PROCEDURES *)
130      (* ALSO SHOWS NAME CALLING! *)
140      (* SEE ALSO PAGE 5-32, 5-33 *)
150

200   VAR                              500   BEGIN (* MAIN *)
210      T,C,R,                        510      WRITELN( 'ENTER AMOUNTS' );
220      Q,D,N,P: INTEGER;             511      WRITELN('TENDERED & COST');
230                                    520      READ( T,C );
300   PROCEDURE DIVIDE                 530
310      (N,D: INTEGER;                540      DIVIDE( T-C,25,  Q,R);
320       VAR Q,R: INTEGER);           550
330       VAR C: INTEGER;              560      DIVIDE( R,10, D,R);
340   BEGIN                            570
350      R := N;  C := 0;              580      DIVIDE( R,5,  N,P);
360      WHILE R >= D DO               590
370         BEGIN                      600      WRITELN( 'THE CHANGE IS' );
380            C := C + 1;             700      WRITELN( Q, ' QUARTERS');
390            R := R - D;             710      WRITELN( D, ' DIMES');
400         END;                       720      WRITELN( N, ' NICKELS ');
410      Q := C;                       730      WRITELN( P, ' PENNIES');
420   END (* DIVIDE *);                800   END (* MAIN *).
430
```

```
PROGRAM  SHORTSORT( INPUT,OUTPUT );
  (* SORTS THREE INTEGER VALUES *)
  (* SHOWS MULTIPLE PROCEDURES  *)
  (* PASS BY VALUE & REFERENCE  *)
  (* SEE ALSO PAGES 3-38, 5-35  *)

VAR
  A,B,C, X,Y,Z: INTEGER;
```

```
PROCEDURE
  SORT2( P,Q: INTEGER;
     VAR L,S: INTEGER );
  VAR T: INTEGER;
  BEGIN
    L := P;  S:= Q;
    IF L < S THEN
       BEGIN (* SWAP *)
         T := L;
         L := S;
         S := T;
       END (* SWAP *);
  END (* SORT2 *);
```

```
PROCEDURE SORT3

  (     (* PASS-IN *)    I,J,K: INTEGER;
   VAR (* PASSOUT *)    L,M,S: INTEGER );

   VAR (* LOCAL    *)    D,E,F: INTEGER;

   BEGIN
     SORT2( I,J, D,E );
     SORT2( E,K, F,S );
     SORT2( D,F, L,M );
   END (* SORT3 *);
```

```
BEGIN (* MAIN *)
  WRITELN( 'ENTER THREE VALUES' );
  READ( A,B,C );
  SORT3( A,B,C,  X,Y,Z );
  WRITELN( 'SORTED VALUES ARE' );
  WRITELN( X:5, Y:5, Z:5 );
END (* MAIN *).
```

Nests of Sub-programs

Sub-programs can be implemented as procedures in various ways. For example, let us consider the previous SHORTSORT (or SORT3). The data flow diagram is drawn twice below, differing only in the labelling.

OLD SHORTSORT separates the input and output variables; it passes in A,B,C and passes out X,Y,Z. Similarly, SORT2 passes in P and Q, and passes out L (Largest) and S (Smallest). This method was used on the previous page.

NEW SHORTSORT passes variables A, B and C by reference, so values A,B, and C are passed in, and the new sorted values still called A,B, and C are passed out. Similarly, SORT2 passes variables U and V through, so variable U becomes the largest, and V the smallest.

Comparison of the OLD and NEW methods shows that the OLD has more variables, but it retains the original values. The NEW method uses fewer variables, but in doing so destroys the original order of the values. Sometimes the destruction is not important; sometimes the original values are important and must be protected.

NEW SHORTSORT can still be implemented in two different ways as shown by the programs NEXT and NEST on the opposite page. NEXT shows all the sub-programs cascaded, one after the other (Next to another). First comes SWAP, because it is used in the following program SORT2, which is used in the main program. NEST shows all the sub-programs nested in one another. SORT3 calls within it SORT2, which in turn calls SWAP within it.

NEXT and NEST behave the same in this example. However, the sub-programs of NEXT are available in the main program, whereas the sub-programs of NEST are available only within the programs they are nested in. These sub-programs are hidden similar to the way variables were hidden. More of this hiding is considered next and in the main text.

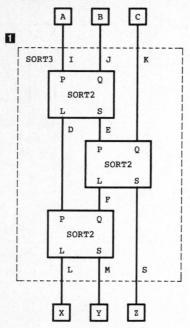

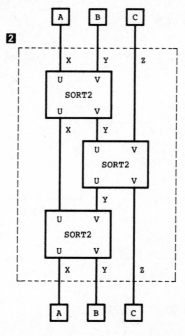

Old SHORTSORT   New SHORTSORT

```
PROGRAM NEXT( INPUT, OUTPUT );
   (* SHOWS SERIES OF SUBS *)

VAR
   A,B,C: INTEGER;


   PROCEDURE SWAP
      ( VAR R,S: INTEGER );
   VAR T: INTEGER;
   BEGIN
      T := R;
      R := S;
      S := T;
   END (* SWAP *);


   PROCEDURE SORT2
      ( VAR U,V: INTEGER );
   BEGIN
      IF U < V THEN
         SWAP( U,V );
   END (* SORT2 *);


   PROCEDURE SORT3
      (VAR X,Y,Z: INTEGER);
   BEGIN
      SORT2( X,Y );
      SORT2( Y,Z );
      SORT2( X,Y );
   END (* SORT3 *);


BEGIN (* MAIN *)
   WRITELN( 'ENTER 3 VALUES' );
   READ( A,B,C );
   SORT3(A,B,C);
   WRITELN( 'SORTED LIST IS' );
   WRITELN( A:3,  B:3,  C:3 );
END (* MAIN *).
```

```
PROGRAM NEST( INPUT, OUTPUT );
   (* SHOWS NESTS  OF SUBS *)

VAR
   A,B,C: INTEGER;


   PROCEDURE SORT3
      ( VAR X,Y,Z: INTEGER );


      PROCEDURE SORT2
         ( VAR U,V: INTEGER );


         PROCEDURE SWAP
            (VAR R,S: INTEGER);
         VAR T: INTEGER;
         BEGIN
            T := R;
            R := S;
            S := T;
         END (* SWAP *);


      BEGIN (* SORT2 *)
         IF U < V THEN
            SWAP( U,V );
      END   (* SORT2 *);

   BEGIN  (* SORT3 *)
      SORT2( X,Y );
      SORT2( Y,Z );
      SORT2( X,Y );
   END    (* SORT3 *);


BEGIN (* MAIN *)
   WRITELN( 'ENTER 3 VALUES' );
   READ( A,B,C );
   SORT3(A,B,C);
   WRITELN( 'SORTED LIST IS' );
   WRITELN( A:3,  B:3,  C:3 );
END (* MAIN *).
```

```
ENTER 3 VALUES
  1  3  2
SORTED LIST IS
  3  2  1
```

```
ENTER 3 VALUES
  2  3  1
SORTED LIST IS
  3  2  1
```

Many Sub-program Examples (12)

There are many aspects of procedures which cannot be conveyed by careful study of only a few examples. The opposite page shows a program of many small procedures, to illustrate the great diversity of details. For example, the header of OUTSTAR is done on one line, whereas the header of POWERP extends over 4 lines. These definitions can be copied into any program, and used within it.

MENU outputs a list of actions in preparation for selection. It involves no variables.

SNAPTRACE outputs the values of three variables. It could be inserted at various points of a program to test it. It also has no parameters, and no local variables.

OUTSTAR15 outputs a line of 15 stars (asterisks), and returns to the next line. It also has no parameters, but has a local variable C to count the stars.

OUTSTAR(N) outputs a line of stars of given length N.

OUTLINE(N,CH) outputs a line of N specified characters CH.

OUTDAY(D) writes out the complete name of the day of the week corresponding to the given shorthand integer form D of the day of the week.

TEMPFC(F,C) is a simple temperature-converting procedure having one input F and one output C, and no local variables.

MAX2(X,Y,M) has two inputs X,Y and an output M. Notice the input and output parameters on different lines.

MAX3(A,B,C,L) has three inputs A,B,C and one output L. It calls the previous MAX2 procedure twice.

POWERP(X,N,P) takes the real value X to the positive integer power N, returning the power P. It could be very useful because Pascal has no other exponentiation operation.

DOUBLE(N) has a single output parameter (passed by reference). It doubles any integer N. It may not be useful, but it illustrates pass by reference alone.

BOOLIN(B) inputs a character 'T' or 'F', and assigns the corresponding truth value to any Boolean variable B. Notice again the output parameter B, passed by reference. This procedure could be very useful because Pascal does not allow READ to enter Boolean values.

A program could call BOOLIN as follows:

```
WRITELN( 'HEIGHT > 72' );
BOOLIN( TALL );
WRITELN( 'AGE > 72' );
BOOLIN( OLD );
```

```
PROGRAM SUBPROGS(INPUT,OUTPUT);
  (* ILLUSTRATES PROCEDURES *)

VAR
  R: REAL;    I: INTEGER;
  C: CHAR;    B: BOOLEAN;
```

```
PROCEDURE MENU;
  (* OUTPUTS MENU OF ACTIONS *)
  BEGIN
    WRITELN( 'ENTER NUMBER' );
    WRITELN( ' 1..FOR MAX ' );
    WRITELN( ' 2..FOR MIN ' );
    WRITELN( ' 3..FOR MEAN' );
  END (* MENU *);
```

```
PROCEDURE SNAPTRACE;
  (* OUTPUTS SNAPSHOT OF 3 VALUES *)
  BEGIN
    WRITELN( 'FIRST =', I:4 );
    WRITELN( 'SECOND=', R:5:2 );
    WRITELN( 'THIRD =', C );
  END (* SNAP *);
```

```
PROCEDURE OUTSTAR15;
  (* PRODUCES A LINE OF 15 STARS *)
  VAR C: INTEGER;
  BEGIN
    FOR C := 1 TO 15 DO
      WRITE( '*' );
    WRITELN;
  END (* OUTSTAR15 *);
```

```
PROCEDURE OUTSTAR( N: INTEGER );
  (* PRODUCES A LINE OF N STARS *)
  BEGIN
    WHILE N > 0 DO
      BEGIN
        WRITE( '*' );
        N := N - 1;
      END;
    WRITELN;
  END (* OUTSTAR *);
```

```
PROCEDURE OUTLINE
  ( N: INTEGER; CH: CHAR );
  (* MAKES A LINE OF N CHARS *)
  VAR C: INTEGER;
  BEGIN
    FOR C := 1 TO N DO
      WRITE( CH );
    WRITELN;
  END (* OUTLINE *);
```

```
PROCEDURE OUTDAY( D: INTEGER );
  (* WRITES DAY OF THE WEEK *)
  BEGIN
    CASE D OF
        1: WRITELN( 'SUNDAY    ' );
        2: WRITELN( 'MONDAY    ' );
        3: WRITELN( 'TUESDAY   ' );
        4: WRITELN( 'WEDNESDAY' );
        5: WRITELN( 'THURSDAY ' );
        6: WRITELN( 'FRIDAY    ' );
        7: WRITELN( 'SATURDAY ' );
      END (* CASE *);
  END (* OUTPUT OF DAY *);
```

```
PROCEDURE TEMPFC
  (F: REAL; VAR C: REAL );
  BEGIN
    C := (5/9)*(F - 32);
  END (* TEMP F TO C *);
```

```
PROCEDURE MAX2
  ( X,Y: INTEGER;
  VAR M: INTEGER );
  BEGIN
    IF X > Y THEN
      M := X
    ELSE
      M := Y;
  END (* MAX2 *);
```

```
PROCEDURE MAX3 (
  A,B,C: INTEGER;
  VAR L: INTEGER );
  BEGIN
    MAX2( A,B, L );
    MAX2( L,C, L );
  END (* MAX3 *);
```

```
PROCEDURE POWERP
  (* TAKES X TO POWER N *)
  (    X: REAL;
       N: INTEGER;
    VAR P: REAL      );
  VAR I: INTEGER;
  BEGIN
    P := 1.0;
    FOR I := 1 TO N DO
      P := P*X;
  END (* POSITIVE  POWER *);
```

```
PROCEDURE
  DOUBLE( VAR N: INTEGER );
  BEGIN
    N := N + N;
  END  (* DOUBLE *);
```

```
PROCEDURE
  BOOLIN( VAR  B: BOOLEAN );
  (* INPUTS BOOLEAN VALUES *)
  VAR CH: CHAR;
  BEGIN
    WRITELN( 'ENTER T OR F' );
    READ( CH );
  (* COULD TEST INPUT HERE *)
    IF CH = 'T' THEN
      B :=   TRUE
    ELSE
      B :=   FALSE;
  END (* BOOLIN *);
```

```
BEGIN (* MAIN *)

    OUTSTAR15;
    OUTDAY(3);
    MAX3(1,4,2,I); WRITELN( I );
    TEMPFC(212,R); WRITELN( ROUND(R) );
    POWERP(2,3,R); WRITELN( TRUNC(R) );
    DOUBLE(I);      WRITELN( I );
    BOOLIN(B);  IF B THEN WRITELN('T');
    OUTLINE(15,'$');

END  (* MAIN *).
```

FUNCTIONS

Functions in Pascal are defined very similarly to procedures. The definition, also shown on the opposite page, has the form:

        FUNCTION name (input-parameters) : name-type;
            declarations-of-local variables
            series-form (with name assigned somewhere)

Notice that the parameter list includes no output variables; the only output variable is the name of the function. This name then must be given a type as shown following the parameter list. Also, the name of the function must be assigned some value within the series form. The function may be used anywhere a variable of that type is used. So a function can appear within an expression.

FACTORIAL is defined on the opposite page, and can be used in the following formula for the number of combinations of N things taken R at a time (a formula often used in counting and probability):

        C := FACT(N) DIV (FACT(R)*FACT(N - R));

PPOWER, the exponentiation function which computes the value of X raised to the positive power N, is shown below. Since Pascal does not have any other exponentiation operator, this function will be useful. It is used in the main program to find the reliability of a system of N independent components, if each has the probability of failure of P.

A typical run would show that if each link in a chain has probability of 0.99 of withstanding a certain load, then a chain of 70 such links connected together has a probability of about 0.5 of withstanding this load. Similarly, 700 links each having a probability of 0.999 have a probability of 0.4964 of success.

```
100    PROGRAM RELIABILITY(INPUT,OUTPUT);
110      (* FINDS FAILURE PROBABILITY *)
120      (* OF N COMPONENTS IN SERIES *)
130      (* SHOWS THE POWER FUNCTION  *)
140
200    VAR
210      P: REAL;
220      N: INTEGER;
230
300    FUNCTION PPOWER( X:REAL; N:INTEGER): REAL;
310      (* COMPUTES POSITIVE POWERS *)
320      (*    DONE ON THE NEXT PAGE  *)
330
500    BEGIN
510      WRITELN( 'ENTER THE NUMBER OF COMPONENTS' );
520      WRITELN( 'AND THE PROBABILITY OF FAILURE' );
530      READ(N,P);
540      WHILE P > 0 DO
550        BEGIN
560          WRITELN( 'RELIABILITY IS ', PPOWER(P,N):5:4 );
570          WRITELN( 'ENTER NEW NUMBER AND PROBABILITY' );
580          READ(N,P);
590        END
999    END.
```

Function definition

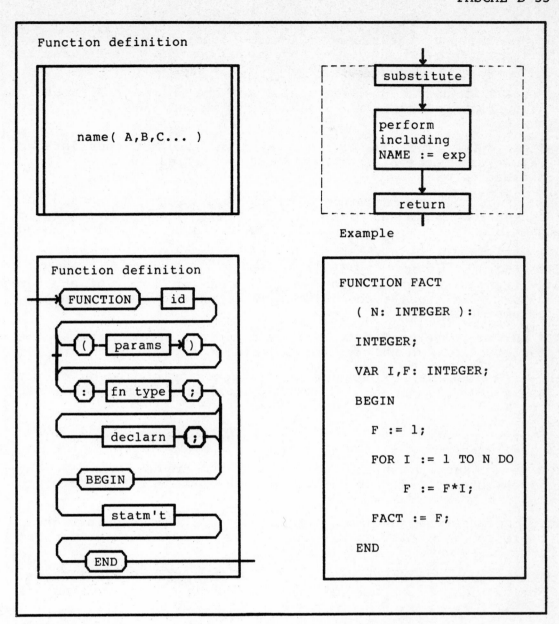

name(A,B,C...)

Example

```
FUNCTION FACT

   ( N: INTEGER ):

   INTEGER;

   VAR I,F: INTEGER;

   BEGIN

     F := 1;

     FOR I := 1 TO N DO

         F := F*I;

     FACT := F;

   END
```

```
FUNCTION PPOWER
   ( X: REAL;
     N: INTEGER )
      : REAL;
VAR
     I: INTEGER;
     P: REAL;
BEGIN
   P := 1.0;
   FOR I := 1 TO N DO
       P := P*X;
   PPOWER:= P;
END (* PPOWER *)
```

```
FUNCTION POWER
   ( X: REAL;
     N: INTEGER )
      : REAL;
BEGIN
   IF N > 0 THEN
       POWER := PPOWER(X,N)
   ELSE
       POWER :=
       1/PPOWER(X, ABS(N) );
END (* POWER *)
```

Many Functions

The opposite page shows many functions created in Pascal. They illustrate the structure of functions, but can also be used as "canned" actions wherever necessary.

FAHRENHEIT converts temperatures, as the name appropriately suggests. Selecting a good name for a function can be very useful.

MAX2 and MAX4 find the maximum value of two and four integer values, respectively. Since MAX2 is called by MAX4, it is defined before MAX4.

MAXR3 finds the maximum value of three real values; it should not be applied to integer values. It is self-contained, but could have been created from a smaller MAXR2 function defined ahead of it.

MAJ3 finds the majority of three values of type ITEMTYPE, which is defined as a type BOOLEAN in this case, but can be another type. This shows a convenient way of specifying and changing parameter types.

FACT is the proverbial factorial computation. Remember that the factorial of N grows very rapidly with N.

TAND is a function to compute the trigonometric tangent of any angle given in degrees. It could be modified to include a test to avoid dividing by zero.

LEAPS is a simplification of the leap year algorithm; it avoids leap centuries.

SIZE is a function which computes the number of digits in any given integer. It could be used to determine the field width in an output statement.

DIGIT converts the "decimal" characters '1', '2', etc into their corresponding integer values. There are other shorter but less clear ways of doing this.

A main program illustrating the use of these functions follows. Notice that functions can be used anywhere expressions are used.

```
    BEGIN (* MAIN *)
      WRITELN( FAHRENHEIT(100):8:2 );
      WRITELN( MAX4( 1, 9, 8, 4 ) );
      WRITELN( FACT(5) DIV (FACT(3)*FACT(2)) );
      WRITELN( TAND( 45.0 )8:5 )
      WRITELN( SIZE( 12345 ) );
      WRITELN( DIGIT('1') + DIGIT('2') );
      IF LEAPS(1984) THEN WRITELN( 'LEAP' );
    END(* MAIN *).
```

More sub-programs are shown on the following pages. PAYROLL illustrates three procedures with rather complex parameter passing. DATES illustrates three functions LEAP, DAYS, and JULIAN and how they are used for some calendar computations.

```
PROGRAM MANYFUNCS( INPUT, OUTPUT );
  (* ILLUSTRATES MANY FUNCTIONS *)

TYPE
  ITEMTYPE = BOOLEAN;

VAR
  R: REAL;      I: INTEGER;
  C: CHAR;      B: BOOLEAN;
```

```
FUNCTION
  FAHRENHEIT( C: REAL ): REAL;
  BEGIN
    FAHRENHEIT := 9/5*C + 32;
  END (* FAHRENHEIT *);
```

```
FUNCTION
  MAX2( X,Y: INTEGER ): INTEGER;
  (* MAXIMUM OF TWO INTEGERS *)
  BEGIN
    IF X > Y THEN
      MAX2 := X
    ELSE
      MAX2 := Y;
  END (* MAX2 *);
```

```
FUNCTION MAX4( A,B,C,D: INTEGER)
  : INTEGER;
  BEGIN
    MAX4 := MAX2( MAX2(A,B), MAX2(C,D) );
  END (* MAX4D *);
```

```
FUNCTION MAXR3( X,Y,Z: REAL ): REAL;
  (* MAXIMUM OF THREE REAL VALUES *)
  VAR M: REAL;
  BEGIN
    M := X;
    IF M  < Y THEN
      M := Y;
    IF M  < Z THEN
      M := Z;
    MAXR3:= M;
  END (* REAL MAX3 *);
```

```
FUNCTION
  MAJ3( A,B,C: ITEMTYPE ): ITEMTYPE;
  (* MAJORITY OF 3  VALUES *)
  BEGIN
    IF A = B THEN
      MAJ3 := A
    ELSE
      MAJ3 := C;
  END (* MAJORITY OF THREE *);
```

```
FUNCTION FACT( N:INTEGER ): INTEGER;
  VAR F,I: INTEGER;
  BEGIN
    F := 1;
    FOR I := 1 TO N DO
      F := F*I;
    FACT  := F;
  END (* FACTORIAL *);
```

```
FUNCTION
  TAND( DEGREE: REAL ): REAL;
  (* TANGENT OF DEGREES *)
  CONST  PI = 3.14159;
  VAR   RAD: REAL;
  BEGIN
    RAD  := 2*PI*DEGREE/360;
    TAND:= SIN(RAD)/COS(RAD);
  END (* TANGENT *);
```

```
FUNCTION
  LEAPS( YR: INTEGER ): BOOLEAN;
  (* SIMPLE LEAP YEAR *)
  BEGIN
    IF YR MOD 4 = 0 THEN
      LEAPS := TRUE
    ELSE
      LEAPS := FALSE;
  END (* SIMPLE LEAP *);
```

```
FUNCTION
  SIZE( N: INTEGER ): INTEGER;
  (* COUNTS DIGITS IN INTEGER *)
  VAR C: INTEGER;
  BEGIN
    C := 0;
    WHILE N > 0 DO
      BEGIN
        N := N DIV 10;
        C := C + 1;
      END;
    SIZE := C;
  END (* SIZE *);
```

```
FUNCTION
  DIGIT( C: CHAR ): INTEGER;
  (* CONVERTS CHAR TO DECIMAL *)
  BEGIN
    CASE C OF
      '0':  DIGIT := 0;
      '1':  DIGIT := 1;
      '2':  DIGIT := 2;
      '3':  DIGIT := 3;
      '4':  DIGIT := 4;
      '5':  DIGIT := 5;
      '6':  DIGIT := 6;
      '7':  DIGIT := 7;
      '8':  DIGIT := 8;
      '9':  DIGIT := 9;
    END (* CASE *);
  END (* CHAR-DIGIT CONVERSION*);
```

```
100    PROGRAM PAYROLL(INPUT,OUTPUT);
110       (* SHOWS BLOCK STRUCTURE *)
120       (* SEE ALSO PAGE 5-37/39 *)
130       (* SUBS COULD BE NESTED  *)
140
150    VAR
160       COUNT, ID: INTEGER;
170       AMOUNT: REAL;
180
300    PROCEDURE  GROSSPAY( VAR GROSS: REAL );
310       (* COMPUTES REGULAR + OVERTIME PAY *)
320          CONST
330             BREAK = 40.0; (* FOR OVERTIME *)
340          VAR
350             HOURS, RATE: REAL;
360          BEGIN
370             WRITELN('ENTER HOURS THEN RATE');
380             READ( HOURS, RATE );
390             IF HOURS <= BREAK THEN
400                GROSS := HOURS*RATE
410             ELSE
420                GROSS := BREAK*RATE +
430                (HOURS - BREAK)*1.5*RATE;
440          END (* GROSS PAY *);
450
460
500    PROCEDURE DEDUCT
510      (  GROSS: REAL;    VAR DED: REAL );
520       (* COMPUTES PAYROLL DEDUCTIONS *)
530          CONST
540             RATE = 0.20;   (* FIXED TAX RATE *)
550          VAR
560             TAXES, MISC: REAL;
570          BEGIN
580             TAXES := GROSS*RATE;
590             WRITELN('ENTER MISC DEDUCTIONS');
600             READ( MISC );
610             DED := TAXES + MISC;
620          END (* DEDUCT *);
630
640
700    PROCEDURE NETPAY( VAR ACCUM: REAL );
710       (* OUTPUTS NET & UPDATES AMOUNT *)
720          VAR
730             GROSS, DED, NET: REAL;
740          BEGIN
750             GROSSPAY( GROSS );
760             DEDUCT( GROSS, DED );
770             NET := GROSS - DED;
780             WRITELN( 'PAY AMOUNT', NET:7:2);
790             ACCUM := ACCUM + GROSS;
800             WRITELN;
810          END (* NETPAY *);
820
830
900    BEGIN (* MAIN PAYROLL *)
910       AMOUNT := 0.00;
920       WRITELN( 'ENTER COUNT' );
930       READ( COUNT );
940       FOR ID := 1 TO COUNT DO
950          NETPAY( AMOUNT );
960       WRITELN( 'AMOUNT PAID IS', AMOUNT:8:2);
970    END (* MAIN *).
```

```
ENTER COUNT
? 2
ENTER HOURS THEN RATE
? 50 10
ENTER MISC DEDUCTIONS
? 100
PAY AMOUNT 340.00

ENTER HOURS THEN RATE
? 10 50
ENTER MISC DEDUCTIONS
? 200
PAY AMOUNT 200.00

AMOUNT PAID IS 1050.00
```

```
100    PROGRAM DATES( INPUT, OUTPUT );
110      (* COMPUTES CALENDAR FUNCTIONS *)
120      (* SEE ALSO PAGE 5-40 AND 5-55 *)
130
200    VAR
210      YR, MON, DAY, N: INTEGER;
220
300    FUNCTION LEAP(YEAR: INTEGER): BOOLEAN;
310      (* FINDS IF A YEAR IS A LEAP YEAR *)
320      BEGIN
330        IF YEAR MOD 4 <> 0 THEN
340          LEAP := FALSE
350        ELSE
360        IF YEAR MOD 100 <> 0 THEN
370          LEAP := TRUE
380        ELSE
390        IF YEAR MOD 400 <> 0 THEN
400          LEAP := FALSE
410        ELSE
420          LEAP := TRUE;
430    END (* LEAP *);
440
450
500    FUNCTION DAYS(MONTH, YEAR: INTEGER): INTEGER;
510      (* FINDS THE NUMBER OF DAYS IN A MONTH *)
520      BEGIN
530        CASE MONTH OF
540          9,  4,  6,  11  : DAYS := 30;
550          1,3,5,7,8,10,12 : DAYS := 31;
560                        2 : IF LEAP(YEAR) THEN
570                              DAYS := 29
580                            ELSE
590                              DAYS := 28;
600        END (* CASE *);
610      END (* DAYS *);
620
630
700    FUNCTION JULIAN(Y,M,D: INTEGER): INTEGER;
710      (* COMPUTES DAYS AFTER FIRST OF YEAR *)
720      VAR I,S: INTEGER;
730      BEGIN
740        I := 1;  S := 0;
750        WHILE I < M DO
760          BEGIN
770            S := S + DAYS(I,Y);
780            I := I + 1;
790          END;
800        JULIAN := S + D;
810      END (* JULIAN *);
820
830
900    BEGIN (* MAIN *)
910      WRITELN( 'ENTER YEAR, MONTH, AND DAY' );
920      READ(YR, MON, DAY);
930      N := JULIAN(YR,MON,DAY);
940      WRITELN( 'JULIAN DATE IS ', N:4 );
950    END (* MAIN *).
```

```
        ENTER YEAR, MONTH, AND DAY
        ? 1984 3 15
        JULIAN DATE IS    75
```

Recursion

Recursive sub-programs are possible in Pascal either as
procedures or functions. This will be illustrated by the
SQUARE program, which was discussed at the end of Chapter 5.

Procedures that are recursive are illustrated in program
SQUARE1. Here, all variables are declared globally, so only
the return points are stored on a stack. In general,
recursive procedures may also pass parameters, and the input
parameters and local variables would also be stored on a
stack.

Functions defined recursively are illustrated in program
SQUARE2. Here, the parameter N is passed in, and
"re-created" (on a stack) each time the procedure is called.
Notice that this definition is self-contained, requiring no
global variables.

Indirect recursion is illustrated by the recursive pair ZIP and
ZAP of SQUARE3. ZIP does not call itself directly, but does
call ZAP, which then calls ZIP; so ultimately (indirectly)
ZIP calls itself.

FORWARD, used on the sixth line of SQUARE3, is a method in
Pascal to indicate that a sub-program is defined later. It
is necessary in such "mutually recursive" programs, because
Pascal insists that a sub-program be defined before it is
used; but in such recursion, that is not possible. FORWARD
is also useful when sub-programs are created out of sequence,
and it is not convenient to rewrite them into their proper
order.

GLOBALOCAL, given below, is a program that emphasizes the
difference between local and global declarations. When the
variable C is declared locally, as shown, it reverses a given
input string; so the sequence "EVIL DID I LIVE." is output
as "EVIL I DID LIVE" (with no period). But when C is
declared globally (by removing line 210), then the same input
sequence yields an output of 15 periods!

```
100    PROGRAM GLOBALOCAL(INPUT,OUTPUT);
110      (* SHOWS LOCAL VS GLOBAL *)
120      (*  SEE ALSO PAGE 5-49   *)
130      VAR C: CHAR;
140
200    PROCEDURE GLOCAL;
210      VAR C: CHAR;
220      BEGIN
230        READ( C );
240        IF C <> '.' THEN
250          BEGIN
260            GLOCAL;
270            WRITE(C);
280          END;
290      END (* GLOCAL *);
300
400    BEGIN (* MAIN *)
410      GLOCAL;
420    END (* MAIN *).
```

```
PROGRAM SQUARE1(INPUT,OUTPUT);
   (* SQUARE BY RECURSIVE PROCEDURE *)
   (* SEE ALSO PAGES 5-45 AND 5-46  *)


VAR
   C,N,S: INTEGER;

PROCEDURE SQUARE;
   BEGIN
     IF C <> 0 THEN
       BEGIN
         C := C - 1;
         SQUARE;
         S := S + N;
       END;
   END (* SQUARE SUB *);

BEGIN (* MAIN *)
   WRITELN( 'ENTER VALUE' );
   READ(N);   C := N;  S := 0;
   SQUARE;
   WRITELN( 'SQUARE IS ', S );
END    (* MAIN *).



PROGRAM SQUARE2(INPUT,OUTPUT);
   (* SQUARE BY RECURSION    *)
   (* OF FUNCTION DEFINITION*)
   (* SEE ALSO PAGE 5-49     *)

VAR
   X,Y: INTEGER;

FUNCTION
   SQUARE( N: INTEGER ): INTEGER;
   BEGIN
     IF N = 0 THEN
         SQUARE := 0
     ELSE
         SQUARE := SQUARE(N-1) +
                     N + N - 1;
   END (* SQUARE FUNCTION *);

BEGIN (* MAIN *)
   WRITELN( 'ENTER VALUE' );
   READ( X );
   Y := SQUARE(X);
   WRITELN( 'SQUARE IS ', Y );
END (* MAIN *).
```

```
PROGRAM SQUARE3( INPUT, OUTPUT );
   (* SQUARE BY RECURSIVE PAIR *)
   (* SEE ALSO PAGE 5-56        *)

VAR
   C,S, M,N: INTEGER;


PROCEDURE ZAP; FORWARD;

PROCEDURE ZIP;
   BEGIN
     IF C < N THEN
       BEGIN
         C := C + 1;
         S := S + C;
         ZAP;
       END;
   END (* ZIP *);

PROCEDURE ZAP;
   BEGIN
     IF C < N THEN
       BEGIN
         C := C + 1;
         ZIP;
       END;
   END (* ZAP *);


BEGIN (* MAIN *)
   S := 0;   C := 0;
   WRITELN( 'ENTER VALUE' );
   READ( M );
   N := M + M ;
   ZIP;
   WRITELN( 'SQUARE IS ', S );
END   (* MAIN *).


ENTER VALUE
7
SQUARE IS 49
```

ARRAYS: Linear Lists

ARRAYS are ordered collections of elements, all of the same type. The type must be declared explicitly in Pascal. Linear lists are the simplest arrays. They may be viewed as a fixed number of variables of some type, indexed by an integer (or sub-range type). Alternatively, they can be viewed as values of the same type stored in a labelled table. In either case, a description of an array involves a name or label (such as LIST), a range of index values (such as 1..100), and the type of values within the array (integer, scalar, etc.).

DECLARATION of an array type in Pascal has the general form:

```
        TYPE name = ARRAY[ index-type ] OF item-type
```

where item-type may be any Pascal type, and index-type is a sub-range type or scalar type. A sample declaration follows.

```
        CONST MAX = 30;
        TYPE LIST = ARRAY[1..MAX] OF INTEGER;
        VAR AGE: LIST;
```

The TYPE declaration describes a general template of a typical array. The VAR declaration indicates a particular object of that type. Examples of more declarations follow to show the diversity of definition of the arrays.

```
        CONST N = 50;  LO = 0;   HI = 200;
        TYPE
           RANGE = 1..30;         SCOPE = LO..HI;
           COUNTDOWN = -10..10;   IDNUM = 100..155;
           WEEKDAY = (SUN,MON,TUE,WED,THU,FRI,SAT);

           LIST     = ARRAY[ LO..HI] OF REAL;
           SEQUENCE = ARRAY[ RANGE ] OF INTEGER;
           STRING   = ARRAY[ 1..N  ] OF CHAR;
           LINE20   = ARRAY[ 1..20 ] OF CHAR;
           TABLE    = ARRAY[ IDNUM ] OF BOOLEAN;
           BITS     = ARRAY[ 0..15 ] OF 0..1;
           WEEKTYPE = ARRAY[WEEKDAY] OF REAL;
        VAR
           AGE, GRADE : SEQUENCE;
           PRICE, QUANTITY, WORKED : LIST;
           NAME, ADDRESS, CITY : LINE20;
           WORD, SENTENCE, PARAGRAPH, POEM : STRING;
           AGED, BIG, MALE, MARRIED, MEMBER : TABLE;
```

ANOTHER, less general, method of declaring an array is as a variable (not as a type):

```
        VAR
           TEMPERATURE : ARRAY[ 1..24 ] OF INTEGER;
           WEIGHT      : ARRAY[ 1..MAX] OF REAL;
           TRAJECTORY  : ARRAY[-10..10] OF REAL;
```

SELECTION of items from arrays is done using the array name with the index value between square brackets, such as

```
        GRADE[ 5 ]  PRICE[ 23 ]  WORKED[ TUE ]  NAME[ ID ]
```

Each of these selectors is treated as a variable which can be assigned, compared, input, output, and used in expressions. Within the brackets may be a constant, variable, or other expression which is evaluated before the selection.

EXAMPLES of programs involving arrays are given on the facing page and on the following two pages. These programs are more fully developed in the main text.

```
100    PROGRAM SIMPLEARRAY(INPUT,OUTPUT);
110      (* ILLUSTRATES LINEAR LISTS  *)
120      (* SEE ALGORITHM ON PAGE 6-5 *)
130
140    CONST
150      L = 100;   (* MAXIMUM ARRAY SIZE *)
160
170    TYPE
180      LIST = ARRAY[1..L] OF INTEGER;
190
200    VAR
210      A: LIST;
220      MAX, VAL, NUM: INTEGER;
230      I, POSN, TERM: INTEGER;
240
300    BEGIN
310      (* INPUT ARRAY USING TERMINATING VALUE *)
320        WRITELN(' ENTER TERMINAL VALUE ');
330        READ( TERM );
335        WRITELN(' ENTER VALUES ');
340        I := 0;
350        READ( VAL );
360        WHILE VAL <> TERM DO
370          BEGIN
380            I := I + 1;
390            A[I] := VAL;
400            READ( VAL );
410          END;
420        NUM := I;
430
500      (* FIND THE MAXIMUM VALUE OF THE LIST *)
510        MAX := A[1];   POSN := 1;
520        FOR I := 2 TO NUM DO
530          IF MAX < A[I] THEN
540            BEGIN
550              MAX  := A[I];
560              POSN := I;
570            END;
580
600      (* OUTPUT COUNT, MAXIMUM, POSITION *)
610        WRITELN( 'NUMBER OF VALUES =', NUM:4 );
620        WRITELN( 'MAXIMUM VALUE IS  ', MAX:4 );
630        WRITELN( 'IT IS IN POSITION ', POSN:4);
999    END.
```

```
┌─ ── ── ── ── ── ── ┐
│  ENTER TERMINAL VALUE  │
│ ? 999                  │
│  ENTER VALUES          │
│ ? 20                   │
│  ? 10                  │
│ ? 30 50                │
│  ? 40                  │
│ ? 999                  │
│ NUMBER OF VALUES =    5 │
│ MAXIMUM VALUE IS     50 │
│ IT IS IN POSITION    4 │
└─ ── ── ── ── ── ── ┘
```

```
100   PROGRAM CHANGEAGAIN( INPUT, OUTPUT );
110     (* CHANGE OF A DOLLAR, ONCE AGAIN *)
120     (* USING A SINGLE DIMENSION ARRAY *)
130
200   VAR
210     COST, REM, DEN, I : INTEGER;
220     A: ARRAY[1..5] OF INTEGER;
230
300   BEGIN
310     A[1] := 50;
320     A[2] := 25;
330     A[3] := 10;
340     A[4] := 5 ;
350     A[5] := 1 ;
360
400     WRITELN( 'ENTER COST' );
410     READ(COST);
420     REM := 100 - COST;
430     WRITELN( 'YOUR CHANGE IS' );
440
500     FOR I := 1 TO 5 DO
510       BEGIN
520         DEN := A[I];
530         WHILE REM >= DEN DO
540           BEGIN
550             WRITELN( DEN:4 );
560             REM := REM - DEN;
570           END;
580       END (* FOR *);
590   END.
```

```
ENTER COST
? 6
YOUR CHANGE IS
   50
   25
   10
    5
    1
    1
    1
    1
```

```
100   PROGRAM NAMECHANGE(INPUT,OUTPUT);
110     (* REFORMATS PERSON'S NAMES *)
120     (* SHOWS ARRAY OF CHARACTERS*)
130
140   CONST
150     SIZE  = 20;
160     BLANK = ' ';
170     PERIOD= '.';
180
200   TYPE
210     NAME = ARRAY[1..SIZE] OF CHAR;
220
300   VAR
310     FIRST, LAST: NAME;
320     I,J, L,M: INTEGER;
330     CH, INITIAL: CHAR;
400   BEGIN
410     (* ENTER NAMES *)
420        WRITELN( 'ENTER YOUR NAME' );
430        WRITELN( 'LAST, THEN FIRST');
440        I := 1; READLN;  READ( CH );
450        WHILE CH <> BLANK DO
460           BEGIN
470              LAST[I] := CH;
475              I := I + 1;
480              READ (CH );
490           END;
500        L := I - 1;
510
600     (* SKIP OVER SPACES *)
620        WHILE CH = BLANK DO
630           READ( CH );
640           INITIAL := CH;
650
700     (* OUTPUT MODIFIED NAME *)
710        WRITE( INITIAL );
720        WRITE( PERIOD  );
730        WRITE( BLANK   );
740        FOR I := 1 TO L DO
750            WRITE( LAST[I] );
800     END.
```

```
------------------------------------
| ENTER YOUR NAME                  |
| LAST, THEN FIRST                 |
| ? MOTIL     JOHN M.              |
| J. MOTIL                         |
------------------------------------
```

```
100   PROGRAM SWAPSORT( INPUT, OUTPUT );
110     (* THE STANDARD BUBBLE SORT  *)
120     (* WITH  LOGICAL  VARIABLE   *)
130     (* SEE ALSO PAGES 6-13, 6-18 *)
140
200   CONST
210     SIZE = 100;
220
300   TYPE
310     RANGE = 1..SIZE;
320     LIST  = ARRAY[ RANGE ] OF INTEGER;
330
400   VAR
410     I, J, N: RANGE;
420     TEMP   : INTEGER;
430     DONE   : BOOLEAN;
440     DATA   : LIST;
450
500   BEGIN
510
520     (* INPUT ARRAY OF N VALUES *)
530       WRITELN( 'ENTER NUMBER OF VALUES' );
540       READ( N );
550       WRITELN( 'ENTER THE VALUES' );
560       FOR I := 1 TO N DO
570          READ( DATA[I] );
580
600     (* SORT THE ARRAY BY SWAPPING *)
610       DONE := FALSE;
620       WHILE NOT DONE DO
630         BEGIN
640           DONE := TRUE;
650           FOR J := 1 TO N-1 DO
660             IF DATA[J] < DATA[ J+1 ] THEN
700                BEGIN
710                   TEMP     := DATA[ J ];
720                   DATA[J]  := DATA[J+1];
730                   DATA[J+1]:= TEMP;
740                   DONE     := FALSE;
750                END (* IF *);
760         END (* WHILE *);
770
800     (* OUTPUT SORTED LIST *)
810       WRITELN( 'THE SORTED VALUES ARE' );
820       FOR I := 1 TO N DO
830          WRITELN( DATA[I] );
840
900   END.
```

```
PROGRAM LINEARSEARCH( INPUT, OUTPUT );
   (* SEARCHES FOR FIRST OCCURRENCE *)
   (* SEE ALSO PAGE 6-21            *)
   (* WITH SIMPLE PROCEDURES AND    *)
   (* AN ARRAY DECLARED GLOBALLY    *)

CONST
  LIMIT = 100;

TYPE
  LIST  = ARRAY[1..LIMIT] OF INTEGER;

VAR
  INFO: LIST;
  SIZE: 0..LIMIT;
```

```
PROCEDURE  INARRAY;
  VAR
    I: INTEGER;
  BEGIN
    WRITELN( 'ENTER NUMBER OF ITEMS' );
    READ( SIZE );
    WRITELN( 'NOW ENTER THE VALUES'  );
    FOR I := 1 TO SIZE DO
      READ( INFO[I] );
    WRITELN;
  END (* INARRAY *);
```

```
PROCEDURE SEARCH;
  VAR
    KEY, I: INTEGER;
  BEGIN
    WRITELN( 'ENTER THE KEY' );
    READ(KEY);
    I := 1;
    WHILE (I <= SIZE) AND
          (INFO[I] <> KEY) DO
            I := I + 1;
    IF INFO[I] = KEY THEN
        WRITELN( 'IT IS IN POSITION', I:3)
    ELSE
        WRITELN( 'IT IS NOT IN THE LIST' );
  END (* SEARCH *);
```

```
BEGIN (* MAIN *)
  INARRAY;
  SEARCH;
END  (* MAIN *).
```

```
ENTER NUMBER OF ITEMS
7
NOW ENTER THE VALUES
20 10 30 40 70 60 50
ENTER THE KEY
30
IT IS IN POSITION  3
```

Passing of Arrays

Passing of arrays is in principle the same as passing any other variables. There are two main methods: pass by value (pass-in) or pass by reference (pass-out). Passing of arrays is, however, sometimes influenced by efficiency reasons.

Passing-in arrays (by value) results in copying of an entire array into the sub-program. If the array is large, or the computer memory space is small, then there could be problems with this duplication of arrays. In such cases, the arrays could be passed by reference. Then care must be taken to be certain that the passed arrays are not modified by the sub-program.

EXTREMA, the given program, involves two general procedures, INLIST and EXTREMES, which may be useful in many main programs. The given main program simply inputs a list of ages, and outputs the count, the oldest and the youngest.

AGE is an array of type LIST which is defined as having at most 100 integers.

INLIST is a procedure which enters values sandwiched by a terminating value. It has two parameters: N, which returns the count of the number of values, and A, which is the array that is assigned the values. Both of these must be passed by reference, for they refer to objects in the main program (in this case they refer to NUM and AGE, respectively). For this reason, VAR precedes each of the names N and A. If they were of the same type, then a single VAR could cover both.

EXTREMES is a procedure which accepts a list DATA and an integer N, and returns the extreme values MAX and MIN. In this case, N should be passed by value, and MAX and MIN should be passed by reference. The array DATA could be passed by value for protection, or could be passed by reference for efficiency of use of memory space. Here we chose efficiency, but the VAR preceding DATA could equally well be removed.

Names in the main program and in the procedures are very different. The procedures are general, applying to any values, and so the variables have general names, such as DATA, MAX and MIN. The main program deals with a specific problem and so has particular names such as AGE, OLDEST, and YOUNGEST. The proper choice of names makes programs very readable.

```
PROGRAM EXTREMA( INPUT,OUTPUT );
   (* SHOWS PASSING OF ARRAYS *)

CONST
   MOST = 100;

TYPE
   LIST = ARRAY[1..MOST] OF INTEGER;

VAR
   AGE: LIST;
   OLDEST, YOUNGEST, NUM: INTEGER;
```

```
PROCEDURE
   INLIST( VAR N: INTEGER; VAR A: LIST );
   (* INPUTS A LIST A OF N INTEGERS *)
VAR
   I, VAL, TERM: INTEGER;
BEGIN
   WRITELN( 'ENTER TERMINAL VALUE' );
   READ( TERM );
   WRITELN( 'NOW ENTER THE VALUES' );
   I := 0;
   READ( VAL );
   WHILE VAL <> TERM DO
      BEGIN
         I := I + 1;
         A[I] := VAL;
         READ( VAL );
      END;
   N := I;
END (* INPUT-LIST *);
```

```
PROCEDURE
   EXTREMES( NUM: INTEGER;
             VAR   DATA: LIST;
             VAR   MAX, MIN: INTEGER );
   (* FINDS THE MAX AND MIN OF DATA *)
VAR
   I: INTEGER;
BEGIN
   MAX := DATA[1];
   MIN := DATA[1];
   FOR I := 2  TO NUM DO
      IF MAX  < DATA[I] THEN
         MAX := DATA[I]
      ELSE
      IF MIN >  DATA[I] THEN
         MIN := DATA[I];
END (* EXTREMES *);
```

```
BEGIN (* MAIN *)
   INLIST( NUM, AGE );
   EXTREMES(NUM, AGE, OLDEST, YOUNGEST);
   WRITELN( 'THE COUNT IS', NUM:3);
   WRITELN( 'THE OLDEST IS', OLDEST:3);
   WRITELN( 'THE YOUNGEST IS', YOUNGEST:3);
END  (* MAIN *).
```

More Dimensions

So far, we have considered only linear lists (or arrays of one
   dimension, one index). Arrays of more dimensions, especially two
   dimensions, are also common.
TWO-DIMENSIONAL ARRAYS are viewed as rectangular grids or tables with
   a ROW index and a COLUMN index, as shown at the bottom of this page.
   Such a two-dimensional table can be viewed in terms of
   single-dimensional arrays as an array of columns, where a column is
   in turn an array of elements as shown at the bottom right. Such an
   array of arrays could be declared as:
         COLUMN = ARRAY[1..N] OF type;
         TABLE = ARRAY[1..M] OF COLUMN;
   It can alternately be viewed more briefly and conveniently as
         TABLE = ARRAY[rowrange, colrange] OF type
   as in the following examples:
         TYPE
         SCORE = ARRAY[STUDENTS, QUIZZES] OF INTEGER;
         MATRIX = ARRAY[IRANGE,   JRANGE] OF REAL;
         GRID   = ARRAY[1..M,   1..N   ] OF CHAR;
         VAR
         LABSCORE, LECTSCORE: SCORE;
         TICTAC : ARRAY[1..3, 1..3] OF ('X', '0', ' ');
SELECTION of items from an array could also be done in two ways. For
   example, the center square of a TIC-TAC-TOE game could be selected
   by either
         TICTAC[2,2]   or less conveniently by   TICTAC[2][2]
   Similarly, the grade of person P on quiz Q from the array G is given
   by G[P,Q].
EXAMPLES of the declaration and use of two-dimensional arrays are
   shown in the program facing this page. It computes the weighted
   average grade of M students on N quizzes. Notice that in this case
   the arrays are declared not as types, but as variables.
THREE-DIMENSIONAL ARRAYS are defined and used very similarly to the
   above arrays. They could be viewed as extensions of two-
   dimensional arrays (which were in turn extensions of one
   dimensional arrays), but they are most conveniently viewed as a new
   entity declared as the type
         TYPE name = ARRAY[range1, range3, range3] OF type
   with items selected by the
         name[index1, index2, index3]
   For example, the hours worked H during month M, week W, and day D
   could be described by the array:
         HOURS = ARRAY[1..12, 1..6, SUN..SAT] OF REAL;
   and the hours worked on the first Saturday of April selected by:
         HOURS[4, 1, SAT];
N-DIMENSIONAL ARRAYS for any value N (only limited by the computer) are
   done similarly.

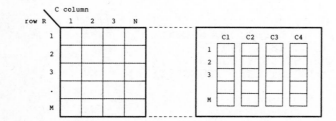

```
100   PROGRAM TWODARRAY(INPUT,OUTPUT);
110     (* COMPUTES THE WEIGHTED AVERAGE
120        GRADE OF M STUDENTS ON N EXAMS
125        SEE ALSO PAGES 6-23 AND 6-24   *)
130
140   CONST
145     MAXSTUD = 50;   MAXEXAMS = 10;
150
155   TYPE
160     STUDENTS = 1..MAXSTUD;
165     EXAMS    = 1..MAXEXAMS;
170
180   VAR
185     W: ARRAY[ EXAMS ] OF REAL (* WEIGHTS *);
186     G: ARRAY[STUDENTS,EXAMS] OF REAL (* GRADES *);
187     F: ARRAY[STUDENTS] OF REAL (* FINAL *);
188
190     I,J,M,N: INTEGER;   S: REAL;
195
200   BEGIN
210     (* INPUT THE ARRAYS *)
220        WRITELN(' ENTER NUMBER OF STUDENTS ');
230        WRITELN(' AND THE NUMBER OF EXAMS  ');
240        READ(M,N);
250
300        WRITELN(' ENTER THE WEIGHTS ');
310        FOR I := 1 TO N DO
320           READ( W[I] );
330
350        WRITELN(' ENTER THE GRADES ');
360        FOR I := 1 TO M DO
370           FOR J := 1 TO N DO
380              READ( G[I,J] );
390
400     (* COMPUTE THE WEIGHTED AVERAGE *)
410        FOR I := 1 TO M DO
420          BEGIN
430            S := 0;
440            FOR J := 1 TO N DO
450               S := S + W[J]*G[I,J];
460            F[I] := S;
470          END ;
480
500     (* OUTPUT THE WEIGHTED GRADES *)
505        WRITELN( 'THE WEIGHTED GRADES ARE' );
510        FOR J := 1 TO M DO
520           WRITELN( J:3, F[J]:7:2 );
530
900   END.
```

```
┌─────────────────────────────────────┐
│  ENTER NUMBER OF STUDENTS           │
│  AND THE NUMBER OF EXAMS            │
│ ? 4  3                              │
│  ENTER THE WEIGHTS                  │
│ ? 0.2  0.3  0.5                     │
│  ENTER THE GRADES                   │
│ ?   40  60  80                      │
│ ?   70  30  80                      │
│ ? 100 100 100                       │
│ ?   80  60  40                      │
│ THE WEIGHTED GRADES ARE             │
│   1  66.00                          │
│   2  63.00                          │
│   3 100.00                          │
│   4  54.00                          │
│                                     │
└─────────────────────────────────────┘
```

RECORDS: Accessing with Dots

A record is a grouping of components (fields) which may be of different types. Records are declared as types in the following form (at the left). An example of a part of some inventory stock is shown specified at the right.

```
TYPE                        TYPE
  name = RECORD               PART = RECORD
    field: type;                PRICE    : REAL;
    field: type;                QUANTITY : INTEGER;
    ...   ...                   REORDER  : BOOLEAN;
    ...   ...                   STATUS   : CHAR;
  END                         END (* PART *)
```

Objects of this type (such as chair parts) can be declared as:
```
VAR
    LEG, SEAT, RUNG, BACK: PART;
```

Access of records is done using a dot notation such as:
```
LEG.PRICE := 3.14;      READ( SEAT.QUANTITY );
```

WITH is a particularly convenient concept to avoid repetition of a record name. It has the form:

```
WITH record-name DO statement
```

where the statement (or series of statements) can involve only the field name, and so read like simple variables, but the WITH attaches the record name common to all the fields. For example, the following are equivalent.

```
                              WITH LEG DO
                              BEGIN
LEG.PRICE    := 1.23;           PRICE    := 1.23;
LEG.QUANTITY := 4000;           QUANTITY := 4000;
LEG.REORDER  := TRUE;           REORDER  := TRUE;
LEG.STATUS   := 'A';            STATUS   := 'A';
                              END (* WITH *);
```

PAYRECORDS, the program on the facing page, shows two records: a date and a person. An alternate definition emphasizing sub-records is shown to the right of the original definition. The month of birth of the Ith worker is denoted by W[I].BIRTH.MONTH. Notice also that WORKER is defined to be an array of PERSONS, illustrating an array of records.

This program first enters information on each worker into an array. Then it finds the maximum hours of the workers. Other computations are suggested at the end of this program.

RECORDARRAY, on the following page, is an example where the student grade record includes an array PROJ of project grades, and an array QUIZ of exam percentages. This example illustrates a record of arrays. STUDENT is defined as an array of records of these arrays.

WORKIN, also on a following page, illustrates briefly the concept of a record variant. More of such concepts can be found on pages 6-26 through 6-31.

```
PROGRAM PAYRECORDS(INPUT,OUTPUT);
  (* COMPUTES PAYROLL INFORMATION *)
  (* ILLUSTRATES ARRAY OF RECORDS *)

CONST
  N = 5; (* NUMBER OF WORKERS *)

TYPE
```

```
DATE = RECORD
  YEAR : INTEGER;
  MONTH: 1..12;
  DAY  : 1..31;
END (* DATE *);

PERSON = RECORD
  IDNUM: INTEGER;
  HOURS: REAL;
  RATE : REAL;
  BIRTH: DATE;
  STAGE: CHAR;
END (* PERSON *);
```
=
```
PERSON = RECORD
  IDNUM: INTEGER;
  HOURS: REAL;
  RATE : REAL;

  BIRTH = RECORD
    YEAR: INTEGER;
    MONTH: 1..12;
    DAY  : 1..31;
  END (* BIRTH *)

  STAGE: CHAR
END (* PERSON *)
```

```
  WORKER = ARRAY[1..N] OF PERSON;

VAR
  I: INTEGER;
  W: WORKER;
  MAXHOURS: REAL;

BEGIN
```

```
  (* ENTER WORKER INFORMATION *)
    WRITELN( 'ENTER ID, HOURS, RATE');
    WRITELN( 'AND THE YEAR OF BIRTH');
    FOR I := 1 TO N DO
      WITH W[I] DO
        BEGIN
          READ( IDNUM, HOURS, RATE );
          READ( BIRTH.YEAR );
          WRITELN( 'NEXT' );
        END (* WITH *);
    (* END FOR *)
```

```
  (* FIND MAXIMUM HOURS *)
    MAXHOURS := 0.0;
    FOR I := 1 TO N DO
      WITH W[I] DO
        IF MAXHOURS < HOURS THEN
          MAXHOURS := HOURS;
    WRITELN('MAX HOURS =', MAXHOURS:3:1);
```

```
  (* FIND MINIMUM WAGE *)

  (* FIND MAXIMUM AGE *)

  (* ACCUMULATE ALL HOURS *)

  (* COUNT PERSONS OVER 30 *)

  (* COMPUTE PAY *)

  (* ETC *)
```

```
END.
```

```
PROGRAM RECORDARRAY(INPUT,OUTPUT);
   (* MAINTAINS STUDENT RECORDS *)
   (* SHOWS A  RECORD OF ARRAYS *)
   (* SEE ALSO PAGE 6-30         *)

CONST
   NOS = 7; (* NUMBER OF STUDENTS *)
   NOP = 5; (* NUMBER OF PROJECTS *)
   NOQ = 4; (* NUMBER OF QUIZES   *)
```

```
TYPE

   LISTCHR = ARRAY[1..NOP] OF CHAR;
   LISTINT = ARRAY[1..NOQ] OF INTEGER;

   GRADE = RECORD
     IDNO: INTEGER;
     PROJ: LISTCHR;
     QUIZ: LISTINT;
   END (* GRADE *);

   STUDENT = ARRAY[1..NOS] OF GRADE;
```

```
VAR
   I,J: INTEGER;
   S: STUDENT;
   SUM, MEAN: REAL;

BEGIN
```

```
   (* ENTER QUIZ SCORES *)
      FOR I := 1 TO NOS DO
        BEGIN
          WRITELN(' ENTER ID ');
          READ( S[I].IDNO );
          WRITELN(' ENTER GRADES');
          READLN;
          FOR J := 1 TO NOQ DO
            READ( S[I].QUIZ[J] );
          WRITELN;
        END (* ENTER QUIZ *);
```

```
   (* COMPUTE AVERAGE QUIZ GRADE *)
      FOR I := 1 TO NOS DO
        WITH S[I] DO
          BEGIN
            SUM := 0.0;
            FOR J := 1 TO NOQ DO
              SUM := SUM + QUIZ[J];
            MEAN:= SUM/NOQ;
            WRITELN( IDNO, MEAN:3:2 );
          END;
```

```
   (* RANK BY WEIGHTED AVERAGES *)

   (* ENTER PROJECT GRADES *)

   (* ETC *)

END.
```

```
PROGRAM  WORKIN(INPUT,OUTPUT);
   (* ENTERS WORKERS INPUT  *)
   (* SHOWS RECORD VARIANTS *)
   (* SEE ALSO PAGE 6-30    *)

CONST
   N = 20; (* MAXIMUM NUMBER OF WORKERS *)

TYPE

   STAGETYPE = (HOURLY, SALARIED);

   WORKER = RECORD
     IDNUM: INTEGER;
     AGE  : INTEGER;
     CASE STAGE: STAGETYPE OF
       SALARIED: (SALARY: INTEGER);
       HOURLY  : (HOURS : INTEGER;
                  RATE  : INTEGER)
     END (* WORKER *);

VAR
   M,I: INTEGER;
   CH : CHAR;
   W  : ARRAY[1..N] OF WORKER;

BEGIN

(* ENTER WORKER DATA *)
   WRITELN( 'ENTER NUMBER OF WORKERS' );
   READ( M );
   FOR I := 1 TO M DO
     WITH W[I] DO
       BEGIN
         WRITELN( 'ENTER AGE' );
         READ( AGE );
         IDNUM := I;
         WRITELN( 'ENTER STAGE OF PAY' );
         WRITELN( 'SALARIED OR HOURLY' );
         WRITELN( 'ENTER S OR H ONLY ' );
         READLN; READ( CH );
         WRITELN;
         IF CH = 'S' THEN
            STAGE := SALARIED
         ELSE (* ALL OTHERS *)
            STAGE := HOURLY;
         WRITELN( 'ENTER PROPER PAY' );
         CASE STAGE OF
           SALARIED: READ( SALARY );
           HOURLY  : READ( HOURS, RATE );
         END (* CASE *);
         WRITELN;
       END (* WITH WORKER I *);

(* QUERY WORKER DATA *)
   WRITELN( 'QUERY WHICH ID' );
   READ( I );
   WITH W[I] DO
     BEGIN
       WRITELN( 'AGE IS ', AGE:3 );
       WRITELN( 'PAY IS ' );
       CASE STAGE OF
         SALARIED: WRITELN( SALARY );
         HOURLY  : WRITELN( HOURS*RATE);
       END (* CASE *);
     END (* WITH *);

END.
```

FILES: Serial

Pascal allows only serial files (in the standard dialect). They consist of an unlimited sequence of components, all of the same type.

DECLARATIONS of files could be done as a type in the form
        TYPE name = FILE OF type
or as a variable in the form
        VAR name: FILE OF type

as in the example:
        TYPE
                DATA = FILE OF INTEGER;
                CHARFILE = FILE OF CHAR;
        VAR A,B,C : DATA;
                STREAM: CHARFILE;
                PRICES: FILE OF REAL;
    Also, in standard Pascal, files must be declared in the program heading after the standard files INPUT, OUTPUT.

FILES, the given program shows the creation of a file of characters, the analysis of the file (finding the average length of words), and the output of this file, a word at a time on a line.

FILEIN, the first sub-program, shows the process of creating or storing a file of characters called STREAM. It uses the two main file operations of WRITE and REWRITE.

REWRITE(file-name) is an operation which prepares a file for writing. It opens a file and sets the window to the beginning, so deleting the previous contents of that file.

WRITE(file-name, expression) writes the value of the expression onto the indicated file.

FILEIN enters characters from the keyboard, appends them to the file STREAM until a terminating dollar sign is entered.

FILEOUT, shows the process of scanning a file. It uses the file operations of RESET and READ.

RESET(file-name) prepares the file for reading, by setting the window to the beginning of the indicated file.

READ(file-name, variable) obtains the value at the window and advances the window.

FILEOUT reads characters from the file STREAM, and outputs them, one word per line, until a terminating dollar sign is encountered. Other useful actions on such a stream are: counting characters, words, and sentences, and then finding the average length of words and sentences.

OTHER file operations include the built-in functions
        EOF(file-name) and EOLN(file-name)
which are Boolean functions indicating the end of a file, or the end of a line, respectively. For example, the EOF function could have been used as a terminator instead of the dollar sign by substituting
        WHILE NOT EOF(STREAM) DO.....
in place of
        WHILE CH <> '$' DO....

TEXT files are particularly useful pre-defined files which sub-divide data into lines (usually separated by the return character). An example is given on page 7-13, where an inventory of items is stored on a text file, where each line contains an item quantity (integer) and its price (real).

```
100   PROGRAM FILES( INPUT, OUTPUT, STREAM );
110     (* SHOWS FILES IN STANDARD PASCAL *)
120
130   TYPE
140     CHARFILE = FILE OF CHAR;
150
160   VAR
170     STREAM: CHARFILE;
180
200   PROCEDURE FILEIN;
210     (* INPUTS FILE FROM KEYBOARD *)
220   VAR CH: CHAR;
230   BEGIN
240     WRITELN( 'ENTER CHARACTERS ' );
250     WRITELN( 'END WITH DOLLAR $' );
260     REWRITE( STREAM );
270     READ( CH );
280     WHILE CH <> '$' DO
290       BEGIN
300         WRITE( STREAM, CH );
310         READ( CH );
320       END;
330     WRITE( STREAM, '$' );
340   END (* FILEIN *);
350
360
400   PROCEDURE FILEOUT;
410     (* OUTPUTS A WORD PER LINE *)
420   VAR CH: CHAR;
430   BEGIN
440     WRITELN;
450     RESET( STREAM );
455     READ( STREAM, CH );
460     WHILE CH <> '$' DO
470       BEGIN
480         IF CH = ' ' THEN
490             WRITELN
500         ELSE
510             WRITE( CH );
520         READ( STREAM, CH );
530       END;
540   END (* FILEOUT *);
550
900   BEGIN (* MAIN *)
910     FILEIN;
920     FILEOUT;
990   END (* MAIN *).
```

```
+-------------------------------------+
| ENTER CHARACTERS                    |
| END WITH DOLLAR $                   |
| ? ONCE UPON A TIME                  |
| ? THERE LIVED THREE BULLS,          |
| ? A DADDY BULL, A MOMMY BULL        |
| ? AND A BABY BULL.                  |
| ? $                                 |
|                                     |
|                                     |
|                                     |
| ONCE                                |
| UPON                                |
| A                                   |
| TIME                                |
| THERE                               |
| LIVED                               |
| THREE                               |
| BULLS,                              |
| A                                   |
| DADDY                               |
| BULL,                               |
| A                                   |
| MOMMY                               |
| BULL                                |
| AND                                 |
| A                                   |
| BABY                                |
| BULL.                               |
|                                     |
+-------------------------------------+
```

REVIEW: Of Appendix B

PASCAL: Programming Practice

This has been an introduction to Programming in the Pascal language. The introduction went beyond the bare minimum, but did not cover the complete language.

CONTROL STRUCTURES at minimum consist of the four forms: SERIES, IF-THEN-ELSE, WHILE, and PROCEDURE. In addition, we met the CASE, FOR, and FUNCTION forms.

DATA STRUCTURES encountered were the Array and Record, along with the simple programmer-defined scalar type. Files were introduced very briefly; there is much more to know about them.

PROGRAMMING STYLE has also been treated briefly. More style will develop with thought, experience, and maturity. Some of the style here is oriented mainly to a beginner. For example, indentation of statements within a BEGIN-END pair was encouraged. For beginners, this makes matching the pairs convenient, but may result in excessive indentation, which a non-beginner may not need. Also all programs are written in upper case, partly to distinguish between the Pascal language and the English "meta-language" used to talk about the Pascal. Non-beginners will often prefer mixed upper and lower case characters because of their readability, especially in very large programs.

OMISSIONS in this appendix are many, and usually done on purpose. For example, there is no mention of either GOTOs or labels; they are simply not necessary in Pascal. Pointer types were also not introduced because they could be badly misused; they should either be covered well, or not at all. They belong more appropriately in a following course in data structures.

MORE PASCAL is considered in the last chapter on Applications, Chapter 7. There some larger systems are shown developed all the way from the general plan to the detailed Pascal program. Other sources of further Pascal can be found in the great many books written about it.

TYPICAL TERMINAL SESSION: On the CDC Cyber

The human's part of the "conversation" is in lower case.
A carriage return follows every input line.
A "friendlier" description is on page 2-25.

```
Log-on     WHAT SYSTEM ? 50
           AFTER 'GO' TYPE      <CR><CR>

           GO

           82/03/11. 09.50.32.
           CSU, NORTHRIDGE CYBER 170/750.
           FAMILY:
           USER NAME: radr123
           PASSWORD:  abcdefg

           TERMINAL:    50, NAMIAF
           RECOVER /SYSTEM: batch
           $RFL,0.
```

```
Enter       /new
Program     FILE NAME: temp
            /100  program convert(input/,output);
            110   var c,f: real;
            120   begin
            130     read( f);
            140     c := (5/9)*(f - 32);
            150     writeln(c);
            160   end.
```

```
Run         pascal3,temp/L-,g+
            ? 98.6
               3.7000000000000E+001
               0.000 CP SECS
```

```
Save        /save
```

```
Modify      /125     writeln( 'enter f' );
            150      writeln( 'degrees c =', round(c) );
```

```
List        list
            100   PROGRAM CONVERT(INPUT/,OUTPUT);
            110     VAR C,F: REAL;
            120     BEGIN
            125       WRITELN( 'ENTER F' );
            130       READ( F );
            140       C := (5/9)*(F - 32);
            150       WRITELN( 'DEGREES C =', ROUND(C) );
            160     END.
```

```
Re-run      /pascal3,temp/l-,g+
            ENTER F
            ? 98.6
            DEGREES C =       ·     37
            0.005 CP SECS
```

```
Replace     /replace
```

```
List        /catlist
Catalog     CATALOG OF RADR123

            INDIRECT ACCESS FILE(S)

            TEMP
```

```
Log-off     /bye

            RADR123  LOG OFF   09.57.19
```

USING THE UCSD SYSTEM

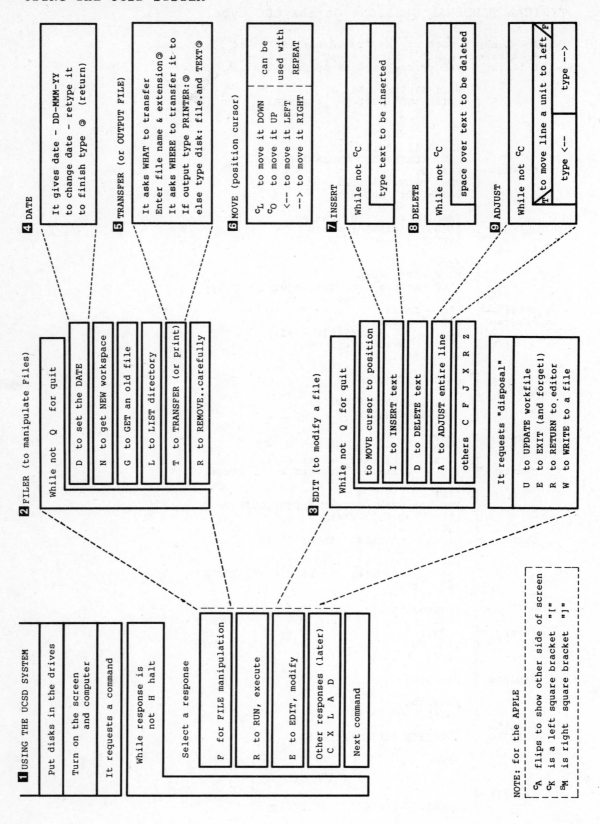

4 DATE

It gives date – DD-MMM-YY
to change date – retype it
to finish type @ (return)

5 TRANSFER (or OUTPUT FILE)

It asks WHAT to transfer
Enter file name & extension@
It asks WHERE to transfer it to
If output type PRINTER:@
else type disk: file.and TEXT@

6 MOVE (position cursor)

c_L to move it DOWN	can be
c_O to move it UP	used with
<-- to move it LEFT	REPEAT
--> to move it RIGHT	

7 INSERT

While not c_C
   type text to be inserted

8 DELETE

While not c_C
   space over text to be deleted

9 ADJUST

While not c_C
   T to move line a unit to left/right
   type <--   type -->

2 FILER (to manipulate Files)

While not Q for quit

   D to set the DATE
   N to get NEW workspace
   G to GET an old file
   L to LIST directory
   T to TRANSFER (or print)
   R to REMOVE..carefully

3 EDIT (to modify a file)

While not Q for quit

   to MOVE cursor to position
   I to INSERT text
   D to DELETE text
   A to ADJUST entire line
   others C F J X R Z

It requests "disposal"

   U to UPDATE workfile
   E to EXIT (and forget!)
   R to RETURN to.editor
   W to WRITE to a file

1 USING THE UCSD SYSTEM

Put disks in the drives
Turn on the screen
    and computer
It requests a command

While response is
    not H halt

   Select a response

   F for FILE manipulation
   R to RUN, execute
   E to EDIT, modify
   Other responses (later)
   C X L A D

   Next command

NOTE: for the APPLE

c_A flips to show other side of screen
c_K is a left square bracket "["
s_M is right square bracket "]"

"INCANTATIONS" FOR THE UCSD SYSTEM

A Typical Conversational Session on the UCSD System
    with US (Unsuspecting Student)
    and IT (Interactive terminal)
See also the algorithm on the previous page.

US: Turn the machine on

IT: WELCOME banner is displayed
    COMMAND: E(DIT, R(UN, F(ILE, C(OMP, X(ECUTE, etc

US: E to Edit a file

IT: NO WORKFILE PRESENT. FILE? (<RET> FOR NO FILE)

US: <RET> i.e. press the return key for new file

IT: E(DIT: A(DJUST, C(OPY, D(ELETE, I(NSERT, J(UMP, R(EPLACE, etc..

US: I to Insert a program

IT: INSERT: TEXT etc...

US: PROGRAM CONVERT;
    VAR C,F: REAL;
    BEGIN
      WRITELN('ENTER F');
      READ(F);
      C := (5/9)*(F - 32);
      WRITELN('DEGREES C =', ROUND(C));
    END.

    Control-C to end the Insert

IT: EDIT: A(DJUST, C(OPY, D(ELETE, etc...

US: Q to quit the Edit

IT: QUIT: U(PDATE, E(XIT, R(ETURN, W(RITE, S(AVE

US: U to Update file into workspace

IT: COMMAND: E(DIT, R(UN, F(ILE, etc...

US: R to run the program of the workspace

IT: COMPILING...to convert to machine language
    RUNNING....
    ENTER F

US: 98.6

IT: DEGREES C = 37
    COMMAND: E(DIT, R(UN, F(ILE, etc..

US: F to enter Filer

IT: FILER: G(ET, S(AVE, N(EW, L(IST, R(EMOVE, etc

US S   To save the workspace permanently

IT: SAVE AS?

US: FIRST

IT: TEXT FILE SAVED AND CODE FILE SAVED

PROBLEMS: on Pascal

CODE: Translate the following flow block diagrams into corresponding pieces of program in Pascal.

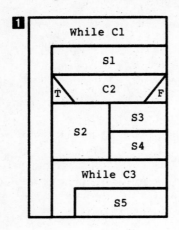

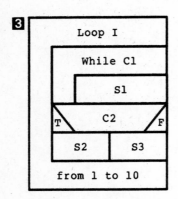

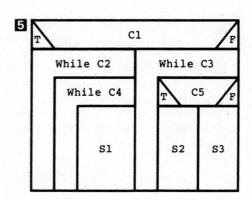

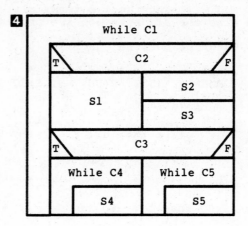

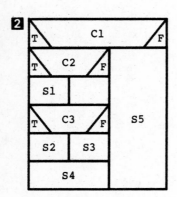

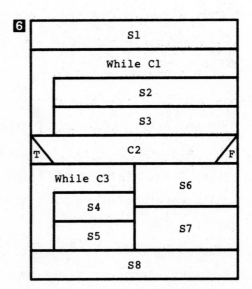

PASCAL QUICKIES

A. For each of the following sentences, indicate your preference by circling the proper capitalized word.

1. The function SQR(X) computes the SQUARE or the SQUARE ROOT of X.
2. To "chop" a number to its next lower integer, we should use ROUND or TRUNC.
3. For every "end" in a Pascal program, there is ALWAYS or USUALLY a "begin".
4. The character "1" CAN or CANNOT be added to the integer 1.
5. To return more than one value, a sub-program should be a FUNCTION or PROCEDURE.
6. If a variable is both passed in and out, it should be passed by VALUE or REFERENCE.
7. It is preferable to declare variables LOCALLY or GLOBALLY.
8. To write many values on a line, you would use WRITE or WRITELN.
9. The components of an ARRAY or RECORD may be of different types.
10. An integer added to a real produces an INTEGER or REAL or ERROR.
11. Arrays normally passed by value may NEVER or SOMETIMES be passed by reference to save memory.
12. The most general, fundamental choice form is the IF or the CASE.
13. The most general, fundamental loop form is the WHILE or UNTIL or FOR.
14. A function in Pascal is used like a STATEMENT or EXPRESSION.
15. A "begin" should NEVER or SOMETIMES have a semicolon in front of it.
16. There is SOMETIMES or NEVER a semicolon before an "else".
17. In a write statement, the field width of an integer MUST or MAY be an integer.
18. Sub-programs should be defined BEFORE or AFTER a main program.
19. Boolean values CAN or CANNOT be directly input to a program.
20. The FOR loop can bump by ONE ONLY or MORE THAN ONE.

B. Indicate all the errors in the following statements. Assume A,B,C,D,E are real; I,J,K,L,M,N are integer; P,Q,R are Boolean.

1. E := .25(A + B + C + D)
2. IF I = J THEN K = L; ELSE M = N
3. IF P THEN Q
4. IF A > (B AND C) THEN WRITELN('MAX IS A')
5. READ(A,E,I,P)
6. WRITELINE('I', I:I+I, A:B:C)
7. WHILE A < B < C DO A := B + C
8. FOR I := 1 TO N + N READ(I)

PASCAL PLOTS

Many interesting programming problems (involving nests of loops) can be encountered in creating plots using a printer. The following plots should be created generally (with sizes entered initially) and done without using arrays.

1. STARBOX   2. TIC-TAC GRID   3. DIAMOND

```
**********              #  #                 *
*        *              #  #                ***
*        *           ########              *****
*        *              #  #              *******
*        *              #  #               *****
*        *           ########               ***
*        *              #  #                 *
**********              #  #
```

4. PINE TREE   5. TRI PATTERN   6. GRID OF CHECKS

```
      *          1          1          xxx   xxx   xxx
     ***         12         22         xxx   xxx   xxx
    *****        123        333           xxx   xxx
   *******       1234       4444          xxx   xxx
  *********      12345      55555      xxx   xxx   xxx
 ***********     123456     666666     xxx   xxx   xxx
     ***         1234567    7777777
     ***         12345678   88888888
                 123456789  999999999
```

7. BAR PLOT UP Create an upright bar plot of a linear list A of N values (percentages), with the length of bars proportional to the values in the array. Each asterisk represents 2% (100% is 50 asterisks). For example: if 7 values in an array are 30,20,10,20,10,5,5, they produce the graph as shown.

8. CALENDAR

```
                                      *
                                      *
                                      *
                                      *
     S   M   T   W   T   F   S        *
                                      *
     1   2   3   4   5   6   7        *   *   *
                                      *   *   *
     8   9  10  11  12  13  14        *   *   *
                                      *   *   *
    15  16  17  18  19  20  21        *   *   *
                                      * * * * *
    22  23  24  25  26  27  28        * * * * *
                                      * * * * *
    29  30  31                        * * * * * * *
                                      * * * * * * *
```

9. BIRTHDAY   Write HAPPY BIRTHDAY N times, twice per line, for someone's Nth birthday, with a gap every 10 wishes (5 lines). The examples represents N = 13.

10. STRING IN BOX Print a given string S of N characters centered in a box of Xs as shown. An array may be used for the string.

```
HAPPY BIRTHDAY   HAPPY BIRTHDAY
HAPPY BIRTHDAY   HAPPY BIRTHDAY    XXXXXXXXXXXXXXXXXXXXXX
HAPPY BIRTHDAY   HAPPY BIRTHDAY    X                    X
HAPPY BIRTHDAY   HAPPY BIRTHDAY    X                    X
HAPPY BIRTHDAY   HAPPY BIRTHDAY    X        MIDDLE      X
                                   X                    X
HAPPY BIRTHDAY   HAPPY BIRTHDAY    X                    X
HAPPY BIRTHDAY                     XXXXXXXXXXXXXXXXXXXXXX
```

MISCELLANEOUS PASCAL PROBLEMS

1. CASE SYNTAX

   Draw a syntax diagram describing the Pascal Case form.

2. TYPE SYNTAX

   Draw a syntax diagram describing the declaration of a TYPE in Pascal (including scalar, array and record).

3. TRACE PASS

   Indicate the output of the following program.

```
PROGRAM MAIN(INPUT,OUTPUT);

VAR A,B,C: INTEGER;

PROCEDURE SUB( A,B: INTEGER; VAR C; INTEGER );
  BEGIN
    A := A + A;
    B := B + B;
    C := C + C;
  END (* SUB *);

BEGIN (* MAIN *)

  A:=1; B:=2; C:=3;
  SUB( A,B,C );
  WRITE(A,B,C);

  A:=4; B:=5; C:=6;
  SUB( C,A,B );
  WRITE(A,B,C);

  A:=7; B:=8; C:=9;
  SUB( A,C,A );
  WRITE(A,B,C);

END (* MAIN *).
```

PETITE PASCAL PROCEDURES

1. BINARY CONVERSION
   Create a procedure BIN(DEC) which accepts a decimal integer DEC, and outputs the binary equivalent sequence of digits.

2. RESISTOR CODE
   Create a procedure COLOR(CODE) which requests a color (input as a three-character sequence), and returns the corresponding digit CODE, as shown on page 1-6. Use this procedure in a main program to determine the values of resistors.

3. ROMANUM
   Create a procedure ROMAN(NUM) to accept any positive integer NUM (less than 300), and output the corresponding Roman number. Assume that four consecutive occurrences of a symbol are proper.

4. CASHIN
   Suppose that the input to a program (such as CHANGE) must have exactly the form

   $D.DD

   where D is one of the ten decimal digits. For example, valid values are

   $5.00, $1.75, and $0.25

   and invalid values are

   $.25, $0.255, $3, and $12.34.

   Create a procedure CASHIN(CENTS) which inputs a sequence of characters (assumed to be in the valid form), and converts it to the corresponding number of CENTS.

5. TELL TIME
   Create a procedure TIME(BIG,SMALL) to accept the clock hand positions BIG and SMALL, and output the time in the four formats given on page 2-44.

6. QUAD
   Create a function QUAD(X,Y) which accepts the coordinates X and Y of some point, and indicates which quadrant the point falls into. If the point falls on an axis, the returned value should be zero.

7. BREAK
   Create a procedure BREAK(N,LSD,MSD,R) which takes a given integer N and "breaks off" its least significant digit LSD, its most significant digit MSD, and returns also the remaining integer R (or a negative 1 if nothing remains).

PROGRAMMING PROJECTS

PROJECT 0: SOME SMALL PROGRAMS

To become acquainted with your computing system, enter one of the following short programs and run it. Make some errors to see what happens. Finally, you may make some modifications. Notice that some programs involve only real values, others involve only integers, and others involve both.

1. CIRCLE CALCULATION
(General oriented)

This program repeatedly asks for a value of radius, and provides the circumference and area of the circle. It stops when the given input radius is negative. You may modify it to calculate something else (such as volumes, metric conversions, sums, etc.).

```
PROGRAM  CIRCLE( INPUT,OUTPUT );
  (* DOES CIRCLE CALCULATIONS *)
CONST PI = 3.14159;
VAR   RADIUS, AREA, CIRC: REAL;
BEGIN
  WRITELN( 'ENTER  RADIUS OF CIRCLE' );
  WRITELN( 'ENTER  NEGATIVE TO QUIT' );
  READ( RADIUS );
  WHILE RADIUS >= 0 DO
    BEGIN
      CIRC := 2*PI*RADIUS;
      WRITELN( 'CIRCUM = ', CIRC:6:3 );
      AREA := PI*RADIUS*RADIUS;
      WRITELN( 'AREA IS ', AREA:6:3 );
      WRITELN;
      WRITELN('ENTER THE NEXT RADIUS');
      READ( RADIUS );
    END;
END.
```

2. COMPOUND GROWTH
(General oriented)

This program shows how an amount (population or interest, etc.) grows when its rate of growth is a fixed ratio of the present amount. The growth stops when it reaches twice the original value.

```
PROGRAM COMPOUND( INPUT,OUTPUT );
  (* SHOWS COMPOUNDING GROWTH *)
VAR
  YEAR: INTEGER;
  AMOUNT, RATE: REAL;
  BEGIN
    WRITELN( 'ENTER THE GROWTH RATE' );
    READ( RATE );
    WRITELN( 'YEAR  AMOUNT' );
    YEAR := 1; AMOUNT := 1.00;
    WHILE AMOUNT < 2.00 DO
      BEGIN
        AMOUNT := AMOUNT*(1 + RATE);
        YEAR   := YEAR + 1;
        WRITELN( YEAR:3, AMOUNT:8:3 );
      END;
  END.
```

3. LOAN PAYMENT
(Business oriented)

This Loan program (of pages 4-6, 4-14, and described also on page 3-32) computes the "Balloon" payment on a loan.

4. PROJECTILE
(Science oriented)

This program enters an initial velocity, and computes the range (horizontal distance) that a projectile would travel for various angles (with no wind). You may wish first to guess what angle produces the maximum range.

```
PROGRAM PROJECTILE( INPUT,OUTPUT );
  (* FINDS RANGE  OF PROJECTILE *)
CONST PI = 3.14159;  G = 32.2;
VAR   DEGREES, R, RANGE, V: REAL;
BEGIN
  WRITELN( 'ENTER INITIAL VELOCITY' );
  WRITELN( 'IN FEET PER SECOND' );
  READ( V );
  DEGREES := 10.0;
  WHILE DEGREES < 90.0 DO
    BEGIN
      (* CONVERT DEGREES TO RADIANS *)
      R := (PI/180.0)*DEGREES;
      RANGE := (2*V*V/G)*SIN(R)*COS(R);
      WRITELN( DEGREES:4:1, RANGE:7:1);
      DEGREES := DEGREES + 5.0;
    END;
END.
```

CHANGE CHANGE PROJECT

You are to modify the change-making program CHANGE (given on the next page) in any five of the following ways, yielding one larger program (not five smaller ones).

1. Make the program more GENERAL,
    by allowing the output of dimes and one dollar bills.

2. Make the program more REALISTIC,
    by allowing the input of any amount tendered

3. Make the program more ROBUST,
    by having it reject any improper input values (such as negative cost).

4. Make the program more INFORMATIVE,
    by writing out the amount of change as:
        THE CHANGE IS 58 CENTS
                    or
        THE CHANGE IS 2 DOLLARS AND 13 CENTS

5. Make the program more CONVENIENT,
    by putting it into a loop and having it continue making change until some negative value is input.

6. Make the program GRAMMATICALLY CORRECT,
    by writing singular and plural counts such as:
        1 QUARTER   0 NICKELS   3 PENNIES

7. Make the program output SHORTER,
    by not writing out the zero count, as:
        1 QUARTER   3 PENNIES

8. Make the program output more VERBOSE,
    by writing out the count in English as:
        ONE QUARTER   THREE PENNIES

9. Make the program more USER FRIENDLY,
    by allowing input as real numbers
    (such as 0.78, 1.25).

10. Make the program more PRODUCTIVE,
    by having it keep track of the number of coins of each type (not attempting to put out any quarters if it has none).

```
100   PROGRAM CHANGE( INPUT, OUTPUT );
110     (* THAT CHANGE MAKER AGAIN *)
115     (* SEE ALSO PAGE 3-48, B-5 *)
120     (* NOTICE  VARIABLE  NAMES *)
130
200   VAR
210      QUARTERS, NICKELS, PENNIES,
215      COST, REMAINDER: INTEGER;
220
300   BEGIN
310     (* INPUT THE COST *)
320        WRITELN( 'ENTER THE COST' );
330        WRITELN( 'IN CENTS' );
340        READ( COST );
350        REMAINDER := 100 - COST;
360
400     (* MAKE THE CHANGE *)
410        QUARTERS := 0;
420        WHILE REMAINDER >= 25 DO
430          BEGIN
440             QUARTERS  := QUARTERS + 1;
450             REMAINDER := REMAINDER - 25;
460          END;
470
500        NICKELS := 0;
510        WHILE REMAINDER >= 5 DO
520          BEGIN
530             NICKELS  := NICKELS + 1;
540             REMAINDER := REMAINDER - 5;
550          END;
560
600        PENNIES := REMAINDER;
610
700     (* OUTPUT THE COIN COUNT *)
710        WRITELN( 'THE CHANGE IS' );
720        WRITELN( QUARTERS,' QUARTERS');
730        WRITELN( NICKELS, ' NICKELS ');
740        WRITELN( PENNIES, ' PENNIES ');
750
900   END.
```

STATISTICS: Rainfall

Create an algorithm and corresponding program to analyse the rainfall over a period of any number of weeks. The rainfall figures (real numbers, giving the daily amount of rain) are input in order, and end with a negative number. The following group of "statistics" is computed as the numbers are read in (they are not stored in arrays!).

1. MEAN is the average rainfall per day, computed by summing all the amounts and dividing by the number of days.

2. MAX is the maximum amount of rain that fell in any day.

3. MIN is the minimum amount of rain that fell in any day.

4. RANGE is the amount of variation between values.

5. DRYDAYS is the number of days of no rainfall.

6. MAXDAY is a day on which the maximum rain fell.

7. MAXDROP is the largest drop in amount of rainfall between two consecutive days.

8. VARIANCE is the difference between the mean of the square of the values and the square of the mean of the values (as given on page 6-7).

9. DEVIATION is the square root of the variance.

10. SECONDMAX is the second largest value of rainfall.

11. DRYRUN is the length of the largest period of days without rain.

12. MAXWEEK is the week which had the most accumulated rainfall.

13. WETRIPLE is the largest accumulated rainfall over three consecutive days.

ISBN PROJECT

The International Standard Book Number (ISBN) is a coding method
for labelling books. It consists of nine digits, possibly
separated by dashes, followed by a check symbol. Some
examples are:

```
0-486-20212-7      0-917930-15-0
3-540-90144-2      0-13-215871-X
```

The check digit is determined by adding the first digit to two
times the second digit to three times the third digit, etc., to
nine times the ninth digit. This "weighted" sum, when divided
by eleven, yields a remainder which determines the check
symbol. If the remainder is ten, then the check symbol is the
character "X"; otherwise, the check symbol is the remainder.
For example, the ISBN code "0-486-20212-7" has a weighted sum
of

$$1*0 + 2*4 + 3*8 + 4*6 + 5*2 + 6*0 + 7*2 + 8*1 + 9*2 = 106$$

Dividing this sum by 11 yields a remainder of 7, which is the
checksum.

You are to create one of the following encoders, and also one of
the following decoders.

ENCODER1 accepts input of nine digits (with no dashes)
and outputs the check symbol.

ENCODER2 accepts input of nine digits (with no dashes)
and outputs the entire ISBN.

ENCODER3 accepts input of nine digits (and possibly dashes)
and outputs the check symbol.

ENCODER4 accepts input of nine digits (and possibly dashes)
and outputs the entire ISBN.

DECODER1 accepts input of an entire ISBN (with no dashes)
and outputs the message "PROPER" or "IMPROPER".

DECODER2 accepts input of an entire ISBN (with dashes)
and outputs "PROPER" or "IMPROPER".

This project illustrates mainly the character type (emphasizing
that digit 0 is not the same as character '0'). Arrays are not
necessary for this project, but could be convenient.

BAR PLOT PROJECT

Create a program to plot a histogram (or bar graph) of some quantity (such as daily rainfall over four weeks, or monthly production over a year). The quantities are input, and the bars are plotted in given proportions. Two typical bar plots follow, the simplest having horizontal bars, and the more complex having vertical ones. The plot should occupy about half a page, and should be "beautified" in some of the following ways. Include runs of at least three different sets of data. Arrays are not necessary except in the vertical plot where the number of bars exceeds 4.

1. Allow the thickness of the bars to be input.

2. Allow bars to be created of symbols other than asterisks.

3. Allow the gap between bars to be input.

4. Draw heading and axes.

5. Print a border around the entire plot.

6. Have the value of the quantities printed on or above each bar.

7. Allow a scaling factor to be input, so that the size of the bars may be controlled.

8. Have the above scale be determined by the program (so that the maximum quantity results in a bar which almost fills the maximum size of plot).

9. Create some other beautifying modification.

(Horizontal bars)   (Vertical bars)

PRODUCTION P IN MONTH M   RAINFALL IN MARCH/82

   M P   INCHES

```
   1 20  ****                            3.0                    2.7
   2 20  ****                                                   ***
   3 30  ******                          2.5                    ***
   4 40  ********                                               ***
   5 30  ******                          2.0   1.7              ***
   6 30  ******                                ***              ***
   7 35  *******                         1.5   ***        1.3  ***
   8 50  **********                            ***        ***  ***
   9 70  **************                   1.0  ***        ***  ***
  10 90  ******************                    ***   0.6  ***  ***
  11 99  ********************             0.5  ***   ***  ***  ***
  12 30  ******                               ***   ***  ***  ***
                                         ----------------------
                                               1    2    3    4

                                                   WEEK
```

DATES PROJECT

Use the sub-programs LEAP, DAYS, and JULIAN, of page B-57 to
create some of the following sub-programs. (Do some in more
than one way, i.e. use MOD instead of loops)

1. VALID tests to see if a given date (Y,M,D) is a proper date.

2. AGE determines the integer age of a person, given the birth
date (and knowing the present date).

3. WEEKDAY finds the weekday that a given date falls on, given
that the first day of the year falls on the Wth day
(where W = 0 for Sunday, W = 1 for Monday, W = 6 for
Saturday).

4. FIRST DATE determines the weekday of New Year's Day, given
the year Y. Use the fact that January 1, 1901 was a
Tuesday. Notice that a year of 365 days has exactly 52
weeks plus one day.

5. ELAPSED indicates the number of days between two given
dates.

6. UNDATE converts a given Julian date of a given year back
into the usual form of date (Year, Month, and Day).

7. LIVED determines the number of days that a person has lived
from a given birthdate to the present date.

8. WEEKDAYBORN indicates the weekday on which a person was
born, given the birthdate.

9. THANKSDATE indicates the day on which Thanksgiving occurs,
given the year. Thanksgiving (in USA) occurs on the
fourth Thursday of November.

10. CALENDAR prints out a monthly calendar given the weekday of
the first day, and the number of days in the month.

11. BIORHYTHM plots out a sine curve supposedly indicating the
rise and fall of a certain ability, such as physical
strength, endurance. The sine wave has a given period
of repetition (say 23 days), starting with 0 at birth.
Create such a plot starting at any given day, and
continuing for one whole cycle.

12. BIG-BIO plots a number of biorhythms, each having a
different period, on one graph. For example, the
intellectual cycle has a period of 33 days, and the
sensitivity cycle has a period of 28 days.

13. UNLUCKY determines, for a given year, the months on which
Friday falls on the thirteenth day.

14. MIDWAY determines the date (Year, Month, and Day), or
dates, half way between two given dates of the same
year.

The grades of person P on quiz Q are given in a two-dimensional array G[P,Q], where there are a maximum of M persons and N quizzes. All proper grades are integer percentages; a missed quiz is indicated by a negative grade.

Create sub-programs to do some of the following.

1. ENTERP enters for each person the grades on all the quizzes (horizontally).

2. ENTERQ enters for each quiz the grades of all the persons (vertically).

3. MEANP finds the mean value of all the quizzes for each student.

4. MEANQ finds the mean value of any particular quiz.

5. FORGIVING MEANP computes a person's mean value with the lowest grade eliminated.

6. WEIGHTED MEANP computes a person's mean after multiplying each grade by a given factor (weight).

7. MEANPQ finds the overall mean value of all persons' overall quizzes.

8. HILO indicates for each person if the "forgiven" grade is above or below (or at) the value of MEANPQ.

9. QPLOT indicates on a bar plot the percentage of people having averages in each of the four quarter ranges:
   0 to 24%, 25 to 49%, 50 to 74%, 75 to 100%.

10. RANKSORT lists the overall grades in decreasing order.

11. PROPORTIONATE SORT lists all grades from 100 to 0 (each on one line) along with the persons (indices) receiving that grade (on the same line).

INDEX OF TOPICS

(A list of algorithms
and programs follows.)